A Career With Meaning

*Recreation, Parks, Sport Management,
Hospitality, and Tourism*

second edition

Keri A. Schwab
Cheryl L. Stevens
James F. Murphy
Lawrence R. Allen
Emilyn A. Sheffield

D1400547

SAGAMORE
PUBLISHING

Publishers: Joseph J. Bannon and Peter L. Bannon
Director of Sales and Marketing: William A. Anderson
Sales Manager: Misti Gilles
Director of Development and Production: Susan M. Davis
Technology Manager: Keith Hardyman
Production Coordinator: Amy S. Dagit
Interior and Cover Designer: Julie Schechter

Cover photo by Dudley Edmondson, http://www.dudleyedmondson.com
Climber on cover: Chelsea Griffie, ED of Los Angeles Wilderness Training,
    http://www.lawildernesstraining.org/about-us/who-we-are/

Library of Congress Control Number: 2014945284
ISBN print edition: 978-1-57167-772-3
ISBN ebook: 978-1-57167-773-0

Printed in the United States

SAGAMORE
P U B L I S H I N G

1807 N. Federal Dr.
Urbana, IL 61801
www.sagamorepublishing.com

Contents

Acknowledgements..v
Preface vii
Editors ix
Contributors.. xi

Chapter 1   Recreation and Leisure in North American Life
             Cheryl L. Stevens and Keri A. Schwab...3

Chapter 2   Understanding Careers in Recreation, Parks, Sport Management,
             Hospitality, and Tourism
             Cheryl L. Stevens and Keri A. Schwab...27

Chapter 3   Community Recreation and Leisure Services
             Clifton Watts and Kindal Shores..49

Chapter 4   Recreation in Nonprofit Organizations
             Jo An M. Zimmermann...75

Chapter 5   Armed Forces Recreation
             Token D. Barnthouse and Asuncion T. Suren 101

Chapter 6   Outdoor Recreation in Federal, State, and Local Parks
             William Hendricks, Tony Sisto, and Cheryl L. Stevens 119

Chapter 7   Recreational Therapy and Therapeutic Recreation
             Richard Williams and Thomas K. Skalko 149

Chapter 8   Campus Recreation, Leisure, and Intramurals
             Doug Kennedy and Tina M. Aldrich 167

Chapter 9   Sport Management and Sport Teams
             Robert J. Barcelona 193

Chapter 10   Event Management
             Emilyn Sheffield and Polly Crabtree...221

Chapter 11   The Hospitality Industry
             Morgan W. Geddie, Yao-Yi Fu, and Chang Lee 245

Chapter 12   Travel and Tourism
             Vinod Sasidharan and Greg Shaw..269

Chapter 13   Commercial Recreation and Leisure Businesses
             Paige P. Viren and Jim Greiner..295

Chapter 14   Preparing for a Career in Recreation
             Craig M. Ross 321

Chapter 15   Forces Shaping the Future
             James Murphy and Daniel Dustin..341

Index 361

Acknowledgements

This complete revision of Kraus's *Career Perspectives* text would not have been possible without the collaborative efforts of many individuals. We started the project determined to produce a book that would introduce student to careers in recreation, parks, sports management, hospitality, and tourism by helping them link their passions to career possibilities. Like most major projects, this one required more time, creativity, and collaborative effort than initially anticipated.

Thanks go first to the editorial team: Emilyn Sheffield, who ignited everyone's passion for the project by sharing her creative vision; Larry Allen, who proved adept at recruiting qualified authors and getting chapters completed; Jim Murphy, who provided necessary, ongoing mentoring, editorial, and visionary guidance.

Second, this book would not be what it is without retired park ranger and contributing author Tony Sisto's vision for the passions, pay and perks, preparation, and possibilities model, which he created in his first draft of the Outdoor Recreation chapter. It took a practitioner to show us (the academics) how to communicate clearly and concisely with our future recreation professionals.

We were committed to providing an edited book that was current, consistent in format, and aligned with our audience's needs. Toward this end, a meeting was held at NRPA in 2008, during which Larry Allen, Bob Barcelona, and Doug Kennedy provided valuable input that shaped the final format. Jim Murphy collaborated with Cheryl to produce the "Leisure Service Delivery System: Evolving Structure" model. The model is important because it allows us to place recreation-related careers on a continuum, which honors an emerging future where organizations have flexible boundaries. In Chapter 15, Jim Murphy and Dan Dustin graciously share their vision for forces shaping the future of recreation, parks, sport management, hospitality, and tourism.

Special thanks go to Dan Dustin, who came up with the "Career With Meaning" title concept; Craig Ross, who shared his expertise on career preparation; and Richard Williams, who allowed Cheryl to practice editing skills with him. All of the contributors deserve special recognition for their time and patience with multiple revisions. Last, but not least, *A Career With Meaning* would not be what it is without all of the recreation, parks, sport management, hospitality, and tourism professionals who took the time to provide informational interviews, break-out box material, and quotes to make the book useful, informative, and interesting to read. We are both grateful to our family and friends, especially Doug Lamont, who supported Cheryl throughout the four-year process to complete the first edition, and to James Shell, who encouraged Keri throughout the second edition revisions. She is also appreciative of the support, guidance, and feedback from the entire editorial team: to Emilyn for her attention to details, to Larry for rounding up authors, to Cheryl for helping to expand many key concepts, and to Jim for sharing and expanding on his vision of a flourishing field.

Our hope is that this text will help move the recreation-related profession toward a new status among undergraduate students: that of intended major rather than discovery major. Too many of our best alumni did not discover this major until they had been in college a while, changing from major to major, searching for the right fit. Eventually, someone pointed them in the right direction, and they "discovered" recreation, parks, sport management, hospitality, or tourism. Every day we hear, "Why didn't someone tell me sooner that I could have a career where I get paid to do this?"

Many thanks to all who contributed to *A Career With Meaning*, which we believe will help resolve this problem by helping students match their passions to the right possibilities earlier in their educational and career planning processes.

—Keri A. Schwab
Second edition lead editor and contributing author

—Cheryl L. Stevens
First edition lead editor and contributing author

Preface

You probably find yourself reading this book because you are enrolled in an educational program related to recreation, parks, sport, hospitality, and/or tourism. You likely are in this program of study because you personally enjoy the same activities and have decided you want a career doing something you love. Who wouldn't want a job where they get up every day wanting to go to work? Plus, you probably have questions such as the following: What kind of a job could I get? How much would it pay? What kind of education and experience will I need to meet my career goals? Perhaps the most important question you have is, would I really love it as much as I think?

The purpose of this book is to connect you with top professionals in all aspects of recreation, parks, sport management, hospitality, and tourism careers so they can help you find the answers you need. Professionals in recreation-related careers tend to have passion for one or more of the following:

- Being outdoors and caring for the environment
- Working to improve quality of life for others
- Playing games and sports
- Creating exciting events
- Entrepreneurism and being your own boss

There are few things we can say that apply to all careers in recreation, parks, tourism, and leisure because so many opportunities are available. As these careers cover many settings, skill sets, and populations, interests and experiences will vary from person to person. However, if you find some (or all) of these qualities apply to you, keep reading:

- You think recreation is fun and exciting
- You want to make a difference
- You enjoy working with people
- You enjoy a challenge
- You're a problem solver and enjoy finding creative solutions
- You like being hands-on and involved in the action
- Sitting at a desk all day doesn't suit you
- You like doing different things and being in different places
- Being passionate about your career is important to you
- You are open-minded when it comes to people—their varied backgrounds, likes and dislikes, and needs and wants
- You can think on your feet without going off the deep end
- You can be both a leader and a team player, depending on the situation
- You do not mind flexible work hours and you are willing to work when other people want to recreate, such as during holidays and vacations
- You believe everyone in a community has the right to play and recreate
- You like the idea of helping to create and implement sustainable, eco-sensitive solutions for communities and the environment
- You would be thrilled to enter a career in which your knowledge and skills are transferable across many fields in recreation, parks, sport management, hospitality, and tourism, providing continual prospects for personal and professional growth

We, the editors and contributing authors, promise that a variety of fulfilling career opportunities exist—careers with pay and perks such as having a job you love, experiencing challenge and personal growth, satisfaction, and benefits. What it takes to find and prepare for these jobs is a little time and effort into your personal career exploration.

This revised second edition offers you new perspectives on the field and updates on trends and research related to each career area. Of note is the renewed emphasis in our field, and thus on understanding the role recreation and leisure play in promoting health and wellness, sustainability, and social justice. Examples of these concepts are woven throughout each chapter and brought to life via anecdotes, quotes, and photos from professionals working in the field. In addition, second edition authors used examples from current research to link each career area to the many benefits that park, recreation, sport, tourism, and leisure services may provide. Finally, each chapter ends with an opportunity for you to actively engage in a little detective work and self-reflection to figure out which aspects of recreation, parks, sport management, hospitality, and tourism may be for right you. Once you figure out your specific interests, the chapter on career preparation will help you create a plan to gain the education and work experiences needed to build your ideal career.

As you read this book, you will discover possibilities you have never dreamed of, or perhaps, if you have thought of them, you were unsure how someone could get a job doing "that." All of the authors and editors are passionate about what they do, and if one of their career areas is right for you, they would love to have you join their team!

Editors

Keri A. Schwab, PhD
Assistant Professor
Recreation, Parks, and Tourism Administration Department
California Polytechnic University, San Luis Obispo

Dr. Schwab is passionate about community recreation and the positive impact recreation may have on youth, families, and communities. She teaches core undergraduate courses including Introduction to RPTA, Evaluation and Assessment Methods, and Programming and Leadership. Dr. Schwab holds a BA degree in media arts/journalism from James Madison University, holds an MS degree in parks, recreation, and tourism from the University of Utah, and earned her doctoral degree in the same department. Her MS and PhD studies focused on positive youth development and family leisure. While earning her degrees, Dr. Schwab continued to use her journalism degree and writing experience to coauthor several articles related to the role recreation plays in positive youth development and individual, community, and environmental health. She also coedited *Just Leisure: Things That We Believe In*, a book of essays on social and environmental justice in parks, recreation, and tourism.

Dr. Schwab's professional experiences in the field include work in several youth and family-focused programs such as after school recreation, early childhood dance/movement, and home-based early intervention and as a grant writer for Head Start. Prior to her work in parks, recreation, and tourism, Dr. Schwab worked as a newspaper reporter and freelance writer and continues to use those skills on projects such as *A Career With Meaning*.

Cheryl L. Stevens, PhD
Professor, Retired
Department of Recreation and Leisure Studies
East Carolina University

Dr. Stevens is a committed recreation educator who facilitated student-centered learning in recreation and outdoor leadership for over 25 years. She taught undergraduate and graduate classes in leisure philosophy, foundations, programming, and outdoor recreation. The recipient of six teaching awards, she continuously developed and advocated for ways to improve student learning in park and recreation education. In addition to serving as lead editor for the first edition of *A Career With Meaning*, she wrote *Service Learning for Health, Physical Education, and Recreation: A Step-by-Step Guide* and numerous articles related to teaching and learning.

In addition to teaching and scholarship, Dr. Stevens served as a member of the Council on Accreditation of Parks, Recreation, Tourism and Related Professions (COAPRT), cochair of the Symposium of Experiential Education Research (SEER), board member of the Society of Park and Recreation Education (SPRE), and editor of the Research Update column in *Parks and Recreation* magazine.

James F. Murphy, PhD
Professor Emeritus
Department of Recreation, Parks, and Tourism
San Francisco State University

Dr. Murphy received his BA in recreation from San Francisco State University (1966), MS with honors in recreation and park administration from Indiana University (1967), and PhD from Oregon State University (1972).

He has authored, coauthored, edited, and coedited eight textbooks including *Concepts of Leisure*, *Leisure Service Delivery System*, *Recreation and Leisure Service for the Disadvantaged*, and *Leisure Systems*. He has written many professional and juried articles and conducted numerous workshops and made many presentations at state, regional, national, and international conferences. He served six years on the SPRE Board of Directors, including one term as president. He was president of the Academy of Leisure Sciences (2008–2009) as well as a charter fellow of the Academy of Leisure Sciences (1980). In 2002, Dr. Murphy received the National Literary Award from the National Recreation and Park Association and, in 2008, he received the Distinguished Colleague Award of the Society of Park and Recreation Educators, NRPA.

Lawrence R. Allen, PhD
Dean
College of Health , Education, and Human Development
Clemson University

In May 2003, Dr. Lawrence R. Allen became dean of the College of Health, Education, and Human Development at Clemson University. From August 2001 to May 2003, he served as interim dean. He received his PhD from the University of Maryland in recreation with a specialty area in counseling and his undergraduate degree in education from West Chester University of Pennsylvania.

Dr. Allen has been active professionally for the past 34 years with memberships in several professional organizations. In 1987, he was elected to the Academy of Leisure Sciences, and in 1995, he served as the president of the Academy. In 1996, he was elected to the American Academy of Park and Recreation Administration. He has a strong commitment to professional practice in leisure and tourism services and has served on various boards of directors and state and national committees.

Dr. Allen has written extensively with his primary interest being the impact of recreation and other out-of-school experiences on individual and community well-being. Along with colleagues at Clemson University, he has authored several articles and manuals revolving around the development and implementation of an outcome-based model (Benefits-Based Programming) of youth program delivery that enhances the youth's ability to overcome and cope with the stress and pressures they face in today's social environment. He has been instrumental in the development of a master's degree in youth development leadership at Clemson University, and he is interested in the integration of free-choice learning experiences with the more traditional educational systems employed within the United States and throughout the world.

Emilyn A. Sheffield, PhD
Professor
Department of Recreation and Parks Management
California State University, Chico

Dr. Sheffield loves every aspect of parks and recreation! She has worked in and taught about tourism, community recreation, fitness, special events, and conference planning in California, Texas, and Missouri. Working with industry sponsors, she develops service learning field schools around themes of national parks, community-based stewardship, hospitality, and conference management. Dr. Sheffield's interdisciplinary team of faculty, students, and field-based professionals complete destination projects for trails, heritage tourism, and scenic byways. The National Park Service, the USDA Forest Service, the Bureau of Land Management, the U.S. Army Corps of Engineers, the U.S. Fish and Wildlife Service are recent project sponsors and partners. She is the past president of the Association of Partners for Public Lands Board of Directors and currently serves on the Executive Committee of the California Roundtable on Recreation, Parks, and Tourism.

Contributors

Tina M. Aldrich was an assistant professor in the Department of Recreation and Leisure Studies at Virginia Wesleyan College. Tragically, she passed away shortly after completing her work for this text and after a brief fight with cancer. Her experience of over 20 years in the field seasoned her in government recreation, campus recreation, administration, and outdoor leadership. She was the past chair of the Recreation Leisure Section of Virginia Association of Health, Physical Education, Recreation, and Dance (VAHPERD) and made numerous presentations at state and national professional conferences. She received a BS in physical education from Keene State College, an MS in adult education from the University of Southern Maine, and an EdD in recreation from The University of Arkansas. She spent 12 years in Maine teaching and administering campus recreation, outdoor skills, leadership, and outdoor ethics at the University of Southern Maine, Outward Bound, and the L.L. Bean Outdoor Discovery School.

Robert J. Barcelona is an associate professor in the Youth Development Leadership Program and the Department of Parks, Recreation, and Tourism Management at Clemson University. Dr. Barcelona received his doctorate from Indiana University after working professionally in the field of athletics and campus recreation. He has worked with numerous recreation and sport organizations in both programming and research efforts. Dr. Barcelona has won awards for his teaching and research at Indiana University, the University of New Hampshire, and Clemson University, and he received a special citation award from the New Hampshire Recreation and Parks Association for his work with youth sports and coaching education. His research on sport and recreation management has been published in refereed journals, trade magazines, and textbooks. Dr. Barcelona is also the coauthor of the textbook *Leisure Services Management*.

Token D. Barnthouse has worked for US Navy MWR for more than 14 years. He currently serves as the MWR recreation director at NAS Fallon, Nevada. He completed a bachelor's in recreation and park administration in 1997 and a master's degree in recreation and park administration in 2004 from Indiana University. His MWR duty stations include NAS Keflavik, Iceland; CFA Sasebo, Japan; NSWC Crane, Indiana; Johnston Atoll, AFB, Hawaii; CFA Chinhae, Republic of South Korea; NSWC Indian Head, Maryland; Naval Base Guam, Marianas Islands; NAS Sigonella, Italy; and currently, NAS Fallon, Nevada. Barnthouse has supervised a diverse set of core and business operations for Navy MWR in varying capacities. He is also a course facilitator for several key managerial and leadership competency courses for Navy MWR professionals. His performance has garnered several managerial excellence awards and recognition.

Polly Crabtree has directed, or provided assistance with, hundreds of events for California State University, Chico in her role as associate director for the Office of Alumni and Parent Relations. These events have run the gamut from small, intimate affairs to events for more than 1,000 attendees. Crabtree started her post-college career with 17 years of retail management, which provided a good training ground for the fast-paced and chaotic lifestyle of an event planner. Her current position provides her the capability and unique resources to train university students who are interested in becoming event planning professionals.

Daniel Dustin is a professor and former chair of the Department of Parks, Recreation, and Tourism in the College of Health at the University of Utah. He served previously as Frost Professor and chair of the Department of Health, Physical Education, and Recreation in the College of

Education at Florida International University in Miami and as professor and chair of the Department of Recreation, Parks, and Tourism in the College of Professional Studies and Fine Arts at San Diego State University. Dr. Dustin's academic interests center on the moral and ethical bases for leisure and recreation activity preferences and behaviors. A past president of the Society of Park and Recreation Educators (SPRE) and the Academy of Leisure Sciences, in 1993, he received the National Recreation and Park Association's Literary Award, and in 1994, he was named an "honorary lifetime member" of the California Park Rangers Association for his contributions to the literature of outdoor recreation planning and policy. In 2001, he received the SPRE Distinguished Colleague Award for a lifetime of achievement. *Stewards of Access/Custodians of Choice: A Philosophical Foundation for Parks, Recreation, and Tourism* (4th ed.); *The Wilderness Within: Reflections on Leisure and Life* (4th ed.); *Nature and the Human Spirit: Toward an Expanded Land Management Ethic; Making a Difference in Academic Life: A Handbook for Park, Recreation, and Tourism Educators and Graduate Students; Service Living: Building Community Through Public Parks and Recreation; Speaking Up and Speaking Out: Working for Social and Environmental Justice Through Parks, Recreation, and Leisure*; and *Just Leisure: Things That We Believe In* are among his recent works as an author and editor.

Yao-Yi Fu is an associate professor of the Department of Tourism, Conventions, and Event Management at Indiana University-Purdue University-Indianapolis (IUPUI). She received her PhD from the Pennsylvania State University in hotel, restaurant, and institutional management. Prior to her current appointment with IUPUI, she taught courses in resort and lodging management and hospitality management at all levels at the Pennsylvania State University and at California State University, Chico. She has work experience in hotel and restaurant businesses, special events planning, and theme park planning. Her teaching and research interests include service failure and service recovery in the tourism and hospitality industry, measurement of customer satisfaction and service quality, tourists' travel decision making, tourist behavior, and tourism destination development and marketing.

Morgan W. Geddie is the department chair and a professor of resort and lodging management in the Department of Recreation, Hospitality, and Parks Management at California State University, Chico. He is also associate dean of the College of Communication and Education at California State University, Chico. Professor Geddie received his doctorate from Oklahoma State University in occupational and adult education with an emphasis in human resources development. He also has an MBA with an emphasis in marketing from the University of Central Oklahoma and a BS in hotel and restaurant management from Oklahoma State University. Before joining the faculty at Chico State, he taught at the University of Houston, Oklahoma State University, Eastern Illinois University, and Arkansas Tech University. He also has several years of hotel experience in the New York City, New York, and Charlotte, North Carolina, markets. Professor Geddie specializes in the areas of lodging and cruise line management. He has published in many journals, textbooks, and trade magazines as well as been a featured speaker at several conferences.

Jim Greiner, founder and president of Wildwater Ltd. Rafting and Starfish Exuma Adventure in the Bahamas, is passionate and committed to outdoor adventures. In addition to his entrepreneurial ventures, Greiner has over 30 years of experience in three cities as a parks and recreation director, and he has been honored with numerous awards in the fields of municipal parks and recreation, tourism, and ecotourism. His wrote *The Middle Atlantic Region Campers Guidebook* and has been involved in leadership roles with a variety of outdoor recreation and adventure organizations such as the Virginia Recreation and Parks Association, Eastern Professional River Outfitters Association, America Outdoors Association (25 years), and Commercial Recreation and Leisure Businesses. Receiving his bachelor's degree in parks and recreation management from North Carolina State University and a master's in leisure services management from Florida State University, Greiner's real-world experience and academic background provide a unique perspective.

William Hendricks is a professor and head of the Recreation, Parks, and Tourism Administration Department at California Polytechnic State University, San Luis Obispo. Dr. Hendricks earned his doctorate at the University of Utah. His research interests in the human dimensions of natural resources and park and recreation management have been complemented by his experience in the field that spans nearly 30 years as a park ranger, employee in the ski industry, and educator. He is currently a member of the California Roundtable on Recreation, Parks, and Tourism and a trustee of the California Foundation for Parks and Recreation. Dr. Hendricks is a recipient of the USFS Rocky Mountain Region Partners in Action Award; the International Journal of Wilderness and USFS Excellence in Wilderness Management Research Award; the Honorary Lifetime Member and Professional Citation Awards of the Park Rangers Association of California; the Cal Poly College of Agriculture Dole Faculty Teaching Excellence Award; the Cal Poly Distinguished Faculty Service-Learning Award; the University of Utah, Department of Parks, Recreation, and Tourism Honored Alumnus Award; and the Cal Poly Distinguished Scholarship Award.

Doug Kennedy is a professor in the Department of Recreation and Leisure Studies at Virginia Wesleyan College. He has also served as the associate dean for campus recreation and oversaw aquatics, fitness, recreational sports, and outdoor activities. Prior to his arrival at Virginia Wesleyan College, he gained experience in environmental resources, employee and campus recreation, fitness, and military recreation while employed in the public and private sectors. He has earned degrees from the University of Delaware, Southern Illinois University, and Temple University. He has also served as the president of the Virginia Recreation and Park Society and chair of the Council on Accreditation. A three-time recipient of the Samuel Nelson Gray Distinguished Teaching Award, Virginia Recreation and Park Society's Fellows Award, and YMCA's Service to Youth Award, Dr. Kennedy has made over 100 presentations at professional events and led delegations to Uzbekistan to assist with recreation planning and democracy education.

Chang Lee is an assistant professor of resort and lodging management in the Department of Recreation, Hospitality, and Parks Management at California State University, Chico. Prior to joining California State University Chico, he taught hospitality and event management related courses at the University of Alabama, New Mexico State University, and Black Hills State University. He earned his PhD from Oklahoma State University in hospitality administrations, education specialist (EDS) degree in human services from University of Central Missouri, master's in commercial aviation (MCA) from Delta State University, and bachelor of science (BS) in hospitality and tourism management from Black Hills State University. Dr. Lee has over 15 years of management experience in the hospitality and travel industry. He has worked in different segments of the industry including hotels, restaurants, resorts, tour companies, events, and clubs in different positions. His research involves the use and impact of diversified workforces in the hospitality and tourism industry. Dr. Lee published in scholarly journals and has made numerous presentations at national and international conferences. He is academically and professionally affiliated with various national and international associations.

Craig M. Ross is a professor in the Department of Recreation, Park, and Tourism Studies at Indiana University (IU) and specializes in sport management. He has been involved in recreation and sport programming and administration in a variety of work settings for over 40 years including municipal parks and recreation, high school athletics, and campus recreational sports. Since 1993, he has been on faculty at IU with teaching responsibilities in recreational sport management. His research activities have focused on collecting and examining data that contribute to the building of the infrastructure and body of knowledge of recreational sport management as well as envisioning the future for the profession. His research focuses on youth sport and physical activity, recreational sport management, and the scholarship of teaching and learning.

Vinod Sasidharan is an associate professor in the School of Hospitality and Tourism Management at San Diego State University. His national and international research and consultation expertise includes the application of sustainability indices for the evaluation of grassroots community development initiatives, implementation of local community participation in planning and decision making for sustainable tourism development, measurement of happiness (and well-being) and Millennium Development Goals (MDGs) accomplishments in community tourism settings, sustainability assessment of destination communities, and formulation of corporate social responsibility strategies in tourism. He holds a master's degree in tourism policy and management from the University of Birmingham, UK, and a doctorate in leisure studies from the Pennsylvania State University. Dr. Sasidharan is past president of the Great Western Travel and Tourism Research Association and the California Society of Park and Recreation Educators. He currently serves on the steering committee for The City of San Diego's Balboa Park Water Sustainability initiative and the Sustainable Tourism Resource Council for Hostelling International. He has also served on the Destination Marketing Association International Student and Educator Advisory Council.

Greg Shaw is an associate professor and department chair of the Department of Recreation, Parks, and Tourism Administration at California State University, Sacramento. Dr. Shaw has served as a board member of the California Parks and Recreation Society Educators Section, the California Geographical Society, and the California State Fair Cultural Advisory Council. He is also on the editorial review board for the *Journal of Tourism Insights* and is the wine editor for *Cuisine Noir* magazine. Dr. Shaw's interests and teaching focuses on wine tourism, architectural tourism, and open space in the urban landscape. Dr. Shaw holds a bachelor's degree in architecture from Georgia Institute of Technology, a master's in recreation administration from California State University, Sacramento, and a doctorate in geography (minor in landscape architecture) from the University of California, Davis.

Kindal Shores is an associate professor at East Carolina University in the Department of Recreation and Leisure Studies. She also serves as the faculty fellow for the Honors College at East Carolina University. Dr. Shores draws on her research experience in both exercise science and leisure studies to investigate the contribution of community parks and recreation for healthy, active living. She has worked on funded research projects linking parks and health for the National Recreation and Park Association, Robert Wood Johnson Foundation, the Association for Prevention and Teaching Research, Be Active North Carolina, the Be Active Appalachian Partnership, the Centers for Disease Control and Prevention, and numerous county commissioners. Dr. Shores is an associate editor for the academic journal *Journal of Leisure Research* and has been recognized with multiple university awards for teaching and scholarship.

Tony Sisto is a retired park ranger with over 32 years of experience in the National Park Service. He stays involved with park issues in his volunteer work with the U.S. Association of National Park Rangers and with the International Ranger Federation. When not traveling to world-protected areas, he lives in California.

Thomas K. Skalko, PhD, LRT/CTRS, FDRT, is a professor of recreational therapy at East Carolina University and an honorary professor, College of Health Sciences at the University of Kwazulu-Natal. Thom has been practicing recreational therapy since 1974 with roles in health care and human service delivery and education including creator of the therapeutic recreation program at the Middle Georgia Community Mental Health Center; director of recreational therapy, Department of Psychiatry, and director and developer of child life services, Department of Pediatrics, Walter Reed Army Medical Center; and director of the ECU Horizons Day Treatment Program. He has been engaged in higher education since 1981. Skalko is a founding member and a past president (1992–1993) of ATRA and has served on committees including ATRA Federal Public Policy; ATRA–WHO

International Classification of Functioning, Disability, and Health Team; ATRA Annual; and ATRA Newsletter. Thom is currently chair of the North Carolina Board for Recreational Therapy Licensure and serves as chair of the Committee on Accreditation of Recreational Therapy Education (CARTE) of the Commission on Accreditation of Allied Health Education Programs (CAAHEP).

Asuncion T. Suren is a former assistant professor in the Department of Recreation, Parks, and Tourism at San Francisco State University. She also directed the campus-wide Youth and Human Services Nonprofit Certificate program. In these roles, she taught multiple courses on recreation and leisure and nonprofit administration. In addition to her years in higher education, Asuncion is considered a multifaceted professional with 15 years of recreation and consulting experience combined. She has facilitated numerous community service needs in the areas of assessment planning, program development, and evaluation. She attributes gaining these transferable skills to working in Armed Forces Recreation. Asuncion has served as a director and program director for community recreation centers both stateside and abroad. She directed the Youth Services Center for Edwards Air Force Base in the Mojave Desert and the 2-2-0 Recreation Center in Korea.

Paige P. Viren is an assistant professor in the Department of Recreation and Leisure Studies at East Carolina University and an affiliate faculty with ECU's Center for Sustainable Tourism. Her research interests revolve around consumer behavior and tourism, with a special focus on adventure travel and sustainable community-based tourism in rural areas. Dr. Viren has worked closely with the Adventure Travel Trade Association examining adventure industry issues and trends and in eastern North Carolina with rural communities in developing sustainable community-based tourism as an alternative means of diversifying the rural economy. She has over 12 years of travel industry management experience, which offers her valuable insight and an understanding of the importance of translating research into practical application for the tourism industry. As a long-time participant and advocate of adventure travel, she believes these types of travel experiences promote cultural understanding, fulfill personal dreams, and encourage environmental sustainability

Clifton Watts Jr. is an assistant professor in the Department of Recreation and Leisure Studies at East Carolina University. Dr. Watts's research and scholarly interests are directed to (1) evaluating how and to what extent communities enact collaborative, interdisciplinary approaches to address the needs of youth; (2) understanding what contexts and transactions are linked to positive youth development; and (3) examining how parks and open spaces promote healthy behavior and environmental awareness in youth. He has an extensive background as an evaluator; assisting with the design and execution of studies for a range of prevention and intervention programs aimed at high-risk youth. He has worked with community-based programs emanating from municipal recreation and park departments, schools, hospitals, criminal justice, and other grassroots agencies. He is a member of the National Recreation and Park Association and serves as an associate editor for the academic journal *Leisure Sciences*.

Richard Williams is an associate professor in the Department of Recreation and Leisure Studies at East Carolina University in Greenville, NC. He teaches primarily in the recreational therapy curriculum but also teaches leisure theory and philosophy and research methods courses. His research interests are varied but are currently focused on the investigation of effectiveness of recreational therapy services for people with spinal cord injuries, stroke, and other disabilities.

Jo An M. Zimmermann, CPRP, has a BS in recreation and park administration from Western Illinois University, an MBA from Olivet Nazarene University, and a PhD in parks, recreation, and tourism management from Clemson University. She is currently an associate professor in the Department of Health and Human Performance at Texas State University. Her professional experience includes recreation program development/management and training and developing training materials while working for and consulting with recreation agencies in both nonprofit and community sectors. Dr. Zimmermann is a Certified Park and Recreation Professional, was named the Al Hattendorf Professional of the Year by the Illinois Park and Recreation Association in 1999, received a Special Recognition Award from the American Camp Association in 2002, and was named a Service Learning Fellow by Texas State University in 2011. Dr. Zimmermann has traveled extensively, allowing her to investigate many approaches to the delivery of recreation services and programs.

"

Recreation improves awareness, deepens understanding, stimulates appreciation, develops one's powers, and enlarges the sources of enjoyment. It promotes individual fulfillment. It encourages self-discovery. It helps give meaning to live.

—David E. Gray, 1972

"

1

Recreation and Leisure in North American Life

Cheryl L. Stevens
East Carolina University

Keri A. Schwab
California Polytechnic State University,
San Luis Obispo

Focus Questions

Q: I understand that this book covers careers in recreation, parks, sport management, hospitality, and tourism, but why is leisure important?

A: If you think of leisure in a casual way, it has limited meaning to most people. As the word is used in everyday language, leisure refers to idle time or being lazy. If you only use these basic definitions, leisure will not seem important. However, once you consider the complex dimensions of leisure, you will learn how leisure experiences are when people feel free, present, and connected. During leisure, we connect to other people and the environment in many meaningful ways. So as you enrich your understanding of leisure, you will come to see how integral leisure is to quality of life.

Q: I heard someone say that recreation is associated with humanism. What does that mean?

A: Humanism, as a philosophical school of thought, attaches great importance to human dignity, concerns, and abilities. Social and environmental justice issues, such as services for often underserved groups (i.e., youth, elderly, minorities, and those who are economically disadvantaged), continue to be important. Also, since many North Americans experience stress because they feel rushed and harried, recreation and leisure have the potential to greatly enhance quality of life for all.

Q: What motivates a person to enter a recreation-related profession?

A: Recreation-related professions provide a great opportunity to align your life's work with something you are really passionate about. Individuals attracted to careers in recreation, parks, sport management, hospitality, and tourism all enjoy some aspect of recreation activities themselves, and they also have a strong commitment to one or more of the following motivations: improving quality of life for others, affinity for nature, love of play, and/or entrepreneurism.

Q: Why do people invest significant amounts of time and money in recreation and leisure experiences?

A: Research has documented numerous tangible (and some less tangible) benefits from recreation and leisure experiences including stress management, improved physical and mental health, personal growth, spirituality, reduced crime and social alienation, economic growth, and environmental stewardship. Perhaps even more important, recreation and leisure experiences add balance and meaning to life, improve quality of life, and lead to greater life satisfaction.

Key Terms

Leisure	Play
Time free from work	Humanism
Discretionary time	Recreation-related profession
Freedom from	Quality of life
Freedom to	Affinity for nature
State of mind	Love of play
Recreational activity	Entrepreneurism
Public recreation	Direct service
Recreation	Inclusive service
Public park	So-importants
Hospitality	Benefits
Tourism	Purple recreation

Inspirational Experiences

Stories of meaningful personal experiences are a great way to better understand why people are passionate about recreation, parks, sport management, hospitality, and tourism. Here are a few stories to show you how leisure experiences are important to quality of life and life satisfaction.

A Senior Leisure Experience: I currently live in a nursing home because I had a severe stroke about a year ago. I can honestly say the only reason I have not gone into a severe depression is our leisure encounter group. The recreational therapists are great and they keep me busy. It's helped me make new friends, it's tested my endurance, and it's something I can look forward to every day.

—Female, Age 72

What's Great About Being a Camp Counselor: Camp was a lot more than I expected because I learned so much about myself. I learned to take leadership for a group of teens and not be afraid of them and what they think of me. I got the chance to make connections with people from different countries and from all walks of life. I got to see the campers overcome their greatest fears, and that put a smile on my face. Some were afraid of horses, others didn't know how to swim, and some didn't want to try a new activity. I learned to gently push them to their limits without making them push back in the wrong way. Some mornings I didn't want to get up, but I did. That says a lot about camp life and the positive state of mind you develop while in the company of your camp family.

—Female, 4-H Camp Counselor, Age 22

Enjoy Work and It Becomes Leisure: I love computers. I have a degree in computer engineering, and I really love spending hours in front of the computer screen. I asked my sister if I could put a computer inside her computer. She had no clue what I was talking about, but she let me do it. It took me hours—uploading, downloading different files and applications—but I had a blast. When I finished, I presented it to her with a smile on my face, and then I showed her how to work her two computers in one.

—Male, Age 27

Competitive Sport: I played women's competitive softball for four years. I have so many great memories from the games. Nothing compares to sharing time with friends and others with a common interest; we laughed all the time. I'm very competitive, so that aspect of the game gave me both a release and a chance to show my skills. The tougher the game, the better I liked it. It was such an adrenaline rush. One thing I really miss now is the fitness—I could run, hit, throw, and exercise in a way that felt more like fun than work.

—Female, Age 50

Framing the Discussion

These personal stories show some of the benefits that recreation and leisure experiences have for individuals and the professionals who provide them. An important first step for you to take to learn about the career options covered in this book is to carefully consider the meaning behind terms used in the profession. Specifically, we will look in depth at the concepts of leisure, play, and humanism. You should also understand the meaning of each word in the book's subtitle: recreation, parks, sport management, hospitality, and tourism. We will start by discussing leisure because it is the broadest term. Then, we will cover the other words and concepts in a way that helps you build your growing understanding into a coherent whole.

What Do You Mean by Leisure?

Do not be too hasty in dismissing leisure as unimportant. The word **leisure** can have a bad rap when it is equated with idle time, being lazy, or time left over when everything "important" is finished. Even though **discretionary time** is the most common view of leisure in North America, the meaning of the word *leisure* is richer and more complex than "time where you get to make a choice." Thus, you should become familiar with the deeper meanings so you will truly know what "leisure services" are about.

Link, a leisure education consultant, said,

Leisure has many different definitions—some involving time, some relating to an activity being done, some relating to state of mind. Personally, I am most at leisure when I feel free, present, and integrated. I like this definition for myself, because it allows me to experience leisure at any moment, even in just a few minutes.[1]

The following sections will introduce you to several historical views of leisure, and further explain leisure as experience and activity.

Leisure and Freedom

Leisure has been associated with **time free from work** since the days of ancient Greece, when the best life was seen as one where male citizens who did not have to labor then had time to pursue truth and self-understanding.[2] The Greeks called this time *schole*—note this word's close association with the English word for "school"—because the Greeks considered learning a privilege and considered having the time and opportunity to learn as part of having the best life possible. Because Greek males who had schole did not have to work, in the sense of physical labor, they were able to enjoy learning and thinking freely about interesting questions such as "How should we best live?" Schole was their leisure (and this view could put a different spin on your college educational experience!).

> Something will have gone out of us as a people if we ever let the remaining wilderness be destroyed; if we permit the last virgin forests to be turned into comic books and plastic cigarette cases; if we drive the few remaining members of the wild species into zoos or to extinction; if we pollute the last clean air and dirty the last clean streams and push our paved roads through the last of the silence, so that never again will Americans be free from noise, the exhausts, the stinks of human and automotive waste. And so that never again can we have the chance to see ourselves single, separate, vertical and individual in the world, part of the environment of trees and rocks and soil, brother to the other animals, part of the natural world and competent to belong in it.
>
> We simply need that wild country available to us, even if we never do more than drive to its edge and look in. For it can be a means of reassuring ourselves of our sanity as creatures, a part of the geography of hope.
>
> —Wallace Stegner

Today, however, we tend to associate school with work, or at least something required to earn a better paying job. In part, this change in viewpoints happened when the meaning of leisure shifted during Roman times when leisure started to be viewed as the opposite of work. Although ancient Roman thinkers helped spread many of the classical ideals in knowledge, arts, music, and literature across Europe, the majority of Roman authors viewed leisure as *otium*, which translates as rest and recreation.[3] *Otium* (i.e., leisure) implied that leisure was a time of nonactivity useful only for recovering or restoring from work. Leisure was viewed as a well-earned rest and reward for a lifetime of hard work (*negotium*).

This work–leisure dichotomy that was introduced into Western civilization over 2,000 years ago is how most people in North America view leisure today; that is, work and leisure are seen as opposite concepts. The Romans believed a person needed to earn his right to rest and relaxation by first working hard. Today, people think about leisure only casually and continue to view leisure and work as opposites. The most commonly understood definition of leisure for people living in North America is time free from work. However, it is important to consider more complex understandings of leisure to understand the true value of leisure services.

Bregha expands our understanding of the connection between leisure and freedom when he urges us to consider that leisure can be both "freedom from" and "freedom to."[4] **Freedom from** is associated with time free from constraint, oppression, or manipulation. For example, if a person views her job as controlling time and choices, she will not have a leisure experience while working. However, if a person has a high-autonomy job and feels in control of and enjoys work (which can be creative and meaningful), then she may experience leisure and meaning during at least some of her work.

Pavelka, author of *It's Not About Time: Rediscovering Leisure in a Changing World*, noted that some people experience more meaning and satisfaction from their work time than their nonwork time.[5] Hochschild, author of *The Time Bind*, explained, "Today's managers have successfully engineered the workplace to serve as surrogate family, and while workers will state they value family more than work, they often find work more personally gratifying than home."[6] There are always internal and external forces that impact our lives, and those forces often place additional constraints on choices and time use. In these instances, an autonomous work environment can feel more like leisure than home life. For example, parents must care for their children all the time, and this limits their sense of "freedom from." In other examples, a person's personal choices may have resulted in a prison term, thus limiting freedom; a child is required to be in school; a person may feel personally guilty for not doing something society considers productive; an unemployed adult or an adult with a disability may feel he has no right to enjoy time not working because he has not earned that right. In sum, a person's perception of "freedom from" constraints, which is necessary for leisure when viewed in the modern sense (which started during Roman times), is much more complicated than just being off of work.

From a different perspective, leisure as **"freedom to"** brings us closer to the deeper meaning of leisure implied by ancient Greek scholars, that is, freedom to engage in an activity meaningful, significant, and authentic to you. Dare, Welton, and Coe stated,

> To live life to its fullest is to live creatively and to understand the freedom which under-lies human existence. To understand and accept this freedom is to be authentic. To live meaningful lives we must understand who we are—that is, we must have reflected on our lives and our projects.[7]

Finding meaning in life is central to a person's satisfaction. Frankl, a concentration camp survivor and author of the book *Man's Search for Meaning*, concluded, "Life is not primarily a quest for pleasure … but a quest for meaning. The greatest task for any person is to find meaning in his or her life."[8] And leisure can be the context in which people connect with whatever is meaningful to them. Pavelka noted, "Leisure is not so much about time as it is the personal meaning of time."[9]

Bregha cautioned that embracing leisure as "freedom to" can be our greatest opportunity and our greatest challenge because it requires the self-knowledge and wisdom to know what we truly want. Many people have great difficulty responding to this challenge when given large amounts of time free from obligation. To embrace this type of freedom, we must be willing to consciously choose goals that will bring long-term happiness and affirm our authentic and unique character. This is not always easy in a world where most of us feel our discretionary time is scarce and subject to restrictions. Most people feel they are under a lot of time stress, so they never have (or make) time to really do the self-exploration necessary to answer the question, "If I was free from all obligations, what would I truly want to do or be?"

In sum, you may be tempted to think leisure is not important in society, but this is only true if you continue to equate leisure with laziness or idle time. As you continue to learn more about leisure, we urge you to remember how leisure as "freedom to" is associated with quality of life. Meaningful leisure has the potential to improve anyone's quality of life because we are human *beings*, not human *doings*. Link hinted at the importance of leisure in a person's quality of life, telling her clients, "Leisure can be experienced every day, even if we only have five minutes. Even small amounts can turn 'surviving' into 'living.'"[10] De Graaf drove this point home, stating that the well-being of people in North America is linked to far more than gross domestic product, and we would do well to ask, "What's the economy for, anyway?"[11] This line of questioning can help policy makers consider the importance and value of health, equality, savings, and sustainability. Thus, a person's attitude toward leisure can make a tremendous difference in quality of life, and this is good news because personal attitude is something every individual can control.

Leisure as a State of Mind

The perspective of leisure as a **state of mind** provides an effective way to move past our tendency to view leisure and work as opposites. If a person enjoys meaningful work, her work becomes leisure for her because of her state of mind. Link described how leisure can be viewed subjectively as a state of mind:

> Leisure can happen when we are in various [mental] states: artistic or creative, physical, intellectual, social, spiritual, learning new things, volunteering, active, passive, or as a spectator or participant. One can be emotionally connected and engaged or not. And we can even have leisure at work and be more productive, healthy, and creative."[12]

The essence of the "leisure as a state of mind" view is that leisure is a special attitude; in fact, time and activity are irrelevant because personal feelings are what matter.[14] Therefore, if a person perceives an experience as leisure, then it is leisure for that individual. Viewing leisure as a state of mind is appealing because it gives value to the individual's subjective feelings about an experience. If your state of mind tells you that "this experience is meaningful and I choose to do it because it has value to me," no one can disagree because leisure depends on your perspective. One downside of viewing leisure as a state of mind is that researchers find it difficult to quantify how much leisure people have and what they are doing for leisure because leisure is unique to each person's perspective.

Leisure as Recreational Activity

Another view of leisure is that of **recreational activity** people choose to do because they expect to enjoy it. Leisure activities may provide personal benefits, reduce stress, or restore peace of mind. Recreational leisure activities can be virtually anything—going for a drive, playing cards or computer games, cooking, or bird-watching. People choose different activities for various reasons, and expecting to have fun is just one. Other reasons may involve social or role obligations. For example, we may go to a movie because our friends or family ask us to go (i.e., social reasons), or sometimes we go to a "fun" event because it is expected of us, such as your boss inviting you to a Christmas party (i.e., role obligations). In reality, most people have multiple reasons for choosing a particular activity. For example, a trip to the gym may be motivated by a desire to lose weight, reduce stress, meet up with a friend, and the intrinsic joy of moving and feeling powerful.

> " The space and quiet that idleness provides is a necessary condition for standing back from life and seeing it whole, for making unexpected connections and waiting for the wild summer lightning strikes of inspiration—is, paradoxically, necessary to getting any work done.
>
> —Tim Kreider[13] "

One advantage to viewing leisure as activity is that researchers can count it by asking people to record activities in time diaries. In this way, researchers can find out how much leisure time people have and what activities they prefer. Time diaries are useful for research purposes, but they are less than perfect. The primary downside to viewing leisure as recreational activity is that people have different perspectives on the same activity (going back to the "state of mind" viewpoint we just discussed). For example, some people find running enjoyable and meaningful, yet others view it as work. The leisure as recreational activity view also excludes nonactive leisure experiences some people may choose for relaxation such as taking a nap or daydreaming.

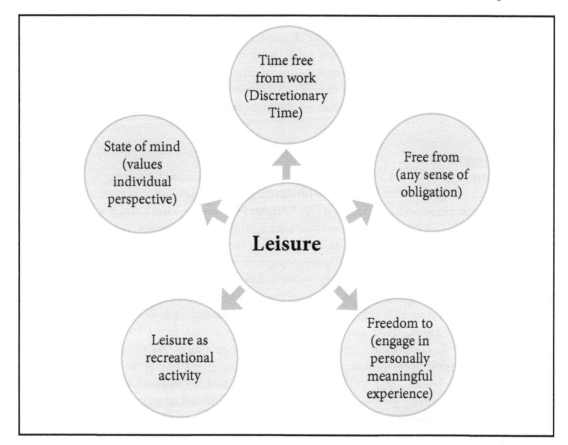

Figure 1.1. Leisure's multiple dimensions.

Now that you know more about the ways you can experience leisure (see Figure 1.1 for a visual representation), the next section provides an overview of common locations and settings for leisure experiences.

Recreation

The National Recreation and Park Association (NRPA) defines **public recreation** as activities that occur at a public park or facility, such as sports, physical activities, experiences in nature, or exposure to arts and culture, among other activities. Recreational activities can be passive or active and can be engaged in by visitors on their own time or they may be organized or conducted by employees of a recreation agency or business (see Chapter 3). DeGraaf, Jordan, and DeGraaf viewed **recreation** as any activity a person freely chooses that has the potential for achieving a desirable outcome.

These same authors defined recreation as "an activity that takes place during one's free time, is enjoyable, freely chosen, and benefits the individual emotionally, socially, physically, cognitively, and spiritually."[15] Thus, although recreation and leisure are often used interchangeably, recreation is more easily linked to measurable benefits because it involves people engaging in activities with specific goals or outcomes in mind. We will discuss the benefits of recreational activities later in this chapter.

Parks

The NRPA defines a **public park** as any area, or portion of an area, dedicated by any federal, state, or local agency primarily for public recreational use. Therefore, parks include boardwalks, green spaces, or playgrounds close to people's homes that they visit on a daily basis; metropolitan and state parks near urban areas where people may visit for a weekend; or large tracts of land such as national parks that have been reserved for all (see Chapter 6). Parks are important to quality of life even when we are not visiting them on a daily basis because we like knowing the park is there for our enjoyment and betterment, as well as that of future generations. Something about being outdoors can bring peace of mind and connect us with our sense of place in the universe. Carson noted, "Those who contemplate the beauty of the earth find reserves of strength that will endure as long as life lasts."[16]

Sport Management

Sport management is a term that is incredibly wide in scope, and can refer to any one of a number of professional careers that involve planning, organizing, leading, and controlling sporting events, programs, personnel, and facilities (see Chapter 9). McLean, Hurd, and Rogers stated that sport management is not restricted to any one sector, so it is important for individuals interested in a sport management-related career to think outside the box.[17] Some career possibilities may come to mind immediately such as collegiate, semiprofessional, professional, and amateur sport, but jobs in these settings often require specialized skill sets or advanced degrees and are highly competitive. If you love sports and are thinking about a sport-related career, think broadly about career possibilities and include other areas of sport management such as sport marketing, guest services, and sport clubs; sport arenas, coliseums, and stadiums (see Chapter 10); intramural sport (see Chapter 8); community recreation youth athletic programs (see Chapter 3); youth sport programs in nonprofit agencies and religious organizations (see Chapter 4); sport programs in military morale, recreation, and welfare (see Chapter 5), and commercial businesses involving sport facilities and sporting goods (see Chapter 13). As you can tell from this extensive list, sport management-related careers can be found in a variety of settings that you probably have not considered yet.

Hospitality

Simply put, **hospitality** is the act of providing food, beverage, lodging accommodations, and entertainment (including recreational activities) to guests. The hospitality industry includes many businesses such as hotels, resorts, cruise ships, theme parks, clubs, and restaurants. Typically, hospitality is considered a component of the tourism industry since all travelers will need hospitality upon their arrival. Hospitality, however, has its own niche since dealing with guests face to face where they sleep and eat comes with its own special set of opportunities and challenges. Lodging must be available to meet the demands of all travelers, whether families, people with pets, people with special needs and interests, people who want luxury, or people traveling on a budget. In addition to food, beverage, lodging, and entertainment, recreation specialists also provide activities or programs for children and families at destination resorts, time-shares, and campgrounds. If you are interested in providing quality customer service and working in a fast-paced industry that advances people more quickly than many, consider a number of career options that fall under the umbrella of hospitality (see Chapter 11, 12, and 13).

Tourism

Tourism can be defined as travel that occurs for recreational, leisure, or business purposes. The World Tourism Organization (UNWTO) defines tourists as people who

> travel to and stay in places outside their usual environment for more than twenty-four (24) hours and not more than one consecutive year for leisure, business, and other purposes not related to the exercise of any activity remunerated from within the place visited.[18]

Today, tourism is big business and is recognized as an expanding field within recreation and leisure services, and some in the field argue that it should be seen as a profession in its own right. However, most experts agree that it is a growth industry and is motivationally tied to a person's recreation behaviors and leisure interests.[19] According to the UNWTO, in 2012 international tourism grew by 4% from 2011 to exceed 1 billion (1,035 million) international tourist visits for the first time ever. This tourism generated $1.075 billion in U.S. dollars worldwide in 2012, up from $1,042 billion in 2011. The travel organization predicts that by 2030, international tourist visits will reach 1.8 billion.[20] Because tourism is a significant business today, and due to its obvious tie to recreation activities and leisure experiences, careers in tourism are addressed separately in Chapter 12 as well as in Chapter 10 and 11.

Play

Play is so integrally connected with having fun that our discussion about the meaning of recreation and leisure would be incomplete without it. All people know what play is from personal experience, and play occurs wherever people find it—play can happen anytime, anywhere. As the *Non-Sequitur* cartoon by Wiley Miller illustrates, children's play today involves both virtual and in-nature experiences, but both types of activity are play.

Huizinga, author of one of the original studies of play and culture, listed seven defining elements of play:

1. All play is voluntary activity, and hence, play is linked to freedom.
2. Play is not ordinary or real life—it is only pretending for fun.
3. Play is limited within time and space in that it has a beginning and an ending.
4. Play creates order by bringing a temporary and limited perfection.
5. Play has an element of tension and uncertainty.
6. All play has rules that determine what "goes" in the temporary world of play.
7. Play surrounds itself with an air of secrecy; that is, "we are different and do things differently when we play."[21]

Play can involve participating in a game of pretend, playing soccer, or playing *World of Warcraft*, and it can occur anywhere—at home, at work, on vacation, and even in a prison—because it occurs in a temporary world that the players construct.

Questions about play have fascinated people for centuries. Why do people play? What benefit is there in play? Ellis, a recognized play expert, explained that people play for two reasons: (1) to have optimal experiences and (2) to gain a sense of competence and control.[22] Consider, for example, a girl "playing" teacher with her dolls—she creates the rules of the pretend classroom and has fun handing out rewards and punishments to her "students." She has placed herself in control (a role she cannot take in real life), and her play world affords her the opportunity to feel competent and effective, just as she perceives her teacher to be.

As to how people benefit from play, the common misconception is that play is only an activity of childhood. Bregha confirmed that is how it starts: "It is a generally accepted belief that, as children, we first discover freedom, its delights and dangers, in playing."[23] However, academic researchers and business managers are increasingly discovering that play is vitally important to adults, too. Adult partners who seek novelty and play together more often stay together. Play also fosters creativity during work by facilitating the cognitive, affective, motivational, and skill conditions of the creative process.[24] For example, Google Inc. removes some of the artificial dichotomizations between work and play by expecting employees to spend 20% of their time on noncore projects, which they are expected to explore without considering profitability or marketability. Why grant people specific permission to play at work? Because companies are finding out that building play into the work culture adds to the bottom line by fostering greater satisfaction and sense of creativity among employees, who then generate more innovative products and ideas. Thus, play in the workplace is a win–win situation: Employees enjoy their work more and those companies who sanction play experience better bottom lines for it.

Clearly, play adds to a person's life at any age. As playwright George Bernard Shaw once stated, "We don't stop playing because we grow old; we grow old because we stop playing." Play is important to quality of life at any age because all humans gain joy from having peak (optimal) experiences and feeling competent and effective, even if only for a moment.

Leisure, recreation, and play are clearly linked to optimal human experience. The next section will explain, from a philosophical perspective, what humanism means to recreation.

Leisure, Recreation, and Humanism

Humanism can be described as a philosophical perspective that attaches great importance to human dignity, concerns, and abilities. Humanism is a point of view about human nature that advocates for "joyous service for the greater good of all humanity in this natural world."[25] Humanists believe that, on a deep level, every person has good inside of them in the form of human spirit, or conscience. Whether a person is in touch with, or uses, his or her conscience is another matter (which we will not debate here), but suffice it to say that recreation and leisure service providers have a long history of striving to help people develop their most human qualities.

Photo courtesy Jay Clark

A humanistic approach to recreation and leisure services is important in today's increasingly stressful and troubled world. De Graaf, coauthor of *What's the Economy for, Anyway?*, pointed out economic success can no longer be measured in only economic terms such as *gross domestic product*.[26] We must also consider other values that constitute the greatest good (health, happiness, knowledge, kindness) for the greatest number (equality, access to opportunity) over the long run (in a healthy democracy and sustainable environment). Parks and recreation visionary Gray noted in 1972 that "America is turning inward. We are reexamining our thoughts, our ideas, our motives. Our method is introspection and our goal is self-discovery...the motive is a deeper participation in life."[27] Before you dismiss Gray's commentary as potentially outdated, consider its keen relevance to today's issues:

- Most North Americans believe they face too many demands on their time on any given day and feel rushed and overwhelmed.[28]
- For most of the final quarter of the 20th century, Europeans gained relative to Americans in almost every quality of life measure.[29]
- Many people face days filled with tension, boredom, feelings of powerlessness, monotony, and frustration and have increasing problems related to physical health (i.e., heart disease, obesity, diabetes) and emotional health (i.e., anxiety, depression, addiction, and alienation).
- Although technology and connectivity have increased work efficiencies, they are merely tools and will not solve problems with the human condition.

A humanistic ethic is important to the delivery of recreation, parks, sport management, hospitality, and tourism in today's world. What this means, in a practical sense, is that we need to reconceptualize recreation from a humanistic perspective and think of health in a manner similar to that of the World Health Organization (WHO), which stated, "Health is a state of complete physical, mental and social well-being and not merely the absence of disease or infirmity."[30] For parks and recreation professionals, this means making it our business to promote health and well-being. It means keeping people well through a focus on preventive health versus treating and curing people after they are sick. It means helping people who are sick back to a path where quality of life is the highest priority. It means viewing recreation as offering psycho-social-emotional-physical benefits, in which the activity is the medium. From a humanistic perspective, recreation is the individual's internal, pleasurable response to the activity. Gray aptly put it:

> Recreation is an emotional condition within an individual human being that flows from a feeling of well-being and self-satisfaction. It is characterized by feelings of mastery, achievement, exhilaration, acceptance, success, personal worth, and pleasure. It reinforces a positive self-image. Recreation is a response to esthetic experience, achievement of personal goals, or positive feedback from others. It is independent of activity, leisure, or social acceptance.[31]

A growing number of people in North America are seeking new ways to experience the fullest of what life has to offer. Grassroots movements and the self-help industry are burgeoning with advice to help people improve the quality of their lives by slowing down, focusing on health and well-being, establishing greater intimacy with others, and creating sustainable lifestyles. These approaches to the good life embrace the fulfillment of individuals' inner experiences rather than the acquisition of things. This is ultimately the work of recreation, parks, sport management, hospitality, and tourism professionals. Humanistic values are not new to recreation; in fact, they have been with the profession since the beginning.

Next, we are going to take a brief historical tour so you can understand, in a general way, where the profession came from and where it is going. This overview illustrates how recreation and leisure programs in North America had beginnings in social services and how the profession has expanded over time to meet the needs of many client groups. This expansion is great news for you because it has opened the door for many diverse career options within recreation, parks, sport management, hospitality, and tourism professions. Meeting humanistic needs is more important now than ever no matter what career focus interests you. Also, as a side note, we will explore a detailed history of each career area in Chapters 3 to 13 because we believe history is more interesting and relevant when studied in context.

A Brief History of Recreation, Parks, Sport Management, Hospitality, and Tourism

The notion of providing recreational activities and parks in the United States has its roots in social services and human needs. The profession was established during the late 1800s as the urban population doubled and the Industrial Revolution and immigration resulted in growing social welfare concerns. Early social reformers, who were mainly private philanthropists, saw play and recreation as antidotes to all nature of ills—physical health could be improved by fresh air and physical activity, and moral character and social skills could be learned through organized recreation and play. As you can see from the break-out box, *Our Radical Roots*, the need was great. Consider that in 1890, 350,000 children were living in New York City, and they had no organized places to play.[32]

Jane Addams and Joseph Lee are two examples of the profession's prominent founders. Addams, the daughter of a wealthy man, helped organize support for immigrant settlers and poor laborers. A settlement house, called Hull House, opened in 1889 in the Chicago slums as a neighborhood center to provide multiple social, educational, and recreational services. Addams channeled her life's energies into programs such as Hull House to create a more humanistic society.[33] She touched the lives of many, including Lee, the father of the American playground movement. Like Addams, Lee came from a wealthy family. He was "appalled by the jailing of children for playing in the streets, [and] he established, at his own expense, an experimental playground in Boston."[34] Philosophically, Lee believed recreation should be an integral part of everyone's life, both adults and children. He wrote an influential book called *Play and Education*, which describes the relationships among play, recreation, and the social problems facing our cities. Lee and Addams both served as officers in the Playground Association of America, which was founded in 1906 and is the forerunner to today's NRPA.

> " In many ways, [our founders] were the radical counterparts of Eldridge Cleaver, Jane Fonda, Caesar Chavez, Gloria Steinem, and Ralph Nader. They continually fought city hall, organized labor strikes, marched in the streets, gave public speeches, and wrote award-winning articles deploring the living conditions of the poor. The issues and problems they faced were well defined: slavery, the aftermath of the Civil War, thousands of new immigrants, slums, child labor, disease, the suffrage movement, World War I, and a rapidly industrializing nation. America was striving to develop its abundant natural resources and was also enjoying a booming economy. The work ethic and the free-enterprise system flourished, thus creating a paradox of strong economic growth at the expense of human suffering and exploitation. Our founders faced these issues. They were not meek and mild, easily intimidated or swayed by local politicians. They worked in, around, and with the political system. The political battles they fought gave them the skills needed in order to establish the park, playground, and recreation services we enjoy today.
>
> —**Mary Duncan**[35]

Table 1.1

Selected Benefits that Have Been Attributed to Leisure by One or More Scientific Studies

I. Personal Benefits
  1. Mental Health and Maintenance of such:
    - Holistic sense of wellness
    - Stress management
    - Prevention of and reduced depression, anxiety, and/or anger
    - Positive changes in mood and emotion
  2. Personal Growth and Development
    - Self-esteem
    - Self-confidence
    - Value clarification
    - Leadership ability
    - Teamwork/cooperation
    - Balanced living
    - Acceptance of one's responsibility
    - Academic and other mental performance
  3. Personal Appreciation and Satisfaction from:
    - Sense of freedom
    - Self-actualization
    - Sense of adventure
    - Perceived quality of life/life satisfaction
    - Nature appreciation
    - Spirituality
  4. Psychophysiological
    - Cardiovascular benefits, including prevention of hypertension and strokes
    - Better muscle functioning and strength
    - Decreased obesity
    - Increased life expectancy
    - Improved perceived quality of life
    - Reduced need for medications
II. Social Cultural Benefits and Improvements
    - Community identity, satisfaction, and morale
    - Reduced social alienation
    - Reduced crime
    - Ethnic social integration
    - Family bonding/better life
    - Conflict resolution/harmony
    - Prevention of social problems by at-risk youth
    - Developmental benefits in children
    - Increased independence of older people
    - Increased longevity and quality of life

(cont.)

Table 1.1 (cont.)

III. Economic Benefits
- Reduced health costs
- Increased productivity
- Less absenteeism
- Local and regional economic growth
- Local amenities help attract industry
- Employment opportunities
- Promotion of places to retire and associated economic growth
- Increased property values

IV. IV. Environmental Benefits
- Stewardship and preservation
- Improved air quality through urban forestry
- Understanding human dependency on the natural work
- Public involvement in environmental issues
- Environmental protection
- Ecosystem sustainability
- Preservation of particular natural sites/areas
- Promotion of ecotourism

Note. Adapted from *Managing to Optimize the Beneficial Outcomes of Recreation* (pp. 10–11), by B. L. Driver (Ed.), State College, PA: Venture.

Other events that dramatically shaped the nature of the emerging park and recreation movement happened at about the same time as Lee and Hull's work. Central Park in New York City was established in 1857 as the first major city park, Yellowstone was set aside as the first national park in 1872, and more than 80 cities initiated construction of their own parks and playgrounds between 1880 and 1900. Thus, the stage was set in North America for a peculiar and uniquely democratic vision that sanctioned the use of public funding to provide for recreational activities, facilities (e.g., playgrounds), and parks on a local and national scale. On a national scale, it was deemed that these activities, facilities, and parks should be available and accessible to the average citizen, not just the wealthy, because the parks and services provided were good and beneficial for individuals, society, and the United States as a whole. Accordingly, recreation agencies, facilities, and parks took on an accepted social role across the country as people came to gradually view recreation, parks, and leisure services as a valid social good, even a necessity, in a democratic society. Table 1.1 outlines selected personal, social, cultural, economic, and environmental benefits of parks and recreation services. We will explore the idea of benefits later in this chapter.

As park and recreation professions matured and diversified, the general populace became more accepting of the idea that leisure was an end in itself to be enjoyed by all. Public recreation drifted away from a social welfare model (with the specific goal being to help those in need) toward a model where services were provided for everyone who wanted them.[36] Hence, new recreation and leisure service providers, which targeted health and wellness benefits, emerged. These more specialized areas included armed forces, therapeutic, campus, and employee recreation. In addition, commercial recreation and leisure businesses such as retail sales of recreational vehicles, boats, and equipment and destinations such as Disneyland became increasingly popular in post-World War II prosperity and beyond. Of course, nonprofit agencies and public parks and recreation continued to operate as well.

As the United States, Canada, and other developed countries moved from manufacturing toward a service economy in the latter half of the 20th century, a more specialized class of recreation, parks, and leisure services began to emerge in response to continuing social service needs and people's growing ability and desire to pay for recreation and leisure. The hospitality industry added value with organized recreation and leisure programs to attract and hold repeat visitor interest. Sport management evolved out of a growing interest in recreation and management opportunities in youth and professional sports. Meeting planning, conference services, and the entertainment industry provided a convergence for business and pleasure. Travel and tourism continued to grow on a national and international scale. Many of these specialized areas are considered professions in their own right, but they are also considered part of **recreation-related professions**.

In the 21st century, recreation and leisure-related professions face tremendous challenges and opportunities. The need for social services, the need for programs that support social justice, and the demand for leisure experiences at all points in the cost spectrum have never been greater. People from all walks of life are reexamining their priorities and consciously seeking out equal access to recreation services and higher quality leisure experiences. All recreation, parks, sport management, hospitality, and tourism organizations are challenged to operate ethically and sustainably and to respond to the needs of diverse populations.

Individuals attracted to careers in recreation, parks, sport management, hospitality, and tourism all love some aspect of recreation activities and also have a strong commitment and attraction to one or more of the following: improving **quality of life** for others, **affinity for nature**, a **love of play** (or playful attitude), and **entrepreneurism**. We will look closely at each of these motivators so we can better understand what drives recreation, parks, tourism, and leisure services professionals.

What Motivates Recreation, Parks, Sport Management, Hospitality, and Tourism Professionals?

Those who work in recreation-related professions are especially passionate about one or more apects that give them great satisfaction in their chosen career. Many students searching for a major discover the recreation field and feel like they have landed in a gold mine because it is obvious to them that this degree will prepare them for a job where they can look forward to going to work every day! Recreation-related professions provide a great opportunity to align your work with something that corresponds with your authentic self. Thus, the recreation, parks, sport management, hospitality, and tourism professionals whose profiles you'll read throughout this book did not arrive there because they were trying to get rich—that may be a secondary outcome—but their first love was something else.

First and foremost, recreation professionals have an intrinsic attraction to some activity or leisure experience that "turned them on" in their youth. What do you love? Maybe it is an activity such as soccer, baseball, backpacking, sailing, summer camp, travel, or kayaking. Or maybe it is an experience, such as an adrenaline rush, a sense of wonder, a competitive spirit, or insatiable curiosity. Mike Gamache, Director of the Oyster River Youth Association (ORYA), told us that his passion connects with his profession:

I played sports and was involved with sports all my life. I've always been interested in sports and fitness. I majored in recreation management with a focus in sport studies. I had a chance to interview with the former Executive Director following my internship, and he hired me. I wanted to be at ORYA because I believed that I would be able to make a difference in people's lives, and learn a lot in the process.

Maybe you love many kinds of recreation and leisure. The possibilities are truly unlimited.

Career Motivation and the So-Importants

Many recreation professionals are driven by the desire to make a positive difference. Our society has many **"so-importants,"** or issues often based in social and environmental justice concerns that are "so important" to address via public, private, nonprofit, and for-profit programs, services, and organizations. Recreation, as you are coming to understand, is a crucial way to bring groups together to address these so-importants. For example, some so-important issues commonly addressed via recreation, parks, sport, hospitality, and tourism include

- offering youth safe and developmentally appropriate recreation opportunities as alternatives to unhealthy behaviors,
- providing opportunities for social involvement and active aging among seniors,
- ensuring resources are available so people with mental, physical, and emotional disabilities can enjoy recreation and leisure experiences in ways they may not in a clinical setting,
- providing recreational opportunities as a way for communities to build common bonds,
- providing sustainable or eco-friendly tourism practices from which communities worldwide can benefit, and
- creating an environment that can be enjoyed and preserved for future generations, when we recreate in a sustainable manner.

There are no limits to the so-important needs and opportunities that can be provided through recreation and leisure experiences. Addressing the so-importants is explored in greater detail via the benefits offered by recreation experiences, as discussed later in this chapter and in Table 1.1. We will lead you through a series of exercises in Chapter 2 to help you assess your passions, but first we would like you to start thinking about what drives your recreational career interests so you can see how your motivators can help you identify the best recreation-related career options for you. The remainder of this section will explore the four motivators that bring people to a career in the recreation field.

Improving Quality of Life

Recreation professionals are all about making a difference in people's quality of life. That difference can be made by working directly with clients or offering opportunities to many people on a broader scale (inclusive service). Tom Carr, certified therapeutic recreation specialist (CTRS) and program coordinator for the Northeast Passage Athlete Development Center, talked to us about what it is like to provide **direct service** to others:

Helping to make a difference was a big thing for me. I like to be involved with beginners and see the instant gratification when they are introduced to a sport and get a positive experience. But I do a lot of my work with high level, competitive athletes. What is even more rewarding is seeing their long-term growth. Seeing them begin a sport, and then 10 years later, they are competing in the Paralympics on the national and international stage.

Sandy Dhuyvetter, founder, executive producer, and host of TravelTalk MEDIA, provides **inclusive services** that have a broader effect. She stated,

The greatest part about my job is to hear from guests about how we have added value to others' lives. Travel positively affects people personally and socially, and our world benefits economically as well. Meeting people and connecting people from all over the world is pure joy.

As you can see from Sandy's comment, some recreation professionals help others on a broad scale.

Matt Polstein, from the New England Outdoor Center in Maine, serves both directly and inclusively.

> First, there is the satisfaction of seeing our guests have a really great time and feeling the enrichment they are receiving from the experience. The second is being a part of helping our community economically, socially, and environmentally by bringing in visitors who are eco-sensitive and sharing the beauty and wonder of this wilderness area with them. We do all this while creating jobs and revenue that support the community.

Affinity for Nature

Are you drawn to the great outdoors? When in nature, do you feel at peace? Those who love working in the outdoors have a strong bond with, attraction to, or empathy for the natural world. Some people would love nothing more than to work outdoors. They may be particularly interested in preservation and protection, providing positive outdoor experiences, or both. Maybe you can relate to this anonymous blogger who wrote, "I love taking long walks, collecting my thoughts as I enjoy the sights and sounds of nature. I like camping, looking up at the stars, breathing in fresh air. The beauty of nature is unmatched, and we should take the time to appreciate it."[37]

Ginny Alfriend, park specialist for the City of Eugene Parks and Open Space in Oregon, told us, "We are outside most every day of the year and time all of our activities to the weather and season. It is a real treat to have my 'office' share space with a Pileated Woodpecker!" So, if you love the outdoors in an extraordinary way, either being in the outdoors, preserving the environment, or both, recreation professions provide a number of ways you can work in, for, and with the natural environment.

Love of Play

Earlier in the chapter we discussed how play is a universal human experience. If you have kept your childlike passion for play as an adult, you may be motivated to share it with others. Jack Wise, CEO of Wildwater Rafting, talked to us about the value of having fun:

I would have to say that the most rewarding [thing about my job] is to have new and exciting experiences in a special environment. It's also a bonus to be able to be involved in all these fun experiences myself.

Given that the desire to play hard and work hard is a widespread phenomenon in North American culture, we are not not surprised that many people would love to have a job where they can do just that!

Entrepreneurism

An entrepreneur is a special type of person who is drawn to the challenge and excitement of combining innovation with risk taking to create and sustain a business venture. This person provides the leadership for the venture and assumes a significant amount of accountability for the risks and outcomes inherent in that enterprise.[38] Phrases that describe entrepreneurs include innovator, creator, risk taker, problem solver, and catalyst for change. Starting and maintaining innovative business ventures is not for everybody, but entrepreneurial skills are increasingly needed in all sectors of the economy. That is, public, nonprofit, and for-profit enterprises increasingly rely on entrepreneurial skills because financial sustainability is no longer a given for any type of organization. Indeed, as we move to a more social economy (more on this concept in Chapters 2 and 15), an increasing number of professionals will be called on to blend their entrepreneurial abilities with their passion for making a difference.

John Hope-Johnstone, CEO of Corvallis Tourism, is one such entrepreneur in a recreation-related profession. Hope-Johnstone told us, "I started my tourism career as a travel agent, then as a tour wholesaler, then as a hotelier, then owned my own bed and breakfast in Hawaii, and now I am finishing my tourism career in destination marketing." He went on to explain how innovation permeates what he does: "Travel and tourism always stays on the cutting edge. When the Internet search engines started to blossom as a marketing tool in the '90s, many of the first online e-commerce businesses were travel based."

If you have entrepreneurial abilities, crave the excitement of solving problems, and crave being on the cutting edge of innovation, you will find a number of recreation-related careers that appeal to you, including sport management, the hospitality industry, travel and tourism, event management, and commercial recreation businesses. Depending on your unique abilities and interests, you may also find ways to combine your entrepreneurial aptitudes with other passions, such as becoming the head of a nonprofit organization dedicated to preserving and protecting open space.

Now that you have become familiar with motives for working in a recreation-related profession, we will look at what motivates clients to engage in recreation and leisure experiences. Understanding the benefits of recreation and leisure experiences will help you better understand how these experiences help people acquire knowledge, skills, and abilities that help them live more satisfying lives.

Motivation for Recreation and Leisure Participation

Generally speaking, people are motivated to engage in recreation and leisure experiences because of a mix of intrinsic and extrinsic motives. For example, I may attend my department's softball game because it is expected of me as part of my work role (extrinsic motive—I feel I have to be there because my boss asked me to come), but I may also think it will be fun (intrinsic motive—I go because I want to enjoy myself). In most cases, people choose recreation experiences because they anticipate receiving one or more benefits.

According to Driver, the recognized expert on outcomes and benefits of recreation and leisure experiences, there are three **benefits** of which to be aware.[39] First, there are benefits associated with a change for the better, or an improved condition. This implies that a new state is viewed as more desirable than a previous state. These changes could occur within individuals, groups, or environmental or cultural resources. Examples include improved health, learning, social bonding, improved economic viability, and improvements in natural or man-made environments. A second benefit is the maintenance of a desired condition, prevention of an undesired condition, or reduction of an undesired condition. An example is protecting natural resources to provide opportunities for visitors to maintain their physical and mental health. A third benefit is, quite simply, the realization of a satisfying recreation experience. It is important to place a high value on people having satisfying experiences regardless of whether any improved conditions can be easily discerned or measured. Estes and Henderson pointed out,

> Professionals shouldn't forget...that the outcomes related to enjoyment are still at the core of what makes our profession unique and valuable among other human service areas—we facilitate fun and intrinsically motivating experiences. Although the values of our profession go beyond 'fun and games,' enjoyment is, at all times, central to our work.[40]

Driver classified benefits into four types: personal, social/cultural, economic, and environmental. See Table 1.1 for a complete outline of these potential positive benefits. As you continue to read this book, be on the lookout for ways in which each leisure setting, experience, or activity could potentially provide benefits. Also, take a moment to reflect on your own recreation experiences and the benefits you have accrued as a result.

Documentation of and research on benefits of recreation and leisure have only come about fairly recently primarily for a need to document impact and benefits, but also because benefits, being of a personal and subjective nature, are hard to measure. However, as you gain more education and experience in recreation, parks, sport management, hospitality, and tourism, you will have a better understanding of benefits and how they can be used to manage the best possible recreation and leisure experiences for your clients. Finally, although most people are motivated to engage in recreation and leisure experiences for positive benefits, you should also be aware of the darker side of recreation motivation.

The Darker Side of Motivation

Let's face it—not everyone who engages in recreation and leisure experiences has moral, health-enhancing benefits in mind. Humans are driven to seek pleasure, and they are often hedonistic—that is, self-indulgent and reckless—in their choice of activities. In fact, our cultural belief system tells us that when we have worked hard for a long time, we have earned the right to play hard. In other words, we are prone to thinking, "Thank goodness that's over. Now it's time to go blow off some steam." Left to our own devices (which means we are free to do what we want), we often choose experiences that are potentially harmful to self, others, or society.

Curtis believed that any recreation professional preparation program should include consideration of **purple recreation**. He coined the term *purple recreation* to refer to "those activities and interests indulged in by youth and adults during non-work, non-study free time that do not fall within the parameters of what society generally views as wholesome or good."[41]

Curtis pointed out that many purple recreation activities are not starkly bad or evil, as they may be victimless crimes, such as a college students drinking too much after final exams (assuming they make it home safely). They have harmed no one but themselves, and the harm may be minimal in the form of a hangover. However, some purple recreation can be harmful even when the person did not intend harm. Consider drinking and driving, binge drinking, heavy drug use, dog fighting, compulsive gambling, pornography, prostitution, and so on.

Our intention here is not to engage in a lengthy discussion about hedonistic behavior, but rather to acknowledge its existence and explain why this knowledge is important for future recreation professionals. Dustin, McAvoy, and Shultz pointed out that the only virtuous act is one that is freely chosen.[42] Therefore, our role (as recreation professionals) is not to force people to do only moral, beneficial activities. However, our job is to ensure that recreation and leisure experiences provided by our agencies are available to all who want or may need them and are as safe and beneficial as possible. In many instances, recreation, parks, sport management, hospitality, and tourism organizations will provide healthy activities that promote positive benefits and moral character development. In other cases, agencies may provide mild purple recreation activities—especially when the paying customer desires them. However, in these cases, it is important that we, as recreation professionals, always remain aware of the potential for harm, practice good judgment about what activities we willingly provide, and practice good risk management to minimize harm.

Living Near Green Spaces Positively Influences Health

New evidence suggests that living near a green space can offer numerous health benefits. A study published in the *Journal of Epidemiology and Community Health* indicates that living near green spaces has quantifiable benefits to human health. The best health benefits come from living less than 1 km (three fifths of a mile) from a green space. The research shows that the impact is particularly noticeable in reducing rates of depression.

Other health indicators that benefit from proximity to green spaces include coronary heart disease; neck, shoulder, back, wrist, and hand complaints; depression and anxiety; diabetes; respiratory infections and asthma; migraine and vertigo; and stomach bugs and urinary tract infections.

Although people often report that time in nature reduces their stress and helps them feel better both physically and mentally, this is the first study to demonstrate that proximity to nature translates into fewer health problems.

Researchers looked at the health records of 195 family doctors and 350,000 individuals across the Netherlands and tracked how often patients were diagnosed with 24 disease types. Researchers mapped the amount of green space near each patient's household by using postal codes and land use data.[43]

Conclusion

The recreation, parks, sport management, hospitality, and tourism professions are rich with meaning, history, and benefits. Many young professionals will find a career under this umbrella, will love their job, and will look forward to going to work every day. To a certain extent, all recreation professionals are leisure educators as well. This is a growing and diverse field, full of challenges and opportunities. A person's desire to make a positive difference while doing a job he or she loves is a unique opportunity, and people in this profession can and should embrace opportunities to improve quality of life for all.

For Further Investigation

For More Research

The seven website resources listed for this chapter will provide you with insight into how organizations or individuals are employing recreation, leisure, sport, and tourism to address the so-importants discussed in this chapter (i.e., issues of social or environmental justice). Some of these groups may discuss ideas for policy change, and others may direct you to self-help information. In either case, reading about these organizations will help educate you as to what citizens are doing to improve life, health, and well-being for themselves and their communities. In every case, you will see that leisure plays a central role.

To continue to further your own education about recreation and leisure-related topics that interest you, browse the Internet and try to locate at least five recent articles or movements related to improving health and well-being via recreation, parks, sport, tourism, or hospitality. Many such movements call for public policy changes to create a real, measurable difference. Which public policy agenda items are most intriguing to you? What do you think about the grassroots movements you come across?

All Web links are also available via the resources section of Sagamore Publishing's website (www.sagamorepub.com/resources) for quick access. Additional Web links specific to each career area are listed at the end of each chapter.

Resources

Take Back Your Time: www.timeday.org
The purpose of this U.S. and Canadian organization is to "challenge the epidemic of overwork, over-scheduling and time famine that now threatens our health, our families and relationships, our communities and our environment."

Right2Vacation.org: www.timeday.org/right2vacation/default2.asp
The organization provides information on why vacation matters and advocates for a law mandating increases in paid vacation time.

Families and Work Institute: familiesandwork.org/site/about/main.html
Providing research on three main areas: the workforce/workplace, youth, and early childhood, this organization's mission is to address emerging issues before they become more serious problems.

The City Project: www.cityprojectca.org
This group strives to make real change in the lives of residents of Los Angeles and the surrounding communities by employing parks and recreation to address issues of social and environmental justice.

Common Good: Restoring Common Sense to America: commongood.org
This organization believes that "people, not rules, make things happen" and has the mission to "restore common sense to all three branches of government...based on the principles of individual freedom, responsibility and accountability."

The USA Affiliate of the International Play Association: Promoting the Child's Right to Play: www.ipausa.org/index.html
The association's purpose is to "protect, preserve, and promote play as a fundamental right for all humans."

Authentic Happiness: www.authentichappiness.sas.upenn.edu
This website provides information on the research of Dr. Martin Seligman and his work to look at positive emotions, to build character strengths, and to improve health and happiness.

Active Investigation

Collect your own stories, or vignettes, about people enjoying recreation and leisure experiences. Ask one or more individuals to tell you about what recreation or leisure activities or services they most enjoy and what benefits they feel they receive. Write a paragraph for each story, and identify the person by sex, age, and geographic location to provide context for the story. Classify the vignette into one of the following experiences:

- a eudaimonic-type leisure experience (i.e., an experience that involves good action and no goal other than enjoyment; the experience is an end in itself);
- a youth benefiting from a recreation program (i.e., after school, summer camp);
- a person with disabilities or an elderly person enjoying a recreation or leisure service or experience;
- a person benefiting from a general sport or play recreation experience;
- a person, or the environment, benefiting from an outdoor recreation experience, such as a park or green space;
- a person enjoying a commercial recreation or leisure experience (e.g., concert at an arena, Disneyland);
- a person or family enjoying a vacation at a resort or adventure travel experience;
- a person or group of people engaging in a virtual leisure experience (i.e., electronic game, social networking); or
- a person enjoying a potentially "purple leisure" experience (e.g., drinking alcohol, gambling).

References

[1]Alboher, M. (2008, May 5). Why leisure matters in a busy world. *The New York Times*. Retrieved November 24, 2009, from http://www.nytimes.com, para. 3.

[2]Dare, B., Welton, G., & Coe, W. (1998). *Concepts of leisure in western thought* (2nd ed.). Dubuque, IA: Kendall/ Hunt.

[3]Neulinger, J. (1974). *The psychology of leisure: Research approaches to the study of leisure*. Springfield, IL: Thomas.

[4]Bregha, F. J. (1982). Leisure and freedom re-examined. In T. L. Goodale & P. A. Witt (Eds.), *Recreation and leisure: Issues in an era of change* (pp. 73–77). State College, PA: Venture.

[5]Pavelka, J. (2000). *It's not about time: Rediscovering leisure in a changing world*. Ontario, Canada: Creative Bound.

[6]Billitteri, T. J. (2005). Time crunched: How busy schedules are sapping our spirit. *U.S Catholic, 70*(5), 12–17.

[7]Dare et al., 1998.

[8]Frankl, V. E. (2006). *Man's search for meaning: An introduction to logotherapy*. Boston, MA: Beacon Press.

[9]Pavelka, 2000.

[10]Link, A. (n.d.). About the leisure link. Retrieved from Leisure Link Consulting website: http://www.theleisurelinkconsulting.com/about.php

[11]de Graaf, J. (n.d.). What's the economy for, anyway? *New American Dream*. Retrieved November 27, 2009, from New American Dream website: www.newdream.org/newsletter/economy_for.php

[12]Alboher, 2008, para. 3.

[13] Kreider, T. (2012, June 30). The busy trap. *The New York Times*. Retrieved from http://opinionator.blogs.nytimes.com/2012/06/30/the-busy-trap/

[14]Russell, R. V. (2009). *Pastimes: The context of contemporary leisure* (4th ed.). Champaign, IL: Sagamore.

[15]Degraaf, D., Jordan, D., & DeGraaf, K. (2010). *Programming for parks, recreation, and leisure services: A servant leadership approach* (3rd ed.). State College, PA: Venture, p. 3.

[16]Carson, R. (1962). *Silent spring*. New York, NY: Houghton Mifflin.

[17]McLean, D. D., Hurd, A. R., & Rogers, N. B. (2008). *Kraus' recreation and leisure in modern society* (8th ed.). Sudbury, MA: Jones and Bartlett.

[18]World Tourism Organization. (1995). *Technical manual: Collection of Tourism expenditure statistics* (Technical Manual No. 2). Madrid, Spain: Author.

[19]Sessoms, H. D., & Henderson, K. A. (1994). *Introduction to leisure services* (7th ed.). State College, PA: Venture.

[20]World Tourism Organization. (n.d.). Fact and figures. Retrieved June 15, 2013, from http://dtxtq4w60xqpw.cloudfront.net/sites/all/files/pdf/unwto_highlights13_en_lr.pdf

[21]Huizinga, J. (1950). *Homo ludens: A study of the play element in culture*. Boston, MA: The Beacon Press, p. 12.

[22]Ellis, M. J. (1973). *Why people play*. Englewood Cliffs, NJ: Prentice Hall.

[23]Bregha, 1982, p. 1.

[24]Mainemelis, C., & Ronson, S. (2006). Ideas are born in fields of play: Towards a theory of play and creativity in organizational settings. *Organizational Behavior: An Annual Series of Analytical Essays and Critical Reviews, 27*, 81–131.

[25]Lamont, C. (2012). What is humanism? Retrieved from http://www.corliss-lamont.org/hsmny/whatishumanism.htm

[26]Baker, D. K., & Batker, D. K. (2011). *What's the economy for anyway? Why it's time to stop chasing growth and start pursuing happiness*. New York, NY: Bloomsbury Press.

[27]Gray, D. E. (1972). Exploring inner space. *Parks and Recreation, 12*(12), 18–19, 46.

[28]Pavelka, 2000.

[29]deGraaf, n.d.

[30]World Health Organization. (2003). WHO definition of health. Retrieved from http://www.who.int/about/definition/en/print.html

[31]Gray, 1972, p. 18.

[32]McLean et al., 2008.

[33]Duncan, M. (1991). Back to our radical roots. In T. L Goodale & P. A. Witt (Eds.), *Recreation and leisure: Issues in an era of change* (3rd ed., pp. 331–338). State College, PA: Venture.

[34]Ibid, p. 335.

[35]Ibid, p. 331.

[36]DeGraaf et al., 1999.

[37]Green – Nature [Blog post]. (2012, July 22). Retrieved from http://thebeautifulmoon.wordpress.com/2012/07/22/green-nature/

[38]O'Sullivan, A., & Sheffrin, S. M. (2005). *Economics: Principles in action*. Upper Saddle River, NJ: Pearson.

[39]Driver, B. L. (2008). Why outcomes-focused management is needed. In B. L. Driver (Ed.), *Managing to optimize the beneficial outcomes of recreation* (pp. 1–17). State College, PA: Venture.

[40]Estes, C. A., & Henderson, K. (2003, February). Research update: Enjoyment and the good life. *Parks and Recreation, 38*(2), 22–31, p. 22.

[41]Curtis, J. E. (1988). Purple recreation. *SPRE Annual on Education, 3*, 73–77, p. 73.

[42]Dustin, D. L., McAvoy, L. H., & Schultz, J. H. (1991). Recreation rightly understood. In T. L. Goodale & P. A. Witt (Eds.), *Recreation and leisure: Issues in an era of change* (3rd ed., pp. 97–110). State College, PA: Venture.

[43]Maas, J., de Vries, S., Spreeuwenberg, P., Schellevis, F. G., & Groenewegen, P. P. (2009). Morbidity is related to a green living environment. *Journal of Epidemiology and Community Health, 63*, 967–973. doi:10.1136/jech.2008.079038

At the end of the day, it's really about a place and a mission to believe in. Yellowstone, and the other national parks, provide people outstanding places to visit and experience, but we must do this in a way that leaves the parks 'unimpaired' for future generations, not just this one, to enjoy. What could be more inspiring than working for the future?

—Collette
Park Ranger
Yellowstone National Park

2

Understanding Careers in Recreation, Parks, Sport Management, Hospitality, and Tourism

Cheryl L. Stevens
East Carolina University

Keri A. Schwab
California Polytechnic State University, San Luis Obispo

Focus Questions

Q: What do you mean by careers in recreation, parks, tourism, and leisure services?

A: High-quality opportunities are available for professional careers with good salaries, benefits, and opportunities for advancement. The good news is that the field of recreation, parks, tourism, and leisure services provides an umbrella that covers a variety of career opportunities.

Q: I love recreation, but how can I determine whether I would like a career in recreation, parks, or tourism?

A: A passion for recreation is a great place to start. Another essential is to have a passion about improving participants' quality of life and for providing the best experiences possible and in an equitable and sustainable manner. This chapter will guide you through two self-assessment exercises to help you discover your personal answer to this question.

Q: What kind of person enjoys working in a recreation profession?

A: Recreation is a hands-on profession. By "hands-on" we mean working with people, planning, facilities, parks, logistics, and so forth. You might be out front working directly with people or behind the scenes making it all happen. If you see yourself as a doer, and if you are a person who likes to be in the middle of what is occurring, you will probably like recreation.

Q: This sounds really great. Why have I not heard about this before?

A: As we mentioned earlier, the good news is that recreation, parks, sport management, hospitality, and tourism professions cover a range of opportunities. That is also the bad news. Recreation-related professions cover so many career possibilities that many people are not aware of how easy it is to build a career doing something they love.

Q: What kind of education do I need, and once I finish my education will I be able to get a good job?

A: Most recreation professionals have a degree, whether it is an associate's, bachelor's, master's, or even a PhD. Whatever level of education you plan to pursue, most recreation, parks, sport management, tourism, and hospitality programs build in practical experiences and internships that help you gain the experience you need to land a full-time position once you have completed school. So, get the education you need and gain plenty of hands-on experience whether it happens through service-learning, volunteering, internships, paid employment, or all of the above.

Key Terms

Leisure service delivery system
Traditional, ownership-based
Public, government-sponsored
Public good
Nonprofit, community-based
Social services
Specialized recreation and leisure services
Needs-driven
Commercial, for-profit
Private enterprise
Emerging boundaries
Blurring the boundaries

Permeable boundaries
Globalization
Virtual leisure
Fourth sector
Hybrid organizational models
Generalists
Preferences
Passions
Continuum approach
Four Ps (passions, pay and perks,
    preparation, possibilities)

Introduction

The good news about recreation and its related professions is that they cover a broad array of career possibilities. The downside is that figuring out where the careers are can be hard because the variety is great. We believe the key to unlocking your career path is matching your passions and personality to the potential careers available, and this book is dedicated to helping you do that!

Maybe you are a student like Shayna, who is considering becoming a recreation major, so she goes to her academic adviser for career advice. For starters, she tells her adviser she loves basketball. Basketball is her authentic passion, and she wants to prepare for a job doing what she loves most. Is recreation the right major for her?

Shayna's passion for basketball is a great place to start, but her career adviser needs to know more to give her a clear sense of direction. Her adviser may ask, "Where do you want to live and work?" Some people want to be an integral part of a smaller community, others see themselves in the middle of big-city life, and still others have a passion for exotic locations and travel. The adviser may follow up with, "What kind of clients do you see yourself working with?" Some people have a passion for helping young people develop their athletic skills, others see themselves working with professional athletes, some really want to help youth at risk or senior citizens, and others like travel and vacation spots where sports are popular. It turns out Shayna really likes youth sport, and she would like to stay and help young people in her hometown. She may find a great match for her passions and abilities within community recreation, nonprofit recreation, or sport management.

Shayna and her adviser have more to talk about, but you get the picture. Whether or not you have an academic adviser to serve as your guide, you can use this book to select and pursue a career path in recreation, parks, sport management, hospitality, or tourism that is perfect for you. Any interested student's passions and interests can be matched with several viable career opportunities in a recreation-related career once he or she knows the right questions to ask. The purpose of this chapter is to show you how to find your own answers to the questions, "What do I really want to do?" and "How do I get that job?" so you can begin to connect with the right combination of education and experiences to have a career you love.

As you begin your personal exploration of recreation-related careers, you first need to understand the unique and varied ways leisure services have been, and are still being, delivered in North America. Consider the phrase, "tradition matters and it is a changing world." Those who do not know the basics run the risk of choosing a focus prematurely only to find that they later have to correct their course because they have spent unnecessary time and resources moving in a direction that is not their best fit. Think of understanding the way leisure services are delivered to people as the key that unlocks the first door. Once you get through this door, you will be able to find which road you want to travel as you hone in on more specific areas that are right for you. Interested yet? Read on!

Leisure Service Delivery System: Tradition Matters and It Is a Changing World

A **leisure service delivery system**[1,2] is a vast network of government-sponsored, nonprofit, for-profit, and specialized organizations that provides recreation, parks, sport management, hospitality, and tourism experiences for people. The system is highly diverse, ranging from the federally owned National Park Service; to nonprofits such as the YMCA; to for-profits such as sport teams, hotels, and resorts; to specialized service providers such as college intramurals and hospitals.

Traditional Leisure Service Delivery System

In recreation, parks, sport management, hospitality, and tourism, tradition still matters, but it is a rapidly changing world. Historically, recreation, parks, sport management, hospitality, and tourism services were organized around a **traditional ownership-based** model, where more formal, defined organizational boundaries were based on ownership (ownership refers to the primary owner).

Before going into detail about who these owners are, we will look at important background on the traditional leisure services delivery system. Before World War II (WWII), most recreation providers in North America could be classified as either public, government-sponsored, or nonprofit community-based organizations serving youth and other people in need of sponsored services. During this time, the owners of park and recreation organizations were the taxpayers (i.e., National Park Service) and not-for-profit social service agencies (i.e., YMCA). The purpose and mission of each organization was fairly easy to understand. However, although the National Park Service and the YMCA still have the same primary missions, they look different today, and the forces affecting them are similar to those affecting all areas of the economy, and hence recreation.

Following WWII, and through the 1990s, recreation, parks, sport management, hospitality, and tourism organizations diversified into four service delivery categories but still remained within fairly clear organizational structures based on ownership, mission, and purpose (see Figure 2.1):

1. **Public, government-sponsored** park and recreation services are primarily owned by the federal, state, or local government for the good of all citizens. This is known as providing parks and recreation for the **public good.**

   Why were public government-sponsored parks and recreation established?

   As the American frontier moved west, it became evident that if the government did not preserve land for the public good, Americans would lose access to wilderness, national treasures, and green space to play near their homes. Yellowstone, the first national park, was founded in 1872 "as a public park or pleasuring ground for the benefit and enjoyment of the people" and was placed "under exclusive control of the Secretary of the Interior."[3] The founding of Yellowstone set off a worldwide national park movement. The recognized need for preservation of timber and water resources and space for play impacted state and local governments, and space was set aside for parks, forest preserves, and city parks, with Central Park in New York City being formally established in 1856 as a place for city dwellers to relax and rejuvenate themselves amid the city chaos. Preserving national treasures, wilderness, green space close to people's homes, and recreation opportunities remains a priority for the park and recreation profession today.

2. **Nonprofit community-based** organizations that provide recreation services, mainly for children and youth, were founded as private nonprofit organizations beginning around the mid-1800s to meet social service needs. **Social services** are activities and programs designed to promote people's social well-being, and they are provided by philanthropic organizations.

   Why were nonprofit community-based organizations recreation providers established?

   Around the mid-1800s, private citizens noted critical unmet social welfare needs among the poor, many of whom were immigrants. Organizations, such as the YMCA, rose from the founders' desires to promote Christian principles through direct service to those in need. Other agencies, such as settlement houses, were started to help poor people, especially immigrants, find their way in America. The work of these organizations and social service pioneers was considered radical and controversial as they fought against child labor, crowding, disease, and other ill effects of industrialization in a rapidly growing nation. Jane Addams, the social work pioneer who founded the Hull House in Chicago was once called "the most dangerous woman in America"[4] for her work, which included providing supervised play facilities. Not surprisingly, many of these organizations still provide recreation and leisure services today by continuing to respond to social service needs such as addressing urban ills and the difficulties facing youth who are considered at risk.

3. **Specialized recreation and leisure services** are recreation service providers that meet clients' specific needs such as therapy and campus recreation that cannot be classified as public, nonprofit, or for-profit. **Needs-driven** organizations are charged with designing and delivering recreation and leisure services based on clients' needs.

Why were specialized recreation providers established?

Although numerous public and nonprofit agencies provided all types of recreation, parks, sport management, hospitality, and tourism services, additional service providers arose that were driven by social and individual needs that did not fit with the missions of public and not-for-profit agencies. Because a healthy leisure lifestyle is essential to a high-quality life, and because people are willing to pay for recreation and leisure services, a number of specialized professional areas have emerged. A cost to participate is often involved, but insurance companies, employers, or educational fees may cover (or highly subsidize) the cost. Examples of specialized recreation providers include recreational therapy (treating individuals with disabilities, injuries, trauma, and illness), employee recreation (serving employees where companies see recreation for employees as central to their mission), and campus intramurals and sports (serving students at schools, colleges, and universities who are interested in health, wellness, and recreational sport).

4. **Commercial for-profit** recreation providers are private enterprises owned by individuals or shareholders who make a profit providing recreation and leisure experiences for which people are willing to pay fair market price. **Private enterprise** refers to privately owned businesses operated for profit in a competitive system.

What are examples of for-profit recreation providers?

People have long demonstrated that they are willing to pay for spa and resort experiences, and companies providing for all aspects of recreation and leisure experiences have flourished in recent years. They range from small family-owned businesses to franchises and major corporations. For-profit recreation providers include hotels, resorts, travel agencies, theme parks, health and fitness clubs, spas, manufacturers of sports and recreation equipment, sport franchises, and entertainment venues such as coliseums and arenas. Ecotourism and adventure tourism are examples of growing leisure services-oriented business enterprises.

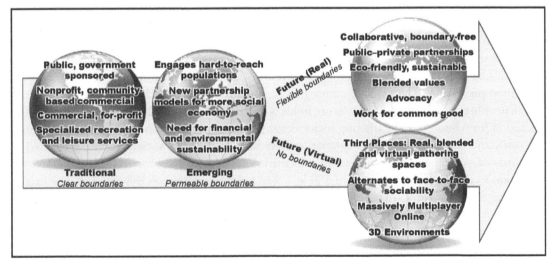

Figure 2.1. Evolving structure of the leisure service delivery system.

While reading this section, you probably noted that the public, government-sponsored, and nonprofit community-based recreation and leisure services have been around longer than the specialized service providers and commercial enterprises. We are not suggesting that people did not receive recreation that was therapeutic or pay for recreational experiences at resorts prior to World War II. However, as we discussed in Chapter 1, recreation started being thought of as a profession around the time of the playground movement in the 1800s, and as with all other professions, over time it has become more specialized and diversified (and popular!). By the 1990s, recreation was a major force in our national and local economies and responsible for millions of jobs in varied fields such as national, state, and local government; sport participation and viewing; youth programs and organized camps; military welfare and recreation; travel and tourism; and other businesses that supported recreational hobbies. By the year 2000, recreation was big business. For example, Golf 20/20, a project focusing on the golf industry and its growth and run by the World Golf Foundation, reported that the golf industry was worth $62 billion—more than the film and recording industries combined. This staggering sum includes golf facility operations; investments in courses, supplies, media, tournaments, and charities; and hospitality, tourism, and real estate associated with golf. By 2007, the same group reported that the golf industry had grown to $76 billion.[5] Many of the people working in these organizations are recreation professionals.

We call these four categories of recreation and leisure services "traditional" because they have traditionally met the needs of particular groups. The plus side of a traditional organization model is that missions and services are fairly clear and specific, which makes it easier to hold the organization accountable. However, a limitation of traditionally organized service providers is that they may not be as quick to innovate because they tend to be limited by bureaucracy. As we will see next, changes in society are resulting in a blurring of boundaries as organizations experience the need to be more flexible and form partnerships across boundaries to stay viable and best meet the increasingly diverse needs of their clients.

Emerging Leisure Service Delivery System

It is a new era, and a new leisure service delivery system has evolved, **emerging** from the traditional structure. Factors such as the need for financial and environmental sustainability, increased accountability, continuing needs of hard-to-reach populations, and the need for services that fit with today's lifestyles have created a new face to recreation, parks, sport management, hospitality, and tourism. In the mid-1990s, a number of important forces started **blurring the boundaries** of the traditional leisure service delivery system. Social justice and programs for the underserved were greatly needed, and trends focusing more on community, family, the environment, sustainability, and well-being were growing. Local governments and nonprofits still fill an important niche in recreation, but they can only respond to some needs due to limited funding. In the current global economy, the demand for innovation, efficiency, and effectiveness affects all sectors—not just for-profit enterprises, as in the past.

Consider how change is accelerating, and you will gain some idea of how it is affecting the recreation profession. The world continues to face increasingly rapid change, and the degree to which people can predict what their future holds is even less now in the 21st century than ever. The transition from hunting and gathering societies to agrarian societies can be measured in thousands of years, and the transition from agrarian society to industrialized society can be measured in hundreds of years.[6] The transition to an information-based society occurred in decades, and the transition to a global economy occurred in less than a decade. Although this rapid change can be unsettling, it is also a time of great opportunities.

As a result of the forces affecting society, the lines that once existed between traditional recreation and leisure services providers have become **permeable boundaries** as leisure expression occurs across traditional lines and partnerships between different agencies are formed. Recreation and leisure occur wherever people want it and find it. Traditionally, leisure services delivery was organized according to ownership and purpose and could be easily classified as public, nonprofit, specialized, or commercial. Although these classifications are still relevant today, these traditional agency structures are becoming springboards for innovative, blended organizational structures. Let's consider a few examples.

- The name of Mesa Arizona's Parks, Recreation, and Commercial Facilities reflects a blending of public services with for-profit ventures. Their stated mission is "to fill our facilities and programs with satisfied guests."[7] You may be interested to know that the term *guests* was popularized by the commercial recreation industry to refer to the way paying customers should be viewed and treated.
- The City of Anaheim, the 10th largest city in California and home to Disneyland, formed partnerships between previously separate departments to form a new department called Community Services. This innovative restructuring was driven by the need to better coordinate service delivery to hard-to-reach populations. Anaheim's Community Services of today encompasses golf, libraries, recreation and human services, parks, urban forestry and neighborhood services.
- More than 650 for-profit concessionaires operate businesses and trips in national parks, and in 2005, concessionaires, working in conjunction with national parks and forests across the United States, grossed more than $34 billion in sales and put $72 million back into the federal government in the form of usage fees alone. Coca-Cola is an official sponsor of the nonprofit National Parks Foundation.
- Gap Adventures, which grew from a one-man show to an award-winning company of over 700 employees, created the nonprofit Planeterra to demonstrate its 20-year commitment to triple-bottom-line sustainability and giving back through travel. Planeterra is dedicated to support sustainable community development through travel and voluntourism, and Planeterra partnered with The International Ecotourism Society (TIES) to host a convention in 2010.

As illustrated in Figure 2.1, the forces affecting this emerging structure can be described as follows:

- Need for financial and environmental sustainability—When public funding and nonprofit donations are tight, agencies look to innovative ways to fund programs, such as forming partnerships with for-profits. Another way agencies increase financial sustainability is partnering with other public and nonprofits to avoid duplicating services. Community grassroots efforts, such as starting a new Boys and Girls Club with funding from private donations, help communities find support for programs they need and want. Furthermore, everyone is going green, and as people direct their time and money toward causes they support, all types of agencies benefit from improving the environment. An example would be a nonprofit kayak and canoe club sponsoring a river cleanup day. River cleanup recruits, equipment, supplies, and leadership may come from a combination of schools, the community, and local businesses.
- Increased accountability and connectivity—People increasingly want to know that their money is going to accomplish something they believe in. Measuring and reporting positive outcomes from leisure services is more important than ever. It used to be enough to report how many people attended a program, but now stakeholders want to know statistics such as whether a youth program is connected to decreasing crime rates and increasing graduation from high school. Regarding connectivity, all types of agencies are using forums such as YouTube, Twitter, Facebook, and automated messages sent via text messages, voicemail, and e-mail. If the local baseball game is called on account of weather, an electronic message can reach parents and coaches before they leave home.

- Need to create outreach programs for hard-to-reach populations—Problems facing youth including gang involvement, drug use and addiction, dropping out of high school, violence, suicide, and mental illness are increasing rather than decreasing. Recreation programs enhance their traditional youth development role through innovative programs such as roving leader outreach. In a roving leader program, leaders move around so they can interact with youth where they are in their communities instead of waiting for them to show up at a program site. For example, to reduce bullying, antisocial, or other aggressive behaviors, the Youth Development Division within the Department of Parks and Recreation in the District of Columbia implemented a roving leader program in which leaders use recreation and leisure activities to neutralize and prevent hostile behaviors among targeted youth groups.
- Service-delivery is increasingly driven by clients' needs and lifestyles—People have high expectations and busy lifestyles, so they expect top-quality programs that occur when they want them. This may mean opening the gym at 5:00 a.m. or even being open 24 hours a day. Increasingly, businesses provide multiple cutting-edge service options in one place, such as the giant Vaughan Mall near Toronto, Canada, that has turned mall shopping into a real event by adding a bowling alley, NASCAR Speedpark with an arcade, Laser Tag, and family friendly racing, including seasonal outdoor tracks.

> For more information on each of these examples, please visit the *A Career With Meaning* website at sagamorepub.com/resources to find links to these resources and much more!

Evolving Leadership Roles

Leadership roles for recreation, parks, tourism, and leisure services professionals under this emerging structure include program facilitator, information referral, developmental leader, outreach specialist, and facilitator. In general, leadership roles require professionals to go where the clients are (rather then expecting them to come to a program site), provide programs that respond to clients' specific needs, and create liaisons between service providers to meet clients' holistic needs. Packaged programs will become part of the past as each professional is expected to adapt to evolving situations and clients' needs.

Future Leisure Service Delivery System

Factors such as globalization, virtual leisure, and the rise of a fourth sector are shaping organizations delivering recreation, parks, sport management, hospitality, and tourism. Friedman, author of *The World Is Flat*,[8] stated that in the 21st century we are experiencing a world with a commercially level playing field. This phenomenon, called **globalization**, is a result of the convergence of personal computer usage, globally available telecommunication, and faster shifts among markets. These changes have resulted in the widespread use of open sourcing, outsourcing, offshoring, insourcing, and informing. Friedman pointed out that although the global playing field is being leveled, Americans are not ready. He projected that if North America does not do a better job keeping pace with these technological advances, it will fall behind.

In Friedman's 2008 follow-up book *Hot, Flat and Crowded*, he added to his "The World Is Flat" concept, suggesting that the United States needs a "green revolution" to renew its place in the global market.[9] He suggested that only by "out-greening" the competition and becoming a leader in sustainable, environmentally friendly products and reducing dependence on expensive foreign oil can the United States expect to have a competitive edge in the global market. Fortunately, this same idea for eco-friendly practices built into a business model is also emerging in the recreation industry, as illustrated in Figure 2.1. We will further discuss this when we talk about hybrid organizational models.

The proliferation of personal electronic devices is responsible for another trend that we predict will continue to grow. **Virtual leisure** experiences such as connecting with friends to socialize via Facebook and Twitter or connecting with the larger world via public blogs and comment boards, online chat rooms, interactive gaming, sports, fitness, virtual tourism, or simulation technologies continue to grow as access to technology and connectivity increase.

As we discussed earlier in the chapter, the future is difficult to predict, but we believe that future organizational models will be collaborative and relatively boundary free because we believe boundaries among traditional sectors will continue to blur and may eventually disappear (refer to Figure 2.1).

According to Fourth Sector Network, the boundaries among public, private, and nonprofit sectors have been blurring for a while, and a **fourth sector** is emerging as many pioneering organizations in the three traditional sectors have blended social and environmental aims with entrepreneurial business models.[10]

According to the Fourth Sector Network,[11] two events are driving the convergence of the three traditional sectors into this fourth sector; the first is a shifting purpose in the private sector, and the second is shifting method in the public and social sectors. The first event, shifting purpose, is characterized by businesses dedicating more resources to delivering social and environmental benefits. Phrases Fourth Sector Network identifies as buzzwords reflecting this trend include the following:

- corporate social responsibility
- cause-related marketing
- cause-related purchasing
- carbon offsets
- corporate philanthropy
- socially responsible investing
- triple bottom line
- employee ownership
- sustainability reporting
- transparency

Parks Make Life Better!

The California Recreation and Park Society (CPRS) has recognized the need to have a brand that is easily recognizable, such as the Starbucks® logo, and stands for something essential to communities. The CPRS has developed a brand as part of its 21st Century VIP project (Vision... Insight... Planning) to help member agencies position themselves as essential community services.

In 2009, CPRS conducted an extensive public opinion research study. This research was used to create our profession's brand promise: Parks and recreation make lives and communities better now and in the future by providing access to the serenity and inspiration of nature; outdoor space to play and exercise; facilities for self-directed and organized recreation; positive alternatives for youth that help lower crime and mischief; and activities that facilitate social connections, human development, therapy, the arts, and lifelong learning.

The brand promise became further condensed into a memorable slogan/tag line: "Parks Make Life Better!" The grand launch of the brand occurred at the 2010 conference in Palm Springs, California. This event illustrates how park and recreation professional organizations are expanding their interpretation of mission, goals, and service delivery mechanisms to embrace change in the 21st century. See www.cprs.org for more details.[12]

The second event, shifting method in the public and social sector, is characterized by buzzwords such as the following:

- effectiveness
- efficiency
- market-discipline
- accountability and measurable impact
- venture philanthropy
- social investing
- program-related investments
- mission-related investing
- earned income ventures
- economic sustainability
- privatization
- reinventing government
- social return on investment

Although addressing the fourth sector in greater detail is beyond the scope of this book, be aware that other terms used to describe the fourth sector include *for-benefit sector*, *quaternary and quinary sector*, and *social economy*. A number of **hybrid organizational models** will also arise as organizations consciously blend attributes and strategies, thus forming organizations that resist classification into one of the three traditional sectors.

Each of these hybrid organizations shares two common characteristics: (1) the pursuit of social and environmental goals and (2) the use of business methodology. Terms you may see as you look at organizations delivering hybrid recreation, parks, tourism, and leisure services include *civic*, *municipal*, *faith-based*, *nonprofit*, *sustainable*, *social*, and *social economy enterprises*, as well as *cross-sector partnerships*, *community wealth*, and *blended value organizations*.

As fourth sector organizations evolve, many are finding that a supportive ecosystem for their practices does not yet exist, and they have to continue to operate within the constraints of the three traditional sectors. These more traditional structures unfortunately can limit the ability of fourth sector organizations to stay on the cutting edge of innovation.[13] For example, if a local city council were to pass legislation requiring a parks and recreation department to provide services to all citizens free of charge, the amount of tax money allocated to the department may not meet the mandate. Policy change to then increase taxes and fund the mandate can take a long time, thus stalling potential change. But in an entrepreneurial (private) organization, these changes could happen almost overnight, demonstrating flexibility and responsiveness to customer or economic demands. However, before the city can partner with private organizations, the city council must vote the new structures into law. Local politics (any politics for that matter) are challenging and complex, so the amount of time these changes take has difficulty keeping pace with growing and diversifying needs.

At present, powerful institutional and structural barriers continue to resist change. However, we predict that as organizations continue to challenge conventional thinking about capital, markets, legal and regulatory rules, ownership, and leadership, a more supportive ecosystem will evolve and innovative organizations unbounded by traditional models will be better supported, perhaps to the extent that the traditional sectors no longer exist.

Although we will comment more on the future of recreation, parks, sport management, hospitality, and tourism services in Chapter 15, we expect the following trends to continue to change current organizational structures:

- Organizational models will become increasingly diverse and continue to be driven by individual and community needs.
- There will be a continuing need for the dual goals of financial and environmental sustainability, which will bring out more public–private partnerships.
- Both virtual and real-life recreation and leisure experiences will be valued.
- Consumers will further expand their influence on organizations because they will use virtual connectivity to explore their choices so they can allocate their time and money exactly where they choose.

- Leadership roles will continue to evolve and professionals in recreation, parks, tourism, and leisure services will become change agents/advocates, servant leaders, guides, collaborators, and experts in many roles, including sustainability.

Making the Connection to the Recreation-Related Career That Is Right for You

Career possibilities in recreation, parks, sport management, hospitality, and tourism are dynamic, meaning they are always in motion. Whether you choose a major in recreation management, therapeutic recreation, leisure studies, sport management, outdoor recreation, resource management, hospitality, or tourism and travel, you will find several career possibilities. Rest assured that you do not have to know exactly what you want to be just yet. If you put time and effort into self-assessment and reflection, you will be better able to hone in on your recreation-related career choices by the time you choose an area of focus and an internship.

The possibilities may seem overwhelming at first, but trust these self-assessment exercises to prepare you for good career matches in the following chapters. If you have a passion for recreation, want to impact quality of life and your community, enjoy a challenge, and love working either with people or behind the scenes to make events happen, be assured you are starting in the right place!

Identifying Your Preferences and Passions

The first step toward making the right choice is assessing your preferences and passions so you can connect your profile to the right potential career areas. Although conducting in-depth personality and values assessments is beyond the scope of this book, you will find guidance on how to conduct these more in-depth assessments in the For More Research and Active Investigation sections of this chapter if you are interested in doing more self-exploration.

What Kind of Person Will Enjoy a Recreation-Related Career?

We believe that all professionals in recreation, parks, sport management, hospitality, and tourism have a few characteristics in common. Look at the following information so you can become familiar with what recreation, parks, and tourism professionals love most about their jobs.

- Recreation, parks, sport management, hospitality, and tourism professionals are people oriented. If you do not like working with people, this is probably not the right profession for you. Professionals should have friendly, outgoing personalities. Some of us may be somewhat introverted, and jobs are available where we work behind the scenes with parks, facilities, animals, and the like, but we still like to get out occasionally and connect with people, too!

- Recreation, parks, sport management, hospitality, and tourism professionals value meaning in their work, and these venues provide a medium whereby professionals can improve quality of life. Whether you are part of a quality of life profession such as youth development or recreational therapy or involved in providing premium experiences at a resort, golf course, or sporting event, you can help people find joy for a moment or teach them skills that may improve their lives for a lifetime. The smiles on their faces and expressions of happiness give recreation professionals frequent positive feedback about the value of their work.

- Recreation, parks, sport management, hospitality, and tourism professionals are willing to put in a good deal of effort and hard work for what they believe in. Day-to-day operations tend to be complex and involve a lot of hard work. Clients do not see the behind-the-scenes work necessary to put on a top-notch program or orchestrate the perfect leisure experience. One of the most exciting aspects of our job is that we conduct an event from start to finish, and we see the participants' satisfaction, accomplishments, and enjoyment.

- Recreation, parks, sport management, hospitality, and tourism professionals can handle autonomy and need to be flexible. Using our skills and resources to solve problems and working irregular hours does not bother us. With a few exceptions, we often work long hours during peak times such as weekends, holidays, nights, and when everyone else has vacation such as the Fourth of July and Labor Day. We often love the excitement and anticipation of working extra hours before, during, and after an event.

- Recreation, parks, sport management, hospitality, and tourism professionals enjoy being hands-on people who apply their knowledge in practical ways to meet people's needs, solve problems, and make things happen. A recreation professional's toolbox contains knowledge about several topics—motivational theory, teaching/coaching, teamwork, facilities and equipment, risk management, budgets, transportation, marketing, program design, assessment, outcomes research, the latest trends—and professionals need to be able to apply that knowledge to solve myriad problems at a moment's notice. If you need certainty and predictability and want to stick to using one skill set, recreation may not be for you.

- Recreation, parks, sport management, hospitality, and tourism professionals find it energizing that a typical day often means performing a number of assignments. They may be analyzing customer surveys before lunch, teaching a parent–youth sport education program at noon, inventorying and buying equipment, and then coaching or refereeing at night. This youth recreation sport scenario is only one of many possibilities—but most recreation professionals perform a variety of tasks during a day.

You probably read something in the paragraphs above that appeals to you. The next step is to get to know yourself better by exploring your preferences.

Preferences: Knowing Yourself

It can be said that careers in recreation appeal to people who are **generalists**—this means most recreation, parks, and tourism professionals share common qualities, but there are a multitude of settings where they can be expressed (e.g., park ranger, guest services for the Yankees, youth recreation services director, tour guide). More than 80% of people in the overall population can be considered generalists. If you are a generalist, you may feel like it has been hard to directly answer the question, "What do you want to do when you graduate?" If the concept of generalist describes you, you may be relieved to know that most people feel the same way. The best way for a generalist to approach a career choice is to learn more about his or her **preferences** and then use that knowledge to look for career areas that are a potential match. In simple terms, a preference is something you favor or prioritize over something else. What this means to you is that likely more than one career option will match your "preferences" profile. Chances are that you would be happy in any of them, and you can make a more informed choice once you understand how the career options fit well for you and why.

Read the list of general qualities of recreation professionals in Table 2.1 and determine whether each is *not like me, somewhat like me*, or *a lot like me*. Check the appropriate box, then go back through the list and select the top five qualities that you would prefer to express in a career position the most. At the bottom of the list, write in the top five qualities in order of how important they are to you.

Chances are that many of these general preferences that describe recreation, parks, sport management, hospitality, and tourism professionals are a fit for you, so we will have you get more specific in the next section.

Passions: What Matters Most to You

Passions are things about which people feel intense emotion. Passions can also be thought of as objects of enthusiasm. As you read through the next checklist (Table 2.2), rate how passionate you are about each item. After you finish the list, go back and review it to select the top five items that matter most to you. Then at the bottom, write them down and list them in the order of how important they are to you.

Table 2.1
General Qualities of Recreation Professionals

	Not like me	Somewhat like me	A lot like me
• I think recreation is fun and exciting.	____	____	____
• I want to make a difference.	____	____	____
• I enjoy working with people.	____	____	____
• I enjoy working behind the scenes.	____	____	____
• I enjoy a challenge.	____	____	____
• I enjoy solving problems.	____	____	____
• I like being hands-on, directly involved in the action.	____	____	____
• Sitting at a desk all day does not suit me.	____	____	____
• I like doing many different things.	____	____	____
• I like being in many different places.	____	____	____
• Being passionate about my career is important to me.	____	____	____

(cont.)

Table 2.1 (cont.)

	Not like me	Somewhat like me	A lot like me
• I am open minded when it comes to people—their varied backgrounds, likes and dislikes, and needs and wants.	____	____	____
• I can think on my feet without going off the deep end.	____	____	____
• I can be both a leader and a team player depending on what the situation calls for.	____	____	____
• I like having flexible work hours, such as working early mornings or nights.	____	____	____
• I am willing to work when other people want time off, such as holidays and vacations.	____	____	____
• I believe everyone in the community has a right to play and recreate.	____	____	____
• I like the idea of helping to create and implement sustainable, eco-sensitive solutions for communities and our environment.	____	____	____
• I want a career that lets me change what I do within the same discipline.	____	____	____

Preferences Worksheet
List, in order, your top five preferences:
   1.
   2.
   3.
   4.
   5.

Table 2.2

Passions of Recreation Professionals

	Not like me	Somewhat like me	A lot like me
• Being part of a mission-driven organization and helping people excites me.	____	____	____
• I see myself working to make a difference with a particular group (choose one):	____	____	____
–Children	____	____	____
–Teens	____	____	____

(cont.)

Table 2.2 (cont.)

	Not like me	Somewhat like me	A lot like me
–Young adults	___	___	___
–Older adults	___	___	___
–Other (i.e., race, ethnicity, religion etc.)	___	___	___
• Social justice and community development are very important to me.	___	___	___
• I'd like to help improve quality of life for people with disabilities.	___	___	___
• I would be happy working within the boundaries of a mission-driven nonprofit or government agency.	___	___	___
• I would like to have the structure provided by a regular schedule.	___	___	___
• I absolutely need autonomy and flexibility to do my best work.	___	___	___
• I am happiest when I have lots of variety, and I actually like multitasking.	___	___	___
• I'm happiest when I get to use the skill set I have developed without having to respond to ever-changing situations.	___	___	___
• Resolving problems, crises, and conflicts energizes me.	___	___	___
• I really enjoy teaching people about … _____ (sport skills, the environment, art, fitness, etc.).	___	___	___
• Working long hours is great so long as I get to play hard later.	___	___	___
• I would really like to own my own business some day.	___	___	___
• The thought of being in charge of a large event excites me.	___	___	___
• I would love to work outdoors most of the time.	___	___	___
• I would rather be hands-on with facilities, planning, or parks than programs.	___	___	___
• I would really enjoy being a part of creating sustainable, eco-sensitive solutions.	___	___	___
• I am highly skilled at and/or especially passionate about a particular, specialized aspect of recreation or leisure:	___	___	___
–Playing or coaching one sport (or several sports)	___	___	___
–Fitness, health, and wellness	___	___	___
–Outdoor adventure/sport	___	___	___
–Arts	___	___	___

(cont.)

Table 2.2 (cont.)

	Not like me	Somewhat like me	A lot like me
–Theater	___	___	___
–Watersports	___	___	___
–Other:	___	___	___
• I would like to live and work in a smaller community.	___	___	___
• I would live and work in a large city.	___	___	___
• Traveling as part of my job is exciting to me.	___	___	___

Passions Worksheet
List, in order, the top five things that matter to you most:
1.
2.
3.
4.
5.

How to Use This Book

Continuum Approach to Understanding Recreation-Related Careers

Due to blurring boundaries, career areas can no longer be neatly classified according to traditional sectors (public, nonprofit, specialized, and for-profit), so we have organized them using a **continuum approach**, meaning the chapter topics begin with government-funded and nonprofit career types, move through specialized areas, and end with commercial enterprises. Traditional sectors, such as community-based recreation and recreation in nonprofit organizations, have been around a long time, whereas other specialized areas, such as therapeutic recreation and event management, are newer on the scene. As we previously discussed, partnerships between agencies and sectors result in more possibilities, and you will notice blending among sectors as you progress through the continuum.

Career Continuum in Recreation, Parks, Sport Management, Hospitality, and Tourism

Chapter 3	Community Recreation and Leisure Services
Chapter 4	Recreation in Nonprofit Organizations
Chapter 5	Armed Forces Recreation
Chapter 6	Outdoor Recreation in Federal, State, and Local Parks
Chapter 7	Recreational Therapy and Therapeutic Recreation
Chapter 8	Campus Recreation, Leisure, and Intramurals
Chapter 9	Sport Management and Sport Teams
Chapter 10	Event Management
Chapter 11	The Hospitality Industry
Chapter 12	Travel and Tourism
Chapter 13	Commercial Recreation and Leisure Businesses

If a career in a recreation-oriented profession appeals to you, you will want to explore the entire continuum because you will likely find potential matches in unexpected places. For example, if you love sports, it will obviously be covered in Chapter 9, but you will also find exciting opportunities for a sport-oriented professional in Armed Forces Recreation—and if you want more opportunity to travel the world, this may be a perfect niche for you. However, do not stop reading there because you will also want to consider the other sport-related opportunities that appear in other chapters to ensure you do not leave any stone unturned while looking for your best match.

The Four Ps: Passions, Pay and Perks, Preparation, and Possibilities

Each career chapter presents career-specific information using a model we are calling the **four Ps: passions, pay and perks, preparation,** and **possibilities**. Each author addresses careers in his or her topic area by describing the four Ps as they relate, in general, to all careers in the chapter. The passions section describes what people who work in the career area feel strongly about. The pay and perks section describes, in a general way, the pay and typical perks that come with these jobs. You may notice that specific salaries are not listed. This was intentional because it is best for you to research what salaries are like for certain positions in your region because salaries differ by location. The preparation section provides information about the education and experience professionals in the career area typically pursue to be successful. You will also find a wealth of information on professional organizations, certifications, and other resources toward the end of each chapter to help you prepare to market yourself successfully. The last P is possibilities. This section provides information about where to look for internships and jobs. Each possibilities section expands to provide details about several specific career tracks. Each career track continues using the four Ps model by including a brief discussion about the passions, pay and perks, preparation, and possibilities specific to that track. What better way to select a career focus that will likely be a great fit for you?

Conclusion

This book is designed to help the interested student link passions, preferences, and interests to the career possibilities available in today's world. Each career chapter begins with fascinating interviews with professionals currently working in the field so you can get in touch immediately with what they love about their jobs. Just by reading this book, you will receive great advice from many active recreation professionals, not to mention expert advice from the contributing authors. The four Ps model provides a consistent frame for determining how well your own passions, preferences, and interests fit with a particular career area. Each chapter also contains ways you can conduct more research and actively investigate the career track, plus more ideas about where to gain experience so you can start building a strong résumé for your future job applications.

For Further Investigation

For More Research

Several online career assessments are available that you can take for free. Self-assessments will help you learn more about yourself by aiding you in further defining your core interests, values, personality traits, and skills. No one assessment can resolve all your career-related questions, but you should use the assessments as tools during your career selection process. Following are a few self-assessments that we recommend. You can find links to these via Sagamore's website at sagamorepub.com/resources.

Keirsey Temperament Sorter II: www.keirsey.com

Click on Take the KTS-II free sorter access and free temperament report. This assessment is designed for college students and adults and provides a brief summary of the user's temperament and career options matching their personality. Free registration is required to take the test.

Complete an iSeek Skills Assessment: www.iseek.org

iSeek is Minnesota's career, education, and job resource site. Click "Assess Yourself" under the "Careers" heading to take the iSeek Skills Assessment complete with matching jobs listing. Users are asked to rate skills positively or negatively according to preference.

Learn more about your work values and motivations: www.lifeworktransitions.com

LifeWorkTransitions.com is the companion website for the book by the same name, and the website has useful and free worksheets, whether or not you buy the book. Go to the website, click on "Career Assessment Exercises," and scroll down to Chapter 3, "Redefining Your Self: Passions, Preferences, Purpose" to access online worksheets corresponding to the book. The worksheets on work values and motivating factors are particularly useful.

Active Investigation

1. Visit your school's career center and find out what self-assessments they have that you can use to explore, evaluate, and measure your various attributes. Self-assessment will help you learn more about yourself by assisting you with defining your core interests, values, personality, and skills. No one assessment can resolve all your career-related questions, but they are definitely useful tools during your career selection process. The Myers-Briggs Type Indicator is especially helpful for gaining understanding of how your personality matches with occupations. If your school does not offer Myers-Briggs, or something like it, you can pay to take a similar test at www.personalitypathways.com.
2. Informational interviewing is a great way to learn firsthand about career possibilities that interest you. It involves setting up an interview with a professional who currently has a job in a career in which you may be interested. These interviews can be done in person, by phone, or by e-mail. When setting up these interviews, be clear you are not seeking a job and are asking for information and advice only. A side benefit of informational interviews is that you will be familiar to potential employers and they may remember you if an internship or job becomes available. You will be pleasantly surprised how many people will enjoy talking with you about what they do and how willing they are to offer advice to an interested student.[14]

What the interview is. The interview is a way of gaining valuable information and advice from a professional in a field that interests you. You conduct the interview for the purpose of seeking information and advice only. A side benefit of informational interviewing is networking with potential future employers.

What the interview is not. The interview is not an interview for a job. Asking for a job during an informational interview is inappropriate.

How to conduct an informational interview.

1. Be clear about your objective before you contact the professional. Write a brief script that explains why you are calling and what you want to know, and rehearse what you will say. Select between eight and 12 questions from the list of potential questions to use during your interview. You may want to write out backup questions in case time allows.
2. When you call (or e-mail) explain why you are calling and be polite, positive, and businesslike.
3. Be flexible. Be prepared to conduct the interview right when you call, but understand that the person may be busy and want to set up an appointment at a future time. Be considerate of their time and keep the interview to 30 minutes as a courtesy. Chances are that you may not be able to ask all of your questions, so know which ones are the most important to you and ask those first.
4. Whenever possible, schedule a face-to-face meeting so you can gain exposure to the work environment and culture as well as make a positive impression.
5. Ask your contact to recommend others to whom you may speak in the field or industry.
6. Always send a handwritten thank-you note by mail (not e-mail) after your call or visit. If appropriate, include your phone number or e-mail address. Ask the contact to let you know if more information becomes available or if they become aware of internship or job opportunities.
7. After you get your internship or first job, notify all your networking contacts. Tell them briefly about your new position, thank them again for their help, and give them your updated contact information.

Questions about the career field.
- How did you get into this career?
- What do you do at work on a typical day? What are your responsibilities?
- What do you like most about your job?
- What are the biggest challenges you face in your job?
- How do you make a difference in people's lives?
- What advice do you have for someone preparing for a career in this field?
- What kind of formal education do you recommend?
- What experience is necessary to get an entry-level job in this field?

Questions about the organization/industry.
- How did you get into this organization? What other organizations have you worked for?
- What would you say is unique about your organization?
- What is your work environment like?
- When there are job openings or internships, where are they advertised and how are they filled? Is this typical of similar organizations?

Questions about future opportunities and salary.
- What are the employment prospects for entry-level employees?
- Are internships common in this industry? What do interns typically do?
- What is the growth and promotional potential in this field?

- What areas are growing/changing in this field?
- Do some regions/countries have a higher demand than others?

Follow-up questions.
- Can you recommend other professionals in this field with whom I should speak? May I use your name when I contact them?
- Is it okay if I contact you again if I have further questions?
- Which professional organizations/publications and other resources do you consider relevant?

References

[1]Murphy, J. F. (1973). *Leisure service delivery system: A modern perspective.* Philadelphia, PA: Lea and Febiger.

[2]Murphy, J. F. (1975). *Recreation and leisure service: A humanistic perspective.* Dubuque, IA: Wm. C. Brown.

[3]National Park Service. (n.d.). *The national park system: Caring for the American legacy.* Retrieved March 2, 2009, from http://www.nps.gov/legacy/mission.html

[4]Duncan, M. (1991). Back to our radical roots. In T. L. Goodale & P. A. Witt (Eds.), *Recreation and leisure: Issues in an era of change* (3rd ed., pp. 331–338). State College, PA: Venture, p. 331.

[5]World Golf Foundation. (2012). Economic impact reports. Retrieved from http://www.golf2020.com/research/economic-impact-reports.aspx

[6]Dare, B., Welton, G., & Coe, W. (1998). *Concepts of leisure in western thought* (2nd ed.). Dubuque, IA: Kendall Hunt.

[7]Mesa Parks and Recreation. (2014). Retrieved from http://www.mpsaz.org/

[8]Friedman, T. (2005). *The world is flat: A brief history of the twenty-first century.* New York, NY: Farrar, Strauss, and Giroux.

[9]Friedman, T. (2010, September). *New thoughts on a hot, flat, and crowded world.* Lecture at Global Climate and Energy Project's 6th Annual Research Symposium, Stanford, CA. Retrieved from http://www.youtube.com/watch?v=E-CSqJl8c14

[10]Fourth Sector. (2008). The emerging fourth sector. Retrieved August 31, 2009, from http://www.fourthsector.net/learn/fourth-sector

[11]Ibid.

[12]Adams, J. H. (2010). Parks make life better: Statewide branding campaign launched. *California Parks and Recreation Magazine, 66*(2), 32.

[13]Supportive Ecosystem. (2008). The emerging fourth sector. Retrieved September 2, 2009, from http://www.fourthsector.net/learn/supportive-ecosystem/

[14]The Career Center. (n.d.). Career success guide 2008–2009: East Carolina University. Retrieved September 4, 2009, from http://www.ecu.edu/e3careers/img/CareerSuccessGuide.pdf on

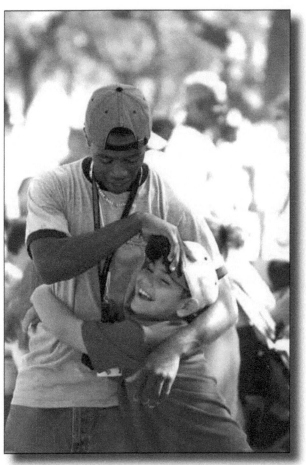

Photo courtesy of City of Austin, Parks and Recreation.

" *The kids are a huge reason for me loving my job. I love talking with teenagers. I work with kids from all types of backgrounds.*

—Chris Goldbecker
Teen Services Program Supervisor
Fairfax County, VA
Department of Community and Recreation Services "

3

Community Recreation and Leisure Services

Clifton Watts
East Carolina University

Kindal Shores
East Carolina University

Focus Questions

Q: Do you have a passion for improving quality of life for others?

A: Having passion to improve quality of life through recreation services is what motivates many who work in this field. This commitment to serving others is rooted in the belief that strong communities need supportive social structures to hold them together. Providers of community recreation services are an important link in this overall service structure.

Q: Do you like working with people and feel you have strong communication skills?

A: Community-based recreation and leisure services jobs require constant interaction with residents, other staff members, and recreation workers in complementary agencies (e.g., other local and non-profit recreation providers). Being calm, comfortable, and responsive when communicating is an important skill to cultivate for a career in community recreation.

Q: Are you a patient person who is willing to go with the flow and put the needs of people first?

A: If you are considering a career working with youth, you will need many of the same skills a good parent and friend may have including patience, understanding, enthusiasm, and more patience! Even well-mannered children can sometimes get out of hand—and you can expect this to happen when they come to your recreation programs. They often come to cut loose, test boundaries, and figure out their identity. Adults as well as seniors can also require constant attention or assistance. Providing programs for diverse public groups requires flexibility!

Q: Are you willing to work a flexible and varied schedule?

A: Especially at the beginning of your career, you may be called upon to work evenings or weekends. After all, since you will be providing leisure for others, you sometimes have to work when they want to play.

Q: What's more important to you: a secure job with benefits and opportunities for advancement or a high salary?

A: You can make a comfortable living in local, county, school, or inclusive recreation careers, although the entry-level salary for such positions is often lower than your starting pay in other careers. The good news is that you can often rise quickly within an agency. As you gain experience and take on responsibility, you will have the opportunity for increases in your income.

Key Terms

Discover the benefits
Senior Games
Inclusive recreation
Risk behaviors
Resilience
Positive youth development (PYD)

Site-based programming
Roving leaders
Pro-social values
21st Century Community Learning Centers
Multidisciplinary perspective

Profile 1: Could This Be You?

Megan Kuhlenschmidt is the sports and aquatics manager for the Champaign Park District in Champaign, Illinois. Megan started as a seasonal employee specializing in lifeguarding and aquatics while in high school and continued in these types of positions through her college years. She completed a bachelor's degree in cultural anthropology and Spanish at the University of Texas and then went on to pursue her master's degree in parks and recreation at Texas A&M University. Her choice to pursue graduate education in this area was driven by her passion for working with people in the areas of aquatics and athletics. While working toward her PhD at the University of Illinois, Megan felt a pull to reconnect with the field and began working part time again in aquatics. Following graduation in 2010, she pursued her current position with the Champaign Park District, which she refers to as her "dream job."

Q: What do you do at work on a typical day?

A: There is not a "typical day" and that is what I like about it. It also changes with the seasons. In general, there is a great deal of communication. E-mails, texts, and phone calls that help us coordinate events and programs. There is also work with human resources around staffing and prepping for our seasonal staff needs. My weekly work is mostly related to administrative procedures. I am planning and I am on committees that work to fulfill the district's strategic events. On the weekends, I spend a lot of time at particular sites for events. It is common to find me bouncing between two or three weekend events and ensuring that operations run smoothly.

Q: What are your responsibilities?

A: Within our division, I oversee youth sports, adult sports, special events, aquatics, fitness, and day camps. I am responsible for managing personnel who supervise and deliver programs in these areas, as well as tasked to consider the budget and resources for supporting these programs. I also supervise our facilities manager who oversees the development of new facilities while maintaining and managing our current facilities. I am basically a middle manager who has to think ahead while processing what is currently happening. I have learned to balance short- and long-range planning in this position.

Q: What do you like most about your job?

A: Being able to express my creativity and having the freedom to experiment really contribute to my job satisfaction. We get to play while we plan and deliver services. Our playing keeps the job fun. I am also lucky to work for someone who trusts my judgment. I have supportive upper administrators who give me the freedom to try new ideas without the fear of failing. Creativity also boils down to the people. Most of my employees love what they do; pay is often secondary. However, I cannot take their passion for granted. I need to be aware of their assignments. I try to avoid constant repetition of duties. I also seek their feedback in program development. Opportunities for expressing creativity go a long way in making happy employees who deliver programs that our community loves. For example, we took on a new approach for our fitness events that seems to refresh our staff. We encourage staff members to develop events that are completely original. We have a "zombie run" in the fall. Staff members come up with ideas for sets, costumes, and mini-events within the event. We also have a "pie run" that features locally made pies. Runners go station to station eating pies and then get a cream pie hurled at them as they finish. The community has also responded well. We have a whole new segment of 20- and 30-year-olds who come to our programs.

Q: What are the biggest challenges you face in your job?

A: Financial decisions are challenging. We are constantly evaluating how we make our services and facilities best for our community while considering the needs and resources of the park district. This requires creativity in planning, budgeting, and service delivery.

Q: How do you make a difference in people's lives?

A: We give adults a place to play. There are very few places where adults, and even families, get to play. I think that idea is often overlooked, but important. We connect families. We connect the community through play. Our events allow for intergenerational participation. We even have events where we award prizes for the most generations competing. For youth, the benefits are obvious. Our programs offer youth opportunities to connect with an activity that instills confidence, offers a lifelong pursuit, and exposes them to other young people and adults who are supportive. It broadens their group of friends. It ties them to more people in the community.

Q: What need do your program and services fulfill within the community?

A: Our services complement, but do not compete with, what is already offered locally. If there are already eight volleyball leagues in the community, why should we offer another? We often look for new niches or areas to address. I think that is why our fitness events work so well. These events are unlike anything offered in the community.

One of the biggest needs we fulfill in the community is employment for teenagers. Our department runs the biggest teen program in the city; it's called employment. We employ hundreds of teens each summer. These young people are smart and energetic. They bring a lot of creativity to our programs, but we also have to be mindful about their needs and development. It is an aspect of the job that I did not envision when starting this position.

Q: What are the employment prospects for entry-level employees?

A: Getting your foot in the door is important. Seasonal work is often a route for career development. Demonstrating a progression at the same place is helpful for getting front-line supervisor positions. I see college students starting as day camp counselors one summer, and the next summer they are working as assistant camp directors. You can land a full-time, year-round job with these kinds of experiences.

Q: What advice do you have for someone preparing for a career in this field?

A: It is important that you learn on the job and show interest in what you are learning. When I hire you as a new staff member, I have to be confident that you love and enjoy what you do. Jobs are committed to budget lines, and there is no guarantee that vacant positions will be filled. As a supervisor, I do not want to risk a position with someone who is not committed. Seeing someone with an established work history helps ease my mind when hiring.

As you move into a career, you will need to articulate what you can do that is unique. When I applied for my current position, I was committed to making the aquatics center financially viable and expanding the number of special fitness events we offer to the community. My past experience in each of these areas made me confident that I could achieve these goals. I had something from which I could frame and execute these ideas.

Q: What kind of formal education do you recommend? What experience is needed?

A: Be prepared to brand yourself; having a degree in parks and recreation is not enough. Pairing your degree with a complementary minor such as accounting or business is important because you will develop applicable job skills. Remember that you are competing with several other people who have a similar degree. Take courses in areas that will expand your marketability. Work in the field. As I mentioned, seasonal employment is great exposure.

Profile 2: Could This Be You?

Sheila Long is the community center coordinator for the Zebulon Parks and Recreation Department in Zebulon, North Carolina. Through high school and into college, Sheila worked in the hospitality industry. During her sophomore year of college, she changed majors from accounting to recreation and park management. She was drawn to working with others and the active nature of the job. She completed her bachelor's degree at North Carolina State University in 2009. She interned with the Athletics Division of the Rocky Mount (NC) Parks and Recreation Department as she finished her senior year of college. She was hired directly after that experience into her current position.

Q: What do you do at work on a typical day? What are your responsibilities?

A: My main responsibility is related to running and maintaining the community center facility. A typical day involves opening the community center and greeting our regular morning users, who are older adults. My staff and I always joke that about 40 percent of our job is socializing with our community members. A lot of what I do is related to our daily programs. I ensure that our rosters are updated, that our staff is prepared, and that the facilities within the center are clean and ready to use. In addition to overseeing these activities, I deliver programs in conjunction with our programming coordinator. I am responsible for networking with neighboring park districts, promoting the programs we offer to the community, and collaborating with other community partners on health initiatives related to community wellness. I also write and manage grants received by the district.

Q: What do you like most about your job?

A: The freedom to try new things is most important to me. I do not want to be stuck behind a desk all day crunching numbers. You are not constantly following a template. Each day is different, and it requires you to think broadly and use perspective. You also get to create relationships with people in your community. It also helps with programming. People feel comfortable telling you what they like and do not like about your programs. Parks and recreation departments are the face that communities see. As a community, we typically see police and fire departments when something bad happens. People from preschool age to seniors deal with our programs on a regular basis. We are the face of our community.

Q: What are the biggest challenges you face in your job?

A: I think the biggest challenge for me is being in a small town. Lots of folks tend to compare our town with larger cities, and the common belief is that we do not have much in the way of programs. The truth is we offer many opportunities. We have to be vigilant about getting the word out and informing the public to fight false perceptions. Another challenge I face relates to separating myself from work. I know my staff is trained and performs well, but I tend to fall into the trap of thinking about work even when I am not working.

Q: How do you make a difference in people's lives?

A: Our town is predominately low income, and we are able to provide opportunities that would not exist in the absence of our department. We have the ability to offer programs at a reasonable cost with little or no travel involved for community members. In terms of contributing to community wellness, we have walking trails and exercise classes that serve people of all ages and we are working with neighboring towns to identify opportunities and emphasize physical activity.

Q: What need do your program and services fulfill within the community?

A: Our emphasis is on exposing people to opportunity. We do not want to compete with niche providers. Our community members might take an opportunity, such as dance, and then decide to specialize later with a more advanced program or school of dance outside of town. We like to open the door to a world of possibilities that extend beyond athletics and fitness. Our community members want to do art, dance, drama, and other noncompetitive expressive activities. We are also unique because we serve the entire community from preschool to older adults.

Q: What are the employment prospects for entry-level employees?

A: In this field, I think it might seem a bit tough for entry-level employees. Following the economic downturn, many people were laid off and recent graduates were competing with people who had master's degrees and experience. However, I see the job market improving. Our state professional organization (NCRPA) has a career connection newsletter that is ripe with job opportunities. I think students who network and develop good relationships with professionals will fare well in the job market. I would not have this job today if it were not for my professional network. You have to be willing to work at relationships and take on employment that will get you to the next level.

Q: What advice do you have for someone preparing for a career in this field?

A: Getting a good background in programming is absolutely important to this job. Our community center serves a multigenerational population and tends to focus on one generation at a time. Our staff members need to understand each population we serve. Having experience with different populations goes a long way in preparing for this type of job. Another important area to consider is grant writing. Our budget is fairly limited, and acquiring grants allows our department to expand services that focus on community needs related to health and wellness. Grant writing is a skill that few people in our field have, but it is one that many departments and districts need.

Q: What kind of formal education do you recommend? What experience is needed?

A: Getting a degree in recreation and parks is a good first step, but it should not be your only basis for training. While students are in school, I would recommend taking opportunities to participate in student organizations, state professional organizations, and department events and getting to know guest speakers and other professionals who come into contact with students. Avoid the trap of thinking that assignments have no practical implications, because I have learned that they do. Prepare yourself before going out on internship. Try seasonal employment. Be deliberate and try out different types of jobs. Take courses or a minor in an area that will augment your skills in the job market. I have a minor in business, and it helps me a great deal in my current position.

Community Recreation and Leisure Services

Like Megan and Sheila, many people who work in county, local, youth, and school recreation choose to do so because they had positive experiences with parks and recreation when growing up or currently in their daily lives. Maybe you want to provide others the opportunity to experience the benefits of community-based parks and recreation that you enjoyed in your hometown. The idea that recreation benefits participants and that a community should provide parks and recreation for its residents is not new. In fact, researchers have traced the origins of local park and recreation programs and youth activities in the United States back to the Industrial Revolution.

Brief History of Community Recreation and Leisure Services

Since the early 1800s, community-based park and recreation offerings in the United States have grown and developed in response to worldwide changes in work, politics, and finance. Community-based parks were first established in the United States during the Industrial Revolution (early 1800s). This period in time was marked by rapid immigration from Europe into U.S. cities, and these cities became a domestic hub for jobs to meet the demands of the increasing population. Even more jobs were created as citizens moved from the countryside into cities to work in crowded factories and live in even more crowded neighborhoods. Both young children and adults worked, and jobs typically required long hours and regimented tasks and took place in dirty and unsafe working conditions. This concerned residents and community leaders in New England and New York factory towns. In fact, in New York City, children were often arrested for playing illegal games such as marbles, throwing stones, or kicking trashcans

> " If we would have our citizens contented and law-abiding, we must not sow the seeds of discontent in childhood by denying children their birthright of play.
> —Theodore Roosevelt, Hon. President, Playground Association of America "

in the street. The need to look out for police led to the formation of informal street gangs, many of which later evolved to commit more serious crimes.[1] To provide children a safe place to play and families a place to gather and refresh themselves for work, towns set aside and landscaped green spaces—the first U.S. parks. The playground movement in these areas expanded nationally, and by the start of the 20th century, more than 80 "sand gardens" or modern-day playgrounds were established.

Community-based recreation expanded over time. In addition to an attractive environment, people realized that children could be taught skills and responsibility through games and recreation programs and that these skills could be beneficial later in life. Joseph Lee, often called the father of the playground movement, felt that work and play were not as different as most people thought, but rather he felt both of them were a cultivation and expression of a desire to explore, excel, achieve, and master.[2] Other early play programs were designed to assimilate the waves of new immigrants to the United States. Later, in the 20th century, recreation programs were expanded to teach adults useful skills, such as basic literacy and household arts. For example, community recreation providers helped women work in "victory gardens" to grow their own produce, as food supplies were limited during the war. Gardening together helped women feel they were contributing to the war effort, and generally boosted morale stateside.

Today, community-based programs are more diverse and far reaching than ever. Community recreation programs are designed to meet the needs of specific groups within the citizenry (e.g., youth, seniors, families, recent immigrants) as well as the general public. Delivery of these services has also changed as partnerships with other community-based services (e.g., public health, schools, social work) provide the opportunity to reach those who most need these services. We will explore how these services function to support communities.

Community Recreation: Discover the Benefits

As part of a movement to emphasize the value of recreation, particularly community recreation, the National Recreation and Park Association (NRPA) developed a campaign focusing on the benefits associated with recreation and leisure services. The campaign's purpose was to help the public understand that park and recreation programs were not only fun and games but also fostered specific outcomes beneficial to individuals, communities, societies, and the environment (including the so-importants discussed in Chapter 1). The Benefits Are Endless campaign was formally launched in 1995 and continued into the 2000s with a slight name change: **Discover the Benefits**. The focus on intentional programming within a benefits-based framework was an important movement and sparked a major resurgence and regard for community-based recreation services. Recreation services were repositioned from being viewed as ancillary to being regarded as valuable resources for meeting the needs of communities throughout the United States. Examples to emphasize each are provided below.

Healthy livable communities. One benefit of community recreation services is that they provide opportunities for residents to improve and maintain their health. This contribution has been increasingly important with the escalating incidence of obesity and lifestyle diseases in the United States. In 2005, the NRPA initiated the Step Up to Health Program, which encourages the role of community recreation and leisure services in contributing to healthy lifestyles and livable communities.

Achieving healthy livable communities is possible by making incremental improvements to ongoing practices, advancing collaboration with other community agencies such as public health departments and city planners, and engaging citizens on individual, family, neighborhood, and community levels. In its first five years, the NRPA conducted 32 Step Up to Health Summits, trained 2,250 individuals, and enrolled over 850 communities in the Step Up to Health Movement.

What Is a Livable Community?

Should all communities have safe and open green spaces for play and recreation programs for youth? Some lawmakers and many park and recreation professionals think so and have asked lawmakers to consider the Urban Revitalization and Livable Communities (URLC) Act. Based on the fact that almost 80% of U.S. citizens live in urban areas, some lawmakers want to provide additional funding to revitalize public parks to provide safe opportunities for citizens to exercise, socialize, and generally improve their individual and community quality of life. The NRPA supports this bill (still awaiting approval as of 2014) and provided the following statistics for those interested. Contact your representative to support H.R. 709.

- Parks in urban spaces attract businesses; many CEOs report access to open space as a top consideration when opening a business.
- Parks create jobs at a higher rate than other sectors. The recreation industry supports
- 6.5 million jobs and contributes $730 billion annually to the U.S. economy.
- Parks increase property values by as much as 25% and attract tourist who generate revenue for the local tax base.
- Parks provide a place for exercise, which is more important than ever as fewer than 25% of adults engage in daily physical activity.[3]

The Step Up to Health initiative is not the first time our nation has addressed livability and public health concerns with a commitment to parks and recreation. The heritage of the parks and recreation movement includes the development of parks to beautify urban communities, improve air quality, reduce the risk of diseases, and provide a place for play, physical activity, and social engagement. Today, community recreation and leisure services agencies are again being asked to enhance existing programs to encourage physical activity and outdoor play for active recreation. Communitywide events hosted by recreation providers are being infused with physical activity. Local parks can be designed to increase physical activity among passive users. Finally, population-specific programs are being developed to encourage physical activity. Thus, more than 100 years later, community recreation services are offered by an estimated 6,000 municipal and county recreation and park systems nationwide that manage approximately 500,000 park and recreation facilities available to support emerging public health and community livability goals.

Photo courtesy Jay Clark

Seniors. One population-specific program that supports healthy active living is the **Senior Games**. In 1985 in St. Louis, Missouri, a group of seven men and women formed the original leadership for what was known as the National Senior Olympics Organization. The organization was dedicated to motivating senior men and women to lead a healthy lifestyle through senior games. In the fall of 1985, they hosted a meeting of individuals who were currently conducting sports and games for seniors in their 33 states. That group planned the first National Senior Olympic Games, which were held in 1987 in St. Louis, Missouri. The games were a great success, with 2,500 competitors. Today, the organization operates as the National Senior Games Association and holds its signature event, the Summer Games, which has grown to one of the largest multisport events in the world with over 12,000 competitors.

Baby Boomers Into Senior Boomers

Since the event began 20 years ago, the Northern Virginia Senior Olympics have more than doubled in size to include 725 participants ages 50 and older. The recreational athletes compete in events such as swimming, track and field, and basketball and in lower impact events such as bridge, cribbage, dominoes, and Wii™ bowling.

In Virginia, as in many states, aging baby boomers are an increasingly large portion of the population, representing about 12% of the state's citizens in 2013, with that number expected to rise to 30% by 2030. As more U.S. citizens live longer, careers in active aging and senior recreation will be available to the prepared recreation professional.[5]

Local recreation and leisure departments that offer senior sport teams and practices and that arrange local and statewide competition most often manage this nationwide event. Senior adults can participate in their state events year-round, and this will keep them motivated to continue to participate and to stay healthy, active, and fit. The Senior Games recognizes that residents of all ages need opportunities to be healthy and active—community recreation providers can provide access to these opportunities. Research backs up the benefits of the Senior Games. In one study, participants reported higher self-image, social networking, a sense of belonging, and improved physical fitness during and after competing in the Games.[4] Healthy and active aging are important components to healthy communities.

Inclusive recreation. The mission of **inclusive recreation** is to create recreation opportunities where all people, regardless of their abilities or disabilities, can achieve their potential and develop their artistic, civic, social, and leadership abilities. Inclusive recreation supports valuing and including all citizens.[6] It goes beyond tolerance and accommodation to allow for full participation and integration into programs. Programs are not separate and include all people. This may require services to adapt equipment, facilities, or programs. At times, it will also require recreation leaders to advocate for individual rights, teach skills, and develop strategies to empower individuals in leisure and assure that other participants respect and include others.

In some cases, community-based recreation and leisure services providers will employ Certified Therapeutic Recreation Specialists (CTRS). CTRSs are trained to implement therapy and techniques to promote skill development, improve function in physical abilities, and meet the needs of clients with disabilities, mental illness, and other challenges. You can read more about the work of CTRSs in Chapter 7.

Inclusive recreation may also connect community members to unique opportunities through adaptive sports. Almost every sport you can imagine can be adapted to encourage participation. Skiing, basketball, and road racing are among the most popular competitive adapted sports. Adaptive sports have grown in popularity with the improvement of technology and advent of universally designed facilities.

Supporting Positive Youth Development

As a community or school-based recreation programmer, you can play a key role in the development of positive assets for youth. The Search Institute lists 40 assets important for youth to grow up as thriving members of their community. As a youth development professional, you can provide safe and engaging opportunities that can assist with the development of assets such as the following:

- high expectations
- positive adult role model
- creative activities
- structured programs
- achievement motivation
- reading for pleasure
- caring
- honesty

- integrity
- responsibility
- restraint
- planning and decision making
- cultural competence
- peaceful conflict resolution
- sense of purpose
- positive view of personal future[9]

Community youth services and positive youth development. In 1992, the Carnegie Council on Adolescent Development published a report titled *A Matter of Time: Risk and Opportunity in the Non-School Hours*.[7] This report had a significant bearing on community recreation services for youth, as research has demonstrated that youth are more likely to engage in **risk behaviors** (e.g., juvenile crime, substance use) between the hours of 2 and 7 p.m. This is especially evident among youth living with a single parent or in households in which both parents have full-time employment, as is increasingly the norm in the United States. Other research has shown that when youth have access to positive nonparental adults and structured extracurricular activities such as after-school or community recreation programs, they may develop protective factors, buffering them from external and internal risk factors. Involvement in such programs, especially when engaged with supportive adults and in (some) structured activities, is linked to the promotion of

resilience, or a state of being where youth bounce back from adversity and feel optimistic about their future. Research has noted that youth with resilient qualities are more likely to perform well in school, avoid risky behaviors, and connect with positive and supportive adults and peers. Promoting resilience continues to be a common goal for many recreation-based programs for youth.

Since 2000, the focus of many programs has evolved from the promotion of resilience into a broader positive youth development framework. **Positive youth development (PYD)** promotes principles to develop youth as assets, and this approach is in opposition to past approaches that focused only on preventing problems or addressing deficits. Similar to the notion of resilience, this perspective examines how youth succeed and develop to be healthy adults who are involved within their communities. Pittman, a noted advocate of PYD, Martin, and Yohalem summed up the PYD approach by stating that "problem free is not fully prepared" and "fully prepared is not fully engaged."[8] This orientation suggests that youth service workers are charged with preparing youth for adulthood by providing opportunities to lead, make choices, and learn from these choices within a supportive environment, leading to substantial benefits to youth, their families, and their communities. Increasingly, youth development programs reflect leisure service delivery systems that are emerging or have permeable boundaries that require new partnership models and methods for targeting hard-to-reach populations. We discuss two approaches in our review of site-based programming.

Site-Based Programming

Over the last 20 years, community-based recreation has experienced growth in the area of **site-based programming**, which is an intentional effort to bring programs to communities where need is most prevalent and where services and facilities are limited. Site-based programs often occur outside public park and recreation facilities and may occur in a school, a neighborhood facility, or even a workplace. This strategy emerged because of the need to engage and retain underserved youth who reported dropping out of programs due to difficulties with transportation or safety concerns with travel to sites managed by public recreation programs. We will focus on two site-based programming methods: roving leaders and 21st Century Community Learning Centers.

Roving leaders. In general, roving leaders are employees of municipal park and recreation programs. These individuals work in underserved communities and meet with youth during nonschool hours. Often, service provision is developed organically. This means programs and services are developed along with youth, who identify what services are needed or wanted within communities. To this end, roving leaders provide meaningful experiences in safe environments, and they also reinforce messages about staying in school, making positive choices, and working to develop **pro-social values** such as trust, respect for others, and cultural awareness. This model is also applied in areas where the

> " The Roving Leader is a community youth worker who works outside the walls and boundaries of the traditional youth work or recreation setting. [They] provide outreach to children where they are: on the street, in the park, with their peers. They involve children in positive activities, breaking down barriers they may face in accessing programs or services in their community and developing their strengths, talents and interests.
>
> —Vancouver, Canada Roving Leader program statement "

presence of new immigrants is high. Oftentimes, new immigrants function outside the dominant culture because of limited opportunities, resources, and understanding from the dominant culture. In these cases, engaging youth and families with services is important, as it may lead to broader access to the dominant culture and other needed services.

The work of roving leaders is often challenging. It can often be difficult to program based on individual needs and preferences. Roving leaders need to have a keen sense of how to respect youth voice and choice and be able to adapt to new ideas, wants, and needs over time. Although challenging, the work of roving leaders can be extremely rewarding.

21st Century Community Learning Centers initiative. The **21st Century Community Learning Centers (CCLCs)** initiative was developed in 1998 to target children attending high-poverty, low-performing schools. These centers share an interesting history with the Lighted School Houses of Milwaukee. Founded in 1911, the Lighted School Houses were developed to enrich the lives of immigrant families through the provision of physical games, dance, the arts, and opportunities for socialization. Today's CCLCs offer similar opportunities for families living in underserved communities.

Since 2002, funding for CCLCs has been managed at the state level and falls under the No Child Left Behind Act. As the name implies, CCLCs promote learning within communities through after-school programs that support academic enrichment. In addition to academic support, CCLCs offer

Photo: DC Greens

services such as activities to support math and science education, the arts, recreational services, and programs to promote parent involvement and family literacy. To meet these service needs, CCLCs often partner with community-based and nonprofit recreation and leisure services providers. This program is an excellent example of how community-based recreation service provision has evolved into site-based service provision, as recreation leaders use facilities that fall under the purview of another community agency (i.e., public schools) and not those managed by a public parks and recreation department.

The CCLC initiative is only one example of how social policy has created opportunities for partnerships between recreation programs and other community-based service providers. Many programs have emerged in the past 10 years, including the Safe Schools/Healthy Students initiative, School to Community Action Grants, and other initiatives introduced by philanthropies and private nonprofit agencies. Funding tied to these initiatives is often designed to promote collaboration between various community-based services, and recreation often plays a substantial role in the services and programs that emerge from these efforts.

As public funding becomes increasingly competitive and limited, leaders in community-based recreation and leisure services must understand the extent to which their services fulfill needs in the broader community. This requires a thorough appraisal of existing human services and the ability to explain to what extent recreation providers can complement, partner, or fill gaps that exist within the broader service structure. This also requires entry-level employees to understand that their work does not exist in isolation. Those within the recreation profession need to develop a **multidisciplinary perspective** or a view of their practice that incorporates an understanding reflective of the broader spectrum of community services. Recreation leaders who realize these objectives can be effective in developing long-term services that benefit communities.

Many benefits related to the provision of community recreation and park programs are evidence based. Godbey and Mowen noted that park and recreation programs are instrumental in supporting physical activity and that the proximity of parks and community recreation programs to residences often leads to greater participation by citizens within communities.[10] After-school programs, such as CCLCs or smaller local and municipal programs, are linked to improved school performance and learning as well as positive impact on self-perception and social behaviors.[11]

These benefits have the greatest impact on youth who are at the greatest risk for academic failure. After-school programs can also improve social-emotional functioning and physical fitness through the provision of evidence-based programs. Senior programs have the potential to reduce disability, promote longer living, improve mental health, and reduce health care costs for older adults. The Centers for Disease Control and Prevention offers several guidelines for implementing evidence-based approaches in community programs. Check out the links to the National Cancer Institute's Research Tested Intervention Programs and the Afterschool Alliance via www. sagamorepub.com/resources.

Careers in Community Recreation and Leisure Services

The majority of the more than 140,000 estimated full-time local park and recreation employees work for a city department of recreation. Today, approximately one third of leisure services careers are in community recreation and leisure services, including programs that are offered in local communities and counties, that are inclusive, that are youth focused, and that are offered through schools. The key goal of community recreation providers today remains the same as it was during the inception of parks and recreation: to provide benefits of parks and recreation in people's daily lives that will help individuals achieve their potential. As discussed earlier in this chapter, plenty of evidence has suggested that community park and recreation professionals contribute to those "so-importants," or social and environmental justice outcomes that contribute to their residents' quality of life. Whether an after-school provider is assisting youth with improving their academic achievement or a recreation supervisor is providing older adults opportunities to be active, the common goal is to help people achieve their potential, enhance their quality of life, and enjoy the process along the way.

Passions

Similar to employees in many of the leisure services careers you will continue to read about, employees in community recreation and leisure services are focused on balancing people's enjoyable experience and sustaining the environment in which this experience occurs. However, two aspects separate careers in community-based leisure services from other public recreation careers. If you recall the passions assessment you completed in Chapter 2 and your passions included helping a particular segment of the population (i.e., children, teens, older adults), or if living in the town or city where you work is important to you, you may enjoy a career in community-based leisure services.

First, in community-based recreation, you interact on a frequent (sometimes daily) basis with park and recreation users. For example, as a school recreation provider, you may work with a group of 20 youth every day after school for an academic year and all day during the summer. This frequent personal contact is a contrast to the experience of a wildlife park manager who interacts most often with tourists visiting for a brief period of time.

Second, as you may have guessed, community-based leisure services providers live in the communities they serve. This means you will be providing facilities and services for residents who may include your friends, family, neighbors, and coworkers.

The desire to give back to the community is a driving force for many professionals in local, county, inclusive, and youth leisure services. In fact, public leisure services providers work hard to provide opportunities for all residents, regardless of their abilities, wealth, background, age, or religion. Public leisure services are for everyone.

Pay and Perks

Pay for many entry-level positions in community recreation and leisure services varies based on the job. Many departments offer seasonal employment to mature high school and college students, and these positions are desirable because they often pay well above minimum wage and offer field experience. Full-time entry-level positions usually require a minimum of an associate's degree with prior experience as a part-time or seasonal employee. The pay for these positions varies by region. Pay increases with education, experience, and nature of responsibilities. Perks for entry-level employees include flexible schedules and duties throughout the year. Many community-based programs offer fixed-site programs during the fall, spring, and winter months with special events, day camps, and other off-site opportunities in summer months. Other perks include the potential of working in one community over a long period of time and the ability to advance within that community. Possibilities also exist to move to other communities by networking in professional organizations.

Preparation

As you think about what makes careers in community-based recreation different from other leisure services, these unique characteristics will help you make a list of personal attributes that are important for employers. Thus, good communication skills, patience, responsiveness, and openness to diversity are key attributes for a career in community-based recreation and leisure services. In addition, a career in community-based recreation requires specific knowledge, skills, and abilities related to managing people, recreation activities, and facilities.

While in school, you can make big strides that will put you in position for a local, county, inclusive, school, or youth position upon graduation. The first step is to earn your bachelor's degree, preferably in recreation and leisure studies or park and recreation administration. Training in business administration, community development, family studies, or employee services will provide you the minimum qualifications to apply for entry-level positions. Also, an associate's degree will meet the qualifications for numerous entry-level positions.

In addition to your major coursework and sampling work in the field, specialized training or experience in a particular field such as youth development, business administration, physical fitness, or gerontology will be an asset for many jobs. Consider earning a minor in these areas or acquiring available certifications. Some jobs will require certification. For example, a lifesaving certificate is a prerequisite for working in water-related activities. A facility manager may be required to be a certified pool operator. Most, if not all, employers will require first aid and CPR certification. Certification in the recreation field itself may be helpful for advancement. Following graduation from an accredited 4-year program and after 2 years of work experience, you may sit for the Certified Park and Recreation Professional (CPRP) exam. The NRPA offers this test to professionals seeking recognition and certification by the national governing body of parks and recreation.

Finally, because there are fewer upper management positions than entry-level positions with local government leisure services providers, you may consider pursuing a master's degree in recreation or a related field to improve your opportunity of advancing into the ranks of higher salaried administration jobs. Those with graduate degrees should have the best opportunities for supervisory or administrative positions.

Importance of Finance, Planning, and Partnerships in Community Recreation and Parks

by Jamie S. Sabbach, MS, CPRP
President of 110% LLC in Boulder, CO
committed to advancing parks, recreation, and related services through education
(www.110percent.net)

GP RED: Research, Education, and Development for Health, Recreation, and Land Agencies (a nonprofit organization)

"Given economic and social realities, cities across the country are grappling with budget problems brought on by a nationwide financial crisis and recession, and ever-changing social circumstances that lead many to believe that the systems of yesterday are antiquated and ill-equipped to adapt to today's conditions. As a result, many municipal park and recreation agencies and others are experiencing unprecedented budget reductions in the midst of heightened expectations. Regardless of governments' financial challenges, citizen interest has not diminished relative to quality of life services. The belief is that municipal parks and recreation, libraries, and others that contribute to or enhance the human condition should be sustained or expanded to meet the needs and desires of increasingly diverse populations. Many organizations have had to make difficult decisions due to budget reductions including eliminating recreation programs, 'mothballing' parks, or permanently divesting of long-held assets.

Due to these economic realities, new professionals must be better prepared when it comes to a myriad of competencies. Among these are financial management, communication, and ethics. These competencies are being vigorously tested in all sectors primarily due to budget reductions and resulting constituent and customer anxieties about how these reductions may affect them and their personal interests.

These competencies can be developed and enhanced through the ability to develop, manage, and monitor budgets; the ability to identify and solicit alternative funding sources such as grants, donations, sponsorships, and other nontraditional methods of generating revenues other than charging and/or raising fees for services; an ability to apply logical pricing methods rooted in fair and equitable strategies; the ability to communicate candidly and diplomatically in diverse settings including political charged venues; and an ability to adhere to ethical principles when presented with ethically conflicting situations."

Possibilities

Now that we have covered the basics of entering the community-based park and recreation profession, we look more closely at specific hiring trends within the ranks of local, county, school, youth, and inclusive recreation.

According to the Bureau of Labor Statistics, a U.S. federal agency that tracks career paths and progressions, employment of local and county recreation workers is expected to keep pace with other occupations through 2014.[12] However, special sectors of the local, state, and school recreation field can expect growth at faster than average rates. For example, the leisure services field is expected to grow as retiring baby boomers bring their disposable incomes, free time, and passion for continued education and health to recreation facilities. Across the United States, city and county recreation centers are adding senior-specific offerings and creating new positions to meet the expected demand from active seniors reaching retirement age. On the employment side, baby boomers—often middle or upper level managers—are retiring at high rates, meaning their jobs will come open for skilled and motivated college graduates.

The obesity epidemic in the United States is another trend causing a shift in the demand for community leisure services providers. Previously content to provide neighborhood parks, crafts, camps, and sport leagues, local and county governments are increasingly turning to park and recreation providers to get children healthy and active within their communities. Graduates from recreation programs with supporting coursework and experience in exercise science, education, public health, or nutrition are attractive to employers looking to address this trend.

What is most exciting about working in community-based recreation and leisure services is the variety of populations served. Community-based service providers work with the population of a community. This means that you may work across different groups (e.g., seniors, youth, families) or specialize in a specific area of programming (e.g., promoting youth development, active living).

Community recreation providers must consider five common career area.

General recreation programming. Imagine your day begins with overseeing a group of seniors who participate in low-impact aerobics and social games. Your early afternoon is spent in meetings with different community groups—schools, public health, and neighborhood associations. The focus of these meetings is related to how your center can integrate efforts to provide a cohesive system of services within the community you serve. The afternoon features after-school programs and teen groups until 6:00 p.m. The remainder of your day is helping the night staff members prepare for family evening programming. Seems like a busy day, right?

General recreation programming is a catch-all term that is used to describe the many duties of community recreation and leisure services specialists and that is reflective of traditional leisure services delivery for public good. In many small communities, program budgets do not allow for specialized services, such as those for youth, families, seniors, and people with disabilities. In these cases, recreation programmers are often the "jack of all trades" who serve the broader population in specialized and inclusive settings. Many of these individuals have worked as seasonal or part-time employees with several populations over time.

Passions. A strong affinity for people. A belief in the benefits of recreation services for communities.

Pay and perks. Salaries vary widely. Employees can be seasonal staff assistants in high schools or city or county park and recreation managers. Oftentimes, community-based recreation specialists live in the communities where they work and become deeply connected to members within that community. These positions also allow for advancement if you wish to climb the management ladder.

Preparation. Seasonal employment can begin as early as the late high school years. Full-time entry-level positions with benefits often require a college degree and work experience. Supervisors usually have 5 years experience beyond college. City program managers have at least 10 years experience beyond college and a master's degree.

Possibilities. Positions are most abundant in suburban and urban communities. Communities are also where the potential for growth is highest.

Youth sports/athletics. Youth sports and athletics is a specialized area that often falls under city- or county-based recreation services. These types of programs fall within the traditional leisure service delivery system and introduce sports to youth in a safe, fun, supportive environment. Youth sports are also an opportunity to promote physical activity and the character values of teamwork, respect for others, and persisting through challenges. If this career area interests you, read Chapter 9 for more details on a sport-related career.

Passions. A love and value of sports, instruction, and management of sport facilities.

Pay and perks. Pay for entry-level employee positions is comparable to other community-based service personnel. Some communities employ a director of athletics who has several years of experience. In many cities and suburbs, good youth athletic facilities and programs offer an opportunity to host county, statewide, and regional tournaments. As sports are generally valued, these programs enjoy good support within communities. Tournaments and other special events related to athletics also have the potential to offer tremendous economic benefit to communities.

Preparation. Similar to other community-based services, positions in youth athletics and sports can range from seasonal to more formal positions with benefits. Positions with benefits require a bachelor's degree with classes or concentration in youth sports, recreational sport management, or youth leadership.

Possibilities. Sports remain popular in the United States, and these programs are well supported in suburban and urban communities.

After-school and teen centers. After-school (sometimes called out-of-school) programs serve many community needs. The majority of after-school programs offer academic enrichment, which provides homework support and tutoring. In addition to academic enrichment, after-school programs offer opportunities to participate in athletics, arts, crafts, theater, and programs where recreation activities embed learning. For example, we once observed a program that focused on boat making. Students learned the craft of making wooden boats, but they also learned math.

Teen centers are after-school programs that cater specifically to this age group. Teen centers offer many of the same activities as other after-school programs, but they are designed to appeal to teen interests and community involvement. These programs may offer the opportunity for teens to develop and implement a community-based project such as a food drive. Teen centers also offer sessions where teens can talk to each other about problems or work directly with mentors. Teen centers represent many of the ideals of positive youth development where youth have the voice to speak their minds and the choice to make decisions in a supported environment.

After-school programs and teen centers often involve collaborative programming with schools or other community agencies. These interdisciplinary opportunities reflect the emerging leisure service delivery systems, which target hard-to-reach populations and often require programming that is outside the boundaries of traditional service.

Passions. Contributing positively to the development of children and teens. Having beliefs about the value of "giving back" to a community. Having an orientation that supports mentoring and positive development for youth.

Pay and perks. Part-time positions are available for college students looking for work experience. Recent college graduates often fill formal youth leader positions. Some communities have recreation departments that have parallel tracks for general community-based programs and youth programs.

Preparation. Educational preparation mirrors that described earlier in community-based recreation services. Specialized coursework in youth development, psychology, and grant writing is a plus for those looking to work in this area.

Possibilities. Public funding for youth programs is currently at historical highs. These emphasize growing public support for developing youth as assets and future community leaders.

Facility manager. Reflective of the traditional leisure service delivery system, many larger towns and counties employ facility managers to oversee the day-to-day operations of arenas, amphitheaters, ball fields, and other built environmental structures. In addition to maintenance and upkeep, facility managers are often responsible for scheduling facility use, developing risk management plans, and managing facility staff. In many cases, facilities become symbols for the communities in which they are housed. If being a facility manager interests you, read Chapter 6 to learn more about working in parks.

Passions. Budgeting, personnel management, risk management, maintenance, scheduling, complex organizations, planning, marketing.

Pay and perks. Salaries for facility managers depend upon the size and number of facilities and experience of managers.

Preparation. Bachelor's degree in recreation or a management-related field. Specific training and aptitude in personnel management and facility maintenance is essential.

Possibilities. Recent growth in the south and southwestern United States means that more opportunities for new construction and new facilities exist in these areas. Cities and towns that have increasing populations of young families and seniors in retirement will be those that have the most potential for new facilities and services.

Seniors. A recreation professional who works with older adults must be confident in a wide range of programming (from crafts to travel to fitness) and have strong social skills. Beyond organizing and promoting senior activities to a wide age of seniors, this professional needs to be a good listener and friend to the seniors who attend the programs. Because of this, individuals who enjoy learning about people, hearing their stories, and sharing their own experiences are likely to enjoy working with older adults. Reflective of the future leisure service delivery system, professionals in senior recreation may be employed by local parks and recreation departments, by assisted living communities, or within a contracted capacity by resident care facilities.

Passions. An appreciation for older adults, their experiences, and their history.

Pay and perks. Entry-level positions in both community and senior resident settings allow new employees autonomy as they often have responsibility for both the design and the delivery of programs that they choose.

Photo courtesy Jay Clark

Photo by Fran Kibler

Preparation. Bachelor's degree in recreation with coursework in gerontology and health promotion is preferred. An aptitude for program planning and organization is essential.

Possibilities. The largest generation of older adults, the baby boomers, are beginning to enter retirement. These older adults are healthier and wealthier than previous generations. Employment prospects working with seniors are at an all-time high and should continue to grow for the next 20 years.

Inclusive recreation. Inclusive recreation specialists are called upon to adapt existing programs and facilities to meet the needs of people with disabilities. In addition, you will have the opportunity to design services for all ages of residents with special needs to ensure that all people can enjoy their leisure time in ways that enhance their health, well-being, and independence. Careers in this field are reflective of the emerging and future leisure service delivery systems, as these professionals are likely to work across agencies and in unique capacities to support the specific needs of their clients.

Passions. Creative, flexible approach to work (each day and resident will be different). Universal design, adapted sports, community outings.

Pay and perks. Pay varies by state and whether employees are Certified Therapeutic Recreation Specialists (CTRSs). This work is often personally rewarding, as it often focuses on empowering individuals through skill development and education.

Preparation. A bachelor's degree in recreation management or therapeutic recreation is preferred (see Chapter 7). Entry-level and seasonal positions are available to individuals with an associate's degree, although advancement will require a 4-year degree in recreation or a related field (child development, social work, adapted physical education). To successfully compete for a supervisory or administrative position, a master of science degree will be beneficial. Volunteer and seasonal work experience in community recreation, education, or clinical settings is a must.

Many staff members begin their path to inclusive community recreation by serving as a volunteer or coach for the Special Olympics.

Possibilities. Inclusive recreation programming is slowly but steadily becoming a more prominent feature of our local communities. Also, new opportunities to work with veterans through Wounded Warrior programs have increased the number and diversity of inclusive recreation programs nationwide.

Summary of Community Recreation and Leisure Services Career Possibilities

Career	Passions	Pay and perks	Preparations	Possibilities
General recreation programming	Community service, giving back	Varies, seasonal employment, entry level to upper management	Varies from high school (seasonal) to master's degree (management)	Superintendent, director, supervisor, coordinator, season
Youth sports/ athletics	Values of sport to skill development	Varies, seasonal employment, entry level to upper management	Varies from high school (seasonal) to master's degree (management)	Director, supervisor, coordinator, seasonal
After-school/ teen centers	Mentoring young people	Paraprofessional leaders and assistants, professional entry and management	High school and community college for paraprofessional, minimun 4-year degree for professional	Director, supervisor, coordinator, youth leader, staff assistant
Facility management	Planning and risk management	Salaries depend upon size and number of facilities and experience	Bachelor's degree in recreation or management-related field and work experience in facilities	Director, supervisor, crew member
Seniors	Working with older adults, personal history	Paraprofessional and professional tracks, demonstrate your creativity	High school and community college for paraprofessional, minimum 4-year degree for professional	Director, supervisor, program staff, staff assistant
Inclusive recreation	Helping others, new challenges	Paraprofessional and professional tracks	High school and community college for paraprofessional, minimum 4-year degree for professional	Director, supervisor, program staff, staff assistant

Future Opportunities, Issues, and Challenges

The future of community recreation and leisure services appears to be ripe with potential. The needs of communities continually change, but we know the need for recreation and leisure is important to developing healthy communities, supporting families, and contributing to the overall welfare of a community. We have identified four areas that present special opportunities and challenges for community recreation and leisure services.

Promoting Healthy and Active Lifestyles

Regardless of age, the need to engage communities in becoming more active is greater than ever. During the past four decades, the obesity rates have at least tripled for youth. Over two thirds of adults are now considered overweight or obese. Diabetes, heart disease, and many cancers are tied to inactivity and obesity, making it the most pressing challenge for community recreation services providers today.

One unique way many recreation departments are helping citizens live healthy and active lifestyles is through community gardens. In recent years, many municipalities have converted patches of unused open space into gardens, with plots available for any residents who wish to cultivate the land. City or county recreation programs often do the general administration of the garden space, and residents do the gardening. Community gardening provides many benefits besides growing your own food. For example, a report of gardeners' experiences with New York City's Parks and Recreation Green Thumb Program found that the gardeners experienced an increase in social networks; a sense of identity; problem solving and decision making; connection to the land; and general education about gardening, food, or specific cultural practices. Their gardening experience not only led to increased physical activity and healthier food choices but also contributed to social and psychological well- being.[13]

> "Unlike traditional parks containing playground equipment or fields designed for organized sports, community gardens encourage creative play and risk-taking in an unstructured, natural environment. Researchers believe risk-taking is an inherent part of play and we cannot remove all risk from play environments without seriously diminishing their benefit to users.
>
> —Edie Stone, New York City Department of Parks and Recreation, Green Thumb Program, New York, NY

Meeting the Needs and Interests of an Increasingly Diverse Population

Communities continue to change and grow with populations becoming more ethnically diverse. Community-based recreation has a long history of serving recent immigrants and their families, and this historical practice will continue into the future. Inclusive recreation practices will ensure service to those with diverse backgrounds. These practices may also lead to a broader "spillover" into mainstream culture as the historical and cultural traditions from those in minority status groups become integrated into the broader population. In recent years, however, recreation programs have moved from merely "serving" diverse populations to a more action-oriented approach to recognize and work for change regarding the often inequitable distribution of park and recreation resources in many urban settings. Several reviews of upper, middle, and lower class neighborhoods have indicated that lower socioeconomic status (SES) neighborhoods have limited access to safe parks, playgrounds, or recreation centers.[14] One study looked at park access nationwide and found that although many low-SES communities have adequate park access, the real problem is with "social access," or the walkability, safety, and sense of welcoming to nearby parks. Simply because a park exists does not mean residents will use it and accrue the benefits.[15] Future recreation programmers must be aware of the sociology and psychology of park and recreation service use, including sense of belonging, culturally appropriate activities, and sense of safety.

Interdisciplinary Collaboration

The need to streamline service and limit duplication requires recreation professionals to continually identify opportunities for collaboration with other community partners. Community-based recreation services have a role in schools and after-school programs, public health, social work, and other human service areas. Recreation professionals need to work closely and collaboratively with their community partners if they are to be valued and called upon as partners. See the Leisure Service Delivery System in Chapter 2 and consider how permeable or boundary free may improve service provision.

Senior Programs

As described previously, the senior population will continue to grow with the aging of the baby boomer generation. In addition to being prepared for this group's retirement, recreation programmers need to be aware of members' unique needs. "Boomers" are better educated and in better health than earlier cohorts, and this means their preferences and needs may be different.

Resources and Getting Involved

Professional Organizations
National Recreation and Park Association: www.nrpa.org
This is the single largest professional organization for recreation professionals in the United States.

American Alliance of Health, Physical Education, Recreation, and Dance (AAHPERD): www.aahperd.org
AAHPHERD is another U.S. professional organization that aims to advance professional practice and research related to health and wellness, physical education, recreation, dance, and sport.

Both AAPHERD and NRPA have state chapters that do an excellent job of being responsive to regional and local communities. State chapters are also great places for professional networking.

State Parks and Recreation Associations

Most states have their own version of NRPA, but on the state level. These associations are excellent resources for internships, seasonal jobs, and full-time careers. Many associations host an annual conference where you could gather information on career possibilities and network for future job opportunities. Check your state associations website for resources such as a job board, newsletter, annual meeting, or continuing education.

Certifications, Licenses
Certified Park and Recreational Professional (CPRP): www.nrpa.org/CPRP/
CPRP is a professional certification offered through the National Recreation and Park Association. Many park and recreation agencies recommend or require CPRP certification when hiring for certain positions.

Certified Therapeutic Recreation Specialist (CTRS)
(Refer to Chapter 7 on recreational therapy for detailed information.)
CTRS is a professional credential designed to ensure professional and ethical standards of practice for therapeutic recreation specialists.

Where to Gain Experience

A large number of temporary seasonal jobs are available in youth sports, event planning and execution, officiating, facility maintenance, youth camps, craft and fitness courses, and community centers. As a general rule, for every full-time position in local government leisure services, two or more part-time positions are available. Volunteering with local agencies during college and back home during vacation periods can help you select an area of community recreation and leisure in which you would like to specialize. These experiences will also give you an advantage when looking for your preferred internship and job at the end of your studies. The contacts you will make "in the field" will provide you with a professional network for job seeking and advice as you establish your leisure services career.

Additional Online Resources

American Association of Adapted Sports Programs: www.adaptedsports.org
This organization works in partnership education agencies to establish programs, policies, procedures, and regulations in interscholastic adaptive sports.

National Alliance for Youth Sports: www.nays.org
NAYS is America's leading advocate for positive and safe sports and activities for children.

National Senior Games Association: www.nsga.com
This is a national organization that promotes healthy lifestyles for seniors through sport and physical activity. It is the national body that oversees Senior Games programs.

NIRSA: Leaders in Collegiate Recreation: www.nirsa.org/wcm
NIRSA is the leading resource for professional and student development, education, and research in collegiate recreational sports.

Active Living by Design (ALbD): activelivingbydesign.org
ALbD creates community-led change by working with local and national partners to build a culture of active living and healthy eating.

National Cancer Institute: Research Tested Intervention Programs:
rtips.cancer.gov/rtips/index.do
The National Cancer Institute identifies and rates specific evidence-based interventions designed to promote health and wellness and prevent disease. Interventions cut across age groups and may be implemented through targeted programming in schools, community centers, and parks.

The Afterschool Alliance: www.afterschoolalliance.org/index.cfm
The Afterschool Alliance is a national organization dedicated to raising awareness of the importance of after-school programs and advocating for more after-school investments. It provides documents related to research-based programs and provides a state-level perspective on the status of after-school services for those wanting to start a program.

Conclusion

Working in community recreation and leisure services is for people who enjoy working with people from all walks of life. One of the important perks of this job is related to the connections you develop within the community. If you value work that positively impacts the lives of the people you serve, your neighbors, and the broader community, then a career in community recreation and leisure services may be the career choice for you. Along with the traditional mission of serving the unique recreation needs of communities, people working in community recreation will play important roles in promoting health through active living, contributing positively to the development of youth, and ensuring equal access to leisure for all citizens.

For Further Investigation

For More Research

1. Check the website of your local parks and recreation department and note what types of services are provided. See if you can find information on the types of staff members that are employed. Are there specialists in youth development, senior programming, and inclusive recreation? If not, who handles these duties? Go to a smaller or larger city's website and try to do the same. What differences do you see in services offered or in staffing?

2. Go to the Internet and look for state schools that feature degrees in parks and recreation. What are the concentrations within the degree program? Do these have coursework to support working with seniors, youth, sports, and/or inclusive recreation?

Active Investigation

Your instructor may guide you to explore one of these opportunities for this chapter:

1. Visit a local recreation center in your area. What services does it provide? List the services and then segment by population served. Note any particular focus (more family oriented, more seniors oriented).

2. Interview five youth served at the local after-school or teen program and find out why they attend this program, how often they attend the program, and what they like best about it.

3. Volunteer with a special event or program. What tasks did the center staff perform? How did the tasks of the permanent staff differ from the tasks volunteers were asked to undertake?

4. Interview Activity: Identify and ask a recreation professional at the center for an informational interview.

5. The questions provided below will assist you with the interview. Refer to the informational interview instructions under Active Investigation in Chapter 2 for more information before conducting your interview.

   - What is the title of your position?
   - What are your responsibilities?
   - What responsibilities do you like most and least?
   - What are your work hours? Does this change during the year?
   - Does your job have a set routine or does it change frequently?
   - In 10 years, what types of services or programs do you feel will need to be offered to the community? Please explain your answer.
   - What advice would you have for someone interested in a career in community recreation and leisure services?

Recommended Reading

Crompton, J. (2007). *Community benefits and repositioning: The keys to park and recreation's future viability.* Ashburn, VA: National Recreation and Park Association.

This book demonstrates how to market park and recreation services based on repositioning. Repositioning is the practice of changing the identity of a product. This text focuses on ways recreation programs can shed the identity of an ancillary service by identifying benefits associated with them and marketing services based on benefits to the community.

DeGraaf, D., & Jordan, D. (2003). Social capital. *Parks & Recreation, 38*(11), 20–27.
This article identifies ways in which recreation programs and services can be used to create social capital within communities.

Schleien, S. J., & Miller, K. D. (2008). *Search for best practices in inclusive recreation: Phase one report.* Retrieved January 15, 2010, from University of North Carolina Greensboron website: http://www.uncg.edu/ctr/phaseonereport.pdf
This monograph identifies practices that administrators and direct leaders can implement to develop more inclusive recreation programs and services.

Wellman, D., Dustin, D., Henderson, K. A., & Moore, R. (2008). *Service living: Building community through public parks and recreation.* State College, PA: Venture.
A must read for anyone considering community recreation as a career, this book underscores the vital role these services play within communities.

References

[1]Frost, J. L. (2010). *A history of children's play and plan environments: Toward a contemporary child-saving movement.* New York, NY: Routledge.

[2]McLean, D. D., & Hurd, A. R. (2012). *Kraus' recreation and leisure in modern society.* Sudbury, MA: Jones and Bartlett Learning.

[3]NRPA Public Policy Office. (2011). The Urban Revitalization and Livable Communities Act [Fact sheet]. Retrieved from http://www.nrpa.org/Advocacy/Resources/Fact-Sheet-Urban-Revitalization-Livable-Communities-URLC-HR-709(1).pdf

[4]Heo, J., Culp, B., Yamada, N., & Won, Y. (2012). Promoting successful aging through competitive sports participation. *Qualitative Health Research, 23*(1), 105–113. doi:10.1177/1049732312457247

[5]Bordenand, J., & Gibson, C. (2013). The Northern Virginia Senior Olympics serve a booming senior population. *The Washington Post.* Retrieved from http://www.washingtonpost.com/local/the-northern-virginia-senior-olympics-serve-a-booming-senior-population/2013/09/17/5a4388a4-1f13-11e3-8459-657e0c72fec8_story.html

[6] Dattilo, J. (2002). *Inclusive leisure services: Responding to the rights of people with disabilities* (2nd ed.). State College, PA: Venture.

[7]Carnegie Council on Adolescent Development. (1992). *A matter of time: Risk and opportunity in the nonschool hours—Report of the Task Force on Youth Development and Community Programs.* Retrieved from Carnegie Corp. of New York, NY website: http://carnegie.org/fileadmin/Media/Publications/A_matter_of_time.pdf

[8]Pittman, K. J., Martin, S., & Yohalem, N. (2006). Youth development as a "big picture" public health strategy. *Journal of Public Health Management Practice, 12*(Suppl. 6), s23–s25, p. 23.

[9]Search Institute. (2013). 40 developmental assets for adolescents. Retrieved from http://www.search-institute.org/content/40-developmental-assets-adolescents-ages-12-18

[10]Godbey, G., & Mowen, A. J. (2010). *The benefits of physical activity provided by park and recreation services: The scientific evidence.* Retrieved from National Recreation and Park Association website: http://www.nrpa.org/Publications_and_Research/Research/Papers/Godbey-Mowen-Research-Paper.pdf

[11]Durlak, J. A., Weissberg, R. P., & Pachan, M. (2010). A meta-analysis of after-school programs that seek to promote personal and social skills in children and adolescents. *American Journal of Community Psychology, 45*(3-4), 294–309. doi: 10.1007/s10464-010-9300-6

[12]U.S. Bureau of Labor Statistics. (2014). Occupational outlook handbook. Retrieved from U.S. Bureau of Labor Statistics website: http://www.bls.gov/ooh/personal-care-and-service/recreation-workers.htm

[13]Stone, E. (2009). The benefits of community-managed open space: Community gardening in New York City. In L. Campbell & A. Wiesen (Eds.), *Restorative commons: Creating health and well-being through urban landscapes* (Gen. Tech Rep. NRS-P-39, pp. 122–137). Newtown Square, PA: U.S. Department of Agriculture, Forest Service, Northern Research Station.

[14]Godbey & Mowen, 2010.

[15]Wen, M., Zhang, X., Harris, C. D., Holt, J. B., & Croft, J. B. (2013). Spatial disparities in the distribution of parks and green spaces in the U.S.A. *Annals of Behavior Medicine, 45*(Suppl. 1), S18–S27.

"*For most people in the nonprofit sector, their work is just a 'job.' It is part of a life of meaning that depends, in no small part, on building a career that makes an impact for good.*

—Shelly Cryer
*The Nonprofit Career Guide:
How to Land a Job That Makes a Difference*"

4

Recreation in Nonprofit Organizations

Jo An M. Zimmermann
Texas State University

Focus Questions

Q: What makes a nonprofit recreation agency different from a public or for-profit agency?

A: There are three major differences between the types of agencies. First, although all three sectors provide recreation programs and/or services, nonprofit agencies are more **mission focused**, meaning they are established to provide a specific type of service based on the organization's purpose. Many nonprofit recreation agencies operate from a social and environmental justice perspective and provide programs and services for people or groups of people who have limited resources or specific needs not being met by public or for-profit agencies. Second, the revenue sources available to each sector are different. Public agencies receive tax money and other forms of government support as well as nominal money from fees for programs or services. Private for-profit businesses earn all of their income via user fees and charges for services. Nonprofit agencies receive money from fees and charges but can also accept grants and contracts for specific projects or services. Finally, each of the sectors has different methods for distributing profit that may be earned. If a public agency has a profit, the excess money goes back into the general operating fund for the agency and/or is used to pay down debt. Private for-profit businesses distribute profits to owners and/or shareholders. Nonprofit agencies can, and many times do, make a profit. Similar to a public agency, profit is reinvested into the organization.

Q: What sort of place do you want to live and work, and what kind of people do you want to be around?

A: The cool thing about working with nonprofit agencies is that you can find them anywhere in the world. You can work for a small local agency or a huge multinational organization such as the YMCA. You can also choose to work with particular population groups such as people with disabilities, children, senior adults, low-income populations, or youth considered "at risk."

Q: Would you enjoy working in a mission-focused environment?

A: The best thing about working in a mission-focused environment is that everyone is trying to achieve the same outcomes. People affiliated with the agency are passionate about either the population or the particular types of programs offered, or both. It is exciting to work with people who are passionate about what they are doing rather than just doing a job.

Key Terms

Mission focused

Nonprofit leisure organization

Volunteers

Mission statement

Vision statement

Social justice

Service provider

Advocate

Facilitator

Unstructured recreation

Structured recreation

Recreational sports

Instructional sports

Out-of-school-time programs

Youth development

Seasonal

Vulnerable populations

Backcountry

Profile 1: Could This Be You?

Margaret Kay-Arora has worked with the YMCA (Young Men's Christian Association, but rebranded in the U.S. as "the Y" to be more inclusive of all populations) in Canada for the past 20 years. After graduating from the University of Toronto, Canada, with a bachelor's degree in physical and health education, she worked for the YMCA of Greater Toronto as the assistant director and then director of health, fitness, and recreation in four facilities during a 10-year period. She later received an opportunity to implement YMCA Canada programs at the YMCA of Metropolitan Singapore. This 2-year project provided her with the chance to adapt health, fitness, and recreation programs to a new culture and to learn about health issues in the Singaporean environment. When she returned to Canada, she moved to the east coast and managed the Dartmouth YMCA in Halifax for 3 years before going international again with the YMCA of Hong Kong, where she managed the Physical and Health Education and Camping programs. In this position, she oversaw two large facilities and developed partnerships with schools, clubs, and government organizations. Now that she is back in Canada, we got together to catch up on her career.

Q: You have been with the Y a long time and have traveled all over the world. What are you doing now?

A: My newest position is with YMCA Canada in the Management Resource Centre where I get to provide training, provide programs, and direct strategic projects for the 14 YMCAs in the Eastern region of Canada. It's an exciting time because our objective is to increase capacity in all the facilities and to leverage our resources to enhance efficiencies, improve productivity, and support association growth throughout the region.

Q: You have been with the Y ever since you graduated from college. How has that worked?

A: I have been very fortunate to grow and develop within the YMCA environment. I started out being the person who implemented programs on the front line with our clients, and now I'm developing strategic initiatives within Canada as well as in other countries. When I took my first job with the YMCA, I never envisioned that I would have so many amazing opportunities to try new things, visit new countries, and meet new people.

Q: I had no idea the YMCA was so big. What can you tell me about its mission?

A: The YMCA is a worldwide movement that strives to develop the body, mind, and spirit of individuals. This can take many forms depending on the community and its issues and focus. For example, in Hong Kong, the YMCA offers a wide variety of programs and services to the community including extensive health, fitness, and recreation programs; employment skills training for immigrants coming from mainland China; secondary school; youth programs; etc. The YMCAs in Canada are all independent associations that meet community needs in a number of ways: Youth Environmental Internship programs, exchange programs for students in the Quebec province (French speaking) to exchange with English-speaking students in other areas of Canada, employment and skills training for unemployed and underemployed, residential and day camps, health, fitness and recreation, and international partnerships with YMCAs in other parts of the world.

Q: You clearly have a passion for what you do. How would you say the Y makes a difference in people's lives?

A: Our slogan is, "We develop strong kids, strong families, and strong communities." Through all of our programs we strive to make a difference in everyone we touch so that overall our communities become stronger. Whether it's teaching a child to swim or helping an adult lose weight, the aim is to do so in a positive and long-term lifestyle modifying way. We also integrate values into all programs so that through the activities, caring, honesty, respect, and responsibility are taught and demonstrated. As a result, not only do participants learn physical activity skills and benefit from improved health, but they also learn how to effectively interact with others in society.

For more information on the Y, and all agencies mentioned in this chapter, visit sagamorepub. com/resources.

Profile 2: Could This Be You?

Elton Fite Jr. is the unit services coordinator for the Boys & Girls Clubs of South Central Texas located in San Marcos, Texas. He has been in that position for 3 years. Prior to working at the Boys & Girls Clubs, he coached Little League baseball starting at age 16 and then worked at an extended day care program while pursuing his bachelor's degree from Texas State University, San Marcos. The Boys & Girls Clubs of America focuses on enabling young people to become productive, caring, and responsible citizens through proven character and leadership programming.

Q: What exactly is a Boys & Girls Club?

A: A Boys & Girls Club (according to its core beliefs statement) provides a safe place to learn and grow by facilitating ongoing relationships with caring, adult professionals, life-enhancing programs, and character development experiences as well as hope and opportunity. The Clubs meet in a dedicated space located within communities or neighborhoods. For example, a neighborhood may be lacking a recreational locale such as a park or recreation center close by. This is often the case in low-income neighborhoods and would be an ideal location for a Boys & Girls Club. Agency administrators would seek to establish a meeting place initially, perhaps using a school, church, or even a conference room in a community building and then work to raise funds to build their own dedicated club facility.

Q: How do you make a difference through your work?

A: Being connected to the Boys & Girls Club, I have the opportunity to influence young lives. In many cases, I have become the only positive adult that our members, children aged 5 to 18 years, have. Through being positive and encouraging, I (along with other staff and volunteers) am able to teach values and promote active and healthy lifestyles to disadvantaged youth.

Q: What do you love about your career?

A: My career as a youth development professional is very rewarding. I am helping prepare young people to live life productively through the same values once taught to me. Daily, we demonstrate social standards and concepts such as manners and respect, which are becoming less and less commonplace in our members' homes. These are only a few things among many that we do to help our youth improve. It's a great feeling to see our youth on a day-to-day basis and have them know that someone is here for them.

Q: How did you get into this profession?

A: I have been working and volunteering for kids programs since I was 16 years old. Three years ago, I was asked to apply for this position because I was teaching writing at a charter school that is on the same property as the Boys & Girls Club. I knew many of the kids in the program, and it seemed like a natural choice for me.

Q: If you could give a young professional interested in this career area one piece of advice, what would it be?

A: This career path is all about being able to share your experiences to make a great impact in a young person's life. You have the opportunity to become the role model that you once had or have heard people speak about.

Nonprofit Recreation and Leisure Services: You Can Make a Difference

A **nonprofit leisure organization** is a legal entity "in which citizens operate outside the government and business apparatuses to improve the quality of life in communities."[1] Four primary characteristics distinguish a nonprofit organization from a public or commercial agency. First, most nonprofits operate based on altruistic goals that reflect their mission statement and clearly outline why they exist and what they are trying to achieve. Core values found in nonprofit agencies include respect for a diversity of people, fairness, stewardship, volunteerism, building community, and service to others. Second, they have a public service mission that focuses on providing an overall public good rather than making a profit for an owner or stockholders. They are seeking to improve the lives of the population they have chosen to serve. Third, nonprofit organizations are tax-exempt because they are public service oriented. Finally, the governance of nonprofit agencies is set up to eliminate self-interest and private financial gain. Boards of directors are usually made up of volunteer members who have a personal and professional interest in the agency mission and can provide strategic direction and links to funding sources.

The provision of recreation and leisure services by nonprofit agencies closely parallels the development of the recreation industry in the United States. We will look more closely at the development of nonprofit recreation and leisure services in North America in the next section.

History of Nonprofit Recreation and Leisure Services in North America

Recreation and leisure programs emerged in the mid-to-late 1800s as a means of addressing social and general welfare issues. Several key organizations were established to serve specific populations. A number of well-known and recognized organizations had their beginnings during this time. For example, the YMCA was first introduced in Boston in 1851 with the National YMCA forming in 1866, the Boys & Girls Clubs of America started as a single Boys Club in Hartford in 1860, and the Young Women's Christian Association (YWCA) began in Boston in 1866. Another early provider of recreation programs was the Hull House, which Jane Addams started in 1889. She designed Hull House to be a center of community life. In many cases, "idealistic young middle class men and women who committed to live for an extended period of time in urban slums" provided the services of these agencies.[2] Although not all of the nonprofit agencies discussed in this chapter have been around as long as those mentioned here, most have a long and interesting history of service to their local communities and beyond.

Public recreation departments began to form to provide public recreation programs and services in 1850, when the state of Massachusetts passed legislation that granted taxing authority to local governments, meaning they could tax residents. Nonprofit organizations were initially developed to provide services that community members saw as being important for health and well-being, but they did not receive taxpayer support. Generally speaking, the same is true today. By law, all money that a nonprofit agency makes must go into operating the programs and services that the organization provides. Nonprofit agencies do not have taxing authority, and they still focus on serving specific segments of the population.

What You Should Know About Nonprofit Agencies

The number and variety of nonprofit leisure services agencies are great, and they share a number of commonalities. "These organizations focus on social welfare and benefits to members in terms of enriched living, community building, character building, and citizenship."[3]

In many cases, one person or a small group of people who saw a need they felt they could meet through a nonprofit agency founded a nonprofit organization. Because most nonprofits start out small and are designed to serve one specific population or provide one specific program or service, they are often able to experiment with new ways of providing services. Although existing for a while as just a group of people trying to accomplish a goal is possible, if they want to grow or expand, they will likely find developing a constitution and registering as a special type of corporate entity, usually a 501(c) 3, which provides tax exemptions and other legal guidance, is necessary. At this point, the organization needs to name a board of directors who will ensure the agency meets all its legal obligations. According to BoardSource, the basic responsibilities of nonprofit boards are to (a) determine the organization's mission and purpose; (b) select the chief executive; (c) provide proper financial oversight; (d) ensure adequate resources, such as donations and sponsorships; (e) maintain accountability; (f) ensure effective organizational planning; (g) recruit and orient new board members; (h) enhance the organization's public standing; (i) determine, monitor, and strengthen programs and services; and (j) support the chief executive and assess his or her performance.[4]

The success of a nonprofit agency is measured in two ways. First, the board of directors will compare the achievements of the organization to its established goals. Second, they will assess how well it has managed to generate "enough revenue and other resources (e.g., volunteers) to stay in operation and continue benefiting their specialized markets."[5] Obtaining funding so that organizational goals can be met is a continuous challenge for many nonprofits. Potential sources of funding include grants, membership fees, individual and corporate donations, general fund-raising, and earned income. The help of **volunteers**, people who offer their time and skills to an organization without expecting to be paid, are the mainstays of many nonprofits' operating staff.

Nonprofit recreation and leisure agencies

> are organized to serve both individual needs and broader community goals. Some are organized to conserve and preserve historical, cultural, environmental, and other traditions. Others are developed to advance social change with a focus on improving the condition of disadvantaged and disenfranchised people who do not feel a part of mainstream community life.[6]

Other Characteristics of Nonprofit Agencies

One characteristic that sets nonprofit recreation and leisure organizations apart from public and commercial agencies is the importance of the agency mission statement. It provides an agency with direction as it describes what the agency is about, its core beliefs, the essence of what it strives to accomplish. Later in this chapter, you will find information about many nonprofit recreation and leisure organizations. Included in the information is either a mission statement or a vision statement. A **vision statement** is more global or far-reaching than a mission statement because it describes what the agency wants to be in the future. It is important to understand what an agency stands for and believes in, but this is even more important when you work in the nonprofit sector. Most nonprofits will want to know that you can and will support what they are trying to accomplish and not only on paper, but also in your actions (both on and off the job). As one YMCA professional stated, "You can work here for a little while without completely buying into what the Y believes in, but if you don't carry the values through to your daily life, you won't be able to make a career here."

Who Nonprofit Agencies Serve

Nonprofit recreation and leisure agencies serve many age groups, specific populations, and income levels. For example, you may work with very young children (and parents or caregivers), preschool age, primary school age, teenagers and adolescents, young adults, adults, and even the elderly. If you are not committed to working with one particular age group, many positions will require you to work with several age groups. Beyond various age groups, you should also consider specific populations with whom you may want to work. Many nonprofit organizations offer programs and services to individuals with some level of disability (and perhaps family members as well). In addition to focusing on people with disabilities, some organizations may target most of their programs to the general population but also make them available on an integrated basis for all ability levels (e.g., YMCA and scouting). Sporting and arts organizations will most likely work with all ability levels as well. Finally, some nonprofit organizations are set up to assist people who, for many reasons, do not have access to recreation programs and services as readily as other groups. This could be due to finances, geography, ethnicity, religion, sexual orientation, age, or ability level. Whatever the reasons, many nonprofits are driven by the desire to work toward **social justice**, which is striving to ensure all members of society have equal access to resources and feel physically and psychologically safe so everyone can participate in his or her society.[7]

> " In the United States, there is no limit to the inventiveness of man to discover ways of increasing wealth and to satisfy the public's needs. The most enlightened inhabitants of each district constantly use their knowledge to make new discoveries to increase the general prosperity, which, when made, they pass eagerly to the mass of the people.
>
> —Alexis de Tocqueville in *Democracy in America*, 1935 "

If you review the list of so-importants in Chapter 1 you will see that working in the nonprofit sector can provide you with many opportunities to address key issues in society. So, if you have a desire to help individuals who may otherwise be excluded, you need to look at a career in nonprofit work.

Where Nonprofits Are Located

Nonprofit agencies are located where both people who need services and programs and people who want to help meet those needs reside. Consider working in a nonprofit in your own community. Local agencies may be small and may depend on a large number of volunteers or may have a number of part-time paid staff. Most serve the interests and needs of a clearly defined local group of people. In addition, they may stand alone and therefore not be connected or affiliated with a national or regional organization (e.g., a community organization established primarily to provide after-school care to a specific area).

If staying local does not appeal to you, consider working or volunteering for a nonprofit agency that has state, regional, national, or even international affiliations. Sport groups tend to have regional or state affiliations to provide statewide or regional competition. Examples of agencies with a national or international presence include Camp Fire Inc., Boy Scouts, Girl Scouts, YMCA, YWCA, and Boys & Girls Clubs.

Nonprofits Fill Varied Roles Within Their Communities

You may assume that all nonprofit recreation and leisure agencies play a similar role or fill similar needs within society. However, nothing could be further from the truth. Organizations may play four primary roles. The most common role is **service provider**. This type of agency's primary role is to develop and deliver programs and services directly to a constituent group, for example, summer camps, dance classes, sport teams, and swim lessons. The YMCA is an example of a service provider. Other nonprofit agencies serve the role of **advocate**. Staff members' primary purpose is to advocate for the rights of people who cannot advocate for themselves. For example, some nonprofits are set up specifically to champion the needs and rights of people with disabilities to participate fully in recreation programs and services. The third role is **facilitator.** Agencies in this role assist people to access programs and services but do not necessarily provide services through their own organization. This approach is frequently used with specific populations such as individuals with a disability, youth at risk, or the elderly. For example, in Melbourne, Australia, the primary function of Rec Link is to connect people with disabilities with appropriate recreation programs. Finally, a nonprofit agency may exist to **provide facilities.** Some nonprofits only provide facilities or maintain outdoor areas for recreation activities. In this case, they do not necessarily offer specific programs or services.

> "Non-profit recreation and leisure agencies benefit society through educating their members, setting professional standards, developing and disseminating information, informing the public...while enriching the lives of their members.
> —Oleck & Stewart[24]

Careers in Nonprofit Recreation and Leisure Services

The nonprofit sector in North America employs a steadily increasing segment of the working population, and the number of those employed in the nonprofit sector continues to grow at a fast pace. Nonprofit employment represents nearly 10% of the American workforce, with 1.6 million nonprofits employing 13.7 million workers.[8] Students interested in a career in the nonprofit sector have many choices including arts, culture and recreation, nursing homes, religious congregations, and social services organizations.

Passions

If you enjoy working with people in a place where the overriding mission is to improve the quality of life of individuals and communities, a career in a nonprofit agency may be for you. According to some studies, people working in the nonprofit sector tend to have a higher level of job satisfaction than either the public sector or the commercial sector. David Mason has had a long career managing local, regional, and international nonprofit agencies. In speaking with nonprofit professionals over the years, he has found that their organizations have provided "direct personal gratification, satisfying activities, and opportunities for cultivating friendships, having one's ego stroked, and socializing."[9] When reflecting on his own career, he realized that for the past four decades he "awoke every morning eager to grasp opportunities, wrestle with problems, create new solutions, and mobilize people."[10] Now that is someone who is passionate about what he does! Look back at the preferences and passions assessments you completed in Chapter 2. Many of your responses may guide you to know whether working in the nonprofit sector is right for you. Specifically, look at your responses regarding populations with whom you want to work, types of programs or services you are interested in delivering, and type of work environment in which you would like to work. As you read through the possibilities in the nonprofit sector, keep your answers in mind as it may help you discover the perfect place to work!

Pay and Perks

Numerous opportunities are available all over the world to find a career in nonprofit recreation and leisure services. People who work part-time or **seasonal** jobs while going to school may have a foot in the door for future employment. If you are working in a seasonal or part-time position, you can expect to be paid slightly above minimum wage, but you will probably not receive benefits in the traditional sense of the word. Some agencies have the capacity to offer amazing perks such as housing and food (perhaps coupled with lower than minimum wage), flexible schedules, the ability to bring children (and sometimes pets) to work, free professional development and/or certification opportunities, and sometimes paid travel to attend conferences.

Many people have had long and fulfilling full-time careers in nonprofit organizations with many of the perks mentioned above. For example, maybe you have heard of career scouts? They are people who have been active in either Boy Scouts or Girl Scouts for most of their lives, starting as participants, moving on to volunteer work, and then moving into paid positions. Many organizations, such as the Y, have a promote-from-within philosophy that enables workers to move up in the agency as they develop skills, as described in the chapter opener by Margaret Kay-Arora. Most nonprofit agencies have come to appreciate that you get what you pay for and have thus improved pay rates during the past 10 years. If you are in an entry-level position, expect to earn about the same as local teachers. The higher the position and the more experience or certifications you obtain will influence how high your salary may go. Although you are unlikely to become rich, you may make a comfortable living doing a job you love by working in the nonprofit sector of recreation and leisure services.

Preparation

Like many areas within the recreation field, professionalism in nonprofit organizations is important. A new perspective has evolved on how important education is compared to work experience. In the past, enthusiasm and experience may have moved you far up the professional ladder, but today, most organizations look for both experience and education. Today's world requires all agencies to be accountable to those they serve, and this includes employees being able to demonstrate professional competence in areas such as financial management, assessment, and evaluation of programs and services and having a complete understanding of risk management in all areas of operation.

Most full-time jobs in nonprofit leisure services require some level of higher education. Depending on the agency and the position, this may be only a 15–credit hour certificate in a specific area, or it may require an associate's or bachelor's degree in a specified area. In many cases, you will also be required to have first aid, CPR, and other safety certifications. Working with people who have disabilities or working in a therapeutic environment may require special training such as the Certified Therapeutic Recreation Specialist (CTRS) certification (refer to Chapter 7 for more information). Or

> I love the fact that I have a career that positively affects people's lives. As adult and child obesity rates continue to grow along with an increase in diseases such as diabetes, there is an escalating need for recreation professionals to educate and provide realistic, safe, and long-term solutions to help individuals acquire a healthy lifestyle.
>
> —Margaret Kay-Arora

if you want to work with a nonprofit that offers youth sport programs, you may need to earn a coaching certificate.

Working in the outdoors or in a specialized facility (aquatic, gymnastics, tennis, rock climbing, etc.) may require other certifications. If you are interested in a particular area, visit the website of a related agency and speak with a manager about specific job requirements (refer to Chapters 6 to 9 for more information about outdoor and specialized recreation opportunities).

Educational requirements are generally paired with a requirement of experience, with either a population group or a program type. The best thing that you can do while in school is to volunteer for at least one nonprofit organization. Agencies engage volunteers in several ways, from helping out with basic administrative tasks to helping operate one-time special events. Figure out what fits into your schedule and interest area, and get out there!

Specific Skills Needed for Success

People who work in the nonprofit sector are often called upon to serve myriad roles. They may prepare a press release in the morning, address the board of directors at lunch, start a grant application in the afternoon, and meet with a youth group before leaving. As such, people who want to work in the nonprofit sector should arrive with several skills—ready to be a jack or jill of all trades. Listed below are competencies (ranked in order) directors noted they look for when hiring staff members:

- ethics and values (align with agency),
- diversity awareness,
- board and committee development,
- nonprofit accounting and financial management,
- community outreach/marketing and public relations,
- program planning, implementation, and evaluation,
- risk management and legal issues,
- volunteer management,
- fund-raising principles and practices, and
- historical foundations.[21]

Possibilities

According to Salamon and Sokolowski, 8,789,300 people are employed in the nonprofit sector.[11] Although the majority of those workers are in other fields, at least 3.5% of them work in recreation and/or cultural organizations. "Nonprofit organizations hire for all types of positions, from chief executive officer to receptionist."[12] Examples of jobs with nonprofits within recreation, leisure, and sport include counselors, teachers, program officers, development directors, public relations managers, and administrative staff.

The potential for employment varies greatly based on the specific program and/or population in which you are interested. Large organizations such as YMCAs are frequently looking for seasonal staff to lead programs or work at the customer service desk. The Scouts, on the other hand, have fewer paid positions at the local level. If you are waiting for a position to open in the nonprofit agency next to your house, you could be waiting a long time. If you are willing to move across town or to another geographic area, your chances of finding full-time employment improve dramatically. Obviously, the larger the agency, the more frequently full-time positions are available. Many organizations will hire full-time program directors who will be responsible for specific areas of programming such as aquatics, early childhood, sports, arts, and so on. Additionally, once you have gained experience, opportunities for administrative roles higher up within the organization may become available.

Most nonprofit organizations have numerous part-time and/or seasonal positions. If you are interested in a career in nonprofits, as stated earlier, one of the best things to do while attending school is to work or volunteer at different agencies to see whether they will be a fit for you. Additionally, by having part-time or seasonal positions, you are gaining experiences that many employers will be looking for when filling full-time positions.

Nonprofit agencies fall under the umbrella of recreation and leisure services, including youth development agencies; faith-based organizations; outdoor and camping organizations; educational institutions; agencies focused on drama, theater, and the arts; and sport organizations. Recreation and leisure services encompass many activities and programs that can range from unstructured to highly structured experiences. People walking on a trail through a park are experiencing what most professionals would call **unstructured recreation**; participants only need the space or appropriate area, and they do their own thing. **Structured recreation** is provided for people who prefer to have activities planned and organized for them. Activities can be loosely structured with participants making many decisions to highly structured where most components are prescribed.

Let's look at four organizations where you may consider looking for a job in a nonprofit recreation and leisure services agency.

Youth-serving nonprofit agencies. Nonprofits serve many populations, and one target market is children and youth. Generally, this means working with people from birth through about 18 years of age. The mission of youth-serving nonprofits tends to center on youth gaining benefits or intentionally chosen outcomes often related to self-image, self-esteem, identity, specific skills, and/or social competencies. In general, the primary objective of such an organization is to assist young people in becoming healthy, successful adults who positively contribute to their community and society. The programs that may be offered are extremely diverse and may encompass sports, the arts, outdoor programs, and high adventure. Public government-supported agencies and for-profit agencies also offer many of these services, so refer to Chapters 3 and 9 for additional information. Job opportunities in this area range from short-term volunteer work to full-time career path positions.

> "According to researchers, successful leaders of non-profit organizations possess the following characteristics: being honest, forward looking, inspiring, and competent.
> —Nanus & Dobbs[25]

Passions. People working in this area are passionate about advancing the interests and capabilities of youth. They may have been youth who received benefits from such a program in the past or know someone who has. Others are appreciative of what they have and want more youth to experience similar opportunities.

Pay and perks. Historically, positions in youth-serving agencies (particularly nonprofit) have paid less than other areas of recreation or leisure. However, this has been changing over the last 10 years or so. Society is increasingly recognizing the value of providing quality programs for children and youth. As the employee education requirements have increased, so has the pay. Perks have not changed much over the years. People work in this area because they love youth and children and want the best for them. If you can do something you love and make a living at it, what more can you ask for? A big perk to this career area is that you will have many opportunities to play and stay current with what children are into. Joyce Taylor, a long-time early childhood teacher once said, "How can I get old or feel bad when I have these smiling faces to look forward to every day?"

Preparation. This area especially requires experience at the leadership level before moving into administration. Children and youth are considered **vulnerable populations**, and therefore particular care is taken when hiring staff for this area. A vulnerable population is any group of people not necessarily capable of making decisions regarding what is in their best interest. To work with children, you will likely need to pass a background check, by either the police or the FBI.

Possibilities. Listed below are examples of key youth-serving nonprofit agencies to give you an idea of the opportunities.

The Y (Young Men's Christian Association, or YMCA). The Y is recognized for its strength in bringing people together; programs and facilities are for people from all faiths, races, ages, abilities, and incomes. Building strong kids, strong families, and strong communities is the Y's mission—worldwide. Ys are at work in more than 120 countries, serving more than 45 million people.

Each Y is unique because it is designed to meet the needs of the community it serves. Because every Y is different, different job opportunities are available in every community (e.g., swim lesson instructors and lifeguards, camp counselors—both day and residential, sport instructors and coaches, child care workers, customer service staff, health and fitness trainers, and community outreach to teens, disadvantaged youth, and the homeless). The Y has many full-time career paths, some tied to the program areas listed above, but other managerial opportunities are available in human resources, facility management, marketing, fund-raising, information systems, and finance.

Boys & Girls Clubs of America. The mission of the Boys & Girls Clubs of America is "to enable all young people, especially those who need us most, to reach their full potential as

productive, caring, responsible citizens."[13] Club programs and services promote and enhance the development of boys and girls by providing a safe place to learn and grow, all while having fun.

Boys & Girls Clubs offer opportunities for volunteering and employment. At the local club level, you may be able to work as a sport instructor or coach, swim instructor, lifeguard, health and fitness instructor, camp counselor, homework tutor, art instructor, computer instructor, community outreach, and much more. Full-time positions are frequently available that offer a career path in the professional areas of youth development, management, and executive leadership. An example of an entry-level full-time position with the Boys & Girls Clubs is as a program director responsible for a particular area of programming such as teens, aquatics, or health/life skills. Additional information can be found on the Boys & Girls Club website (www.bgca.org) under "Careers."

Community Youth Services. In almost any mid-sized community across the U.S, you will find Community Youth Services. Generally, they receive some level of funding from the United Way. Listed below is information from one such agency to give you an idea what a Community Youth Service agency is about.

Community Youth Services (CYS) in Olympia, Washington, was founded in 1970. "It has grown steadily, responding to the diverse and ever-changing needs of our community."[14] Currently, CYS offers programs that serve nearly 4,000 children, teens, and families each year. The Mission of CYS is to "empower youth at-risk and their families to meet their goals for safety, stability, belonging and success by providing a continuum of individualized services and advocacy."[15] CYS operates a number of programs: AmeriCorps, Career TREK, Choice for Change, Diversion, Family Reconciliation and Preservation, Foster Care, Haven House and Safe Shelter, Independent Living Skills, and Readiness to Learn.

Girls Inc. Girls Inc. is dedicated to inspiring all girls to be strong, smart, and bold. Since 1864, "Girls Inc. has provided vital educational programs to millions of American girls, particularly those in high-risk, underserved areas."[16]   Today, the organization concentrates on innovative programs to help girls confront and deal with societal messages about their value and potential and to prepare them to lead successful, independent, and fulfilling lives. Individual clubs encourage girls to try new activities and to master physical, intellectual, and emotional challenges. Currently, their major programs address math and science education, pregnancy and drug abuse prevention, media literacy, economic literacy, adolescent health, violence prevention, and sport participation.

4-H clubs. The National 4-H Council Mission is "to empower youth to reach their full potential, working and learning in partnership with caring adults."[17] 4-H is funded in multiple ways, including federal and state funding, and some groups are becoming official nonprofit organizations. Within its mission, 4-H focuses on three priority areas: science, engineering, and technology; healthy living; and citizenship. 4-H offers a number of programs including environmental stewardship, rural youth development, family strengthening, health, and wellness and safety, among others. 4-H Afterschool is a program offered by the organization that is designed to increase young people's opportunities to have fun while developing lifelong skills through experiential learning in safe, healthy, and enriching environments. If you are looking for jobs with the national office, they are shown on the website. On the bottom of the homepage (www.4-h.org) click on "Careers" under "4-H Information."

Camp Fire USA. Camp Fire USA's mission is to build caring, confident youth and future leaders. The organization serves nearly 750,000 boys and girls from birth to age 21 on an annual basis. Youth participate in comfortable, informal settings that allow them to learn and play. They are committed to providing inclusive, fun programs to all children and families, including youth leadership, self-reliance, after-school groups, camping and environmental education, and child care. Camp Fire USA's programs are designed and implemented to reduce sex-role, racial, and cultural stereotypes and to foster positive intercultural relationships.

Volunteer and part-time opportunities exist at the local club level to help plan and lead activities, educational programs, and events. Seasonal positions are available at more than 100 day

and residential camps nationwide and include counselors, kitchen help, specialty instructors, and aquatics staff. Full-time positions are available and may be located on the website (www.campfireusa. org/cfjobs.aspx).

Big Brothers Big Sisters. The mission of Big Brothers Big Sisters is to "provide children facing adversity with strong and enduring, professionally supported one-to-one relationships that change their lives for the better, forever."[18] The main focus of the organization is providing a one-on-one match between children and youth aged

6 to 18 and adult volunteers in a professionally supported mentoring program. The program can be either community based or site based, but both involve regular weekly interaction between a "big" (volunteer) and a "little" (child or youth). Although most of the opportunities in Big Brothers Big Sisters are volunteer, full-time professional positions are available at local and national levels. Local positions include program directors, program specialists, matching specialists, and development officers. National positions are in areas such as executive leadership, fund development, program management, marketing and communications, and information technology. See the website (www. bbbs.org) and look at "Careers" in the "About Us" section for more information.

Faith-based agencies. Not only are many religious organizations interested in reaching their current members, but they also are looking for ways to reach out to the community around them. Sport and recreation programs provide an excellent venue for faith-based agencies to provide practical support and life-changing experiences within neighborhoods and communities.

Passions. Recreation and sport is one of many tools that may be used in communicating to the world about a particular religious belief or perspective. A common theme in this area is the opportunity to advance your faith while pursuing a career about which you can be passionate.

Pay and perks. Many assume that the pay in religious organizations is low compared to a similar position in local government, and although they may be correct, the working conditions can make up for it if they are appealing. Work hours tend to be concentrated on weekends and afternoons or evenings. As with other recreation jobs, you need to work so that others can play during their time off from school and work. One of the biggest perks offered in this type of position is the alignment with your own spiritual beliefs. People who work in this area appreciate working with others who have a like mind-set.

Preparation. Although a religious degree is not necessary for working for a faith-based organization, you will need to believe in and accept the philosophy of the organization. These organizations will want a person skilled in an area of recreation and/or sport but who is also able to discuss issues of faith with participants.

Possibilities. Job opportunities in this area can be found in a number of settings from local churches to organizations with large networks of service. Listed below are examples of key agencies.

Church recreation. Many local churches offer recreation or sports for their members, whether focused only on children and youth or the entire family. Activities within a church may include outdoor activities such as picnics and camps; social gatherings; vacation schools; workshops stressing arts, crafts, and music; fellowship groups and clubs; sport leagues; study and discussion groups; and innovative worship programs. In small churches, volunteers would probably conduct recreation programs, although in some communities, churches band together and contribute to employ a qualified person. Larger congregations may have multiple positions in recreation services. If you are interested in this area, look for information under specific denominations or check with your local clergy.

Salvation Army. The mission of the Salvation Army is "to preach the gospel of Jesus Christ and to meet human needs in His name without discrimination."[19] The basic social services are a visible expression of the Army's strong religious principles. In addition, new programs that address contemporary needs have been established. Recreation or community centers owned and operated by the Salvation Army can be found in many communities. Examples of programs and services include disaster relief services; day care centers; summer camps; holiday assistance; services for the aging; AIDS education and residential services; medical facilities; shelters for battered women and children; family and career counseling; vocational training; correction services; and substance abuse rehabilitation. Depending on the local corp (the name for a local Salvation Army group), you will be able to find jobs working with sport leagues, child care, after-school programs, various summer and holiday camps, and senior citizens programs. Full-time positions may be found at each local corp, and positions at the national headquarters are listed at www.salvationarmyusa.org under "About Us."

Jewish Community Centers (JCC). "JCC Association is the continental umbrella organization for the Jewish Community Center Movement, which includes more than 350 JCCs, YM-YWHAs, and campsites in the U.S. and Canada."[20] JCC Association supports the largest network of Jewish early childhood centers and summer camps in North America and also is a U.S. government–accredited agency for serving the religious and social needs of Jewish military personnel through JWB Jewish Chaplains Council. Due to the size of this national organization, full-time jobs are frequently available. Check with the local center in your area or browse www.jcca.org at the bottom of the page under "Find a Career at a JCC" or www.jccworks.com where they offer not only a listing of available jobs but also tips on interviewing and preparing applications.

Outdoor and camping organizations. Although many nonprofit organizations are tied to specific populations such as children and youth or people with disabilities, many are equally tied to the outdoors.

Passions. People who work in outdoor, camping, and resource-related organizations are generally passionate about spending time in the out-of-doors. Not only do they want to do all they can to preserve the natural wonders of the world, but they are convinced that nature can assist people with personal growth in ways that other facilities cannot.

Pay and perks. Pay may be structured differently for agencies in this group. For instance, if you are working at a camp, you may have housing and/or food covered, which may be considered part of your pay. A side benefit to working at a camp is that saving money is easy because you do not have much on which to spend your paycheck. You may also be hired on a contract basis to complete a specific task such as leading a group on a longer outdoor adventure trip. You will be paid, but it will not be calculated on an hourly basis. In some cases, an organization will provide you with specialty gear, but in others, the organization will expect you to purchase it. Many organizations offer a pro rate (professional rate) that allows employees to obtain a significant discount on brand-name gear. If you truly love spending a lot of time in the outdoors, you may not want to pass up the opportunity to work in the natural environment, hopefully with a population you enjoy. Breathing clean air on a regular basis and exercising plenty is a great health benefit!

Preparation. Working in the outdoors involves many safety aspects. If this is your chosen career area, you will want to investigate the specific requirements for what you want to do. Depending on where you work, you will need specific knowledge of various populations and to be able to teach skills or lead activities. Expect that most organizations will require you to have personal experience in the environment in which you want to work, in addition to your formal education. If you are going to work in a **backcountry** setting, you will need special certifications such as Wilderness First Responder (WFR) certification or training in specialized sports such as rock climbing, white-water rafting, or ropes course facilitation and safety.

Possibilities. This section will discuss specific organizations related to the outdoors and camping, including scouting, international opportunities, camping and retreat centers, parks and reserves, and advocacy groups.

Scouting. Scouting has a long tradition that can be traced back to the early 1900s in both North America and England. Since that time, scouting has become one of the primary means of introducing young people from all backgrounds to the outdoors. Listed below is information on Boy Scouts and Girls Scouts. Information on international scouting programs is listed under international opportunities.

Boy Scouting is a year-round program for boys aged 10 to 18. The program offers fun outdoor activities, peer group leadership opportunities, and an exploration of personal career, hobby, and special interests, all designed to achieve the Boy Scouts of America's objective of strengthening character, personal fitness, and good citizenship. Local councils operate and maintain scout camps. The National Council operates high-adventure areas at in New Mexico, Minnesota, Canada, and the Florida Keys. About 70 local councils also operate high-adventure programs. These outdoor centers provide seasonal positions for everything from counselors to cooks to specialty instructors to aquatics staff. If you are interested in a career in scouting, check with your local council, as most employ full-time executive directors and positions such as director of special needs. If you are new to scouting or have trouble locating a local council, visit www.scouting.org and click on "Careers" at the bottom of the page for information on requirements, benefits, and diversity as well as internship and career opportunities.

The mission of Girl Scouts is, "Girl Scouting builds girls of courage, confidence and character, who make the world a better place."[22] Girl Scouts offers programs that have the potential to change the way girls see the world and their place in it. The overall objective of the program is for girls to learn the importance of personal responsibility, the value of goal setting, the spirit of teamwork, and the thrill of accomplishment. Girl Scouts is based on four fundamental goals that encourage girls to develop to their full potential; relate to others with increasing understanding, skill, and respect; develop a meaningful set of values to guide their actions and to provide for sound decision making; and contribute to the improvement of society. In addition to seasonal jobs at the local level, Girl Scouts offers career opportunities at local and national levels. The organization employs 400 people in the national office and over 9,500 in local councils in areas such as marketing, program development, technology, research, advocacy, publishing, fund development, and sales.

Photo by Jessica Cangiano

To see what opportunities await you, visit www.girlscouts.org and look under "Careers" at the top of the page.

International opportunities. As mentioned at the beginning of this chapter, many nonprofit organizations have international connections. YMCAs, Boy Scouts, Girl Scouts, and many others have international branches in their operations. Listed below are examples of two organizations; both operate worldwide and offer opportunities for careers in nonprofit work. If you are interested in pursuing an international job or career, check out the Global Directory of Nonprofit website (The Idealist) at www.idealist.org. The site provides links to more than 10,000 nonprofit websites in 120 countries.

The World Organization of Scouting is an international nonprofit organization comprising recognized national scouting organizations around the world. According to the organization's website (www.scout.org), scouting is about more than the outdoors. Scouts are involved in a number of issues facing the local communities in which they operate. A large component of scouting involves working with other community groups to achieve mutual objectives. Although volunteers conduct most of the work of scouting, a small staff of full-time professionals in 12 offices around the world is employed. Current openings at the world level are shown at www.scout.org under "Our Organization, Job Opportunities."

Outward Bound International is an umbrella organization for Outward Bound Schools worldwide. Outward Bound has schools on six continents and offers courses for individuals, families, corporate groups, and other organizations. Programs may vary depending on the country and the environment. Outward Bound is recognized as a world leader in outdoor experiential education. Although the international office does not often have full-time job opportunities available, it can help connect you with job openings in one of the schools operated in over 30 countries including the United States. If you want to know what the possibilities are, go to www.outwardbound.net/schools and follow the links to the countries where schools are operated. Some schools only offer seasonal programs, but many have year-round positions.

Camps/retreat centers. Organizations and programs that fall under this heading typically will have a meaningful and intentional relationship to the natural environment. Too many job and career possibilities are available to list in this brief section as thousands of seasonal positions are available across the United States in which you can do anything from cooking to being a camp counselor, a specialty instructor, or a program or unit coordinator. Many full-time positions are available with camps and retreat centers as well. A starting point would be the American Camp Association

(ACA), as they provide accreditation for both day and residential camps as well as conference and retreat centers. Check out their website (www.acacamps.org) and register for their job notification service.

Parks/preserves. National, state, and local parks and forests and related nonprofit organizations such as The Nature Conservancy and Sierra Club as discussed in Chapter 6.

Other Career/Leisure Services Areas

In addition to the major career areas already discussed, other opportunities are available to you in the nonprofit sector. We will discuss three options in this section.

Out-of-School-Time Programs (may also be called after-school programs)

In addition to traditional recreation and leisure nonprofit agencies, many schools offer **out-of-school-time programs**, which include recreation and/or sport experiences. Programs may be offered as before- and after-school programs, may be offered as intramural sports or weekend/vacation activities, and may be academically oriented. In most cases, each school offers programs that will benefit its students and perhaps other members of the local community. This area has developed rapidly in the past two decades as work patterns in the United States have changed, with more families headed by single parents or, in the case of two-parent households, both parents working full-time. Programs for school-aged children can be found in most communities and may be offered by schools, local recreation departments, or nonprofit organizations set up for that specific purpose. Although some agencies may rely on volunteers, most employ people on either a part- or full-time basis as they have realized the value of consistency in staff. We discuss the topic of youth development in more detail in Chapter 3.

Drama, Theater, and the Arts

This is an area where the nonprofit sector has traditionally taken the lead. Most towns and cities will have at least one (if not many more) nonprofit organizations dedicated to various forms of art, including performance arts (dance, drama, music), visual arts (painting, photography, ceramics, etc.), and folk arts. A search on the Internet reveals literally hundreds of thousands of organizations around the world. Although many organizations survive due to volunteers, do not make the mistake of thinking jobs are not available in this area; you would be wrong! If you think about the number of theaters, museums, and art centers in any metropolitan area, you will realize that they all need people to conduct programs, organize events, manage staff, develop marketing programs, and much more. Jobs in the arts area tend to be listed at a more local level than what this section is going into. At the end of this chapter in the section For Further Research, several arts organizations are listed. Follow the links to local or regional groups, and that is where you will find the jobs.

Sport Organizations

As mentioned in the focus questions, sport programs are offered on several levels depending on the skill level and preference of the individual involved. Nonprofit agencies organize many youth sports for competition and instruction (e.g., baseball, softball, soccer, football, swimming, and golf). Websites for a few sport organizations are listed in the further resources section of this chapter. More information on sports is available in Chapter 9.

Summary of Nonprofit Organizations Career Possibilities

Career	Passions	Pay and perks	Preparations	Possibilities
Youth-serving nonprofit agencies	Advancing the interests and capability of youth	May start out a bit low, but the more education or experience required, the higher the pay	Experience at the leadership level before moving into administration. Must pass background checks	Seasonal positions are widely available, permanent full-time jobs are competitive
Religious-affiliated agencies	Advancing your faith	Similar to teaching, flexible work hours	Positive educational requirements, belief in the organizational philosophy, experience important	A variety of settings, various opportunities at the lower levels, permanent full-time positions are competitive
Outdoors and camping organizations	Preservation of natural wonders	Varies from minimum wage to contracts including housing and gear	Positive educational requirements, experience important, some specialty certifications	Seasonal positions almost limitless, permanent positions can be difficult to get

Future Opportunities, Issues, and Challenges

This chapter has covered information about the various nonprofit agencies in recreation and leisure services. Although this interesting and exciting sector offers diversity in terms of jobs and careers, challenges need to be addressed. The nonprofit sector of recreation has long faced many challenges. We will explore three major challenges facing nonprofits today including funding, efficient operations, and locating volunteers and staff and conclude with thoughts on how nonprofit agencies are dealing with them.

One of the biggest challenges most nonprofits face is a lack of funding and financial sustainability. Because many nonprofits start out as small organizations serving a specialized need of a population group, the sources of funds have traditionally been limited. Today, this is being overcome in a number of ways. First, small groups have begun to band together to gain efficiencies of operation and a voice in the public sector. By forming partnerships with agencies providing similar services or working with similar population groups, they also benefit from knowledge gained by others. Another funding source that has benefited many nonprofit organizations is the availability of government grants or contracts for providing specific social services. However, these funding sources often specify how and where services must be provided. Local, state, and federal government agencies are being challenged to operate in a more efficient manner, and in many cases, they are no longer providing all services themselves but are contracting with specialized agencies. Contracts are a great way to increase funding for nonprofits as long as the funded efforts are consistent with their mission and core business. If you want to work in nonprofit organizations, you will need to gain an understanding of how contracts are managed, be comfortable working in partnerships, and know how to conduct traditional fund-raising activities.

Most nonprofits are started by a group of people with good intentions, but "new organizations often start without the necessary skills to manage their resources effectively."[23] One key ingredient to long-term success for a nonprofit is a clear vision of what it hopes to achieve and a sound strategy for achieving it. Once the vision and strategy are in place, the need for sharper business skills is great so that finances and other resources, such as volunteers and staff, are managed properly. Large organizations with a long history will probably have more developed management systems, but this is not always the case. One of the best things you can do if you are planning to work in a nonprofit organization is to obtain business skills. Most current position descriptions will ask for business knowledge and experience.

The third challenge facing nonprofits is locating, training, and retaining quality staff and volunteers. Volunteers are the lifeblood of an organization. Without them, the agency would have no hope of achieving its vision. There are two types of volunteers: those who believe in the mission of the organization and will help with anything and those who are only interested in helping with specific projects. Both are needed for sustained success, so it is important to understand what motivates a person to volunteer. As you are investigating the possibilities of working in the nonprofit sector, volunteer for one or more organizations. If you let someone at the agency know you are interested in a career in nonprofits, he or she likely will be willing to share his or her knowledge and expertise about the sector.

Although the challenges above may seem daunting, agencies in the other recreation sectors are facing similar issues in today's rapidly changing world and economy. If you refer to Chapter 2, you will recall the discussion on the emerging leisure service delivery system and evolving leadership roles. In that section of the book, we talked about lines being blurred between the various service sectors almost to the point that it is difficult to discern who "owns" the programs and services being delivered. Partnerships between sectors are no longer the wave of the future but rather a primary method that nonprofits use to continue offering services to their clientele. The nonprofit sector has experience working with specific target markets that can assist public and commercial sectors in achieving their service delivery goals. Partnerships also offer a way to use scarce resources to continue to provide much needed programs and services. The lines between sectors will continue to blur as the world becomes more globalized. Current and future clients come with expectations formed via the Internet and social media. Nonprofit agencies wishing to stay relevant and financially solvent will need to become better at documenting and communicating the benefits that participants can achieve from being in their programs. This increased expectation of documentation is currently linked to many forms of funding including those received from the United Way. Current and future leaders in nonprofit organizations will need to have a better business sense and be prepared to be a collaborator with leaders in their community regardless of the sector to which they belong.

Resources and Getting Involved

Professional Organizations

One good way to find out more about the nonprofit sector is to join a professional organization. These membership agencies have been established to support people working in specific industries or sectors and offer many educational and networking benefits to a student. Listed below are some you may want to consider. Keep in mind that you can locate many more by searching the Internet.

American Camp Association: www.acacamps.org

If you are interested in organized camping, this is an excellent organization to join. It offers leadership institutes, certification programs, and assistance with finding jobs.

Art in the Public Interest (API): www.apionline.org
The API is part of the Community Arts Network, offers a monthly newsletter, and publishes a quarterly magazine focused on the arts.

Association for Experiential Education (AEE):www.aee.org
The AEE is a nonprofit, professional membership association dedicated to experiential education and the students, educators, and practitioners. It offers publications, conferences, accreditation for programs, and postings about jobs.

The Charity Channel: www.charitychannel.com
This is an online subscription resource that allows you to connect to nonprofit professionals around the world. You can take online classes, subscribe to various newsletters and alerts, and register for a career search feature.

Christian Camping International (CCI): cciworldwide.org
CCI is an alliance of Christian camping associations throughout the world, helping each association to be more effective in serving its membership of Christ-centered camps, conference, and retreat ministries, to the glory of God and for the building up of His Church.

Idealist (also known as Action Without Borders): www.idealist.org
Idealist is one of the most popular communities of nonprofit and volunteering resources on the Web and offers information for nonprofit professionals, students, parents, and teachers. One of the prime benefits of the site is the access to searchable nonprofit job, internship, and volunteer opportunities (U.S. and international). It also offers tips and resources for nonprofit job seekers.

International Association of Conference Center Administrators (IACCA): www.IACCA.org
This professional organization offers a student membership, provides conferences, has a certification program, and offers listing of current job postings.

National AfterSchool Association (NAA): www.naaweb.org
This organization offers accreditation programs for programs and sites, conferences and training programs, and numerous resources to assist the practitioner. The website also features a section for affiliated organizations to post job openings.

National Council of Nonprofit Associations (NCNA): www.ncna.org
This organization advocates that professionals and organizations join their state associations for professional development and networking. Many NCNA state associations have job boards on their websites where nonprofits advertise job openings.

National Institute on Out-of-School Time (NIOST): www.niost.org
NIOST provides resources and training for practitioners working in the field and provides technical assistance to programs having difficulty with particular issues. One of the best features of its website is the links page, which offers resources including information on national and international organizations, funding sources, education, public policy and advocacy, and professional development.

Nonprofit Leadership Alliance: www. nonprofitleadershipalliance.org
This is a good organization to consider if you are interested in nonprofit work as it offers training and certification for students and professionals.

Outward Bound: www.outwardbound.org
Outward Bound is a nonprofit educational organization that serves people of all ages and backgrounds through active learning expeditions that inspire character development, self-discovery, and service both in and out of the classroom.

Wilderness Education Association (WEA):www.weainfo.org
The mission of the WEA is to promote the professionalism of outdoor leadership through establishment of national standards, curriculum design, implementation, advocacy, and research-driven initiatives.

Certifications/Licenses

Certified Nonprofit Professional Alliance: www.nonprofitleadershipalliance.org
This certification is earned by graduating from a university that is partnered with the Nonprofit Leadership Alliance and completing the required courses that demonstrate essential competencies in the nonprofit sector. The website for the Nonprofit Leadership Alliance has links to a number of national organizations for jobs and internships.

Leave No Trace/Leave No Trace Training: www.lnt.org
Master Educator Courses train people to become comprehensive Leave No Trace educators, or Master Educators. Master Educators, in turn, teach people who become Leave No Trace Trainers. Trainers (or Master Educators) are then able to conduct Awareness Workshops, which are designed for the general public and promote Leave No Trace.

Red Cross: www.redcross.org
CPR, first aid, and automated external defibrillator (AED) training are available.

Wilderness First Responder and Wilderness First Aid: www.nols.edu/wmi/courses/wildfirstresponder.shtml
This is a nationally recognized program that trains participants to respond to emergencies in remote settings. The 80-hour curriculum includes standards for urban and extended care situations.

Aquatics certifications include Certified Pool Operator, Water Safety Instructor, and Lifeguard. Information on these and other specialized certifications can be obtained by searching the Internet.

Where to Gain Experience

As we mentioned earlier in the chapter, you should gain experience while you are going to school. Doing so will help you make good decisions about future employment opportunities, including field placements and internships. Even if you have a busy schedule, try to find time to volunteer at local events, whether it is a plant sale at the local community garden or a fundraiser for the local chapter of the Boys & Girls Clubs. If you have a little more time and can volunteer on a more regular basis, coach a soccer team for the YMCA or help out with a local Boy Scout troop. We also encourage you to consider seasonal positions with nonprofit agencies. Many opportunities to work at both day and residential camps are available during the summer. Nonprofits are always looking for enthusiastic staff with a passion for service. Everything you do builds your understanding of the nonprofit sector and builds your résumé for a future career.

Conferences

Conferences are a great way to meet people in a particular industry or sector of work. As we mentioned in the section on professional associations, many conferences are available to people working in the nonprofit sector. The advantage that you have as a student is that many offer reduced fees and membership rates for students who want to attend. Some organizations even offer full scholarships if you are willing to volunteer at the conference. To search for conferences, start with professional associations, talk to people in the field, and search on Internet.

Volunteer Opportunities

Volunteering involves you giving up some of your free time and skills to assist your community or an organization. The commitment could be a one-time event or an ongoing involvement. As we discussed earlier in this chapter, most nonprofits lack resources, both financial and human. You can make a difference in helping an organization to achieve its mission or vision! It is not a one-way street, though; the organization will benefit, but so will you. Helping others feels good, and you will gain a broader perspective on life at the same time you are gaining valuable experience to add to your résumé. Literally millions of opportunities exist for you to volunteer with nonprofit organizations. Start with your local area, and you will see much that you can do in your own backyard. Need more information? Enter the word *volunteering* into any Internet search engine, and see what happens; you will be overwhelmed! Another great way to locate opportunities is to check with your school's volunteer center. Volunteer centers are dedicated to connecting people with their community's volunteer needs.

Conclusion

This chapter has provided a glimpse into the exciting work that is being done in recreation and leisure services by nonprofit organizations throughout the world. Many opportunities are available in this area, from small neighborhood programs to large international organizations and everything in between. If you are still not sure about working in this sector (or even if you are), check out the final section of the chapter, which offers information for further investigation including numerous websites and additional resources that you may find interesting.

For Further Investigation

For More Research

If you are interested in looking for employment in the nonprofit sector, visit these websites in addition to the recreation-specific websites listed in the chapter (note that these websites are not recreation specific):

Energize Inc.: www.energizeinc.com/placements.html
Jobs and internships involving volunteer management.

Community Career Center: www.nonprofitjobs.org
Search jobs and post jobs.

The Chronicle of Philanthropy: philanthropy.com
Browse jobs by position and receive career advice.

Nonprofit Career Network: www.nonprofitcareer.com
Offers a complete one-stop shop for job seekers in the nonprofit sector.

The Nonprofit Times: www.nptimes.com
Whether you are looking for a new job or you are ready to take the next step in your career, this is the website for you.

Philanthropy News Network Online: www.philanthropyjournal.org
Allows you to search job openings by region or category.

For more information on nonprofit organizations in the arts and sport industries, try these websites:

Art Search: www.artsearch.us
This unique website offers listings of art galleries, artists, art museums, art services, art supplies, education, jobs, and much more. This is a perfect jumping-off point to learn more about the art world.

National Alliance for Youth Sports (NAYS): www.nays.org
NAYS partners nationwide with more than 3,000 community organizations to promote the value and importance of physical activity and sport. The website offers a list of resources for parents, coaches, officials, and anyone interested in youth sports.

Sports Outreach Institute: www.sportsoutreach.net
This organization seeks to use sports as a means of reaching communities through the local church, with an overall goal of reaching kids, connecting families, and equipping leaders through providing vision, training, and resources.

Active Investigation

Throughout the chapter, you have seen mission and/or vision statements for several nonprofit recreation and leisure agencies. Most nonprofits will want to know that you can and will support what they are trying to accomplish—and not only on paper but also in your actions (both on and off the job). The message is, knowing what you believe in makes it easier to decide whether you can work in an agency that has strong beliefs about how and why they function. You should be thinking about and developing a personal philosophy about recreation service provision and be able to clearly state it to potential employers.

Try writing a personal philosophy statement:

A. Start by writing down three to five things that are important to you.

B. Explore nonprofit agencies further by doing the following:

Look back through the agencies listed in the chapter and find two or three are particularly interesting to you. Go to each website and look at what the agency stands for and what types of programs and services they offer to what type of people. Write down key phrases or statements from each that stand out or strike you as being personally meaningful. Once you have finished with several websites, look and see what you have written down; that should give you a starting point for refining and expanding what you first wrote down into a personal philosophy statement.

Recommended Reading

Bird, F. B., & Westley, F. (2011). *Voices from the voluntary sector: Perspectives on leadership challenges.* Toronto, Canada: University of Toronto Press.
This book contains essays and reasoned reflections by practitioners on significant challenges that not-for-profit organizations in Canada face today. Topics include organizational and managerial challenges, social

entrepreneurship, and how to foster effective global movements. The essays also include a reflection on the ways that young people can find the courage to become leaders.

Borrup, T. C. (2006). *Creative community builder's handbook: How to transform communities using local assets, arts, and culture.* St. Paul, MN: Fieldstone Alliance.

This book offers tools that may be used in communities to bring together individuals and groups from diverse backgrounds, perspectives, and skills to build upon the strengths within a community to make it a better place for all to live, work, and play.

Bronfman, C., & Solomon, J. (2012). *The art of doing good: Where passion meets action.* San Francisco, CA: Jossey-Bass.

This book is a must read for anyone considering starting their own nonprofit organization. The authors offer guidance and real-world advice for sustaining the spirit, ambition, and ingenuity to keep their vision alive and thriving.

Cryer, S. (2008). *The nonprofit career guide: How to land a job that makes a difference.* Saint Paul, MN: Fieldstone Alliance.

This book explores rewarding career opportunities in the nonprofit sector beyond those in recreation, parks, sport management, hospitality, and tourism.

Putnam, R. C., & Feldstein, L. M. (2003). *Better together: Restoring the American community.* New York, NY: Simon and Schuster.

This book takes the reader on a journey around America to learn about organizations and communities that are being strengthened through making connections with people, establishing bonds of trust, and understanding and building community.

Wheeler, C. (2009). *You've gotta have heart: Achieving purpose beyond profit in the social sector.* New York, NY: American Management Association.

Using examples from national nonprofit organizations, this book demonstrates that a mission statement is not the same as a sense of mission.

References

[1]Ashcroft, R. F. (2006). Nonprofit sector. In Human Kinetics (Ed.), *Introduction to recreation and leisure* (pp. 143–162). Champaign, IL: Human Kinetics, p. 145.

[2]DeGraf, D. G., Jordan, D. J., & DeGraf, K. H. (1999). *Programming for parks, recreation, and leisure services: A servant–leader approach.* State College, PA: Venture.

[3]Edginton, C. R., Hudson, S. D., & Lankford, S. V. (2001). *Managing recreation, parks, and leisure services: An introduction.* Champaign, IL: Sagamore.

[4]BoardSource. (2004). Ten basic responsibilities of non-profit boards. Retrieved from www.ncnb.org

[5]Brayley, R. E., & McLean, D. D. (2008). *Financial resource management: Sport, tourism, and leisure services.* Champaign, IL: Sagamore.

[6]Ashcroft, 2006..

[7]Bell, L. A. (2007). Theoretical foundations for social justice education. In M. Adams, L. A. Bell, & P. Griffin (Eds.), *Teaching for diversity and social justice* (2nd ed., pp. 3–16). New York, NY: Routledge.

[8]Salamon, L. M., Wojciech Sokolowski, S., & Geller, S. L. (2012). *Holding the fort: Nonprofit employment during a decade of turmoil* (Nonprofit Employment Bulletin No. 39). Baltimore, MD: John Hopkins University Center for Civil Society Studies.

[9]Mason, D. E. (1996). *Leading and managing the expressive dimension: Harnessing the hidden power source of the nonprofit sector.* San Francisco, CA: Jossey-Bass.

[10]Ibid, 1996.

[11]Salamon, L. M., & Sokolowski, S. W. (2005). Nonprofit organizations: New insights from QCEW data. *Monthly Labor Review, 128*(9), 19–26.

[12]Vaugan, A. (2005). Career options in the nonprofit sector. Retrieved October 3, 2006, from Learning to Give website: http://www.learningtogive.org

[13]Boys & Girls Club of America. (n.d.). Our mission. Retrieved from http://www.bgca.org/whoweare/pages/mission.aspx

[14]Community Youth Services. (n.d). Retrieved from http://communityyouthservices.org

[15]Ibid.

[16]Girls Inc. (2013). About Girls Inc. Retrieved from http://www.girlsinc.org

[17]4-H Youth Development Organization. (2014). Retrieved from http://www.4-h.org

[18]Big Brothers Big Sisters. (2013). Retrieved from http://www.bbbs.org

[19]Salvation Army. (2013). Retrieved from http://www.salvationarmyusa.org

[20]Jewish Community Centers of North America. (n.d.). Retrieved from www.jcca.org

[21]Nonprofit Leadership Alliance. (2011). *The skills the nonprofit sector requires of its managers and leaders*. Retrieved from http://www.nonprofitleadershipalliance.org/cnp/cnprevalidation/pdf

[22]Girl Scouts. (2014). Facts about Girl Scouting. Retrieved from http://www.girlscouts.org/who_we_are/facts/

[23]Zimmermann, J. A. M., Stevens, B. W., Thames, B. J., Sieverdes, C. M., & Powell, G. M. (2003). The DIRECTIONS nonprofit resource assessment model: A tool for small nonprofit organizations. *Nonprofit Management and Leadership, 14*, 79–91. doi: 10.1002/nml.22

[24]Oleck, H. L., & Stewart, M. E. (1994). *Nonprofit corporations, organizations and associations* (6th ed.). Englewood Cliffs, NJ: Prentice Hall.

[25]Nanus, B., & Dobbs, S. M. (1999). *Leaders who make a difference: Essential strategies for meeting the nonprofit challenge*. San Francisco, CA: Jossey-Bass.

" *After spending two years on the U.S.S. Nimitz aircraft carrier in the middle of the Gulf—where I provided recreation and leisure for 5,500 military personnel—I knew the services that I provided served a valuable purpose of building camaraderie as the soldiers maintained a stance of combat readiness.*

—Kerrie Smith
Athletic Director "

5

Armed Forces Recreation

Token D. Barnthouse
NAS Fallon, Nevada

Asuncion T. Suren
San Francisco State University

Focus Questions

Q: What is Armed Forces Recreation?

A: Armed Forces Recreation is a comprehensive network of support and leisure services designed to enhance the lives of military personnel, their families, civilian employees, retirees, and other eligible participants. Often referred to as the individual service branches' Morale, Welfare, and Recreation (MWR) department, Armed Forces Recreation contributes to the health and well-being of servicemen, servicewomen, and their families.

Q: Are Armed Forces Recreation programs similar to recreation programs in civilian communities?

A: Armed Forces Recreation departments operate in a similar manner as civilian recreation agencies. Many of the programs such as entertainment, outdoor adventure, club sports, and fitness trends mimic those offered at civilian recreation agencies.

Q: Why choose a career in Armed Forces Recreation?

A: A career with Armed Forces Recreation allows the recreation professional to contribute to the strength and readiness of United States military personnel by offering comprehensive services designed to enhance the quality of life and personal physical readiness.

Q: How can I get started with a career in Armed Forces Recreation?

A: The key to selecting a rewarding career with Armed Forces Recreation is to do your research. Start by conducting a thorough overview of which branch of service best meets your interests; for instance, are you interested in working for the U.S. Navy because of its mission to defend our nation's waterways and to support the U.S. Army, or are you interested in the U.S. Air Force because of its mission to protect the nation from the air and cyberspace threats? You will then want to identify at least three program service areas (e.g., fitness and aquatics, travel and tourism, youth and child development) that will both meet your career goals and satisfy your personal recreation and leisure needs. With this preliminary information in hand, you can then complete a Web-based search by looking up your selected branch of service's informational website and respective Civilian Personnel Office.

Q: Do I need to complete an internship with one of the Armed Forces Recreation departments in order to secure a position?

A: Don't be concerned if you want to intern with an agency or company outside of the Armed Forces; you will be just as marketable. The key is to seek work opportunities to gain the traits and characteristics necessary to be successful in the Armed Forces Recreation system. Use your internship to gain a well-rounded experience that will prepare you to be competitive in multiple program service areas (e.g., budgeting, supervision, programming, marketing, computers). You should select meaningful projects at your internship site that will expose you to public speaking opportunities, allow you to apply customer service techniques, and allow you to lead different target groups through programs and activities.

Key Terms

Department of Defense (DoD)

Morale, Welfare, and Recreation (MWR)

Armed Forces Recreation

Branch of service

Esprit de corps

Nonappropriated fund (NAF)

Profile 1: Could This Be You?

John Lenz works as the athletic director for the U.S. Navy Morale, Welfare, and Recreation (MWR) program at the Naval Air Station, Sigonella, Italy. He oversees fitness and sport programs for U.S. Navy personnel and visiting military personnel from NATO countries, including active duty, dependents, retirees, reservists, and **Department of Defense** (DoD) civilians. He manages a multimillion-dollar full-service recreation complex with all the services and equipment found at a private fitness center. The recreation center also includes a snack bar, swimming pool, bowling center, movie theater, and classroom. He also manages several multiuse athletic fields and courts. In this position, John is responsible for several recreation-related programs, including

- intramural sport programs,
- Navy fitness program including group exercise classes and self-directed fitness programs,
- communitywide special events bowling center,
- training and recreational aquatics facilities,
- two fitness centers, and
- multiple outdoor sport courts and lighted/multipurpose sport fields.

Q: What attracted you to a career in military recreation, and what do you like most about your role with Navy MWR?

A: I went into military recreation knowing nothing about the program and have stayed with Navy MWR for over 20 years. Military recreation is so diverse, and it has never mattered what my title was or is; you jump in wherever needed to provide the best event or service to the military service member or their family. I have witnessed firsthand the impact of hearing a sailor or his family say thank you to MWR staff.

Q: Your career with Navy MWR has allowed you to move around quite a bit. What types of challenges are unique to working overseas?

A: Supervising MWR staff overseas brings different challenges. Many mid-level candidates bring a good skill set to the job, but not necessarily in a recreation field. I find myself doing more hands-on training and coaching. Also, because we rely heavily on military spouses, the turnover rate is much higher than MWR departments that are stateside. This, of course, requires more recruitment and training.

Q: It sounds like you have a variety of important tasks to accomplish in your current role with Navy MWR. How have you been able to learn and progress in your career?

A: I was fortunate early in my career to work for some very experienced MWR senior managers who had high expectations for their staff and managers. I also volunteered to become a facilitator for the Navy MWR Managers' Course. As a facilitator, I became very familiar with a wide range of topics from recreation to food and beverage and financial instructions and policies.

Profile 2: Could This Be You?

Pamela Law has worked for multiple MWR departments since 1995, when she launched her career following two internships. She has worked in Diego Garcia, a British Indian Territory, as an athletic director; Atsugi, Japan, as a community activities director; Vicenza, Italy, as a preteen director; and Hickam Air Force Base, Hawaii, as an outdoor recreation programmer. She has been successful at building supervisory skill sets and applying them to enhance Navy, Army, and Air Force MWR programs. As the fitness and aquatics manager for Commander Fleet Activities in Sasebo, Japan, Pamela's duties include the following:
- operation of multiple recreation facilities
- maintenance of fitness equipment
- coordination of lifeguard and water safety classes
- coordination and leading fitness classes
- special events planning and implementation

Q: Your career with the Navy has allowed you to travel quite a bit. What is it like supervising MWR staff overseas?

A: I enjoy working with the staff and seeing them learn why I want things done in a certain way. I have bilingual staff, so that is a huge challenge for me. I have lived in Japan for more than seven years total, and I still don't know enough of the language—something to work on! I also enjoy creating new events. I like hearing ideas from customers and making their ideas come alive. When you listen to your customers and then they see the results, it makes everyone happy.

Q: You are learning from your staff and customers. What do you like least about working for MWR?

A: Budgets! The Navy doesn't require us to be responsible for the budget. I really enjoy knowing how my programs are doing financially whether it's good or bad. In MWR, there is always a need for qualified staff who know about recreation and leisure.

Q: As a Navy MWR career professional, do you think you are making a difference in the lives of the people you serve?

A: I know I make a difference every day! Being able to let people know that they are cared for and appreciated can set the tone in the community. I will have commands ask for me to help with swim lessons or physical training sessions. I have run a contest similar to the television show The Biggest Loser. The participants came back several months later to show me their waistlines and tell me that what I taught them really does work. Their smiles, in return, make me want to do a better job.

Did You Know?

Armed Forces Recreation, also known as **Morale, Welfare, and Recreation (MWR)**, is a multifaceted operation where each branch of service (Army, Navy, Air Force, Marine Corps, and Coast Guard) offers many program and service career options throughout the United States and overseas. MWR personnel contribute to the readiness, productivity, **esprit de corps** (or camaraderie), and overall quality of life for soldiers and their families. MWR exists because the Armed Forces are committed to the well-being of the military community who stand ready to protect the nation. MWR employees worldwide are dedicated to providing the best facilities, programs, and services possible. Career opportunities are available for any recreation professional interested in family and youth programs; single (unmarried) service member services; community events; sports and fitness; or information, travel, and tourism.

> " Providing services that help create a 'home away from home,' military recreation professionals have the opportunity to positively affect the quality of life of our dedicated military service members and their families.
>
> —Edward Cannon, Director of Navy Fleet and Family Readiness. "

Photo courtesy of Frederick Solheim, Warriors on Cataract

Do You Know How MWR Got Its Start?

The U.S. Navy MWR tradition is said to have started in pre–Revolutionary War America as sailors and maritime soldiers organized light-hearted harbor games for ship bragging rights and prize money in their downtime. These games actually served as core skill development for crews to test their preparedness for real-time action when underway or in battle. Morale-boosting activities bolstered esprit de corps and served as valuable practice for wartime skills. Shipboard life centered on food service, preparedness and the provision of basic life support requirements, and the provision of simple games to keep crew members occupied with social activities.[1]

Legend has it that the U.S. Army MWR tradition was born on a rainy World War I day in France, when a Salvation Army soldier cooked up the first batch of doughnuts to go with a homesick Arkansas soldier's hot coffee. Not until July 1940 was the U.S. Army's Morale Division established within the Adjutant General's Office, and then during the following 9 years, civilian and active duty military members created and staffed core recreation programs.[2] In the next few decades, the U.S. Army Community and Family Support Center was established as the headquarters for MWR operations. This structure provided oversight and policy support as well as management of the Armed Forces Recreation Centers. As this system evolved, the Family and MWR Command were established in 2006 by the Department of the Army, resulting in numerous recreation and leisure career options.

The U.S. Coast Guard's MWR department has similar roots to the U.S. Navy's. Since 1790, the U.S. Coast Guard has safeguarded our nation's maritime interests and environment around the world. The U.S. Coast Guard is an adaptable,

Photo courtesy of Frederick Solheim, Warriors on Cataract

responsive military force of maritime professionals whose broad legal authorities, capable assets, geographic diversity, and expansive partnerships provide a persistent presence along our rivers, ports, and littoral regions and on the high seas.[3]

Supporting this force requires an equally adaptable and creative team of recreation professionals dedicated to the well-being of the entire U.S. Coast Guard team.

What Is MWR Like Today?

Between 1946 and 1955, active duty military and civilians across all branches of the Armed Forces established and staffed core recreation programs. From that foundation, today's Armed Forces MWR effort continues to thrive in its mission to support the combat readiness of military personnel through myriad programs and services designed to meet specific needs of service members, family members, and civilian employees around the world. In the 21st century, Armed Forces Recreation professionals operate everything from small community centers to state-of-the-art fitness facilities and exotic resorts worldwide.[4] Some centers and programs are offered for free within a military installation, and other specialized activities are offered for a fee, such as golf, horseback riding, or scuba diving. Requiring a fee for services generates revenue for the programs to cover operating expenses.5 No matter what type of facility, though, the programs and services play a starring role in keeping service members and their families physically healthy and socially connected.

Recreation for military members, especially those who have experienced physical or emotional trauma during their service, can be especially beneficial and therapeutic. As MWR departments commonly offer such programs, this could be a career option for students who want to work with service members. Research is underway to examine how and why recreation, especially outdoor adventure activities, can positively impact the psychological, emotional, and social well-being of returning service members.6 Studies have found that when injured (physically, emotionally, or psychologically) military members participate in an outdoor adventure experience or multiday trip, they may learn to better interact with the physical and social environment. This could be because the trip provides opportunities for personal challenge and growth, time to build new friendships, and time and space to share thoughts and feelings with others who have had similar experiences.7 One example is the Wounded Warrior Project, which is detailed in the box below.

The Healing Power of Nature

In recent years, the military and civilians have increasingly noticed the intangible impacts of serving in a war. With more service men and women returning home with emotional or psychological trauma, many recreation-based programs have been launched to address the unique needs of this population. If you like the outdoors and serving others, this may be a career option for you.

The mission of the Wounded Warrior Project® (WWP) is "to honor and empower wounded warriors" and the vision of the WWP is to "foster the most successful, well-adjusted generation of wounded service members in our nation's history."8 The WWP takes a holistic approach, meaning programs address mind, body, and emotions, when working with service members. Programs such as skiing, bike skiing, camping, and outdoor challenge courses encourage service men and women, and sometimes their family members, to learn how to trust again, relate to others, create safe peer connections, set new goals, and learn how to live in their "new normal." Visit http://www.woundedwarriorproject.org for more information.

Careers in Morale, Welfare, and Recreation

Based on the branch of service, careers in recreation and leisure can be found on small tropical islands, in large urban cities, on ships, and underwater in submarines—in other words, worldwide. Recreation professionals can find career opportunities under categories such as Family and Morale, Welfare, and Recreation with the Army; or Fleet and Family Readiness with Navy MWR; or Combat Support and Community Service with the Air Force; or Marine Corps Community Services. Each branch of service has myriad program service areas for students either to pursue as an intern or to establish professional career tracks that will allow them to move from one program service area to another. Overall, MWR professionals work hard so that military personnel and their families can have fun and enjoy life at any time of the day or week.9

Passions

If you have a sense of duty to humankind and believe in a holistic approach to enhancing the well-being of men and women whose mission in life is to protect and serve, then you have the passion needed to be successful in MWR. For instance, do you embrace the Army's philosophy, which is that soldiers are entitled to the same quality of life as the citizens they are pledged to defend? If you answered "yes" to the above question, continue reading to explore what career professional Mr. Edward Cannon believes to be necessary for a successful career in military recreation. Cannon currently works as the director of Navy Fleet and Family Readiness (FFR). He is a member of the Senior Executive Service. As the director, Cannon oversees a worldwide network of professionals supporting military members, their families, reserve forces, retirees, and civilian employees of the Department of Defense. He told us,

> Working in Armed Forces Recreation, Quality of Life Programs, or Military Support Programs can be one of the most challenging and rewarding career options available to a person interested in truly making a difference. Providing services that help create a 'home away from home,' military recreation professionals have the opportunity to positively affect the quality of life of our dedicated military service members and their families. Careers in Military Recreation, or the more expansive Quality of Life programs include, but are not limited to, Child Development and Youth programs, crafts and hobbies, food and beverage, catering and conferencing, fitness, sports, forward deployed support (recreation and fitness on ships or remote and/or temporary sites), family and individual counseling, family housing, single service member housing (dorms or "barracks"), hotel services, special events, movie theater management, tickets and travel, golf course management, marina and sailing programs, bowling center management, resort management, cabins, cottages and campground management, and much more. The options are limitless, and knowing you are providing support to those who are defending our country is extremely rewarding!

Preparation

Cannon stressed that preparation for work in military recreation is extremely important. Coursework is essential to building a solid foundation in the theories and practices of the recreation profession. Learning the basics, and eventually more advanced practices, including legal, social, business, and political aspects of recreation programming and facility sustainment is key to building a solid foundation for your career. However, in the recreation field, nothing prepares you for potential future career challenges more than performing practical work in the field. Because of the unique bond recreation professionals form with customers, especially those in close quarters such as military professionals, you need to gain as much experience as possible by actually performing functions in the recreation field. This experience will help instill confidence in working with different demographics and in various settings. These combined experiences will allow you to succeed upon graduation and in a full-time position.

In addition to practical experience, securing a degree in recreation and leisure with an emphasis in sport management, fitness and wellness, commercial, outdoor, tourism, nonprofit, or even therapeutic recreation will give you a solid foundation for your career. Most colleges and universities require field experience prior to pursuing an internship. When selecting an agency for field experience, make sure you gain the necessary skills as previously described; however, success is predicated on your willingness to experience and practice the following:

- program planning creativity
- budgeting and financial management
- team building and partnerships
- leading activities and people
- risk management planning
- conducting inventories
- exhibiting sound customer service
- maintaining databases and registrations
- writing and documenting
- encouraging accountability and integrity
- listening and effective verbal communication

Advancing Your Career With MWR

More than ever, the need to continually sharpen your skills is imperative. The foundational education you receive in college and through internships or your first job is what will make you a successful entry-level employee (and probably a popular service provider since you will come to the job with new and refreshing ideas). But, more than many career fields, what helps you succeed as an entry-level employee must be improved if you wish to advance your career. As a young professional, you must learn to grow and adjust as an employee, manager, mentor, and leader. Career development needs to be thought of as a lifelong ambition. Challenge yourself by taking on tough assignments to demonstrate to your supervisors that you are eager to contribute to the greater interests of the organization and are willing to learn. If you are not a supervisor, understand the roles and responsibilities of supervisors in your organization. Seek out a mentor who can explain to you how he or she built his or her career. In short, know as much about your boss's job, and your boss's boss's job as you know about yours so you can help them succeed.

The benefits of working in the Armed Forces as a civilian recreation professional are endless. First, in this day and age of uncertainty and reduced benefits, civilian military careers still offer defined retirement, health, and vacation benefits equal to or better than most Fortune 500 companies and the ability to move around within the organization. These internal moves can be as short as the cubicle next to yours or 10,000 miles away! With military installations offering many programs and activities as well as locations on every continent (Antarctica is even an option for a few lucky volunteers), the potential for career and personal growth is limitless. Whether the Air Force, Army, Coast Guard, Marine Corps, or Navy is the branch of service you choose, you have the ability to move among the service branches, further expanding your options. A military recreation career is an honorable and rewarding choice that offers something for almost everyone.

To be competitive for career opportunities with MWR, consider taking the Army MWR's **Nonappropriated Fund** (NAF) Management Training Program. This program is designed to train college students in select program service areas (e.g., hospitality, marketing, and recreation) and then hires them for full-time employment. Trainees are placed at various military installations within the United States to complete up to 18 months of on-the-job training. After successfully completing the field training experience, trainees are encouraged to compete for permanent placement worldwide.

Similar to the Army's NAF program, both the Navy and Coast Guard MWR offices provide internship opportunities in recreational programming, sports, and leisure programs and community- based services. The MWR Intern Program offers students currently enrolled in a college program and working toward an MWR-related degree the opportunity to gain hands-on experience by assisting with program services. For more on the NAF or intern program, please refer to the online resources at sagamorepub.com/resources.

Example MWR Program Service Areas

Physical fitness Outdoor recreation	Youth recreation
Single soldier recreation	Special events and entertainment
Child development Library services	Information, travel, and tourism
Auto hobby shop	Resort management - Hospitality
Aquatics	Golf course
Arts and crafts	Music and arts/crafts
Food and beverage	Sports and intramural clubs
Recreation centers	Marketing and public relations

Pay and Perks

A career with MWR has a competitive salary at professional levels ranging from student intern to supervisory classification and benefits package that includes medical, dental, life insurance, 401(K) savings plan, and a comprehensive retirement plan.

Career-minded MWR personnel ranked at the professional level (one of the highest performance levels) can, as of 2013, earn an average salary of $75,000 annually. Check military human resources departments for current salary information. Other benefits derived through the performance-based personnel management system include

- annual pay raises and/or bonuses on performance and contributions and
- higher base pay raises and/or bonuses for high-performing employees.

Possibilities

Recreation and leisure career opportunities are available in areas such as special events, marketing, youth services, fitness and wellness, and much more. If you love the arts, building classic automobiles, or even boxing, you can build a career around your personal interests, skills, and talents. In addition to the more traditional recreation possibilities described above, positions are also available for those who seek adventure through travel and tourism. If this sounds like you, then working for the MWR Information, Travel, and Tourism program may be right up your alley. Although traditional recreation and leisure program service areas are available across the Armed Forces, unique service areas may be available for your individual career interests and talents.

Army MWR - Armed Forces Resort Center (AFRC)

"Whether strolling barefoot on the sands of Waikiki Beach, sightseeing historic European castles, shopping Seoul's exciting shopping district or visiting the enchanting Walt Disney Resort, there is a vacation getaway that will leave you with fresh memories and new perspectives."[10]

How would you like to be the hospitality professional to write a similar advertisement to invite military personnel to a relaxing yet exhilarating vacation experience? Hospitality professionals are hired to organize and plan such vacation experiences for military personnel and their families at one of five Armed Forces Resort Centers (AFRCs) worldwide, which are operated by the Army Family and MWR Command. As with other civilian resort destinations, AFRCs offer a full range of hotel opportunities and amenities. Refer to Chapter 11 for additional information that complements this career option.

Passions. Someone in this career path must be friendly and team oriented, enjoy working with all types of people, freely engage in public speaking, and be skilled at creative writing, program planning, special events coordination, and customer service, as well as enjoy facilitating relaxing and memorable vacation experiences.

Pay and perks. A number of factors such as previous work experience in the hospitality industry, education, and time in the military system will determine the annual salary range. Professionals working for AFRCs may earn an average salary, at the low end, of $30,000, but can earn $60,000 or more. Wages are comparable with industry standards. Depending on the AFRC resort location, professionals may be eligible for meal programs, dormitory-style housing accommodations, and access to the amenities during downtime.

Preparation. A bachelor's degree in recreation, special events planning, hospitality management, or a closely related field is often required.

Possibilities. AFRCs are resort hotels located in five vacation destinations: Florida (Shades of Green–Walt Disney World®), Hawaii (Hale Koa Hotel–Diamond Head), Korea (Dragon Hill Lodge–Asia Style), Germany (Edelweiss Lodge and Resort), and Virginia (Cape Henry Inn–Atlantic

Coast). Professionals with the AFRC will provide high-quality yet affordable resort experiences with a focus on endorsing the Army MWR's mission to provide rest, relaxation, and recreation for military personnel and their families, to foster combat readiness and retention.[11]

Marine Corps Community Service–Single Marine Program (SMP)

The well-being and recreation needs of single soldiers have been a vital service component of MWR programs for more than a decade. The Single Marine Program (SMP), or Better Opportunities for Single Soldiers (BOSS) for the other branches of service, is a highly energetic program designed to identify and address issues and concerns affecting the living environment of the soldier. Additionally, it gives a voice to single soldiers in developing recreational events that best meets their needs.[12]

Passions. In this career path, you need a passion for program planning, needs assessment, and evaluation; an interest in providing opportunities for single individuals to participate and contribute to local community efforts and recreational activities; to be able to facilitate efforts to improve conditions to enhance the well-being of others; and to enjoy advocacy work and organizing fund-raising events.

Pay and perks. Professionals working in the SMP/BOSS program are usually considered recreation specialists (single soldier coordinator) under the community activity center. Pay range for recreation specialist, as of the 2013 pay scale, can range from $40,000 to $50,000 annually depending on location and other factors. Positions with the SMP/BOSS program are available worldwide. One of the perks of working in the SMP/BOSS program is that it allows recreation professionals to assume a leadership role on base and work closely with military leaders there. Standard perks include a generous retirement program, flexible work environment, alternative work schedules, paid employment-related training, education, and possible student loan repayment. Other incentives include assistance with paying tuition for academic degrees, pay band bonuses, and performance awards.

Preparation. A bachelor's degree in recreation and leisure with competencies in leadership and team building, budgeting, and financial management is highly desirable. The recreation specialist working for the SMP/BOSS program must also exhibit the highest standard of self-confidence, integrity, dependability, and knowledge of program delivery. A significant amount of time spent either through an internship or a volunteer experience gaining skills in the area of needs assessment and evaluation is essential.

The Future of Armed Forces Recreation

An exciting opportunity for MWR professionals is the chance to work with "Generation Next," or the 85% of military families made up of young parents (born between 1980 and 2000) who have young children. MWR professionals foster family communication and bonding via enjoyable, safe recreational opportunities. For families who may move frequently, who live far from relatives, or in which a parent is deployed, recreation professionals and services are essential to maintaining family physical health and social and emotional well-being. In addition to wanting traditional recreation activities, this generation is technology savvy, meaning the recreation professional may be called upon to help families communicate with loved ones via webcam in a recreation center computer lab or assist in building a virtual community among those with similar interests.[13]

Possibilities. The single soldier coordinator will work closely with the soldier, senior military personnel, and other essential community service staff to ensure the best possible quality of life for single and unaccompanied men and women in the Armed Forces. Career advancement is available worldwide.

Navy MWR – Fleet Recreation

Because being at sea for lengths of time can be difficult and demanding for sailors, quality leisure-time activities that fit into the limited space available aboard ship are essential. Therefore, recreation professionals are expected to provide holistic leisure experiences for sailors whether in port or overseas. For instance, these career professionals provide individual and group activities such as tours, picnics, athletic competitions, or fitness and wellness classes. The recreation professional working for Navy MWR is responsible for developing programs and services, as well as providing resources such as equipment for 5,000 or more Navy personnel. Refer to Chapter 3 for details on similar jobs.

Passions. Those interested in this area must be passionate about sailing and living in coastal communities; be an independent thinker who can also embrace team camaraderie; be interested in special events, planning, fitness and wellness, sports, and budget management; and enjoy marketing and public relations.

Pay and perks. Depending on a number of factors such as job responsibilities specific to programming activities or managing budgets, the average salary for a recreation specialists ranges from $30,500 to $40,000 annually. A primary perk of working for the Navy MWR Fleet recreation is extensive travel.

Preparation. A bachelor's degree in the field of recreation management from an accredited university or college is preferred. Recreation specialists working for the Navy should be knowledgeable of activities suitable for individuals or groups of various ages, interests, and capacities based on participants' interests and needs and able to implement such activities into limited spaces. Furthermore, the ability to effectively communicate both verbally and in writing is important. Students can gain experience from an internship or by volunteering at local agencies to learn more about managing people and material resources.

Possibilities. Career options are available at fleet sites around the world for people interested in shipping out to sea and providing quality recreation and leisure programs for hard-working sailors and civilian crew members.

Air Force Combat Support and Community Service–Outdoor Recreation

Outdoor recreation programs provide military personnel (airmen and women) and their families with opportunities to recreate in the outdoors by planning and offering activities and adventures. Emphasis is placed on outdoor recreation skill development and opportunities for airmen to acquire lifetime leisure skills that assist them in remaining combat-ready. In many cases, outdoor recreation specialists are charged to assist base commanders in maintaining readiness by providing outdoor adventure training opportunities.[14] Chapter 6 has additional information that will be helpful if this is a career area that interests you.

Passions. For those with a passion or interest in the great outdoors, natural resources, adventure, and/or skill building, then MWR outdoor recreation will be the best path with the military system. Other areas of interest are rock climbing, skiing, sailing, kayaking, and camping.

Pay and perks. The average salary, as of 2013, for MWR outdoor recreation specialists is approximately $31,000 annually. Similar to other recreation specialist positions within the MWR system, perks include a generous retirement program, flexible work environment, alternative work schedules, and paid employment-related training and education. The programs and services ranging from planning outdoor adventure excursions to managing family camp groups can be a fantastic perk for the outdoor enthusiast.

Preparation. A bachelor's degree in outdoor adventure, park management, or recreation management is beneficial. Exposure to experiential learning opportunities in the out-of-doors is also beneficial.

Possibilities. All service branches have thriving outdoor recreation and adventure programs; however, based on geographic location, availability of natural resources, and patron demand, employees may find themselves managing a riding stable, marina, picnic areas, outdoor equipment "checkout centers, or family campgrounds.

> As the Director of Sierra Club Outdoors, I get to work with active duty military, families, and veterans, as well as non-veterans to get literally thousands of people outdoor each year. This is great because we're teaching a lot of leadership skills. Our goal is not to take people outside, but to go outside with them and make sure they can go out long after they leave the trip with us.
>
> "I didn't take the normal path to a career in the outdoors that included being a long-standing guide or instructor at NOLS, instead I followed a passion of helping other people and myself for a couple of years when I came home from Iraq and realized the outdoors could take care of most challenges all in one simple walk around the block or climbing mountains. Follow your passion, and whatever it is, I bet you can do it outside!
>
> —Stacy Bare, Director, Sierra Club Mission Outdoors,
> Former Captain, U.S. Army OIF Veteran

As you learn more about military recreation careers, you will notice the numerous position levels and titles available, all of which come with various duties and responsibilities. In general, however, you will see that jobs fall at one of three different levels.

Entry level. These are either part- or full-time positions with minimal management responsibilities. With this type of position, the employee may assist a director or specialist with activity planning and maintain basic day-to-day customer service operations such as equipment checkouts and activity registrations.

Mid level. These are full-time positions with the responsibility of managing people, programs, services, and facilities. This level generally requires a college degree and experience in the program service area. With a pay band increase, the MWR professional may be in charge of approximately 10 employees.

Upper level. These are full-time director positions where the MWR professional would oversee duties of mid-level personnel. At this level, the director is expected to oversee budgets, understand and apply all military operating standards, and ensure that all employees are adequately trained to apply their skills in an efficient and effective manner.

Career advancement generally follows a path from entry level, through the intermediate level, to managerial or executive positions. Individual progression depends on a variety of factors including demonstrated performance, assignments completed, formal education, functional and geographical mobility, and completion of training programs.[15]

Summary of Morale, Welfare, and Recreation Career Possibilities

Career	Passions	Pay and perks	Preparations	Possibilities
Army MWR-Armed Forces Resort Center (AFRC)	Friendly and team-oriented, customer service	Ranges from entry-level pay similar to educators to administrative levels	Bachelor's degree in recreation or special events planning	Various opportunites in fine vacation destinations
Marine Corps Community Service-Single Marine Program (SMP)	Program planning, needs assessment, and evaluation	Ranges from entry-level pay similar to educators to administrative levels	Bachelor's degree in recreation and leisure services	Career advancement is available worldwide
Navy (MWR) Fleet Recreation	Passionate about sailing and be an independent thinker	Pay level similar to educators, depending on education and experience	Bachelor's degree in the field of recreation management	Career options are available at fleet sites around the world
Air Force Combat Support and Community Service	Great outdoors natural resources, adventure, and skill building	Pay level similar to educators, depending on education and experience	Bachelor's degree in outdoor adventure, park management, or recreation management	All branches of the service have thriving outdoor recreation and adventure programs

Resources and Getting Involved

To remain competitive and move up the ladder from a recreation assistant position, for example, to a director or specialist position, you will need to gain new skill sets from various trainings offered via workshops, via specialized courses, or by attending national conferences. Individual professional development is a high priority for the military, so much so that it has a training center known as the U.S. Army's MWR Academy. "It provides employees with quality management and customer service training, in support of continuous professional growth and meeting the U.S. Army's MWR mission."16   Professionals in the field can select from more than 50 courses and training programs through this professional development system. Many of these courses will not only help you with continuing education units but also help you earn college credits.

Professional Organizations

You may want to also consider joining a professional organization such as the National Recreation and Park Association (NRPA) or the Armed Forces Recreation Network, a branch of the NRPA.[17] As you become more familiar with a specific program area and develop a passion for what you are doing to meet the military mission, it will be essential to connect with a professional association. Many professional associations are available at state and national levels where you can network with others in your area of expertise and stay abreast of current trends and practices.

Certifications and Licenses

There are no licenses or certifications specific to MWR, but you should investigate those that relate to your specific area of interest. In the absence of a specific military-oriented recreation certification, we highly recommend that career-minded professionals obtain certifications from nationally recognized organizations such as the NRPA. These will be covered in the chapters on community recreation, outdoor recreation, therapeutic recreation, and sport management.

Where to Gain Experience

MWR internships are educational experiences designed to give college students studying recreation and leisure or related curriculums an opportunity to gain real-life experience while earning credits toward their degree. Universities are committed partners with MWR departments from any of the branches of service. Through this partnership, students gain practical hands-on experience before graduation and MWR program departments bridge the gap between theory and practice that students learn while in school. The benefit of this partnership is the enhanced service to military personnel and their families.[18]

Conclusion

MWR departments provide a valuable service to military personnel, their families, civilian personnel, military retirees, and other eligible participants. MWR exists because the Armed Forces are committed to the well-being of the military community who serve and stand ready to defend the nation. MWR offers comprehensive recreation and leisure service areas ranging from sports and fitness to travel and tourism, to single soldier special events to family recreation. Thousands of MWR employees worldwide are committed to delivering the highest quality programs and services at each Armed Forces installation. A career with MWR allows the recreation professional to contribute to the strength and readiness of soldiers by offering services that reduce stress and build skills and self-confidence.

Numerous positions are available for students interested in earning a degree in recreation and leisure or a related discipline with MWR throughout the United States and overseas. To be competitive for career opportunities with MWR, consider taking the NAF Management Training Program (mentioned previously), participating in the Navy MWR's Internship program, and joining a professional organization such NRPA's Armed Forces Recreation Network.

To fully comprehend the vast structure of MWR, its hiring structure, job opportunities, and employee benefits, you must think critically about what program service area interests you and do your homework by asking specific career planning questions. Furthermore, you should conduct this inquiry with the notion in mind that MWR services are equivalent to recreation and leisure services found at civilian agencies. If you have a passion for helping others and working to uphold the ultimate mission of keeping U.S. service members combat-ready and their families taken care of, then you should strongly consider military recreation for your future career.

Active Investigation

In preparation for an internship with military recreation, or to determine whether you are interested in making a 3-year commitment to the NAF training program, conduct an informational interview with any career professional within the MWR system. See Chapter 2 for more details on conducting this type of interview, and consider the following questions to guide your personal quest to secure an MWR position:

1. What can I do right now to prepare myself for a career with MWR?
2. Are there specific skill sets I should gain that will make me competitive for a position as a recreation specialist?

3. What should I consider before pursuing a position overseas?
4. Are there financial perks available to me if I qualify for and accept an overseas position with MWR?
5. Once I secure a position with MWR, how can this experience help me if I want to pursue a position with a civilian agency or a corporate business?

For Further Investigation

Websites

To help you address these questions and others, you will want to surf the following websites and their links:

U.S. Navy MWR
www.navymwr.org

U.S. Marine Corps Community Services
www.usmc-mccs.org

U.S. Army and MWR Family Command
www.armymwr.com

**U.S. Air Force Combat Support
and Community Service**
usafservices.com

U.S. Coast Guard MWR
www.uscg.mil/MWR

Air Force Services Career Program
www.nafjobs.org/nafcareers.aspx

Army Civilian Personnel On-Line
www.cpol.army.mil/library/naf/

Civillian Personnel On-line
www.cpol.army.mil

U.S. Coast Guard MWR
www.uscg.mil/MWR

**Department of Defense's Civilian
Employment Center**
www.godefense.com

**Fundamentals of NSPS:
An Overview of Proposed Regulations**
www.cpms.osd.mil

MWR Training Academy
www.mwraonline.com

**Nonappropriated Funds Employment
Opportunities**
acpol.army.mil

USAJobs.com
www.usajobs.gov

Recommended Reading

Lankford, S., & DeGraaf, D. (1992). Strengths, weaknesses, opportunities, and threats in morale, welfare, and recreation organizations: Challenges of the 1990s. *Journal of Parks and Recreation Administration, 10* (1), pp. 31-45.

This article, although written in the 1990s, lends much to the reader on the topic of trends and issues in MWR. The authors provide strategies to aid Armed Forces Recreation directors on how to best assess future leisure service delivery systems. This reading provides an excellent framework for MWR trends and issues that young professionals may face in the 21st century and effective methods for making operational decisions.

McLean, D. D., Hurd, A. R., & Rogers, N. B. (2005). *Kraus' recreation and leisure in modern society.* Sudbury, MA: Jones and Bartlett.

This textbook provides a brief yet thorough overview of six specialized leisure service areas, including Armed Forces Recreation. Chapter 9 will offer the reader insight into how the military is an untapped industry and why recreation students should consider it as a career option.

Human Kinetics. (Ed.) (2006). *Introduction to recreation and leisure.* Champaign: Human Kinetics.
Temple and Ogilvie, authors of the "Recreation in the Armed Forces" section, discuss the similarities between military and civilian recreation in this introduction to recreation and leisure textbook. See Chapter 11 for more in-depth reading on the history of morale, welfare, and recreation. The interested reader will also get a peak at the educational credentials and career path taken by Mr. John Kelly Powell. There is a brief discussion on Canadian Armed Forces and recreation principles.

References

[1]*Navy Fleet and Family Readiness Internship Program Manual 2013.* (2013). Retrieved from http://www.navymwr. org/mwrprgms/trngann/internmanual.pdf

[2]Gibbs, H. K. (2007). MWR 2007: This is not your father's morale, welfare, and recreation program. *AmeriForce.* Retrieved from http://www.ameriforce.net/PDF/mag.pdf

[3]U.S. Coast Guard. (n.d.). About us. Retrieved from http://www.uscg.mil/top/about

[4]U.S. Army MWR. (n.d.). Family and MWR programs. Retrieved from http://www.armymwr.com/mwr-about-us.aspx

[5]Center for Military Health Policy Research. (2011). Programs addressing psychological health and traumatic brain injury among U.S. military service members and their families. Retrieved from Defense Technical Information website: http://www.dtic.mil/cgi-bin/GetTRDoc?AD=ADA553351

[6]Lundberg, N., Bennett, J., & Smith, S. (2011). Outcomes of adaptive sports and recreation participation among veterans returning from combat with acquired disability. *Therapeutic Recreation Journal, 45*(2), 105–120.

[7]Duvall, J., & Kaplan, R. (2013). *Exploring the benefits of outdoor experiences on veterans* (Report prepared for the Sierra Club Military Families and Veterans Initiative). Retrieved from Sierra Club website: http://www. sierraclub.org/military/downloads/Michigan-Final-Research-Report.pdf

[8]Wounded Warrior Project. (n.d.). Retrieved from http://www.woundedwarriorproject.org

[9]Temple, J., & Ogilvie, L. (2006). *Recreation in the armed forces: Introduction to recreation and leisure.* Champaign, IL: Human Kinetics.

[10]U.S. Army MWR. (n.d.). Armed Forces Recreation Center resorts: Destination paradise. Retrieved from http://www.armymwr.com/travel/recreationcenters

[11]Ibid.

[12]Marine Corps Community Services Camp Lejeune. (n.d.). Retrieved from http://www.mccslejeune.com

[13]Davis, B. E., Blaschke, G. S., & Stafford, E. M. (2012). Military children, families, and communities: Supporting those who serve. *Pediatrics, 129*(1), S3–S10.

[14]Aberdeen Proving Ground Family and Morale, Welfare and Recreation. (n.d.). Outdoor recreation. Retrieved from http://www.apgmwr.com/recreation/odr/index.html

[15]Campus Career Center. (n.d.). Job seekers. Retrieved from http://www.campuscareercenter.com/students/honorrolldetail

[16]U.S. Army MWR. (n.d.). Retrieved from http://www.armymwr.com

[17]National Recreation and Park Association. (n.d.). Retrieved from http://www.nrpa.org

[18]U.S. Navy MWR. (n.d.). Retrieved from http://www.navymwr.org

"*We simply need that wild country available to us, even if we never do more than drive to its edge and look in. For it can be a means of reassuring ourselves of our sanity as creatures, a part of the geography of hope.*"

—Wallace Stegner
Author and advocate for Utah's
landscapes, people, and culture

6

Outdoor Recreation in Federal, State, and Local Parks

William Hendricks
California Polytechnic State University,
San Luis Obispo

Tony Sisto
National Park Service (retired)

Cheryl L. Stevens
East Carolina University

Focus Questions

Q: Do you really love parks, love spending time in the outdoors, and have an affinity for nature? Do you also enjoy being with and helping other people?

A: Those who love working in the outdoors have a strong bond with nature. If you do not know whether that is you, spend extended time in the outdoors and find out. Some park jobs can be isolated and require employees to work alone in the outdoors for long periods of time, whereas others require constant interaction with park visitors. If you would like a job with variety that balances the peace and quiet of the natural world with the noisier world of park visitors, this may be the job for you.

Q: Do you like working with people in the role of teacher or educator?

A: Many park jobs require working with visitors who may have little understanding about how to behave in the natural world so that its beauty and serenity are sustained for future visitors. Park employees often emphasize visitor education about appropriate park uses through media or personal contact. This often requires patience and a positive attitude because new visitors often ask the same questions you have been asked the previous day, week, or month.

Q: Are you willing to work on creative solutions to create a sustainable future for outdoor recreation areas?

A: Shifting federal, state, and local priorities will continue to challenge the funding options available for outdoor recreation professionals who must be ready to continually seek out new and innovative ways to secure funding and resources. Employees must be willing to seek support from public, nonprofit, and private sectors.

Q: Do you have a particular interest or passion related to the outdoors that drives you?

A: If you have a favorite outdoor recreation activity, it is possible to turn that passion into a career. Similarly, if you find yourself attending rallies or meetings in which people are trying to change governmental policy to promote environmental sustainability, you will discover many nonprofit organizations and entrepreneurs with similar interests who partner with government outdoor recreation agencies.

Q: How important are financial rewards to you?

A: Although most career positions in outdoor recreation will pay comparable salaries to similar non-recreation jobs, you almost certainly will not get rich in this profession. It is important to know this at the beginning of your career. Many people find that the perks of living close to nature and doing what they love are more important to them than large financial rewards.

Key Terms

Village greens
Boston Common
Central Park
Frederick Law Olmsted
Landscape architecture
Yellowstone National Park
Secretary of the Interior
John Muir
Forest Reserve Act
Gifford Pinchot
Antiquities Act of 1906
U.S. Forest Service
Department of Agriculture

Multiple Use Sustained Yield Act (MUSY)
Nonprofit organizations
Stephen T. Mather
Concessionaires and commercial recreation
    businesses
Carrying capacity
Interpretation
Law enforcement
Public safety
Emergency medical technician
Resource management
Government Land Management Agencies
Nongovernmental Organizations (NGOs)

Profile 1: Could This Be You?

Erica Francis is a park ranger with the National Park Service. As a park ranger, she is responsible for many visitor services and resource protection duties, including the following:

- backcountry patrol, by foot, horseback, boat, 4 x 4, and aircraft
- firefighting
- search and rescue
- law enforcement
- resource protection
- emergency medical services
- park operations

Erica Francis

Q: What do you do in a typical day?

A: When working in Klondike Gold Rush National Historic Park in Alaska, my daily activities include patrol, making sure people are doing okay, being friendly, providing interpretation, and making sure nobody is violating any laws. The park has a small campground, a few historical buildings, an old historical town site, and a trail.

Q: What do you like most about your career?

A: It is pretty thrilling! I like the adventure part and how varied it can be. One second I could be organizing a search for a missing person and the next second I could get a call to fight a fire or respond to a domestic violence. There is never a boring moment. I get paid to do some pretty cool things such as rafting down the Colorado River and living in the bush in Katmai National Park with brown bears all summer. You could be a climbing ranger, located at a dive park, doing law enforcement only or a variety of duties.

Q: What are some of the biggest challenges you face in your job?

A: The job requires you to be very diversified from firefighting to law enforcement to resource management to emergency medical services. There are so many skills you need to know that it is difficult to become proficient in one.

Q: How does your career make a difference in the lives of others?

A: Doing visitor resource protection, you come in contact with the public on a daily basis to serve their needs. They often tell me it is the first time they have seen a park ranger. It is a very unique law enforcement job because people appreciate what you do. They don't just see you as "the law," and they frequently say thank you.

Q: What advice do you have for someone preparing for a career in this field?

A: It is very competitive to become a ranger with the National Park Service. Volunteering or an internship with The Student Conservation Association (SCA) will help. Getting seasonal or unpaid experience while a student can help you get an edge on the competition. Joining the Peace Corps gives you a year of status so you are not competing with everyone else on USAJobs.gov. To get a law enforcement job you must first go to a seasonal law enforcement academy. A season or two as a noncommissioned ranger helps get a commissioned position. Have the knowledge and know the requirements to get into the academy.

Profile 2: Could This Be You?

Chelsea Modlin is the director of social media and the marketing manager for Monterey Lakes for The California Parks Company, a for-profit park concessionaire. She is responsible for promotions, advertising, events, social media, and print media for two parks in the California Central Coast and 19 total concession locations.

Q: What do you do in a typical day?

A: It changes daily. Every week and every season is different. I might be doing graphic design, contacting vendors for an event, going to a trade show, working on an online newsletter, creating new social media sites, coordinating direct mailing, handling a concession management agreement, coordinating a market research survey, or putting on events such as a fishing derby, summer kickoff party for wakeboarders, or a lake cleanup.

Q: What do you like most about your career?

A: The amazing view out my office window of Lake Nacimiento! I do something different every day. I get to work with each department—the marina, store, restaurant, Monterey County Parks. I am 20 years younger than most of the other senior managers. It is cool that I am so young and able to do all of this.

Q: What are the biggest challenges you face in your job?

A: Because we are a concessionaire, we need approval within our company and from a public agency, which often takes time. Things don't get done right away. Working with many different entities is the biggest challenge.

Q: How does your career make a difference in the lives of others?

A: I am part of a team that helps people and families create memories for a lifetime. I love hospitality, making sure others have a good time. I provide opportunities to others with fun events and outdoor recreation experiences.

Q: What advice do you have for someone preparing for a career in this field?

A: Learn as much as possible. Make sure you have a passion for what you are doing and what you are marketing. You need to have a connection to your career. If you are young, you will often have to prove yourself. But you can do it!

Chelsea Modlin

The Wide, Wild World of Outdoor Parks and Recreation

Every day in the U.S. National Park Service (NPS), over 47,000 people report for work in 401 national park areas. Nearly half of these are NPS employees working in professional and trade careers. The other half includes concession employees working for private hospitality firms under contract to the NPS (operating lodges, restaurants, stores, and campgrounds). In addition, the **U.S. Forest Service** (USFS) manages 155 national forests, 20 national grasslands, and 19 research and experimental forests, as well as other special areas covering nearly 193 million acres and employing approximately 30,000 permanent and 15,000 seasonal employees.[1] These numbers do not include the vast number of employees working to support outdoor recreation in myriad other federal, state, and local agencies; nonprofit organizations; and businesses. Most of these employees have one thing in common, however, and that is working in or near a great outdoor environment, with spectacular scenery just over their shoulder.

> Everybody needs beauty as well as bread, places to play in and pray in, where Nature may heal and cheer and give strength to body and soul alike.
>
> — John Muir

Indeed, many employees have the job of providing and maintaining space for outdoor recreation in North America. These careers offer exciting and rewarding job experiences for those passionate about open space and outdoor recreation.

At the federal level, in addition to the aforementioned NPS and USFS areas, there are 545 fish and wildlife recreation areas and over 4,000 other public land recreation sites. Canada has 44 national parks and hundreds of provincial parks. In the United States, all 50 states have similar areas, from the 6 million-acre Adirondacks State Park in New York (the largest publicly protected area in the contiguous United States), to a large variety of seashore, lakeshore, and forest parks in every state.

A Brief History of Open-Space and Recreation in North America

Brief History of Open Space and Recreation in North America Many volumes have been written about the history of North American open space and outdoor recreation, so we will only cover the highlights. People who choose outdoor recreation as a career area should expect to learn more history as it is critical to understanding how to manage the land for future generations. We will also discuss key people whose passion and influence shaped the creation and management of the spaces we know and love today.

Open Space for Recreation in Urban Areas

From the earliest days of western Europeans settling North America, the vast and forbidding western American frontier seemed limitless, so there was little concern for preserving land for recreation or resource sustainability. Soon, however, problems arose with deforestation, overhunting, and crowding in populated urban areas, which resulted in the establishment of village greens and laws regulating forests and hunting game.[2] The earliest parks were **village greens**, which were established during the colonial period and still exist in several New England states. America's oldest municipal park is the **Boston Common**, which was set aside by Boston residents in 1634 for cattle grazing and public gatherings. Bostonians made a conscious decision to keep this open, green space, and not allow any buildings to be constructed without approval of all citizens.[3]

Central Park today seems such a natural part of the New York City landscape that many people do not realize it is human made.[4] The design for Central Park by **Frederick Law Olmsted** and Calvert Vaux (a British architect) was selected from 33 competitors in 1857, and set the stage for a particularly American vision for urban park design that stands in stark contrast to formal European gardens. Park creation was not simple; the rocky, swampy, and muddy area required 500,000 cubic feet of topsoil from New Jersey for park construction.[5]

Frederick Law Olmsted (1822–1903) was an American journalist and landscape designer who was responsible for designing many well-known urban parks, including Central Park and Prospect Park in New York City and the Emerald Necklace in Boston, MA. Olmsted's unique way of, designing urban parks was to make everything—paths, trees, and bushes—fixed in a particular place with a purpose—and that purpose was to bring the atmosphere of wildness to the urban dweller. Olmsted stated:

> We want a ground to which people may easily go after their day's work is done, and where they may stroll for an hour, seeing, hearing and feeling nothing of the bustle and jar of the streets, where they shall, in effect, find the city put far away from them. …We want, especially, the greatest possible contrast with the restraining and confining conditions which compel us to walk circumspectly, watchfully, jealously, which compel us to look closely upon others without sympathy.[6]

When Olmsted, a landscape architect, delivered his lecture "Public Parks and the Enlargement of Towns in Cambridge, Massachusetts" in 1870, Boston was an overcrowded, noisy, and dirty city. Concerned with the health and happiness of Bostonians restricted to these unhealthy surroundings, the city hired Olmsted to design a park system. The series of parks he designed over the next several years is known as the Emerald Necklace. Each unique "jewel" in the Emerald Necklace—from lovely waterways to botanical gardens to peaceful meadows to tree museums—plays a vital role in linking the citizens of Boston together through nature.

In addition to providing vision for urban parks, Olmsted recommended an innovative management style that included an executive office, skilled landscape architect, and an unpaid board of directors to oversee park decisions.[7] Olmsted is considered the founder of American **landscape architecture**, a profession that deals with arranging land and buildings for human use and enjoyment. Olmsted's work

> forged a design ethic for natural parks which would be carried into the twentieth century by landscape architects, be adopted and adapted by the National Park Service designers, and flourish in the park conservation work of the 1930s in national, state, and metropolitan parks.[8]

National Parks and National Forests

When Congress established **Yellowstone National Park** in 1872 by preserving land "dedicated and set apart as a public park or pleasuring ground for the benefit and enjoyment of all the people,"[9] it sparked a series of unanticipated events. The NPR noted, "This idea of a national park was an American invention of historic consequences, marking the beginning of a worldwide movement that has subsequently spread to more than 100 countries."[10] Ken Burns, director of *National Parks: America's Best Idea* (2009) suggested that the idea of the national parks "is as uniquely American as the Declaration of Independence and just as radical."[11] Many citizens take for granted the idea "that the most special places in the nation should be preserved, not for royalty of the rich, but for everyone,"[10] but at the time this was done, it was indeed a radical concept.

The newly established national park led to a quarter century of protracted struggle to define a code of policies to guide the administration, protection, and development of public parks.[12]

> " In these special places we've resolved together as a people to preserve, we feel a sense of commonality. You come to a national park and some of the barriers between people, between classes, even between nationalities, are broken down and you share and have the experience of an essential, collective humanity.... At a park we experience something that's collective. It's a common wealth, and my goodness, especially today we need that reminder of what we share in common.
> —Excerpted from an interview with Ken Burns, documentary filmmaker of *The National Parks: American's Best Idea* "

In the book *Early History of Yellowstone*, some key policy decisions that crystallized over 25 years were "so universally concurred that it does not occur to us now that they could have ever been questioned,"[13] and others were thoroughly established as national policy through the first 25 years of Yellowstone's administration. The following are four policies of particular relevance to outdoor recreation professionals:

1. The federal government may reserve and keep control of the management of land. Notably, the experiment of turning great scenic regions over to the state for management was not deemed successful.

2. There are twin purposes to the land reserved: (a) the enjoyment and use of the area as a "pleasuring ground for the benefit and enjoyment of the people" and (b) at the same time, "the preservation, from injury or spoliation of all timber, mineral deposits, natural curiosities or wonders within said park and their retention in their natural condition."

3. The parks are to be administered primarily for the enjoyment of the people and leases and concessions in the park are decided on in accordance with "the welfare of the visitor" as the first consideration.

4. Enjoyment of the areas shall be free to all the people. At first, it was thought leases of utilities would provide needed monies for park management, but it was soon realized that the federal treasury would need to appropriate money for development and maintenance. (Today, however, you need to pay an entrance fee or purchase a National Parks and Federal Recreational Lands pass.)

Other policies describe how parks will be under the control of the **Secretary of the Interior**, will be a game preserve, not a hunting reservation, and guided by national interests rather than those of local benefit. And, important for recreation professionals is the statement noting that "Recreation is an essential purpose of park use even though secondary or incidental" to preservation.[14] However, recreational use does not take precedent over preservation. As stated in the NPS's 2006 management policies, "The fundamental purpose of the national park system… begins with a mandate to conserve park resources and values."[15] Park enjoyment means not only domestic visitors, but also those visiting from afar. Clearly, the enjoyment of those distant can only be ensured "if the superb quality of park resources and values is left unimpaired [and] … when there is a conflict between conserving resources and values and providing for the enjoyment of them, conservation is to be predominant."[16]

John Muir would have been pleased with the NPS's current management policy that places preservation of park resources as the top priority. However, it has not always been clear that preservation would win out because many other voices promoted uses such as timber, tourism, watershed, and range use, and these uses are often in conflict with preservation—especially when preservation is taken to mean "left unimpaired."

> **John Muir** (1838–1914) is often considered America's most influential naturalist and conservationist. During his lifetime, he worked tirelessly to help preserve wild, open spaces. His work led to the establishment of Yosemite National Park in 1890, and he worked to convince Theodore Roosevelt to begin the national wildlife refuge system and to convince the government to preserve some 21 million acres of forestland. Outdoor enthusiast and Patagonia® founder Yvon Chouinard said of Muir, "If you think about all the gains our society has made, from independence to now, it wasn't government. It was activism. People think, 'Oh, Teddy Roosevelt established Yosemite National Park, what a great president.' BS. It was John Muir who invited Roosevelt out and then convinced him to ditch his security and go camping. It was Muir, an activist, a single person."

Preservation was ultimately balanced with the need for multiple uses. As early as the late 1800s, lawmakers noted that the national parks would not meet all land management needs of future generations. Setting aside land for multiple uses first began with the **Forest Reserve Act of 1891**. Several early leaders and visionaries, including President Theodore Roosevelt and the first Chief of the Forest Service, **Gifford Pinchot**, led the nation in efforts to retain and manage millions of acres of federal forest land for future generations.

Roosevelt was known as the conservation president. He not only impacted the national parks system by establishing five new parks, but he was also the first president to invoke the Antiquities Act of 1906 and use his executive authority to override others to preserve natural wonders before special interests could make such preservation impossible.[17] Recent presidents have invoked the same act including President Jimmy Carter, who set aside millions of acres of Alaskan wilderness; President Bill Clinton, who called upon the act to create Grand Staircase-Escalante National Monument in Utah; and President Barack Obama, who used it to establish eight national monuments, including five as recently as March 2013. Such acts were not without controversy and public outcry, however.

When Roosevelt acted, he worked to balance ideas of preservation with the need for multiple uses. Following much debate about appropriate use of federal forestland, the **Multiple Use-Sustained Yield Act** (more generally referred to its acronym **MUSY**) was passed in 1960, which directs the **Department of Agriculture** to develop and administer land for five renewable resources: (a) outdoor recreation, (b) range, (c) timber, (d) watershed, and (e) wildlife and fish values.[18] In brief, one important difference between national parks and national forests is that parks are set aside for preservation and enjoyment and national forests are for multiple uses.

By now, you should realize dozens of agencies oversee the management and visitor experience in the United State's 401 national parks. As such, hundreds of outdoor recreation jobs are available at federal, state, and local levels.

Stephen T. Mather (1867-1930) recognized magnificent scenery as the primary criterion for establishing national parks. He was careful to evaluate choices for parks, wishing the parks to stand as a collection of unique monuments. He felt those areas that were duplicates may best be managed by others. Within the framework of "scenery," his preservation ethic covered issues such as the locations of park developments, provision of vistas along roadways, and the perpetuation of the natural scene. Mather always wished to have the parks supported by avid users who would then communicate their support to their elected representatives. His grasp of a grassroots support system encouraged the rise of "nature study" and modern interpretation, as well as other park services, and was followed by increases in NPS appropriations.[19]

Photo: AAPRA.org

Outdoor Recreation and Nonprofit Organizations

The Sierra Club, founded by John Muir and other supporters in 1892, was one of the first **nonprofit organizations** to complement the missions of agencies responsible for outdoor recreation (see Chapter 4 for more information). Additional outdoor recreation-related nonprofit agencies exist today, and these will be listed later in the chapter. A review of the Sierra Club's mission statement illustrates the connection between nonprofit organizations and outdoor recreation:

> To explore, enjoy, and protect the wild places of the earth; to practice and promote the responsible use of the earth's ecosystems and resources; to educate and enlist humanity to protect and restore the quality of the natural and human environment; and to use all lawful means to carry out these objectives.[20]

Outdoor Recreation Today

Today, outdoor recreation opportunities are as important to Americans as they have ever been. Increasingly, recreation and public health professionals are lauding the benefits of natural settings for human mental and physical health. These so-importants available in parks contribute to healthy lifestyles, children who appreciate the natural world, and opportunities for all citizens to enjoy the great outdoors. In fact, First Lady Michelle Obama is leading the country's efforts to get kids outside and active with her Let's Move! initiative.

In the most general sense, outdoor recreation professionals need to know about managing outdoor resources, working with visitors, and techniques for ensuring the financial sustainability of outdoor areas. As you read about these topics, be aware that most jobs require specialized knowledge, skills, and abilities you will learn about later in the chapter.

Managing Outdoor Resources

With visitation to national park areas alone in 2011 nearing 279 million visits, not counting the millions of visits to other public lands across the nation, the science and practice of outdoor recreation management provide several job opportunities. How do we provide for the increasing use of recreational visitors and protect park and recreational resources for future generations?

Public lands, whether local, state, or federal, encompass various purposes and recreational opportunities. Much land allows for multiple activities, including hiking, camping, climbing, mountain biking, skiing, horseback riding, off-road vehicle use, fishing, and even hunting. Local and regional parks also may include organized sporting opportunities such as swimming, competitive field sports, and other activities. On the other end of the spectrum are lands set aside specifically for long-term protection, such as designated wilderness areas where only recreation activities compatible with the protection of these valuable resources are allowed.

© Photographerlondon| Dreamstime.com

With such a wealth of recreational opportunities, job opportunities remain abundant. Beyond the more obvious jobs of park ranger, recreation planner, and naturalist is a whole field of opportunities including law enforcement, search and rescue, resource management, education, hospitality, outdoor recreation leadership, wilderness education, biology, history, and interpretation. For example, enlightened public land management requires understanding the possible impacts of visitors on park resources and the social impacts that increased use will have on the visitors. Careers in both scientific and social research will continue to play a large role in public land management. In addition to the job opportunities just mentioned, many federal parks contract out concessions, so more jobs are located in national parks, but the park service does not administer them.

Working With Park Visitors

Most jobs in outdoor recreation involve working with visitors and outdoor recreationists. Even if the job entails indoor work, interaction with the people who visit the area is both inevitable and rewarding.

One key aspect to this job is providing information and environmental education so visitors can have a safe and rewarding experience. Many people coming to a park area, particularly a wilderness area, may face environmental conditions completely unlike what they face daily. Providing visitors the tools to have a safe and rewarding experience is an important part of any recreation professional's job. There are three key factors in providing protection and safety to visitors:

- **Protecting people from the resource:** Natural conditions, such as wild animals, rough trails, fast-flowing rivers, changing weather, or steep cliffs can pose dangers to visitors unaccustomed to such features.

- **Protecting the resource from human impact:** Similarly, some people think that taking fossils or plants, cutting trees, or even shooting wild animals is acceptable when there appears to be so much open land around. This, of course, is seldom the case.
- **Protecting people from people:** Unfortunately, even when on vacation in public lands, people still experience crime and altercations with other people. Making people aware of these possibilities, even in a tranquil-looking campground, is important.

To provide this protection to people and the resource, education and interpretation are the first tools outdoor recreation professional's use. The term *interpretation* can have different meanings. Although many people may think of it as language interpretation, in the environmental, cultural, and historical education context, the goal of all interpretive services is to increase each visitor's enjoyment and understanding of the parks and help visitors care about the parks on their own terms. With the diverse interests people bring with them on vacations and outdoor visits, the ability of an outdoor recreation employee to relate to these interests is critical.

> "The best part of my job is I do something different every day—wilderness patrols, front country law enforcement, searching for lost backpackers, high angle rescues, treating injured hikers, and fighting wildland fires.
>
> —Duane Poslusny, Protection Ranger Yosemite National Park

Interpretation may take the form of providing basic information at an entrance station; preparing effective interpretive signage and other media; giving prepared talks or presentations about the human and natural history of the area; teaching organized environmental education classes through public and private schools; and assuring that websites and other remote services provide enough advance information for people planning trips to outdoor areas. Because of the key role interpretation and education play, a range of careers specific to these professions is available. Nearly all land management agencies provide opportunities for environmental educational and interpretive careers. This can be one of the most rewarding jobs that outdoor recreation can provide and is a key tool of many park employees.

Planning, Financial Sustainability, and Partnerships

We generally help pay for outdoor recreation lands through our taxes and other means. Because of this, it is important that outdoor recreation employees understand the financial components of working with public resources. Funding for public land recreation programs comes from three main sources.

First, federal, state, and local taxes often support park and public recreational lands. Consequently, seeking and listening to public input into major land management decisions is important to a land manager.

Second, many individuals and private institutions often provide supporting funds for park and recreation programs. This can range from the small personal donation of a frequent park user to a nonprofit "friends of the parks" group, to the planned corporate sponsorship of a visitor center, recreation center, or other facility. Working with nonprofit and for-profit entities is an important part of any recreational management activity.

Third, fees can be an important aspect of park or recreation area finances. Though seldom if ever able to cover all costs, some state park agencies are able to cover a large portion of management costs. These fees range from visitor fees such as park entrance fees, to campground fees, to activity fees.

Because of the increasing costs agencies face in managing park areas and providing for recreational use, careful financial planning, in the context of overall planning activities, is essential.

For example, the NPS works with the nonprofit National Parks Conservation Association (NPCA) to provide jobs for recent MBA graduates. In exchange for scholarships from the NPCA, the NPS provides positions in park areas related to financial planning, budget, or other careers. As a consequence, many national parks have developed business plans that clearly show the expected funding sources, private revenue opportunities, and costs to effectively manage the area for public use over a period of time. Such financial management plans are only a part of the overall planning requirements that any public park or recreation land faces.

Most land management agencies at all levels work with defined partners to reach shared recreational and land management goals. Moreover, President Obama's America's Great Outdoors initiative encourages grassroots conservation efforts and emphasizes the importance of community engagement in the protection of our natural resources. This includes both in-kind assistance (e.g., organizing volunteer or other project work assistance in a park) and financial assistance for project or long-term management activities. These partners, often but not always nongovernmental organizations, can provide key assistance to recreational managers through their ability to attract financial resources and other support. Partners range from local "friends" groups that provide volunteers to staff local visitor centers, provide interpretive programs, or assist visitors in campgrounds; organized associations that run educational bookstores and other facilities in park areas; or groups such as the NPCA that provide students of outdoor recreation with career opportunities. Another important example is universities that work on a cooperative basis with agencies to provide scientific research, cooperative park study units, and other educational and management assistance.

Any career in recreation management will generally allow you to be involved with similar support and educational groups, without which the level of services in many areas would not be as easily possible. As public and private agencies face difficult future financial decisions and planning issues, the importance of such partnerships will only grow.

The management of outdoor recreation resources and visitor services clearly requires a dedicated and educated staff of permanent and seasonal employees as well as long-term planning efforts to ensure sustainability. Next, we will discuss how you can take your passion for the outdoors and match it with almost any job you can imagine.

Careers in Outdoor Recreation

Would you like a job in outdoor recreation? Think back to your assessment of your preferences, passions, and the qualities that describe you as a potential recreation professional. Do you want to make a difference? Are you willing to work when other people are on vacation? Do you like the idea of implementing sustainable solutions that help the environment? Is a career doing something you are passionate about important to you? Do you love outdoor adventure and adventure sports? How can you get a job working in a park or outdoor setting?

When people hear about a career in outdoor recreation, they typically think of a "park ranger," and in the past this would have been fairly accurate. Today, however, the need for financial and environmental sustainability, combined with the potential of partnerships that enhance the scope of influence for outdoor recreation enthusiasts, means good careers can be found in the public sector with government agencies, in the nonprofit sector with organizations dedicated to preservation and enjoyment, and with for-profit commercial organizations providing concessions and guiding others in outdoor recreation activities. We will talk about outdoor recreation careers in all three sectors, and you can also reference related chapters in this text for more information.

USFWS National Digital Library

Passions

Careers in outdoor recreation attract people with a keen interest in learning, playing, preserving, sharing, or simply being in the natural world. These careers encompass the broad world of natural and cultural resources management, land use planning and facility development, hospitality and tourism, adventure travel, environmental education, and similar careers. If your interest is in natural or cultural resources, look at careers such as park ranger, outdoor recreation planner, resource manager, interpreter, wilderness educator, or law enforcement officer. Jobs in these areas are found within governmental agencies at federal, state, and local levels. If you are interested in working at the local level, the job of city or community recreation planner or park employee may be for you. If you are interested in large space resource management, consider state and national government agencies.

If your passion is sharing the outdoors with youth, consider the nonprofit sector with a career such as camp director or counselor, outdoor educator, and even jobs working with at-risk youth through wilderness therapy (refer to Chapter 7). The nonprofit sector also includes opportunities with agencies such as The Trust for Public Land, a national nonprofit organization working to protect land as parks and open space whose mission is to "conserve land for people to enjoy as parks, gardens, and other natural places, ensuring livable communities for generations to come."[21]

Finally, if you are more interested in the commercial aspect of outdoor recreation, the career field opportunities are even broader. Work in the outdoor concessions industry includes commercial campgrounds, hotels, restaurants, golf courses, swim centers, ski areas, outdoor event centers, tours, and the large and vibrant world of tourism services that are located within many national, state, and local parks. Jobs are available in all aspects of outdoor recreation and travel and at all levels, from community based to international in scope.

Pay and Perks

In choosing a career focus, your financial goals and desires are important. If your goal is to get rich, then you should probably consider a different career area. Unless you become a high- level manager of a concession company or start your own successful outdoor business, then this is not a field in which many people become wealthy. However, you can be financially comfortable; have job security, excellent health care, and retirement; and enjoy opportunities for promotion, all while doing a job you love and believe in.

If your goal is to work for a public agency, positions start at minimum wage and advance to around $150,000 for the few high-level positions. Permanent full-time government jobs in outdoor recreation come with good insurance and retirement plan opportunities, and many agencies promote from within. Keep in mind that permanent positions are competitive. If your goal is to work in a nonprofit organization, you may start as a volunteer, move to an entry-level salary, and then advance to a salary comparable to corporate managers of smaller companies, especially if you have a strong track record with fund-raising. For-profit companies also range from minimum wage to corporate management salaries. As with any other job with a corporation, education and experience are keys to success.

Preparation

A successful career will demand specific knowledge, skills, and abilities. These abilities begin with general experience and education, becoming more specific and targeted as you move forward in a career. An entry-level park ranger job in a federal or state agency will require a high school diploma and basic life experiences that show an ability to work effectively with people. As you develop ranger skills, you may seek to move up and into a job with increased responsibilities and challenges, perhaps supervisor or technical specialist. This will often require a bachelor's or master's degree in areas such as recreation management, forestry, natural resources, communications, law enforcement, education, planning, business administration, hotel management, or biology. It will also require more work experiences. To prepare for such a career, look beyond the specific job to the bigger picture of how you would like your career to advance. An employer is often not looking just for a person skilled in a particular job, but one who can someday move beyond and contribute to the larger goals and responsibilities of the agency.

Possibilities

Hiring and career trends in outdoor recreation, park management, and related fields generally follow the trend of economic well-being or anxiety in the population. Outdoor recreation activities require a certain expenditure of time and money, often associated with a vacation and travel away from home. These activities can be adversely affected when the economy is down. Nonetheless, even in periods of economic unease, people often seek the outdoors for relief. After the tragic events of September 11, 2001, international travel plummeted, but travel to local park areas increased. Yosemite National Park noticed, at least anecdotally, an increase in day visitors to the park. The outdoors and park settings seemed to provide solace for many in a grieving nation.

In the field of outdoor recreation, we believe you can have a rewarding career and financial security. We will examine possibilities in each of the three major areas where outdoor recreation jobs are located today.

Government land management agencies. Government land management agencies involved in outdoor recreation are managed based on specific legislated governmental purposes, including the protection and preservation of particular resources, scientific research, or multiple uses including outdoor recreation. The purpose of many federal parks, public lands, and state and local parks is to conserve natural and cultural resources for long-term protection so they are available for generations to come. For instance, parks may have research, wilderness, or specific environmental protection objectives that may take precedence over recreation. In other instances, the primary purpose may be resource extraction (mining, oil exploration, timber) or other resource uses (grazing, hydroelectric). Or many public recreation areas include recreational activities such as boating, hunting, hiking, camping, skiing, snowmobiling, and off-road vehicle use. In areas with multiple users, interests and motivations may conflict, which results in interesting challenges for employees.

Passions. Conservation/environmental ethics, natural resources, historic preservation, extreme activity (firefighting, smoke-jumping, law enforcement, search and rescue), wild open spaces, physical challenge, being part of a team, public service, working with outdoor resources as well as visitors.

Pay and perks. Federal hourly wage pay scales apply to both seasonal/part-time and permanent full-time jobs. However, permanent positions often begin at a higher scale than seasonal positions and are usually tied to a career track of progressively higher wages over a defined period of time. State pay varies according to prevailing wage, as does pay in municipalities. Most agencies, at least for career positions, offer health coverage, pensions, and/or matching savings plans similar to 401(k) plans.

Preparation. For agency employment, although some professional jobs require a degree or other credentials (outdoor recreation, biologist, geologist, hydrologist, law enforcement, etc.), many entry-level jobs only require a high school diploma. However, most professional

USFWS and Recreational Boating and Fishing Foundation

career employees with federal and state agencies usually have a college degree, in subject areas such as park and recreation management, law enforcement, education, or one of the sciences.

Most entry-level jobs require a high school diploma and related experience. A 4-year college degree will also make the difference when competing for career positions, especially as you move up the career ladder. The U.S. government recommends the following degree fields for park and recreation management and natural resource management:

- fish and wildlife administration, general biological science, program analysis
- wildlife biology
- wildlife refuge management
- outdoor recreation planning
- forestry
- recreation management, and law enforcement (ranger)

The key to most agency jobs, at the federal, state, or local level, is experience. Education can substitute for experience and can get you in the door at a higher pay level. For example, many job announcements may require one of the following:

- 1 year general experience OR 2 years of education beyond high school with 6 semester hours of related coursework (includes most entry-level jobs, such as park aid, information desk, or ranger aid)
- 1 year of specialized experience OR 4 years of college leading to a bachelor's degree with 24 semester hours of natural science, social sciences, or recreation management (includes

more challenging jobs such as park ranger, education specialist, biological technician, or similar)

- 2 years experience in the aforementioned positions and education at the graduate level in an accredited college or university (meets the requirements for positions including professional level jobs such as supervisory ranger, biologist, or site manager)

Possibilities. Most agency jobs are open to everyone on a competitive basis. Broad opportunities are often available for seasonal and part-time employment. However, gaining a permanent career is more difficult, often requiring passing a written test, having previous governmental service (e.g., the military), or having relevant education (degrees or certifications).

At federal and state agencies, many employees begin in a seasonal or temporary position, usually while attending college. At the federal level, although jobs are always available to qualified applicants, entry into many permanent positions is often restricted to those currently employed with the government.

At state and federal levels, a career can often move from entry level to a supervisory position and eventually to a management position in charge of park planning, maintenance, recreation, and finances. However, many successful careers may be based on staying at one level of expertise and enjoyment without moving into management, including district ranger, public affairs officer, firefighter, or field research biologist.

Progression through a career, at least at the federal level, often occurs more rapidly if you are able to move to different parks and areas of the country. For example, you may work for several years at a park or wildlife refuge in California and then transfer with a promotion to an area in Michigan or Alaska. Although moving is not required to progress, promotions within one geographic area may be harder to accomplish.

Employment is available with numerous agencies at federal, state, and local levels. The Department of the Interior houses the NPS, Bureau of Land Management, U.S. Fish and Wildlife Service, and Bureau of Reclamation. The USFS is located in the Department of Agriculture, and the U.S. Army Corps of Engineers is under the auspices of the Department of Defense. These agencies manage the vast federal lands available for outdoor pursuits, and you can seek outdoor recreation and conservation related careers with each of them.

Every state has a department of natural resources, parks department, or similar agency. For the approximately 57,000 outdoor recreation jobs in all states, each state will have its own hiring procedures. Many of the jobs are similar to those in federal agencies. According to America's State Parks Foundation, more than 7,000 state park areas comprise over 14 million acres, with approximately 720 million visitors annually.[22]

Most cities of any size maintain a city parks and recreation department. County, municipal, and city parks provide a large operational base to begin a job and develop an outdoor recreation career. Park programs provide urban families with recreational programs, often directed at youth. (Local agency outdoor recreation career opportunities are covered here because they are similar to opportunities found at state and federal levels).

Nonprofit outdoor recreation agencies. These organizations, often called **nongovernmental organizations (NGOs)**, are numerous in the world of parks and recreation and have different objectives:

- supporting conservation agency objectives (National Park Foundation, The Trust for
- Public Land, The Nature Conservancy, Yosemite Association, etc.),
- providing conservation and recreation employment or training (The Student Conservation Association, Outward Bound, National Outdoor Leadership School, Leave No Trace, etc.), and
- encouraging lifestyle choices using outdoor recreation (Boy and Girl Scouts, YMCA/ YWCA, religious and spiritual youth organizations and camps, etc.; these human services nonprofits are discussed in Chapter 4).

© Shao-chun Wang | Dreamstime.com

These organizations hire both part- and full-time employees, from camp counselors, to recreational instructors, to professionals in planning, legal, and scientific endeavors. Work experience gained at NGOs often serves as a springboard to careers with a government conservation agency or for-profit company with similar objectives. They should not be overlooked in considering a career in outdoor recreation and parks. Consider the following to determine whether a career in an NGO is right for you.

Passions. Conservation/environmental ethics, natural and cultural resources, education, advocacy for a cause, politics, fund-raising, change the world.

Pay and perks. Beginning pay often is nothing, as these organizations attract many volunteers for little or no compensation (other than stipends for cost of living). However, all but the smallest have some paid staff, which can be substantial for the largest organizations. Depending on the size of the NGO, full-time staff employees can be paid comparable to starting salaries at agencies, though high-level management positions for the larger NGOs can be negotiated for comparable professional salaries similar to some for-profit companies. Many provide health and other financial benefits.

Preparation. Unless seeking particular business, legal, or scientific credentials—which many of the larger NGOs do seek—positions with most NGOs rely more on past experience than on positive educational requirements. There is often crossover between for-profit and nonprofit entities, so experiences gained in either can transfer. As with agency employees, most NGO volunteers and employees are well educated, at least in their field of interest. Career fields with NGOs often require experience or training in fund-raising, business, and supervision.

As with public agency careers, experience is as highly respected as education. Larger organizations that are national in scope may have regional offices with paid staff overseeing field projects, whereas smaller NGOs often have volunteers providing much of the support work of a small or limited staff.

The Truth About Career Possibilities in NGOs

Long careers with a single nonprofit organization are not as common as those with government conservation agencies. Some CEOs of nonprofits began with the organization when it was first formed, or were indeed involved in forming it, and stayed with it through a feeling of ownership. However, advancement in a career of nonprofit work will more likely occur if you work with different organizations through your career, even in fields of interest in which you did not begin.

Many people with careers in agencies, or with for-profit companies, often will be active as volunteers with a related nonprofit organization. Serving on the board of a related organization (if it is not a conflict of interest with your "day" job) can be tremendously rewarding for both personal satisfaction and career development.

Education is the key to higher level paid positions at larger nonprofits. Because nonprofits must actively seek funding, education and experience in business management or fund-raising are important. A funding or regional manager for a larger nonprofit may require a minimum of a bachelor's degree, 5 years direct experience, and demonstrated success in foundation and corporate fund-raising or marketing. Project leaders may require technical degrees in the sciences rather than business-related skills. As you move up the career ladder, the requirements for education and experience increase. For example, a project supervisor or crew leader may require a bachelor's in environmental education/science or a related field and 3 years of progressively responsible program management experience.

Possibilities. Possibilities are broad and varied but limited. NGOs operate at international, national, and local levels. Although all nonprofits have some staff to support their work, full-time positions are relatively limited and often volunteer in nature (except for the largest organizations). Also, positions are often office-based, indoor environments even for NGOs with park and recreation missions. Today, you can readily locate nonprofits related to your area of interest via the Internet. Once you locate the agency website, learning more about job and career options is relatively easy. The following are examples of agencies where you could seek a job or career with an NGO.

National Park Foundation. The National Park Foundation (NPF) was established by Congress to serve as the national charitable partner of the U.S. national parks. Its purpose is to "lead the national park cause by raising critical private support to directly aid national parks, playing a pivotal role in sustaining the work of the National Park Service, and expanding the community of supporters."[23]

The Student Conservation Association. The Student Conservation Association (SCA) is a leading conservation service organization for young people. Founded in 1957, SCA hires over 3,000 "conservation volunteers" annually to work on park and conservation programs in all 50 states. Many federal agencies and many states with recreational responsibilities use SCA's popular volunteer programs. Many SCA alumni go on to have careers with the NPS and other similar endeavors.

The Trust for Public Land. The Trust for Public Land (TPL) is an advocacy group that works to support the protection of lands for public recreational use and preservation. Working on a willing buyer–willing seller basis, TPL purchases properties of significant historical or natural qualities and then holds them until it finds an entity, often an agency, that can manage them for these causes.

The Nature Conservancy. The Nature Conservancy is a leading conservation organization that is committed to preservation and addressing threats to conservation. They work around the world to protect ecologically important lands and waters for nature and people. The focus of their work is to "preserve the animals, plants and natural communities that represent the diversity of life on Earth—by protecting the lands and waters they need to survive."[24]

Sierra Club. The Sierra Club, founded in 1892, is America's oldest grassroots environmental organization that is committed to helping people explore, enjoy, and protect the planet. Each state has a local chapter, and each has numerous goals including safeguarding communities, clean energy solutions, green transportation, and resilient habitats.

National Outdoor Leadership School. The National Outdoor Leadership School (NOLS), established by Paul Petzoldt in 1965, teaches leadership and wilderness skills. Students of all ages participate in NOLS courses in outdoor settings while pursuing diverse outdoor recreation activities. NOLS courses emphasize leadership development that transfers to outdoor and nonoutdoor leadership and life roles.

For-profit commercial outdoor recreation businesses. Few park or recreation areas operate without the support of or coexistence with businesses directly related to the provision of recreation activities. One example familiar to all people is food vendors at organized sporting events. However, the world of park concession management provides great opportunities for those business-oriented careerists with an underlying support and love for recreation, travel, or conservation objectives. Career opportunities exist in areas such as lodges, food and beverage services, campgrounds, guided backcountry trips, ski areas, extreme sports, and climbing/rafting schools. Some employees in these businesses either came to them initially because of a love for the outdoors and recreational pursuits or gravitated to them after a time spent working in other similar recreational endeavors. This is an excellent opportunity to mix a passion for business with a love of the outdoors and recreation.

For-profit businesses are competitive by nature and intent. Consequently, they are always seeking talented, educated people to pursue a career with them. Within the outdoor recreation field, for-profits operate lodging, campgrounds, food services, and specialized tours such as white-water rafting, fishing, and camping. Is a career in a for-profit outdoor recreation–related business for you?

How to Prepare for a Career With a For-Profit Commercial Outdoor Recreation Business

The key is to understand that many permanent or management employees often started their careers with a company in entry-level positions and were then promoted from within. Fortunately, the availability of seasonal and entry-level jobs is great, and few require education requirements other than a high school diploma. These positions are often seasonal, but they can be a springboard for beginning a career or gaining permanent employment. Higher level permanent jobs almost always have additional educational requirements. Qualified candidates for food and beverage positions must have at least 2 or 3 years of supervisory experience in a food and beverage environment. Most full-time positions will also require a degree in a related field.

Passions. Business, financial, entrepreneur, competition, travel, reward/risk, unique work environment, customer service, belief in the power of capitalism, in addition to a love of outdoor recreation.

Pay and perks. Minimum wage to "name your price." Concession operations in park and recreation areas have job experiences similar to businesses in any small city (food and beverage, hotel, bookkeeping, computer technology, labor, management, etc.). Pay at most levels will reflect local community salaries in comparable positions. Lower level management positions, such as hotel manager, campground manager, and the like, will also pay comparable salaries of similar non-recreation services. However, other benefits may include room/board compensation based on remote locations. Higher management level jobs are similar to any business, may be negotiable, and are often higher than a comparable management position in an agency.

Preparation. An MBA can be a gold-star education for these positions, and it will help support your quest for higher salaries. At the 4-year college level, courses in marketing, business, recreation, hospitality, and finance degrees can provide an entrée to this world, although few entry-level positions have education requirements beyond a high school diploma. Gaining education and experience in your particular interest in the parks and recreation field and then applying this to the corporate world of a recreation-oriented business can be useful in addition to pursuing general financial or business experience. Gaining experience through seasonal or part-time work can be helpful in competing for permanent positions in companies.

Possibilities. The possibilities are unlimited. With the growth of outdoor recreation and tourism, an expanding number of companies and concession operators cater to the park and recreation environment.

Delaware North Companies Parks and Resorts, Xanterra Parks and Resorts, and Aramark are major concessionaires operating within many federal, state, and local parks and outdoor recreation areas. They operate some of the largest concession operations in places such as Yellowstone, Grand Canyon, and Yosemite National Parks. These are but three examples of hundreds of similar concessionaires, large and small, operating in public park and outdoor recreation areas. See www.concessions.nps.gov for a more complete listing.

Commercial outfitters and guides offer their clients guided experiences such as camping, hiking, horseback riding, hunting, fishing, and rafting. Although many of these companies are sole proprietorships with modest job potential, nearly all hire staff to carry out their often seasonal guide work. Working a season or two with one that meets your interests would be helpful if you were considering starting your own business or were not ready or interested in the formalities of a large agency, NGO, or business.

Summary of Outdoor Recreation Career Possibilities

Career	Passions	Pay and Perks	Preparations	Possibilities
Conservation agency	Public service	Minimum wage to professional salary	Positive educational requirements in many jobs	Competitive, permanent positions are more difficult to get
Nonprofit organizations	Change the world	$0 to ? professional and corporate comparable	Positive educational requirements in some jobs, experience is most important	Various opportunities at the lower levels, permanent positions are relatively few
For-profit companies	Power of capitalism	Minimum wage to corporate management	Positive educational requirements in some jobs, experience is most important	Unlimited

“ I never imagined that with a degree in psychology and a passion for sports, I would end up traveling the world as a whitewater riversurfing guide for ten years. But after college, I decided for once in my life to live without a clear destination and see where my interests and opportunities took me. So instead of taking up a scholarship for graduate school in Cambridge, I accepted an opportunity to play in an Australian soccer competition. Then stopped in New Zealand, and despite feeling lost and alone, took the chance to travel and try new outdoor adventure activities. Those 'uncharted' choices led me to Queenstown, where I took a three-day whitewater riversurfing guide course. I had no experience and was so scared. But I asked myself two things: 'What's the worst that could happen? (I quit and 'fail') Will I regret this if I don't try? (Yes!).'

After three days on an all-male course, the owner said he doubted I would ever be a guide. But another guide encouraged me to keep at it and slowly my confidence and skills grew. Not only did I eventually become a guide, I ended up running operations, training other guides, consulting, and helping draft new adventure tourism industry guidelines. Although this was not the path I envisioned, it has enriched me personally and professionally. I learned how to mentally overcome fear and try things that seemed impossible. Although life as a seasonal guide is difficult in many ways (physically, financially, mentally), the perspective it gives you will enrich every aspect of your life. So go in with your eyes open, be prepared to work hard, and ask yourself, 'What's the worst that could happen? Will I regret this if I don't try?'

—Susan Houge Mackenzie, Assistant Professor
at California Polytechnic State University, San Luis Obispo ”

Future Opportunities, Issues, and Challenges

The demand for outdoor recreational uses will probably always exist. Year to year visitation statistics may ebb and flow, but over the past 50 years, they have generally showed a steady trend upwards. Although this trend may shift in the future, in particular during stressful economic times, the human population will certainly continue to grow. Consequently, career opportunities in outdoor recreation will more than likely remain viable. Several key factors will, as always, determine job opportunities.

Funding

Because funds from taxes are a large part of financial support for public recreational land management and preservation, public financial status can significantly impact jobs. For example, during the recession that began in 2009, the state of California considered closing some state parklands until the financial picture improved, and this occurred again in 2012 due to federal budget uncertainties. This obviously seriously impacted careers and jobs within state parks. Similar financial problems can manifest themselves in any publicly supported endeavor. Following and understanding the political process in developing a public budget is important when considering at future career opportunities.

> Funding issues continue to be a challenge, and following the money usually shows where the employment opportunities lie. For example, federal money to support stormwater management has created several new jobs within parks to manage riparian and wetland areas. The public sector has shifted from relying solely on tax funding to pursuing grant monies and public–private partnerships. And, in other cities, routine maintenance duties (e.g., restroom maintenance and garbage/litter pickup) are now contracted out to the lowest bidder. Although this may save money for the municipality, it creates a lower class of employees (and taxpayers!) and forces remaining city employees to be contract administrators.
>
> —Ginny Alfriend, Park Specialist IV,
> City of Eugene Parks and Open Space, Oregon

Population

The 2010 U.S. census provides key data for predicting regional and national growth, financial status, and other important information to chart possible growth areas. An increasing population, especially concentrated in larger and congested cities, will probably continue to seek relief from these conditions through open space or other outdoor recreational endeavors, if the past is any guide.

Environmental factors

As more is learned about global climate change, animal populations, pollution, and other environmental indicators, recreation patterns may change. For example, off-road vehicle use, allowed in many areas, may change either by restricting such use in some areas or by evolving the use to less impacting technologies. Similarly, hunting or fishing patterns most likely will change as streams and watersheds are further impacted or restored.

Education

Education about the environment and the outdoors, from grade school through college, and in everyday life, will play a critical role in how people relate to their environment. Keeping environmental and outdoor education topics alive in the classroom is instrumental to providing the interest of future generations to take advantage of outdoor use and recreation. This in itself offers possible education and teaching career opportunities. By keeping attuned to these issues, you will better understand how future outdoor recreation opportunities will evolve.

Technology

As people from all walks of life become more "connected" and rely on technology for everyday activities, cell phones, GPS units, the Internet, destination-specific applications, and a host of other technological advances will increasingly be present in parks, wilderness areas, and other natural areas. Future professionals will need to adapt to the changing use patterns and desires of outdoor recreationists, maintaining a balance in programming and services that allows for the conveniences afforded by technology and encourages people to "disconnect" to experience the true benefits of outdoor recreation.

Resources and Getting Involved

The Internet is a major tool for investigating career opportunities. Many websites related to parks and outdoor recreation were cited earlier in the chapter under Possibilities. However, you should be aware of a few more organizations as you prepare for your future career.

Professional Organizations
Natural Resources Defense Council (International): www.nrdc.org
"NRDC is the nation's most effective environmental action organization. We use law, science, and the support of 1.2 million members and online activists to protect the planet's wildlife and wild places and to ensure a safe and healthy environment for all living things."

Conservation International (International): www.conservation.org
"A U.S.-based, international organization, Conservation International (CI)...applies innovations in science, economics, policy, and community participation to protect the Earth's richest regions of plant and animal diversity in the biodiversity hotspots, high-biodiversity wilderness areas as well as important marine regions around the globe. With headquarters in Washington, D.C., CI works in more than 40 countries on four continents."

National Parks and Conservation Association (National): www.npca.org
This 85-year-old NGO is a key advocate for the national parks, and sometimes the strongest critic of the National Park Service. Headquarters in Washington, DC, with regional offices throughout the country.

Bay Area Ridge Trail Council (Local): www.ridgetrail.org
This organization is attempting to complete a 300-mile public trail that circumnavigates the San Francisco Bay area. It works "in close partnership with local governments, public agencies, nonprofit land trusts, and local grassroots activists in the nine counties of the Bay Area to complete the Ridge Trail."

Association of National Park Rangers (National): www.anpr.org
Organization founded by national park rangers, "created to communicate for, about and with National Park Service employees." Publishes quarterly magazine Ranger for all members.

International Ranger Federation (International): www.int-ranger.net
A federation of ranger associations from over 50 countries. Holds a World Ranger Congress every 3 years in a different country. Seventh Congress held in 2012 in Tanzania. Headquarters in the United Kingdom.

Washington [State] Outfitters and Guides Association: www.woga.org
This association bills itself as "the only industry organization in Washington that represents outfitters, sport-fishing guides, horse and llama packers, white-water rafters, hunting guides, and other outdoor professionals who supply 'outfitted services' to the recreational public in our state." It is an excellent source to seek out companies, who are members, that provide these activities. New York, Oregon, and many other states have similar organizations that can provide an easy way to research similar opportunities across the country.

America Outdoors: www.americaoutdoors.org
"America Outdoors is an international association representing the world's finest active travel outfitters, tour companies and outdoor educators."

National Association for Interpretation: www.interpnet.com
Members of the National Association for Interpretation serve in educational positions in areas such as parks, recreation areas, museums, zoos, botanical gardens, and historical and cultural sites. These professionals and docents interpret cultural and natural resources for visitors to these areas.

National Recreation and Park Association: www.nrpa.org
The "National Recreation and Park Association (NRPA) is the leading advocacy organization dedicated to the advancement of public parks, recreation and conservation." This organization is the primary professional organization for nearly 40,000 park and recreation professionals and citizen volunteers nationwide.

Certifications/Licenses

There are not any particular certifications needed to work in the NPS or any other public lands agencies. However, the National Association for Interpretation (NAI) offers six certifications including: Certified Interpretive Manager, Certified Interpretive Planner, Certified Heritage Interpreter, Certified Interpretive Trainer, Certified Interpretive Guide, and Certified Interpretive Host. See www.interpnet.com/ for more information.

Within land management agencies, you can expect to find required training and certifications related to certain positions, such as firefighting, law enforcement, park dispatch, and so on. Some companies may require, or recommend, certification or licenses for outdoor guides depending on regulations and training available in a particular region. Also, you may want to check out the Eppley Institute for Parks and Public Lands at Indiana University, which offers courses to the public for those interested in educational opportunities related to outdoor recreation and interpretation. Many of the courses are free of charge. Visit eppley.org for more information.

Where to Gain Experience

Because of the nature of park, recreation, or tourism work, many opportunities exist for seasonal (often summer) or part-time work. Working during the summer at a job that strikes your interest is an excellent way to see whether you like what you think you are interested in and builds work experience that will significantly help you to obtain a full-time job after school.

Always look for and consider opportunities to enter an internship program while attending school. Internships allow you to add experience and skills to a comparable field of study. Some offer opportunities to begin a full-time job after graduation. Federal agencies have several programs.

For example, The Student Conservation Association (SCA) has postings for internships and employment, and its goal is to provide college- and high school-aged members with hands-on conservation service opportunities in virtually every area of outdoor recreation. Their goal is to prepare the next generation of conservation leaders. See the SCA website (www.thesca.org) for more information.

USAJobs.gov is the official job site for the U.S. federal government. The Student Educational Employment program offers access to work experiences directly related to your academic field of study, and you may be eligible for permanent employment after successfully completing your education and meeting work requirements.

You can apply for an internship through one of these programs, but you can also often apply directly to any agency or company where you are interested in working. Many state and local agencies and NGOs also have special internships that are supported by a grantee seeking a particular outcome, such as having underrepresented groups employed in outdoor recreation.

Many for-profit companies also seek students for entry-level positions in which they can groom qualified employees for careers within their company. See the concessionaires' websites earlier in the chapter under Possibilities.

Additional Online Resources

Coolworks: www.coolworks.com

This "cool" website, which bills itself as helping to find "thousands of jobs in great places," can help you find a seasonal job or career in some of the greatest places on earth. Get a summer job in Yellowstone, Yosemite, or another national park.

OutdoorIndustryJobs.com: www.outdoorindustryjobs.com

This website provides links to outdoor jobs and careers in the outdoors, bicycle, action sports, fitness, hunting and shooting, fishing, and snow sports industries.

Conclusion

This section has provided a brief introduction to the career opportunities in parks and recreation. If you have read this far, you appear to have the prime requirement for any successful career—interest!

Go back to the start of the chapter and review the Focus Questions and review your passions and preferences from Chapter 2. If you have not spent much time in a park or recreation venue, go now. While there, watch the people working there who match up with the jobs that interest you. Can you see yourself in that ranger uniform/guide raft/visitor center/lodge front desk? If so, talk to them. Ask them what they think about their jobs. Write down what they say, and give it serious thought.

Next, look around the location where they are working. Are a lot of people around? How do they interact with these people? Would you like working with and talking to these visitors or coworkers on a daily basis?

More important, you can have the experiences of a lifetime and live in some of the most unique real estate in the country. Old Faithful geyser in Yellowstone is fun to watch as you drive through on a 2-week vacation. Living at Old Faithful in the winter, skiing along the Firehole River on a moonlit night, and hearing wolves howl outside your cabin cannot be matched.

Study, plan, and think about your career. It is your future. But at some point, you will just have to get out there. In the words of retired Yellowstone park superintendent Bob Barbee, "If you look too closely at a crystal ball, you wind up with glass in your mouth." Good luck! Hope to see you on the trail some day!

For Further Investigation

For More Research

1. **Implement:** Before the school year ends, you need to test your dreams. Is there a reasonable opportunity to get a job in your area of interest? Is the beginning (and future) pay enough?

   Choose one each from each type of organization covered under Possibilities: (a) government conservation agencies, (b) nonprofit organizations, and (c) for-profit companies. Through phone, through e-mail, or preferably in person, contact each group. Ask about seasonal job opportunities, the types of job, locations, and salaries. Then apply for a job. Even if you are not completely sure, or even if the chances appear slim, by applying for a job, you will be forced to seriously think about the work and the pay. And if you succeed in getting a summer or part-time job, you will be provided with an easy way to seriously test your interests and passions for such a career.

2. **Investigate:** On the next rainy/snowy/windy day, when you do not want to go outside, pick a website from the discussion of nonprofit organizations. Look at the website for a few minutes, and then contact the organization either by phone, by e-mail, or preferably in person. (Note. You may also do the same thing for a local organization that interests you). Ask them the following:
   a. How do you primarily fulfill your mission? With whom do you primarily work in doing this?
   b. Do you advocate for change? Discuss what they advocate for and how they do it. follow-up?
   c. Explain your career interests or ideas. Do they have suggestions for you on which to follow-up?
   d. Ask to set up a meeting with the executive director or another employee for a more in-depth informational interview. Buy him or her a cup of coffee and discuss what the job entails.

Active Investigation

Now that you have finished this chapter, make use of what you have learned. Take action and set goals. Here are a few suggestions:

Explore: This week, take an overnight trip with a friend to a nearby park or spend the day in a park. If you have time to visit a park, either camp or stay in a park lodge. Play like a tourist:
- Take a guided tour.
- Eat in a restaurant.
- Visit a state park and take a self-guided tour, using the provided interpretation (signs) to learn about the area.
- Get a trail map and go for a hike.
- Ask for information or directions.
- Take a friend or younger sibling to a park and practice your tour guiding skills. Teach them about the history of state and local parks or build their environmental awareness.
- Talk with a park or lodge employee about their job (see the informational interview activity in Chapter 2 for suggestions).

- Watch any of the PBS series *The National Parks: American's Best Idea*.
- Explore a map of the land surrounding your campus and learn who manages it.

When you return home, review the Focus Questions at the start of the chapter. Did your overnight stay or day in a park help you to answer some of these questions? How? Write down your thoughts. Then write down brief answers to the following questions:

a. Would you want to do what some of the people you met did? Why or why not?
b. Think of what you and your friend did and how you interacted on your trip with the people you met. If you were an employee in the park or lodge you visited, would you have wanted to play host to yourself (e.g., answered your questions, helped you find the trail, served you dinner)? Why or why not?

Recommended Reading

These are key environmental and conservation books that continue to greatly impact the establishment of parks and the beginning of recreation.

Leopold, A. (1949). *A Sand County almanac*. New York, NY: Random House.
Leopold's book contains a classic collection of conservation essays that greatly influenced th establishment of wilderness areas and modern game management.

Udall, S. L. (1963). *The quiet crisis*. New York: HarperCollins.
Ex-assistant secretary for the U.S. Department of the Interior writes about the history of a conservation land ethic of the United States, and thoughts on the future.

Tilden, F. (1951). *The national parks: What they mean to you*. New York, NY: Alfred A. Knoff.
The classic book on the national parks and what they mean to all of us. Also, by the same author, *Interpreting our Heritage* (1957) is the "bible" for environmental interpretation.

Sax, J. L. (1980). *Mountains without handrails*. Ann Arbor: University of Michigan Press.
Professor of law, writer, and thinker, Sax focuses on the political and emotional battles regarding recreation, wilderness, and the preservation of America's parks.

Abbey, E. (1968). *Desert solitaire*. New York: Random House.
Gonzo journalism about the national parks and governmental policies in the management of the national parks and the western public lands, particularly in the desert and canyon country of Utah and Arizona.

Pinchot, G. (1947). *Breaking new ground*. Washington, DC: Island Press.
Autobiography of the founder of the U.S. Forest Service, and of forestry management in America, with a contemporary perspective of the early 20th century conservation movement.

Recent Writings

Much has been written since the beginning of the modern environmental movement in the late 1960s. Below are just a few of the thousands of appropriate readings.

Bytnar, B. W. (2010). *A park ranger's life: Thirty-two years protecting our National Parks*. Tuscon, AZ: Wheatmark.
Bytnar provides a glimpse of a ranger's career and experiences.

Lankford, A. (2010). *Ranger confidential: Living, working, and dying in the national parks*. Guilford, CT: FalconGuides.
Lankford shares true stories about her career with the National Park Service.

Smith, J. F. (2006). *Nature noir: A park ranger's patrol in the High Sierra.* New York, NY: Houghton Mifflin Publishing Company.
A California state park ranger reflects on his job and on the meaning of park lands to the American public.

Sellars, R. W. (1997). *Preserving nature in the national parks: A history.* Boston, MA: Yale University Press.
Sellars, a historian with the Park Service, shows how the Park Service has, throughout its existence, allowed the preservation of endangered species and habitats to be governed by politics. His book discusses the NPS's conundrum between traditional tourism management and growing ecological concerns.

References

[1] The Forest History Society. (n.d.). Gifford Pinchot (1865–1946). Retrieved from http://www.foresthistory. org/ASPNET/people/Pinchot/Pinchot.aspx

[2] McLean, D. D., & Hurd, A. R. (in press). *Kraus' recreation and leisure in modern society* (10th ed.). Sudbury, MA: Jones and Bartlett Learning.

[3] National Park Service. (n.d.). Theodore Roosevelt and the National Park system. Retrieved from http://www.nps.gov/history/history/hisnps/NPSHistory/teddy.htm

[4] Central Park Conservancy. (n.d.). The history of Central Park. Retrieved from http://www.centralparknyc. org/visit/history/

[5] Ibid.

[6] National Park Service. (n.d.). *The Emerald Necklace: Boston's green connection* (Teaching With Historic Places Lessons Plans). Retrieved from http://www.nps.gov/history/nr/twhp/wwwlps/lessons/86bostonparks/86bostonparks.htm, para. 1.

[7] Central Park Conservancy, n.d.

[8] McClelland, L. F. (1998). *Building the national parks: Historic landscape design and construction.* Baltimore, MD: Johns Hopkins University Press, p. 41.

[9] National Park Service. (2006). *Management policies 2006.* Washington, DC: U.S. Government Printing Office.

[10] Ibid.

[11] Public Broadcasting Service. (n.d.). About the series. Retrieved October 2, 2009, from http://www.pbs. org/nationalparks/about/, para. 1.

[12] Cramton, L. C. (1932). *The early history of Yellowstone National Park.* Retrieved from National Park Service website: http://www.nps.gov/history/history/online_books/yell/cramton/letter.htm

[13] Ibid, para. 3.

[14] Ibid, para. 15.

[15] National Park Service, 2006, p. 10.

[16] Ibid, p. 11.

[17] U.S. Forest Service. (n.d.). History. Retrieved October 2, 2009, from http://www.fs.fed.us/aboutus/history/

[18] Ibid.

[19] Sontag, W. H. (Ed.). (1990). *National Park Service: The first 75 years.* Philadelphia, PA: Eastern National Park and Monument Association

[20] Sierra Club. (n.d). Sierra Club policies: Mission statement. Retrieved from http://www.sierraclub.org/policy/

[21] The Trust for Public Land. (2009). The Trust for Public Land: Mission statement. Retrieved September 27, 2013, from http://www.tpl.org/about/mission/

[22] America's State Parks Foundation. (2013). Help support the America's State Parks Foundation. Retrieved from http://www.americasstateparks.org/

[23] National Park Foundation. (2014). New look. Same great mission. Retrieved from http://www.nationalparks. org/connect/blog/new-look-same-great-mission

[24] The Nature Conservancy. (2014). Where we work. Retrieved from http://www.nature.org/ourinitiatives/regions/

"

The master in the art of living makes little distinction between his work and his play, his labor and his leisure, his mind and his body, his information and his recreation, his love and his religion. He hardly knows which is which. He simply pursues his vision of excellence at whatever he does, leaving others to decide whether he is working or playing. To him he's always doing both.

—James Michener "

7

Recreational Therapy and Therapeutic Recreation

Richard Williams
East Carolina University

Thomas K. Skalko
East Carolina University

Focus Questions

Q: Are you interested in devoting your professional life to using recreation-based activities as a means of treatment or to help improve the health and quality of life for people with disabilities?

A: Students who choose to major in recreational therapy (RT) have often discovered in their own lives that recreational activities are not only fun but also beneficial in many ways. Through a range of activities, children and adults alike develop physical skills, learn to interact with others, improve decision making, and learn a host of other everyday functional skills. Having experienced these benefits, students often have an interest in a career that uses recreation and other activities as a means to help people with illnesses and disabilities improve functioning, health, and quality of life.

Q: Do you have a background in sports, art, music, dance, theater, or another activity that you can use to develop skills and share with others?

A: Recreational therapists use recreation-related skills they already have to develop and implement programs that have positive outcomes for people with illnesses or disabilities. For instance, if you are an accomplished skier, you may engage an individual with a physical disability in skiing as a means to develop balance, coordination, and engagement in community life. Perhaps you have a background in dance. You may use that expertise to help others improve their abilities in that activity or improve cardiovascular functioning.

Q: Are you interested in the challenge of being a part of continuous improvement in a young and growing allied health profession?

A: According to the U.S. Department of Labor, RT is listed among a host of allied health professions. Although a relatively new profession, RT continues to grow and change in exciting ways. Young professionals entering the field have immediate opportunities to shape its future.

Q: Where would you like to work? In health care at a hospital or rehabilitation center? Or perhaps in a community setting such as a parks and recreation department or school?

A: Recreational therapists may be found in settings that serve people with illnesses and/or disabilities. Some people prefer to provide clinical services in a medical setting such as a hospital, and others choose community-based settings such as group homes, schools, and public parks and recreation departments. The opportunity to work across settings is endless.

Key Terms

Recreational therapy
Leisure focused
Therapeutic recreation specialist
Recreational therapist
Clinical outcomes
Leisure ability model
Health protection/health promotion model

Recreation service model
International Classification of Functioning,
    Disability, and Health
Third parties
Evidence-based practice
Standards of practice

Profile 1: Could This Be You?

Debbie Robinson, MS, CTRS/L, FACHE, is a recreational therapist with a specialty certification in behavioral health who works at New Hampshire Hospital in Concord, New Hampshire. After graduating from the University of Florida, Debbie worked in adult inpatient psychiatry in Jacksonville, Florida, and then moved to the northeast. Debbie began her years at New Hampshire Hospital as a recreational therapist on an extended care unit, then moved to a supervisory position, and is now the director of the Rehabilitation Department. In her current position, Debbie is responsible for recreational therapy, occupational therapy, physical therapy, vocational therapy, and volunteer services.

New Hampshire Hospital is a 158-bed state psychiatric hospital that serves children, adolescents, adults, and seniors. Recreational therapists are responsible for implementing evidence-based practices that enhance quality of life for patients and aid in their recovery to return to community living. We recently spoke to Debbie about her job.

Q: What goals do you have for your clients and how do you help them achieve them.

A: Nearly ninety percent of patients at New Hampshire Hospital are involuntarily admitted because they pose a danger to themselves or others. Individuals arrive scared, confused, angry, and very often exhibiting out-of-control behaviors. Our initial efforts are focused on establishing rapport and reinforcing that they are safe and that we can help. Goals for treatment are individualized, based on the symptoms each patient experiences. We teach social skills, coping skills, relaxation, stress management, anger management, and creative expression. In addition, we provide individual and group treatments that focus on acquiring recreational skills for positive use of free time after discharge.

Q: What is the most challenging aspect of your job?

A: Years ago it was common for patients to stay at the hospital as long as they needed treatment. Now, with mounting pressures from insurance companies and managed care, patients are often leaving within 5 to 7 days, and that may not be enough time for symptoms to fully resolve or for medication to take full effect. The focus is on treatment in the community, which is certainly preferred, but in situations when the community services aren't adequate, we see patients coming back into the hospital rapidly.

Q: Tell us about a memorable experience you had with a client.

A: I worked for years with a highly educated woman who had bipolar disorder. Because of the effects of her symptoms, she never got to be a professional person and that was difficult for her. She struggled with interpersonal effectiveness and managing her distress. We engaged in a variety of group and individual treatment over the years, focused on recognizing impending manic symptoms and making choices that would prevent full-blown mania from beginning so that she could take action and avoid repeat hospitalizations. Because of my rapport with her, I was chosen to accompany her to a family funeral out of state and be part of her support team for getting through that terrible loss. I am constantly grateful for the lessons she taught me.

Profile 2: Could This Be You?

Al Kaye is a recreational therapist who works at the Patricia Neal Rehabilitation Center (PNRC) in Knoxville, Tennessee. After graduating with a master's degree in recreational therapy, Al began working in a physical rehabilitation unit specializing in brain and spinal injury. The PNRC is the largest inpatient rehabilitation center with 73 beds within a hospital in the United States and among the top 3% of all CARF-accredited facilities by holding 15 accreditations. PNRC focuses on helping people of all ages with stroke, brain, spinal, or orthopedic injuries and a variety of other neurological impairments.

Recreational Therapy Services at PNRC provides services across the continuum of care to include initial rehabilitation soon after a traumatic event to transition back into the community. The recreational therapy staff works in a programmatic model affiliated to specific diagnostic teams of interdisciplinary health care professionals. Recreational Therapy Services developed a national award-winning education and awareness program known as the Innovative Recreation Cooperative (IRC) for persons with disabilities and their families to transition back into life through adaptive sports and recreation. Overall, the recreational therapy staff is dedicated to rehabilitating individuals to rebuild lives. We recently spoke to Al to ask about his job.

Q: What goals do you have for clients, and how do you help them achieve them?

A: When we first meet patients, they are transitioning through traumatic events in their lives. No one asked to be compromised by a life-changing event such as a stroke, amputation, brain, or spinal injury. One moment they are fine and the next they are hospitalized, often fighting for their lives on a touch-and-go basis. Once medically stable, they have options for their recovery process, and physical rehabilitation is an option. Recreational therapy within physical rehabilitation is an elective service for recovery.

Our goal is to return people to as close a level of functioning as they were previously. Thus, on the acute side of rehabilitation, we assess the patient's premorbid lifestyle and level of involvement as well as assess their current level of functioning. As a recreational therapist, I look at the whole person and his or her abilities in a realistic here-and-now environment. This encompasses a review of basically four domains—physical, behavioral, cognitive, and spiritual functioning—often reflected in the individual's lifestyle. The basic goal for acute rehabilitation is to get the patient home in as independent and manageable status as we have time allotted by the insurance company. We are charged to help reduce the burden of care on the individual from a financial accountability and on the humanistic side help patients adjust to their current situations to take care for basic needs as they will transition into the next level of continued therapy, usually on an outpatient basis.

Outpatient treatment works on goals to improve the quality of life for the patient with the goal of still reducing the burden of care of their disabling condition upon their life. The IRC program we created helps people transition into community settings, such as their homes, by educating them on what they can still do and enjoy what life has to offer.

Life is about constant change. Often we cannot control change but have to deal with it. We challenge patients and their support networks to live with the change in a positive way.

Q: What is the most challenging aspect of your job?

A: Other than dealing with the challenges of health care financing, the most difficult part of my job has to do with reality checks for the patient. Often it has to do with the human spirit and keeping a person moving forward in a positive direction. We have patients measure progress sometimes by inches vs. yards…as long as we can keep their perspective on moving forward. It is like trying to ride a bike up a steep hill. We don't look at the top because it can be frightening, but we duck our head and look right in front of our front tire until the next thing we know, we have reached the top. We celebrate the little as well as major achievements, as life is also about celebrating.

The trick is to convey to the patient the importance of focusing on the here and now. I might say to a patient, "You currently are not walking, so let's work on wheelchair skills until we see changes in your legs as you have to be able to get around so you can get home. If we see some progress, we will work with what we see to help you with your goal, but for now let's work on getting from point A to B the best way we can and hope for some return."

Q: Tell me about a memorable experience you had with a client.

A: I have been blessed to have impacted many lives. I guess one of my most memorable experiences was with an 18-year-old senior in high school who got a spinal injury from a motorcycle accident. He was on his family property with friends, and they challenged him to jump a small stream on his motorcycle. He made the jump but crashed on the other side, breaking his back and suffering a mild brain injury. He would never walk again without significant bracing assistance but would be able to gain normal functioning from his brain injury.

I worked with him through rehab and adjustment back into life. If he wanted to try something, I explored options for him and modified equipment so he had the resources he would need. I watched him get back to social life with dating, completing college, getting married, and having a family all from a wheelchair as a spinal injured survivor. He now works like everyone else, but through all of his time, I have been able to help him find a passion in his life outside of his family. He is a wheelchair road racer. He found his niche, and through it, he has become one of the top

20 road racers in the U.S. He travels all over the U.S. and has been to Asia and South America racing. In 2007, he was on the U.S. team at the Pan Am games and was on the wheelchair 4 x 100 team that won gold and broke the current U.S. record for time. He is now 31 and trying to make the U.S. Paralympic team for Brazil.

Matthew Porterfield, wheelchair racer

What is neat about this story is that he gives back. He is a mentor for our IRC program in road racing, meaning that he will help teach others how to achieve the things that he has achieved in his life. He is a model of excellence in my eye as he not only overcame his traumatic life-changing event but continues to help others overcome theirs. He talks to high school kids about life decisions and safety, he does fund-raising for various charities in the community, travels to about 15–20 races a year for competition, helps run a family business, and has a great family. He truly is a model of what rehabilitation may do to help get a person back into life.

What Is Recreational Therapy?

When asked, recreational therapists echo Cameron's and Al's sentiments about why they became recreational therapists: They make positive differences in people's lives. These positive changes do not happen randomly. Rather, they are the result of systematic planning and implementing a therapeutic process known as recreational therapy that takes advantage of the benefits of recreation activities.

One terrific aspect about recreation is that it is good for you physically, psychologically, and socially, and people are inclined to participate in their treatment because it is enjoyable. Take soccer. Although you may never earn a penny playing soccer, you certainly receive physical benefits through cardiovascular health and endurance. Success may lead to improved self-confidence, and if you become an avid soccer player, you may start to identify as an athlete, thus promoting a healthy self-image. Soccer, which is normally played with others, leads to friendships and social support.

Another example is tai chi (or yoga). If you were working in an assisted living facility, and if, through your assessment, you determined that several individuals were at risk of falling, you could prescribe participation in tai chi to improve balance and physical functioning. In addition, they may benefit socially and cognitively from participating. For many, tai chi and yoga become meaningful and enjoyable lifelong activities.

If a company could develop a pill to simultaneously lead to cardiovascular fitness, improved self-confidence and self-image, and improved social support, it would sell billions of units. People would line up around the block to get it and would pay a fortune for it. No such pill is available, but thank goodness there is recreation, or more to the point of this chapter, there is recreational therapy.

Simply put, **recreational therapy** is practiced by trained and certified (and in some states, licensed) professionals who use recreation and other activities to help people with illnesses and disabilities gain new skills and restore skills that have diminished due to injury or illness.

A Brief History of Recreational Therapy as a Profession

It is difficult to point to a specific moment when RT became a profession. Rather, over the course of decades during the 20th century, people with the understanding that recreation could be therapeutic organized themselves into a profession. The American Red Cross provided recreation to soldiers as early as World War I and began to offer services deemed hospital recreation to wounded soldiers.[1,2,3] By 1949, the Hospital Recreation Section of the American Recreation Society was formed, creating a central organization for the budding profession. However, a hallmark of the profession since the beginning has been a philosophical debate among its members about the nature of recreational therapy. Some believe that services should facilitate meaningful leisure experiences, and others believe services should use activities as interventions that lead to functional gains. In 1953, this philosophical difference led to the founding of a competing organization named the National Association of Recreational Therapists. Despite fundamental disagreements between members of these national organizations, they joined forces in 1966 to become the National Therapeutic Recreation Society (NTRS), a branch of the National Recreation and Park Association (NRPA).

Throughout the latter half of the 20th century, numerous academic programs began offering courses and degrees in therapeutic recreation (TR) and RT. However, there was little consensus about the training needed for practitioners, and there was no control over who could identify as a therapist. After years of diligent effort to lay the groundwork for an independent credentialing body, the National Council for Therapeutic Recreation Certification (NCTRC) was formed in 1981. Among its many roles, NCTRC determines who may use the title Certified Therapeutic Recreation Specialist (CTRS) and serves as a gatekeeper of the profession by administering a certification exam.

In 1984, however, philosophical differences (leisure focused vs. functional outcomes focused) between members of the profession led to the founding of the American Therapeutic Recreation Association (ATRA). This new national organization provided a philosophical home to people who viewed RT as a health care profession best used to facilitate functional improvements rather than enhanced leisure. Until 2010, only two national organizations remained: NTRS and ATRA. In 2010, NRPA dissolved NTRS. Today, ATRA is the only national professional membership organization representing RT interests. ATRA recognizes that the use of recreation is an important element in promoting an individual's quality of life and that qualified recreational therapists are essential providers of these services.

Four Models of Practice

Models of practice guide practitioners in the organization of their programs and service delivery. Although many models of practice have been proposed, the first three models presented in this section are widely cited and represent an evolution of practice models over time. They also illustrate the evolution from leisure-focused practice to functional outcomes–focused practice. The fourth model, the International Classification of Functioning, Disability, and Health (ICF), is not specific to RT, but rather it is a model endorsed by the World Health Organization (WHO) that health care professionals worldwide have adopted. This model may be applied to RT practice, and according to many professionals, it is critical that RT abandon its own practice models in favor of placing RT services within the comprehensive model that the majority of other health care professions have embraced. Each model is explained in turn.

An Ongoing Discussion: Two Philosophical Views

Although RT is a relatively new profession, until recently, recreational therapists had two national organizations, each with somewhat different philosophies. Similarly, two terms are often used to refer to the profession: *therapeutic recreation* and *recreational therapy*. These terms reflect the different philosophies of the two national organizations.

Leisure Focused (Therapeutic Recreation Specialists)

Practitioners and scholars who have a leisure-focused philosophy of the profession generally believe that the purpose of RT services is to facilitate leisure for people with illnesses and disabilities and refer to themselves as **therapeutic recreation specialists**. Services are designed to facilitate knowledge, skills, and abilities that lead to satisfying leisure expression. The fullest expression of this philosophy is the leisure ability model proposed by Peterson and Gunn.[4] A version of this model was adopted in 1979 by NTRS as its official model for delivery of services. Peterson and Gunn identified the development of an appropriate leisure lifestyle as the ultimate outcome of services.

Functional Outcomes Focused (Recreational Therapists)

Alternately, **recreational therapists** have a **functional outcomes focus** and generally believe that services should be designed to increase the functional abilities of clients including strength, balance, endurance, memory, mood control, and stress management. Although recreation activities likely play a large part in developing these skills, recreational therapists with a functional outcomes focus use both recreation- and non-recreation-based activities to promote functional outcomes.

Today, therapeutic recreation specialists and recreational therapists work in many health care and community settings, including acute care and rehabilitation hospitals, long-term care facilities, correctional facilities, schools, and public parks and recreation departments. Because professionals in the field work in so many settings and with so many people, models of practice have been important tools that help practitioners to organize their services.

Leisure Ability Model

The **leisure ability model** is widely recognized as one of the field's early models.[5] According to its adherents, the purpose of RT is to facilitate a leisure lifestyle. The model has three main components: treatment, leisure education, and recreation participation. Within treatment services, clients gain knowledge, skills, and abilities needed for full leisure participation. In leisure education, participants engage in an educational process designed to help them understand the value of leisure, gain social skills, and develop self-determination. Recreation participation services provide the opportunity for leisure expression, relaxation, fun, and a chance for clients to practice skills learned in treatment and leisure education. At any given time, participants may participate in any combination of services from all components of the model.

Health Protection/Health Promotion Model

The leisure ability model has been a lightning rod for controversy ever since it was introduced, so it did not take long for alternative service delivery models to be proposed. One of the first alternatives was Austin's **health protection/health promotion model**.[6] Drawing on Maslow's hierarchy of needs, Austin designed a model with three components: (a) prescribed activities, (b) recreation, and (c) leisure. According to Austin, the purpose of RT services is to help clients move from a state of illness and dependence to a state of self-actualization and health. The ultimate goal is for RT clients to engage independently in leisure that promotes health.

Recreation Service Model

In an effort to provide RT with a model suitable for clinical practice in health care settings, burlingame proposed a service delivery model based on a the WHO model. This model was organized into levels of care and "provided a framework for the diagnosis, treatment, funding and outcome measurement of all health care services (including recreational therapy) worldwide."[7] The levels of care contained in the WHO model included (a) disease, (b) impairment, (c) disability, and (d) handicap. Essentially, burlingame's model adapted the WHO model and described the nature of RT services within each level of care. In addition to the four levels of care of the WHO model, the recreation service model includes three levels of care specific to RT: (a) education, (b) organized recreation programs, and (c) independent activities.

International Classification of Functioning, Disability, and Health

In 2001, the WHO adopted a new comprehensive model for health care known as the International Classification of Functioning, Disability, and Health (ICF).[8] More than 190 countries have endorsed the ICF as the worldwide standard for measuring and classifying disability and health. By taking the stance that all people face suboptimal health at some point in their lives, the ICF discourages the concept of people with disabilities as a separate group. Instead, the model encourages practitioners to focus on the impact rather than the cause of a disability. In this light, health care practitioners and others account for not only medical and biological aspects of disability but also social and environmental factors that impact and are impacted by disability.

Because the ICF is a universal model for health care, many leaders in the field of RT have strongly encouraged practitioners to use it as the framework for organizing their clinical activities including assessment, planning, programming, and evaluation of programs and client progress. A primary advantage of adopting the ICF in RT is giving practitioners a common professional vocabulary and theoretical stance in their interactions with fellow health care providers.

Careers in Therapeutic Recreation and Recreational Therapy

Because recreational therapists work with many people with disabilities, they may choose among many work environments, from hospitals to public recreation departments. In general, individual recreational therapists develop specialties related to certain disabilities and interventions. For instance, a recreational therapist in a community setting may develop into an expert at teaching and facilitating adaptive sports for people with physical disabilities. Another may receive training in aquatic rehabilitation and work in a major medical center or a community-based agency.

Most recreational therapists are primarily responsible for providing direct services to people with illnesses and disabilities. With experience, frontline practitioners may be promoted to departmental and other management positions.

Passions

Motivations for becoming a recreational therapist differ from person to person, but common motivations include a passion for helping people with disabilities and a belief in the power of specifically designed recreation and leisure activities to positively transform lives. Although the pay for well-trained recreational therapists continues to improve, no one goes into the field to become wealthy. The primary motivation for many is the passion they have for helping their clients. Recreational therapists experience joy when watching clients gain valuable skills, confidence, and self-esteem while engaging in meaningful activities. If you have doubt about this, reread the profiles at the beginning of this chapter. To see whether your passions may fit well with the RT or TR world, refer to the passions you noted in Chapter 2.

Many recreational therapists report that having a family member or friend with a disabling condition was the initial motivation they needed to pursue this profession. Others have experienced

RT either directly or through observation and knew immediately that RT was a career they wanted to pursue. Although the authors of this chapter came to the RT field in different ways, the personal commitment to engage in a profession with meaning was central to their decisions.

Pay and Perks

As with many professions, resources in RT tend to go to the most highly trained and highly skilled practitioners. Additionally, certain facilities typically pay their employees more than others. For instance, the national average pay of recreational therapists in rehabilitation hospitals is higher than for their colleagues in long-term care facilities. Other factors such as geography and education level determine practitioners' salaries. The best sources for current salary information are the U.S. Bureau of Labor Statistics (www.bls.gov) and the National Council for Therapeutic Recreation Certification (www.nctrc.org). Both report regularly updated salary trends for the field.

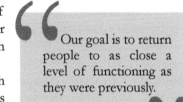

Our goal is to return people to as close a level of functioning as they were previously.

The perks are an attractive feature of RT jobs. Although RT lacks high pay, it makes up for it (at least in part) with perks that many find self-motivating. Practitioners often experience extraordinary autonomy in their jobs. Recreational therapists commonly have flexible schedules and the freedom to design and revise interventions and processes. Although tasks such as documentation and staff meetings are more structured (and important parts of the job), recreational therapists also spend much of their time planning and facilitating interventions directly with clients. Facilitating recreation programs is challenging and invigorating and is often the part of the job that clinicians like most. Since interventions may occur in a pool, in a gym, in a classroom, or on an outing to the community, they provide welcome variety and excitement that is difficult to find in traditional office work.

Preparation

The NCTRC specifies the minimum requirements for use of the title Certified Therapeutic Recreation Specialist (CTRS). These standards continue to become more stringent and include requirements related to amount and type of formal higher education, practical experiences in the field (e.g., internships), and passing a national standardized exam.

Once certified, recreational therapists must annually renew their certification and become recertified every 5 years. To qualify for recertification, recreational therapists must demonstrate that they have actively practiced RT and continued their professional education by attending professional conferences, taking college courses, receiving in-service training, and participating in other educational opportunities and scholarship. Several states also have licensure acts and use the NCTRC examination as a mechanism to establish competence for practice.

Possibilities

Most recreational therapists are frontline clinicians who work directly with clients. With experience, training, and additional education, recreational therapists have taken on administrative duties, serving as managers of RT and other departments within health care settings. Many of those recreational therapists who take on administrative duties also maintain a caseload of clients.

According to the NCTRC, most recreational therapists work in either a hospital (40%) or a skilled nursing facility (18%). The remainder work in settings such as residential/transitional facilities (9%) and community parks and recreation departments (8%).[9] As a recreational therapy student, you may already have strong ideas about the type of facility where you would like to work as a professional. However, it is worthwhile to consider the characteristics of many of the common settings where RT is practiced.

Recreational therapy in hospital settings. Many types of hospitals exist. Typically, recreational therapists work in acute care hospitals and rehabilitation hospitals. Acute care hospitals offer services to meet the immediate medical needs of many illnesses and disabilities, including physical and psychiatric conditions. Because of the expense of hospitalizations and medical treatment in general, the goal of acute care is to medically stabilize patients as quickly as possible. Long-term hospitalizations used to be common, but according to the Centers for Disease Control and Prevention, the average length of stay in U.S. hospitals is now less than 5 days.[10] Once stable, patients may be treated long term through outpatient and other services.

After becoming medically stable, some patients are admitted to rehabilitation hospitals for long-term treatment. Although many types of patients receive treatment in rehabilitation hospitals, some of the common diagnoses include spinal cord injuries, stroke, and brain injuries. Patients in rehabilitation receive treatments designed to restore physical and cognitive skills that have been lost or diminished and to develop new skills that will be needed for independent functioning in the community. RT programs in hospitals include fine and gross motor skills training using crafts and games, aquatic therapy, therapeutic exercise, community reentry outings, and stress management. Recreational therapists in hospital settings commonly work on treatment teams with other health care professionals such as occupational therapists, physical therapists, physicians, nurses, and social workers.

Passions. If you would like to work in a medical environment and be a member of a treatment team with professionals such as doctors, nurses, occupational therapists, physical therapists, and speech and language pathologists, becoming a recreational therapist in an acute care hospital may be your best alternative. These fast-paced and demanding environments are not for the faint of heart. Only highly trained and highly skilled professionals thrive in acute care settings. Recreational therapists who work in acute care hospitals tend to focus on clinical outcomes dictated by the clients' needs. A large RT department in an acute care hospital may offer services to patients in physical rehabilitation, behavioral health, acute pediatric care, cardiovascular rehabilitation, and other specialty areas.

> " As a recreational therapist, I look at the whole person and his or her abilities in a realistic 'here and now' environment. "

Pay and perks. Most RT jobs in acute care hospitals will be full time and will carry benefits such as health care insurance, retirement benefits, paid vacation, and sick leave. The NCTRC reports that hospitals offer among the best paying jobs for recreational therapists.[11]

Preparation. A student who would like to ultimately work in a hospital setting should begin preparing while in school by completing practicums and an internship in an acute care hospital. Such experiences will help students gain skills that will be valued in the job market. These experiences will also help students gain valuable contacts in settings where they may ultimately work. Additionally, students should consider taking elective classes such as aquatic therapy or biofeedback to develop specific and marketable skills valued in hospital settings.

Possibilities. The best advice for young professionals and students who would like to work in a hospital setting is to steer clear of geographic limitations. In other words, to get the job you want, you may have to move to a city or region with a highly desirable RT position. Students who steadfastly insist on staying in a limited geographical area may struggle to find the perfect job simply because relatively few RT positions are available in any given location that match an individual's professional interests.

For instance, the Shepherd Center in Atlanta is a world-renowned rehabilitation hospital with a large and active RT program. Programs at the Shepherd Center include adaptive sports, adaptive art and music, horticulture therapy, community outings, and leisure skills development. These services are designed to help patients develop skills so they may be independent, active, and healthy when they return to the community.

Recreational therapy in skilled nursing facilities. As the U.S. population continues to live longer, it is anticipated that more people will receive services from skilled nursing facilities. Clients who receive treatment from a skilled nursing facility are usually not unhealthy enough to require hospitalization in an acute care hospital, but they have health limitations that prevent them from living safely at home.

Skilled nursing facilities are not nursing or retirement homes meant for custodial care. Rather, clients in skilled nursing facilities receive active treatment designed to promote improved functioning. Recreational therapists in these settings help clients develop and restore fine and gross motor skills, balance, strength, and cardiovascular health. Additionally, recreational therapists may work with clients to alleviate depression, learn to cope with stress, and remain socially integrated. As in acute care and rehabilitation hospitals, recreational therapists in skilled nursing facilities often serve on treatment teams with other professionals and often cotreat with physical therapists, social workers, and occupational therapists.

Passions. Many students know immediately that they want to work with older adults. Perhaps they have had influential experiences caring for an older relative or neighbor, or perhaps they have had meaningful volunteer or professional experiences that have sparked their professional interests. Even if it has never occurred to you to work with older adults, consider exploring the possibilities of working in a skilled nursing facility, as many professionals find this work to be extremely rewarding. Older adults have accumulated decades of wisdom, skills, and knowledge that they are often eager to share.

> Often it has to do with the human spirit and keeping a person moving forward in a positive direction.

Pay and perks. The pay for recreational therapists in skilled nursing facilities, as in many settings, varies based on agency and region of the country. However, unlike the relatively short lengths of stay in hospital settings, patients in skilled nursing facilities may receive services for weeks, months, or longer. These extended stays facilitate meaningful therapeutic relationships and permit therapists time to significantly impact their patients' health over time.

Preparation. Students who would like to work in skilled nursing facilities should consider completing practicums and an internship in a skilled nursing facility. Additionally, students may consider taking courses in gerontology to gain knowledge and skills that will be both marketable to employers and helpful once employed. Some schools offer gerontology certificates or similar concentrations. Finally, students should consider building their résumés and their abilities by volunteering at skilled nursing facilities.

Possibilities. By all accounts, the U.S. population is aging, and it is anticipated that more recreational therapists will be needed to meet the demands for services for older adults. Although employment trends are hard to predict, well-trained students with volunteer experiences, practicums, and internships in skilled nursing facilities can expect to be in high demand in the future.

Therapeutic recreation in community settings. States and all but the smallest municipalities provide park and recreation services for their citizens. Since the passage of the Americans With Disabilities Act (ADA) in 1990, these services must be accessible to people with disabilities. Ideally, park and recreation programs and facilities are designed to be inclusive, meaning that people with and without disabilities participate in the programs together. Although many park and recreation professionals strive to make their services inclusive, many still provide separate programs designed exclusively for people with disabilities. Two well-known programs are Challenger League Baseball and Special Olympics. Often, recreational therapists are hired by parks and recreation departments to coordinate, plan, and facilitate recreation services for people with disabling conditions (see Chapter 3 on community recreation for more details).

TR programs in community parks and recreation departments are as varied as people's recreation interests. Therefore, cultural arts programs, adaptive sport programs, and outings to local sites of interest are commonplace and popular. Other communities hire qualified recreational therapists to work as community support personnel for people with psychiatric and cognitive disorders living in the community. The support often comes in the form of facilitating social interaction and helping people learn activities of daily living and to use community resources (e.g., public transportation).

Although not many recreational therapists currently work in public schools, federal legislation (Individuals With Disabilities Education Act, or IDEA) has identified RT as a service that may be requested as part of a student's Individual Education Plan (IEP). Recreational therapists have worked in public schools as support personnel for children with disabilities, leisure educators, and community transition specialists. Considering the important role recreation and leisure play in children's development, schools are logical places for expanded involvement of RT in the future.

Some of the standards typical of clinical RT settings are more relaxed in community settings. For instance, recreational therapists working in the community may not document client progress as thoroughly as their counterparts in an acute care hospital. One benefit to working as a recreational therapist in the community is the ability to interact with clients and those around them for long spans of time. Thus, community-based recreational therapists often get to know the family and friends of their clients and have the potential to make lasting and deep impacts on their clients' quality of life.

Passions. Recreational therapists in community settings often become deeply involved with their clients, their clients' families, and their communities. These therapeutic relationships may last years, and community-based recreational therapists are often in the enviable position of contributing to (and witnessing) significant development of their clients over time.

Some people never imagine themselves being "tied to a desk" and hope to find a job that gets them up and moving. Most RT jobs fit that description, but perhaps none more so than community-based jobs. Depending on the nature of the agency, recreational therapists may expect to spend much of their time outdoors, on community outings, in residences, in recreation centers, and in schools.

Pay and perks. The pay in community settings varies depending on the size and nature of the employing agency. Parks and recreation departments in large municipalities may have large budgets, but too often these services are underfunded. Recreational therapists have become experts over time at learning to accomplish much with relatively few resources and to form collaborative relationships that provide support.

The hours of recreational therapists in community-based settings may be irregular when special events need to be planned and delivered, and many services are offered in the evenings and during weekends. Flexible scheduling may be frustrating to some people, but for others, it is a valuable perk.

Preparation. It is particularly important for community-based recreational therapists to have recreation knowledge and skills related to sports, arts and crafts, and games. Cultivating a large repertoire of such skills will help in planning and providing services to people with individual interests. Additionally, recreational therapists in these settings must be particularly familiar with their communities to connect their clients with resources and to serve as advocates for their clients and agencies.

Possibilities. The passage of the Americans With Disabilities Act led to a sea change in the delivery of many services for people with disabilities. Specifically, large state-operated residential facilities have become decentralized, and clients who formerly lived in often-locked and substandard large institutions have now been placed in community settings such as group homes. The shift to least restrictive environments has created many opportunities for recreational therapists. Additionally, although the number of recreational therapists working in public schools is low, legislation such as IDEA opened the door for recreational therapists in schools.

To reduce the ever-increasing cost of health care, many experts have suggested providing fewer services in hospitals and other medical facilities in favor of less expensive community-based settings. As long as clients are medically stable, adaptive sports, community living skills, healthy living, exercise, and other programs may be as easily offered in the community as in hospitals and often at a fraction of the expense. Such a reform will create additional opportunities for recreational therapists interested in working in the community.

Summary of Career Options

Many career opportunities are available for recreational therapists in addition to the ones discussed here. Most commonly, recreational therapists work in hospital and long-term care settings, but other alternatives are available. Working in parks and recreation departments, schools, and other community settings may lead to rewarding careers that provide practitioners the chance to have long-lasting therapeutic relationships with their clients. Career choice is individual, and RT students are encouraged to seek out volunteer, practicum, and internship experiences to determine the work setting that best fits their goals and skills.

Future Opportunities, Issues, and Challenges

The debate about the essential nature of RT is ongoing. Many professionals contend that the field should be primarily aligned with parks and recreation, focusing on leisure-related outcomes. Critics of this vision of the profession advocate abandoning leisure-related outcomes and associations with parks and recreation in favor of aligning the field with allied therapies such as occupational therapy and physical therapy. As stated earlier, this young profession has a bright future that is still being shaped by its practitioners.

A primary argument against the leisure-focused RT goals is that **third parties** usually do not pay for leisure-related outcomes RT services. These third parties include private insurance companies, Medicare, Medicaid, workers' compensation, and other entities in the business of providing funding for health care. However, recreational therapists who provide (and document) health-related outcomes for their clients often are considered covered services by third parties. In fact, in health care settings such as hospitals and skilled nursing facilities, RT has been practiced for decades as a clinical intervention and is widely recognized as an effective treatment option for a range of illnesses and disabilities. Medicare and many private insurance companies cover RT services via mechanisms similar to other health care services.

In the recent past, ATRA promoted its ATRA Medicare Project to lobby federal policy makers to further clarify Medicare's coverage of RT. Medicare is such a large source of health care funds that it often sets the tone for private insurance companies and their willingness to cover specific services. Although RT has long been included in the budget for Medicare, the regulations governing Medicare are inconsistent and often confusing. As a result, money earmarked for RT services in health care settings has often been spent in other ways. Financial consideration is only one hurdle RT will face in the coming decades.

Most RT practitioners work in a highly competitive health care arena. Such an environment requires efficiency and effectiveness, and recreational therapists must develop several features to secure the future of the profession. Among the most important priorities for the profession is the continued development of a body of knowledge that will allow practitioners to provide **evidence-based practice**. Additionally, practitioners must adhere to **standards of practice** and develop and adhere to standard treatment protocols. Having valid and reliable research documenting outcomes will enable practitioners to provide efficient, effective, and standardized services and to justify their services to health care administrators, colleagues in allied professions, clients, and the public.

Finally, the future of RT will be shaped, in part, by large social forces beyond anyone's control. For instance, as populations continue to age, the demand for recreational therapists to provide services to older adults will increase. As health care industries continue to focus on efficiency, evidence-based practice and cost containment opportunities for recreational therapists will increase in areas such as home health and outpatient services.

> " Other than dealing with the challenges of health care financing, the most difficult part of my job has to do with reality checks for the patient. "

Ever-advancing technology has opened new doors for recreational therapists, and no end is in sight for this trend. For instance, recreational therapists routinely use video game systems such as Nintendo® Wii™ as therapeutic interventions, and recent research validates the positive effects on health and functioning that some video games may have. Recreational therapists are already using biofeedback, an interdisciplinary modality that relies heavily on computer technology, in a variety of settings, and this will likely continue to grow in popularity.

RT will continue efforts to position itself as an effective and efficient health care and human services profession. An important initiative already underway is the joint effort of ATRA and NCTRC to achieve RT licensure in all 50 states. Additionally, NCTRC offers specialty certifications, as well as its standard CTRS certification. These and additional efforts will be needed to ensure that recreational therapists and RT continue to meet the increasingly complex demands of future clients.

Resources and Getting Involved

RT is a relatively small profession, and it is important to establish and maintain professional relationships within and outside of the profession. With the advent of new technology, networking has never been easier. Students and others are encouraged to join and participate in RT and health care e-mail newsgroups, Facebook pages, and Twitter feeds. One of the best ways to meet other professionals and students in RT is to attend RT conferences, and students routinely pay significantly less than others for conference registration fees. Finally, volunteering at agencies that provide services to people with disabilities is a great way to give back to the community, to explore professional options, and to create important professional ties.

Professional Organizations
American Therapeutic Recreation Association (ATRA): www.atra-online.com
Committee on Accreditation of Recreational Therapy Education (CARTE): www.caahep.org/carte
National Council for Therapeutic Recreation Certification (NCTRC): www.nctrc.org

Certifications and Licenses
All recreational therapists must attain and maintain certification through NCTRC. More information may be obtained by visiting NCTRC's website: www.nctrc.org.

Currently, only a handful of states require a license to practice RT, but several movements are underway in states to require licenses to practice RT. For more information, contact your state or regional RT organization. You may find contact information for your state or regional organization via the Internet.

Where to Gain Experience
Prior to practicing RT, individuals must be certified by the NCTRC. However, job opportunities are available working with people with disabilities in recreation contexts. For instance, many public

park and recreation agencies hire people to manage programs designed for people with disabling conditions such as camps, adaptive sports, and Special Olympics. Although these are not RT positions, they provide an opportunity for people to to work in the field.

One of the best ways to gain experience in RT is to find a dedicated recreational therapist and ask to volunteer. Almost all recreational therapists were required to volunteer in community and health care agencies when they were students, and they will likely be accepting and willing to accommodate enthusiastic volunteers.

Remember that recreational therapists work in agencies that have strict rules related to client confidentiality, infection control, and safety. Volunteers in RT settings often are required to complete extensive training and a background check and will be expected to follow certain rules of conduct.

Conclusion

If you are an energetic and creative person interested in working with people with disabilities and illnesses, RT may be the profession for you. Most people have an intuitive sense that recreational activities are beneficial, and recreational therapists use the inherent enjoyment in recreation to help people gain these valuable benefits. As a relatively young and growing profession, RT has made great strides in recent decades, yet work remains to be done as the profession continues to evolve and improve. If you choose to become a recreational therapist, we encourage you to gain experience and technical skills while you are in school. These experiences and skills will help you not only attain a job you will like when you graduate but also become a better therapist. Recreational therapists do not earn the same living as investment bankers, but a serious case may be made for a career that daily provides the opportunity to make real and positive differences in the lives of others.

For Further Investigation

For More Research
1. Visit the websites for ATRA, NCTRC, and CARTE (listed under professional organizations above). Compare and contrast the information about the RT/TR profession (e.g., mission, vision, standards of practice). Also, check out membership requirements and see when and where the next regional and national conferences will occur or the requirements for academic accreditation.
2. Visit the website for U.S. Department of Labor's Bureau of Labor Statistics (http://bls.gov) and conduct a search using the term recreational therapists. The Bureau of Labor Statistics tracks employment and salary trends for most professions.
3. Visit your school's library and find bound volumes of the Therapeutic Recreation Journal and ATRA's Annual in Therapeutic Recreation and then catalogue the types of research studies that have been published about RT.

Active Investigation
1. **Benefits of recreation activity:** On a piece of paper, write down three recreation activities that have been meaningful to you during your life and then list all of the physical, psychological, and social benefits that you have received from each activity (or that may reasonably be received). Finally, consider what sort of individual with a disabling condition may benefit most from the activities you chose. Would the activities need to be adapted in any way for people with various disabling conditions?

2. **Disability in perspective:** This activity may not apply to you if you have already experienced a disabling condition, but for others, it is eye-opening. Sit quietly for 1 minute and consider how your life would change if this afternoon you were in a car accident and acquired a spinal cord injury. Write down 10 ways that your life would be impacted. Consider your involvement in school, work, recreation, and other life activities, and consider how your family and friends will be impacted. How will your relationships be impacted?

Recommended Reading

Austin, D. R. (2004). *Therapeutic recreation: Processes and techniques* (5th ed.). Champaign, IL: Sagamore.
This text covers a broad array of information and offers a strong foundation that TR professionals may use to improve quality of their services.

Long, T., & Roberstson, T. (2008). *Foundations of therapeutic recreation*. Champaign, IL: Human Kinetics.
This text showcases how TR professionals can address various clients' needs throughout the life span through therapeutic programs, modalities, and activities.

Porter, H. R., & burlingame, j. (2006). *Recreational therapy handbook of practice: ICF-based diagnosis and treatment*. Enumclaw, WA: Idyll Arbor
This handbook of recreational therapy clinical applications is designed to implement the ICF. The authors' goals are to standardize communication, research, and therapy within RT and facilitate clearer communication with other disciplines.

References

[1]Bedini, L. (1995). The 'play ladies'—The first therapeutic recreation specialists. *Journal of Physical Education, Recreation, and Dance, 66*, 32–35.

[2]Dieser, R. (2008). History of therapeutic recreation. In T. Robinson & T. Long (Eds.), *Foundations of therapeutic recreation*. Champaign, IL: Human Kinetics.

[3]James, A. (1998). The conceptual development of recreational therapy. In F. M. Brasile, T. Skalko, & j. burlingame (Eds.), *Perspectives in recreational therapy* (pp. 7–38). Ravensdale, WA: Idyll Arbor.

[4]Peterson, C. A., & Gunn, S. L. (1984). *Therapeutic recreation program design: Principles and procedures* (2nd ed.). Englewood Cliff, NJ: Prentice Hall.

[5]Ibid.

[6]Austin, D. R. (2004). *Therapeutic recreation: Processes and techniques* (5th ed.). Champaign, IL: Sagamore.

[7]burlingame, j. (1998). Clinical practice models. In F. M. Brasile, T. Skalko, & j. burlingame (Eds.), *Perspectives in recreational therapy* (pp. 83–106). Ravensdale, WA: Idyll Arbor.

[8]World Health Organization. (2001). *Towards a common language for functioning, disability, and health: ICF*. Retrieved from http://www.who.int/classifications/icf/training/icfbeginnersguide.pdf

[9]National Council for Therapeutic Recreation Certification. (2009). 2009 CTRS profile brochure. Retrieved http://www.nctrc.org/documents/CTRSProfile09-FINAL081809.pdf

[10]Centers for Disease Control and Prevention. (2009). Hospital utilization. Retrieved December 31, 2009, from http://www.cdc.gov/nchs/fastats/hospital.htm

[11]Ibid.

[12]Fortune, D., Thompson, J., Pedlar, A., & Yuen, F. (2010). Social justice and women leaving prison: Beyond punishment and exclusion. *Contemporary Justice Review: Issues in Criminal, Social, and Restorative Justice, 13*(1), 19–33.

[13]Selby, A., & Smith-Osborne, A. (2013). A systematic review of effectiveness of complementary and adjunct therapies and interventions involving equines. *Health Psychology, 32*(4), 418–432.

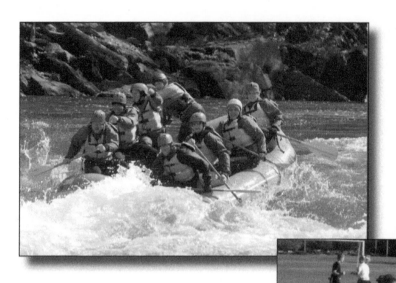

8

Campus Recreation, Leisure, and Intramurals

Doug Kennedy
Virginia Wesleyan College

Tina M. Aldrich
Virginia Wesleyan College

Focus Questions

Q: What is campus recreation?

A: Campus recreation is the intentional effort by schools to provide leisure-time programs that contribute to enhancing the well-being of the campus community. These programs may include formal sport leagues and special events as well as informal opportunities to use a school's recreation facilities. Campus recreation often includes cocurricular and diversional activities provided by a student activities office. For instance, a cocurricular program would support an academic course or major. For example, a debate competition may be held in conjunction with a political science course. Diversional activities are provided to allow a break from school and their value is not tied to the academic mission.

Q: Why choose a career in campus recreation?

A: Campus recreation professionals are passionate about working around young college-aged students and the chance to positively impact their lives. Many students have never had a fitness program before, attended a particular cultural event, or tried an activity such as scuba diving or kayaking, and campus recreation staff help them develop interests and skills that last a lifetime.

Q: Is campus recreation mostly about sports?

A: Sports and intramurals are a big part of campus recreation, but it is about a whole lot more. Campus recreation programs not only provide an opportunity to balance the hard work of being a college student, but also may be cocurricular and relate to a specific class. Programs may include camping, wellness, entertainment, clubs, and other ways students, faculty, and staff spend their leisure time. The slogan "work hard, play hard" describes a number of campus recreation programs.

Q: What kind of things would a campus recreation professional expect to do on a day-to-day basis?

A: Most campus recreation professionals oversee one or more program areas. They enjoy managing both people and facilities because life in campus recreation is about both. College students are often looking for creative recreation programs that at times may be serious but are also fun. For example, the popularity of the Harry Potter novels and movies has caused over 200 colleges and universities to create Quidditch teams. There is even an International Quidditch Association with its own world cup! Starting such a program at any school would require a great deal of creativity and excellent management skills to be successful.

Q: How do you see technology changing campus recreation?

A: Like many areas in higher education, campus recreation has embraced technology to provide an enhanced experience. Today many schools have gone paperless. That means students can register for programs online. Personal electronic devices such as iPods and smartphones are being integrated into exercise equipment so you can listen to music or watch movies. Even traditional activities such as backpacking have been changed by technology such as GPS receivers. The integration of technology will undoubtedly continue as will challenges that come with it.

Key Terms

Campus recreation

Student learning imperative

Cocurricular programs

Intramural sports

Extramural sports

Recreational sports

Club sports

Student activities

Profile 1: Could This Be You?

Kevin Marbury is the director of the Department of Physical Education and Recreation at the University of Oregon. On a daily basis he has departmental oversight responsibilities for physical education classes, intramural sport programs, informal recreational opportunities, fitness programs, outdoor pursuit programs, and aquatic programs. Along with these areas, he is responsible for personnel management, problem solving, planning, and financial management.

Kevin started his career in municipal recreation, but his love for working with college students led him to start his career in campus recreation. After 28 years in the profession, he has received a number of awards from state, regional, and national associations and recently completed a term as the president of NIRSA: Leaders in Collegiate Recreation. NIRSA—now known only by its initials—is the largest national association for collegiate recreation professionals. After playing a significant role in building and managing Old Dominion University's $25 million student recreation center, he recently relocated to Eugene, Oregon, to oversee the building of the University of Oregon's $51 million recreation center expansion.

Q: How important is campus recreation?

A: I realize every day that what we do in campus recreation makes a positive impact on students now, and that impact will carry over for the rest of their lives. Everyone in my department is committed to the programs we provide and realizes that being involved in something like a sport club not only is fun for our students but also offers them an opportunity to learn leadership skills, develop new friends, improve their communication, and develop other areas they'll use in their work and personal lives.

Q: Do most staff and participants come from similar backgrounds?

A: No, they don't. Campus recreation is very diverse. What makes a huge difference is having a real variety of staff and participants. As a matter of fact, we recently had a student come to us for a part-time job who knew nothing about recreation; her major was accounting. She started as a scorekeeper for our intramural leagues, and over time, as she developed management skills, she's taken on more and more responsibilities. The same is true for our participants. Very often in our fitness programs, we'll get participants who have never worked out. It's so exciting then to see them make huge gains in their health and develop lifestyles that will help them for the rest of their life.

Q: What recommendations do you have for anyone considering campus recreation as a career?

A: There are a few things I think are critical. You have to like working with young people. Some schools have more nontraditionally aged students, but at the core of most schools are 18- to 22-year-old students. It's a great group to work with, and they'll keep you young! You should also develop two or three mentors who have been in the profession for a while. Challenges will come up on a daily basis, and the advice of others who have been in campus recreation longer than you will help you make good decisions. Your mentors will also be incredibly valuable in helping you develop as a professional and finding other positions. Last, you have to enjoy managing people and facilities. Both can be a challenge at times, but nothing's more rewarding than watching your staff develop and your facilities serve your participants.

Q: Where do you see campus recreation going in the next 20 years?

A: Right now we're in a tremendous building phase across the country. At some point, that will slow down. When it does, we'll really need to focus on providing programs when people want them. We're moving away from things like group exercise programs and developing individual fitness programs that will allow participants to complete them on their timetable and get immediate feedback. As technology becomes more a part of our lives, we'll increasingly have to make use of that, or down the road our programs will seem too "old fashioned!" The next 20 years are going to be an exciting time!

Profile 2: Could This Be You?

Willie Harrell and Jason Seward are on the other end of the spectrum from Kevin Marbury. Both have careers that are less than 10 years old and each directs half of the campus recreation program at Virginia Wesleyan College.

Willie is the director of aquatics and fitness, and he oversees the college's indoor pool, fitness center, and racquetball courts. The total operation of these areas includes programs, staff, and facilities. Willie's counterpart, Jason, is the director of recreational sports and outdoor activities and also serves as the director of the college's student recreation center. His office plans and oversees all the intramural leagues, sport clubs, and sport tournaments, in addition to planning the year-round outdoor recreation activities and running the climbing wall. By working together and contributing to the college's campus recreation program called "RecX," they have seen participation in their programs quadruple since 2010.

Q: Do you need specialized education and training in these positions?

A: (Jason) My degree in recreation and leisure studies has been important in my being able to provide the right programs. Beyond that, I'm a certified park and recreation professional, I've completed a course in wilderness first aid, and I continue to attend educational sessions at conferences to keep up to date.
(Willie): I'm a certified aquatic facility operator as well as a certified personal trainer and certified park and recreation professional. I believe it's mandatory for someone in my position to have these certifications from a reputable agency.

Q: What do you two like most about your jobs?

A: (Willie) Working with students. This is a great group that really appreciates everything you do for them. We follow the principles of what's called the "**student learning imperative**." Specifically, we really believe that we contribute to one of the main principles, which says that experiences in and out of the class contribute to learning and personal development. So whether you are a participant in one of our programs or working in our department as a lifeguard, you're developing skills that you can use in the classroom and will help you after graduation. I also love the fact that I get to teach students to kayak, scuba dive, become triathletes, and even train for marathons. (Jason): Willie's right. At this school (and others) you have the opportunity to expose students to experiences outside the classroom that carry over into their studies and will stay with them long after they graduate. We call what we do in campus recreation "serious fun," and that's just what it is. We get to plan fun programs, but what the students get from them can make a serious difference in how happy they are to be in college and how well they'll do in their classes. When I take a group to the Florida Keys to kayak and snorkel, or to West Virginia for some white-water rafting, they not only enjoy the activity, but they also learn how to be independent, communicate with others, deal with adversity, and develop new interests.

Q: What's helped you get started in your campus recreation career?

A: (Jason) My experience in the profession allowed me to develop my management skills. Before I started in campus recreation I worked in resort recreation. What I've really discovered is how important it is to get involved with professional organizations and try new programs. Students don't want to do the same old thing. Sharing new ideas with others and not being afraid to try some crazy ideas can really make a difference in how well you do your job.
(Willie): Before starting this position, I worked for a few years as an aquatics director with the YMCA. I agree with what Jason said and would only add that trying new things will not only keep your students, faculty, and staff happy but will make you look forward to your job every day!

Q: You both mentioned new programs as being very important. Give examples.

A: (Willie) Some programs we do are just plain fun, and some might be a little more serious. Last year we tried a Belly Flop Contest and invited schools from around the state. It was a ton of fun and great competition for participants and spectators. On the other hand, we recognized that many people couldn't find the time to participate in our fitness programs during the day. So we've partnered with online fitness programs and offered fitness classes at nontraditional times.

(Jason): I guess the one thing that comes to mind was something we started this year at the end of the fall semester when everyone needed to blow off some steam. We wanted to also get our dedicated runners out with some people who didn't run much, if at all. So one night at 11:00 we had an Underpants Run, where students, faculty, and staff ran around campus in their underwear! It raised some eyebrows but everyone had a great time and now it will become an annual event.

What Is Campus Recreation?

Odds are you have come into contact with a campus recreation professional. Campus recreation professionals take on the challenge of providing fun, enjoyable, and beneficial recreation programs for their target populations in ways that are similar to community recreation professionals. Community recreation is responsible for the leisure-time activities of the general public, but campus recreation's clients are predominantly college or university students, faculty, and staff. As of 2013, over 11 million college students use their campus recreation facilities. More than 2 million students are part of college sports clubs and over 1 million intramural events are held every year.[1] NIRSA has identified several goals for campus recreation programs, including providing programs that enhance recruitment and retention; attract diverse groups such faculty, staff, and students; serve personal needs that aid good mental and physical health; and assist academic units preparing students for a career in campus recreation.

Take a minute to review the results of your preferences and passions assessment from Chapter 2. If you enjoy working with college-aged people and in the campus environment, want to make a difference, and are interested in organizing large events, campus recreation may be a good choice for you.

How Did Campus Recreation Get Its Start?

Campus recreation traces its roots back to the earliest colleges in the United States. Phi Beta Kappa, now an honor society, was the first Greek-letter social organization with its founding at the College of William and Mary in 1776.[2] The early 1800s saw an increase of other fraternities with sororities following suit in the mid-1800s. This same period saw the first extramural event in 1852, when Harvard met Yale in a rowing race that is still held every year. Other events became formal intercollegiate competitions with baseball occurring in 1859 and football in 1869. During the same period, intramural events were held with the first recorded track meets appearing in 1870. As time progressed, and the value of student recreational activities was seen, both athletic and social programs continued to grow.

The early 20th century saw the first campus recreation professionals hired as valued members of higher education communities. As World War I and II unfolded, and the value of rigorous physical training was better understood, physically active campus recreation programs increased in number. The postwar growth in student enrollment seen in the 1950s also produced a large increase in campus recreation programs.[3] At the same time, the first professional organization, NIRSA, was formed. The 1970s and 1980s saw this continued growth as coeducational participation increased as a result of Title IX and enhanced opportunities for women.[4] More recently, campus recreation has experienced a boom as schools rushed to complete increasingly elaborate recreation centers. This trend developed as schools found themselves facing increasing competition for students coupled with recognition of the value of recreation facilities not only in recruitment of students, faculty, and staff, but also in their being able to retain them. For the campus recreation professional, the start of a new century has seen unprecedented opportunities for professional employment and participation by all members of the college community.

Photo courtesy of Cal Poly ASI

Campus Recreation Today

Today, we are witnessing an emphasis on campus recreation like never before. All areas of campus recreation are becoming fully integrated within the strategic plans of colleges and universities. The incredible investment in recreation facilities on many campuses is proof that schools have discovered the benefits of providing a quality of life, outside the classroom, that is attractive to prospective students. As campus recreation's value is better understood through ongoing assessment, its growth should continue for some time.

The specialized nature of the campus recreation delivery system is traditional as outlined in Figure 2.1 of Chapter 2. Public good and social service roots are characteristics. Leadership roles include packaged programming such as Zumba, direct service as in being an organizer of an event, facility manager, and activity specialist such as an instructor for rock climbing. Though traditional in nature, new and unique campus recreation delivery systems are also emerging, which we will discuss later in this chapter.

Goals and roles: Before, during, and after. The director of the Department of Physical Education and Recreation at the University of Oregon emphasized the importance of campus recreation's accomplishments: "I realize every day that what we do in campus recreation is make a positive impact on students now and that impact will carry over for the rest of their lives."

Campus recreation is much more than unlocking the doors to the pool or posting a sign saying a softball league is forming. It is a comprehensive set of programs and facilities with goals designed to help the school, its students, its employees, and its alumni. Campus recreation works hand in hand with all areas on campus such as academic programs. Many professors will encourage participation in out-of-class activities that complement the in-class instruction. For example, a debate provided by a student activities office between two candidates for a local mayoral election office may be tied to a political science class. Or a clinic on strength training provided by a fitness coordinator may be scheduled at a time when an exercise science class is studying that topic. These **cocurricular programs** demonstrate how learning in the classroom applies to life now and later in the real world.

Table 8.1 illustrates the role of campus recreation over the course of a student's life at a college or university. Campus recreation helps achieve important goals before a student chooses what school to attend, after the first day of classes, and after graduation.

Facilities. Between 2006 and 2011, over $3.17 billion was spent on new construction and renovations at a combined 220 college and university campus recreation facilities (Table 8.2).[5]

Table 8.1

Role of Campus Recreation Over a Student's Life at College or University

Time period	Benefits of campus recreation
Before: High school	Increases attractiveness of college or university to prospective students. Promotes a sense of joining a community. Enhances a sense of inclusion for all types of students
During: New student	Aids in assimilation to the college community. Reinforces the decision to enroll. Aids retention during the critical first semester. Develops bonds within residence halls and between residents and commuters.
During: Established student	Helps balance work–leisure needs. Helps with stress management and other wellness. Provides ongoing social opportunities. Allows students to socialize with faculty and staff. Increases academic performance by enhancing quality of life.
After: Alumni	Provides opportunities for alumni to return to campus. Facilities such as fitness centers may be used by alumni and generate revenue for school. Participation in campus recreation enhances alumni appreciation for the school and may lead to increased financial support.

Table 8.2

Recently Completed Campus Recreation Facilities

School	Facility	Cost	Features
California State University	East Bay Recreation and Wellness Center	$19.1 million	Two-court gymnasium, track, fitness center, wellness center, multipurpose rooms, locker rooms, juice bar
Drexel University	Recreation Center	$42 million	Multipurpose gym, jogging track, squash courts, climbing room
Rice University	Barbara and David Gibbs Recreation and Wellness Center	$32.6 million	Two-court gymnasium, MAC, dance studios, racquetball courts, squash courts, fitness center, group fitness room, classrooms, offices, wellness suite
University of Iowa	Campus Recreation and Wellness Center	$51.3 million	Natatorium, fitness center, gymnasium, track, MAC, climbing wall, activity rooms

Management of these facilities will be the job of a campus recreation professional. Since any facility is only as good as the staff that supports it, an effective facility manager will need to address many aspects of facility management, including human resources, budget, maintenance, scheduling, and risk management. Looking more closely at human resources, we find that the manager will need to recruit both full- and part-time staff and develop an annual training program. Since many recreation centers are staffed by student workers, a plan must also be in place to ensure that employees are available during breaks and the summer when most schools have fewer students on campus.

Now, consider that students returning from one year to the next may expect a raise in pay or increased responsibility. You will need a good performance appraisal system in place. Next, consider the day-to-day challenges that will pop up. The campus recreation professional needs to be flexible and love a challenge when the local high school comes to use the pool for a meet and minutes before a lifeguard has called in sick. Or suppose a storm has produced a leak right over the basketball court hours before the intramural championship is scheduled to be played! Above all else, recreation center management takes a love of challenge, the ability to be flexible, and a desire to balance all the needs of participants, staff, and the facility.

Careers in Campus Recreation

You will find a number of professionals dedicated to enhancing the college experience for students inside all campus recreation facilities. Their life's work is to add something meaningful to the life satisfaction of students, faculty, and staff alike. A quick look at bluefishjobs.com, the online home of NIRSA's career center, usually reveals openings in campus recreation in every state and in international schools. Professionals from all levels of experience, whether they are graduate assistants just starting or seasoned professionals ready to lead the biggest departments, are always needed. What makes this especially important to a student interested in campus recreation is the ability to start a career right out of college. It is also possible to pursue a master's degree while gaining experience as a graduate assistant in campus recreation. Students and new professionals often gain specialized training in their specific area of campus recreation while working and become involved early in professional associations that further their career.

Passions

If you asked most campus recreation professionals what they liked most about their career, they would probably share the same feelings as the professionals profiled at the beginning of this chapter. They recognized their love for working with students; the role of recreation in making their campus a wonderful place to work, study, and live; and the impact their work has on student development. College students bring a constant feeling of energy, inquisitiveness, independence, determination, creativity, and passion to their leisure-time activities. Campus recreation professionals love the college atmosphere and working with students, faculty, and staff at their school. They like the pace of planning activities according to the school calendar and working long hours, and they look forward to school breaks when they can recharge! They also have a great deal of creativity and desire to try new ideas. Above all else, campus recreation professionals love working with students, get their satisfaction from seeing student growth, and know that their work is critical to making their school one that students want to attend, be a part of until graduation, and value as alumni.

To understand the work of professionals within the areas of campus recreation, you must recognize what makes campus recreation professionals tick. College and university campuses are communities where a great deal of diversity typically is found. Students make friends from different parts of the country, different religions, different races, all of whom come to campus with a love for a variety of recreation and leisure interests. Campus recreation professionals accept the challenge of this great diversity and are driven by the desire to improve their campus so it is a fun place to study, work, and live. Critical to being successful at this is the ability to partner with people from across the campus. Campus recreation professionals understand that their jobs may have them partnering with the campus health service one day to provide a wellness program and then working with music majors next to cohost a concert. In fact, embracing a cocurricular philosophy means the campus recreation professional believes in the value of providing programs that complement classroom learning to drive home the importance of what a professor is teaching.

Campus Recreation Creativity

Bringing together groups from across campus is often the goal of campus recreation. Many schools including Notre Dame, Central Michigan, and Southern Illinois now hold cardboard boat regattas where clubs, dorms, and organizations compete to see whose cardboard boat can be navigated around a course before sinking (with students in it)! In fact, this activity was named one of the "101 things to do before you graduate" by *Sports Illustrated*.

Pay and Perks

There are some pay and perks that are similar for all campus recreation career areas. Entry-level salaries depend upon responsibilities, education, experience, region, and school budgets. Perks include flexible work hours and schedules that follow the academic year. You may work long hours during the fall and spring semesters, but you will usually get a break after each semester is over. So if the schedule you lived on when you were in college appeals to you, that is a plus. Reimbursed travel to professional conferences and workshops is often available. In addition, many schools will support you to obtain specific certifications that will help you do your job better and make you more marketable. Also, campus recreation facilities are normally available for use by employees and often their families.

Entry-level salaries in campus recreation are similar to those in public and commercial recreation and they will be roughly comparable to those entering the teaching profession in any particular region. Of course, assistant director and director positions have higher pay levels, which are commensurate with education and experience. Educational requirements vary slightly depending on the area of campus recreation. We will discuss specifics in the possibilities section.

Preparation

At a minimum, to be well prepared for a career in campus recreation, you will need a bachelor's degree with a major in an area of recreation and leisure services. This degree is critical in understanding how to determine participants' needs, planning and conducting programs, managing your facility and human resources, and marketing your programs effectively. Key to preparing for a career in campus recreation is the experience you gain. Campus recreation offers many opportunities for student workers to serve as referees, assistants with promoting events, or perhaps belaying people on a climbing wall. At many schools, the campus recreation staff is filled with students! After gaining experience through part-time work, you should next complete an internship. These internships are intensive; typically semester-long experiences are an excellent way to gain a deeper understanding of the field and complete work that will show potential employers your value. Because the field is so diverse, you may intern at a school of your choice. For example, if you attend a large school, consider complementing your experience by interning at a small one. If you are not sure what area of campus recreation to pursue, think about interning where you will be allowed to rotate among many areas. Last, it is always a good idea to earn as many certifications as possible. When queried, 88% of colleges and universities reported that they currently require various certifications.[6] Some such as first aid and CPR are useful in all areas. Others such as the Aquatic Facility Operator certification offered through the National Recreation and Park Association (NRPA), or the Certified Personal Trainer offered by the American Council on Exercise (ACE) or another certifying agency will increase your qualifications to work in specific areas of campus recreation.

Consider Graduate Assistantships

An excellent way to start your career in campus recreation is by continuing with a graduate assistantship while earning your master's degree. Many schools use graduate assistants to work in campus recreation. In return for working 20 to 30 hours a week, you will receive a monthly stipend and often a waiver for your tuition. Graduate assistantships are listed at www. bluefishjobs.com and on each school's website. Do not wait too long, though. Most schools fill assistantships early in the spring for the upcoming fall semester.

Discovery and Gaining Experience

The best way to better understand what campus recreation is all about is to get a part-time job in campus recreation while you are in school. Most campus recreation programs are happy to employ students as office assistants, referees, instructors, and other positions. It is a great way to learn more about this area and earn a few extra dollars doing something you enjoy. Check with your campus recreation staff and your financial aid office.

Possibilities

There has probably never been a better time to be a campus recreation professional. More than ever before, schools view campus recreation as a critical element in making the college experience satisfying. This is evident through an increase in hiring and an increase in the variety of positions within campus recreation. Although some schools, predominantly smaller ones, may still employ the "jack of all trades," many have turned to a staffing model that requires specialists to be responsible for the variety of recreation programs. Also, higher education has seen a dramatic escalation in the number of campus recreation facilities that have been built or are in the planning stages.[7] With the competition for students increasing, schools are constructing more elaborate student centers, recreation centers, outdoor recreation areas, and similar facilities in an effort to attract and retain students. As well, yearly operating expenditures have increased since 2010 and are projected to increase in the future.[8]

As new facilities are created, it is the campus recreation professional who is responsible for facility operations. This provides an excellent opportunity for career growth. At the entry level, you may be expected to plan and implement recreation programs. As your career develops, you may have opportunities to become more involved with the highest levels of management. Figure 8.1 illustrates a typical career progression.

When professionals start a campus recreation career, they may be responsible for direct program development such as intramural sports. As a programmer, success will be judged on the number of participants in programs as well as participant satisfaction reports. Entry-level professionals design programs, market them, manage their budget, hire and train student assistants such as referees, oversee scheduling and field preparation, and basically complete all the steps required of any recreation programmer. If the professional's passion is for intramural sports, the next step may be to serve as an assistant director of intramural sports, eventually leading to a position as the director of intramural sports. In either of these higher level positions, the employee will take on increasing responsibility for oversight of programs, facilities, and staff. An alternative path for advancement is facility management. A professional may become interested in managing facilities, such as a student recreation center and its associated facilities (e.g., pool, intramural fields, ropes course, etc). Eventually, a campus recreation career path may reach a position with responsibility for overseeing a complete campus recreation division or facility.

Campus recreation is a broad career area, and there are several specialties you may want to consider. A few are described below, along with the passions, preparation, and possibilities for each area.

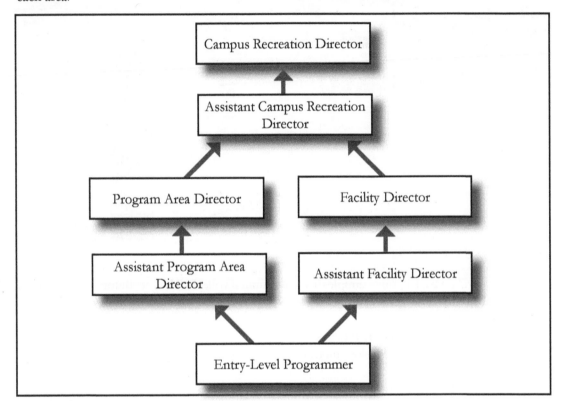

Figure 8.1. Campus recreation typical career progression.

Intramural and recreational sports. It is the end of a long day in the classroom. You have worked hard all day and answered many questions when called upon. You were prepared for today's classes, and now you have to start preparing for tomorrow. Assignments are coming due, and the end of the semester is coming quickly. You feel your stress building, but you know you have an opportunity to blow off a little steam with friends. In a couple of hours, your intramural volleyball team will meet and take on…who knows? The preceding scenario may describe you, your professor, or someone else who attends your school. Intramural and recreational sports break down barriers to bring everyone together. Behind the scenes, the intramural or recreational sports staff make this possible.

Although many schools are known for their intercollegiate sports teams and have a great number of students who are intercollegiate athletes, intramural sports serve more students than intercollegiate sports every year. **Intramural sports** include activities where students compete against other students at their school. Sometimes they may even compete against intramural teams from other schools. In that case, the event is known as an **extramural sport**. Some schools use the classic term *intramural sports*, and others see their role as being broader and use **recreational sports**.

Photo courtesy of Cal Poly ASI

Now, we will go back to our example of the intramural volleyball league. Before this intramural league can begin its first game, the intramural sports professional must complete many steps, including the following:

- determining start and end of the season
- marketing the league to develop interest
- recruiting teams to play
- reserving volleyball courts
- scheduling all games
- ensuring that equipment is available and risk management procedures are followed
- recruiting, training, scheduling, and handling payroll for officials
- recording results, updating standings, and overseeing league progress
- rescheduling games that are canceled
- repeating most of the steps above for playoffs
- awarding prizes

Of course, within each step above, many smaller tasks need to be completed. Campus recreation professionals must pay a great deal of attention to detail and have an infectious enthusiasm that will help recruit participants to team and individual events. For every sport that a college student may want to play, a league, tournament, or contest may be organized.

Passions. Recreation programming, organization, fun, creativity, teamwork, sports, communication, competition, student and community development.

Pay and perks. The national average for a director of campus recreation is $64,691.[9] However, the value of this career field is much greater than any salary. The perks of working in campus recreation include the great availability of starting positions around the country, the excitement of ever-changing programs, following a school calendar, and plentiful opportunities to become involved with professional organizations such as the NIRSA.

Don't Forget Clubs!

Schools are also increasingly emphasizing their club sport programs. These clubs range from the competitive and formal that will compete against other schools (extramural) to the fun and casual that will gather together to share their common interest in an activity. A good example is Sam Houston State University, which offers the following club sports: martial arts, cycling, volleyball, paintball, dodgeball, bowling, baseball, in-line hockey, hapkido, outdoor adventure, powerlifting, racquetball, rugby, soccer, tennis, ultimate Frisbee, and wrestling.

Preparation. Bachelor's degree in recreation or a related recreational sports field. Experience in intramural programming and management of sport clubs is essential. Becoming a Certified Park and Recreation Professional (CPRP) as defined by the NRPA is an excellent way to demonstrate entry-level knowledge of the profession.

Possibilities. This area has excellent opportunities for mobility within campus recreation. With colleges in every state, the number of potential employers is great. Additionally, this area provides many opportunities to gain experience in related fields and offices within higher education.

Student activities. Keeping students happy outside of the classroom has been an increasing goal for every school because it aids in retention. **Student activities** are a part of campus recreation and include activities such as concerts, celebrations, cultural events, and assisting student clubs and organizations. Student activities are critically important because they have the capacity to reach such a broad cross section of students. Also student activities are often cocurricular in nature; thus, the programs and activities are connected to material being covered in an academic course. The opportunities that cocurricular programs provide support not only the academic mission but also the overall student development mission of the institution.

The student activities director is a challenging but exciting position because of the range of activities schools provide. One day the student activities director may plan a homecoming parade, oversee the details of a state or U.S. senator speaking to political science students and members of the student government association, and before the day ends, work on promoting a major rock concert to be held the next weekend. Clearly, if you work in student activities, you will have variety.

It's All About Variety!

Darton College in Georgia is one example of a school that offers a variety of programs through its student activities office. Here are a few: geocaching, music trivia, midnite madness, campus clean up scavenger hunt, welcome back party, fun flicks—make your own video, honors day, hypnotists, magicians/comedians/ventriloquists, fall fling, blizzard of bucks wild and crazy game show, Darton beach party, bring your own banana day—free banana splits, one hit wonder—make your own CD, munch-a-mania, old tyme photos, art fairs, cartoon portraits, and peanut boil.

Passions. Working with students and faculty, organizing special events, using creativity, marketing programs, working with performers and agents.

Pay and perks. For a director of student activities, the average salary is $56,338.[10] Perks include working closely with faculty on cocurricular programs, exposure to the entertainment industry, and following a school calendar. Opportunities also exist to be involved with professional organizations such as the National Association for Campus Activities.

Preparation. Bachelor's degree in recreation, student personnel, or higher education administration.

Possibilities. This position is often at the center of campus life, so the opportunity to significantly impact campus life is excellent. In doing so, you would have the chance to partner with local performers and explore your creative interests. If your dream career includes producing events such as concerts and festivals, then the possibilities are endless (as long as your budget holds out)!

Fitness and wellness. Campus recreation professionals often specialize in the area of fitness and wellness. This includes personal training, supervision of a fitness facility, or even providing wellness programs such as weight loss and smoking cessation. This area also requires specialized training and certification beyond a bachelor's degree. For the safety of participants, it is critical that fitness professionals hold recognized certifications in the areas they teach. The campus recreation professional overseeing fitness and wellness programs must have an outgoing personality with an endless sense of enthusiasm if he or she is going to attract and retain participants who may be out of shape. It is that person with the smiling face that students expect and want to see every day as they head for a workout.

Passions. Fitness, health promotion, working with participants of all fitness levels, desire to improve the health of others.

Pay and perks. Salaries for full-time fitness and wellness coordinators are usually in the mid-$30,000 range, but of course, this depends on the size of the program. The main perk of this position is the ability to gain great satisfaction from aiding people in meeting their fitness and wellness goals. If you have an interest in wellness areas such as yoga, Pilates, weight loss, and the newest forms of fitness, then this area lets you explore all of those. Opportunities may also exist to work with a school's sports teams.

Preparation. Bachelor's degree in recreation, exercise science/physiology, health promotion. Fitness trainer certification through a recognized organization such as the American Council on Exercise or the American College of Sports Medicine.

Possibilities. This position has responsibility for impacting the health and wellness of all members of the college community. Of all the positions within campus recreation, this one has the greatest potential for showing the direct impact of the services offered. In addition, services may be offered to employee family members so the reach of the fitness staff may extend well beyond students.

Aquatics. Like campus recreation professionals who specialize in fitness and wellness, aquatic staff who work within campus recreation are also highly specialized. Beyond teaching aquatics-related skills, this professional may also work with outside groups, host events such as swim meets, be responsible for the maintenance and operation of an aquatic facility, and oversee a staff of lifeguards. Because of this, aquatic specialists also require training and certification beyond a bachelor's degree. More and more, aquatic facilities that mirror small waterparks are being added to schools. It is not uncommon now to see waterslides and lazy rivers turning up on campus.

Passions. Teaching others to swim, aquatic fitness, management of aquatic facilities, working with intercollegiate and outside swim teams.

Pay and perks. Salaries for full-time aquatic directors are usually in the mid-$30,000 range, but of course, this depends on the size of the program, and are often higher when there are more facilities to oversee. Besides the opportunity to work with a school's intercollegiate swimming team, another perk is the chance to assist local public and private swimming programs that may use your facility.

Preparation. Bachelor's degree in recreation, physical education, management. Specific training and certification related to aquatic facility management is also required. This includes the Aquatic Facility Operator's certification provided by the NRPA and the Certified Pool Operator provided by the National Swimming Pool Foundation, as well as training offered by the Red Cross covering lifeguarding and swimming and water safety certifications.

Possibilities. Aquatics may be a lifetime leisure pursuit. Aquatic professionals have the opportunity to provide programs for all age and fitness levels. As innovative facilities are added to schools, the aquatic professional has the opportunity to network with aquatic professionals from commercial waterparks and explore their practices through organizations such as the World Waterpark Association.

Swimming: Continued Popularity

According to the U.S. Census Bureau, in 2009, over 50 million Americans went swimming six or more times a year. This places swimming as the fourth highest activity after exercise walking, exercising with equipment, and camping. Over the past decade, swimming has consistently been in the top five activities for participation.

Recent trends point to the continued growth of nontraditional aquatic facilities on campus. Schools are now adding features often seen at waterparks. Southern Methodist University's Dedman Center features an area called "The Falls," where students may sunbathe in and around an outdoor pool that doubles as a fountain.

Georgia Tech University's Crawford Pool complex includes not only a traditional 25-yard pool but also a current channel, free-form play area, 16-person spa, and 184-ft waterslide!

Outdoor recreation. Many schools recognize the importance of promoting outdoor recreation opportunities so students can gain an appreciation for everything the local environment can provide. Whether students come from nearby or from around the country or world, outdoor recreation can open their eyes to activities they may have never known existed. A look at the outdoor recreation programs offered by colleges and universities shows a broad variety that includes camping, hiking, snowboarding, triathlon, wakeboarding, mountain biking, kayaking, rock climbing, ultimate Frisbee, rodeo, sailing, and slacklining. With an increasing concern for the environment on a national level, outdoor recreation on campus is seeing a great resurgence of interest. Professionals offering outdoor recreation opportunities may outsource their leadership to companies with the technical expertise required. If not, this specialty requires both proficiency in leading a program and training in first aid and risk management specific to activities that occur in remote settings.

Double-Dipping

If you have an interest in an area of outdoor recreation, you should speak to your campus recreation director. It is not unusual for schools to hire students as assistants during programs and on trips. This is a great way to participate in your activity, gain experience, and perhaps be paid as well.

Passions. Camping, outdoor leadership, travel, climbing, mountain biking, canoeing, skiing, backpacking, sailing, surfing, and other outdoor pursuits.

Pay and perks. Full-time positions in outdoor recreation are not as numerous as others in campus recreation. Full-time salaries may be comparable to those in fitness and wellness. The main perks to this position are the chance to make your work what other people consider their recreation and being able to make the outdoors your office!

Preparation. Bachelor's degree in recreation, outdoor leadership or recreation, environmental education. Specific training and certification related to outdoor pursuits and safety are required. This may include wilderness first aid certification, canoe and kayak instructor training provided by the American Canoe Association, and various instructor courses offered by the National Outdoor Leadership School.

Possibilities. Outdoor recreation continues to grow. According to the U.S. Census Bureau, camping was the third most popular activity in 2009 after only exercise walking and exercising with fitness.[11] As well, the National Sporting Goods Association reported that in 2011 camping equipment purchases were up 14%.[12] Schools also recognize the importance of outdoor recreation and see it as a way to better connect students with the community and to enhance retention.

First-Year Orientation Programs and Outdoor Recreation

For over 20 years, Harvard University has offered a First-Year Orientation Program (FOP). This voluntary program includes 6-day trips to Maine, New Hampshire, and Vermont. It is described as an "introduction to Harvard that takes place in the woods."[13]

At the University of the Puget Sound, multiday freshman orientation programs are offered that take students camping, backpacking, and canoeing. These programs are designed to match students with their interest and skill level and allow them to bond with other students and forge friendships that carry over into the school year.

Facility management. The start of the 21st century has shown a significant growth in the renovation of existing campus recreation facilities and the construction of new ones. This includes a trend toward integrated campus recreation facilities that include elements of a student center, athletic facility, food service area, library, and wellness center. These mega-centers seek to unite many student service areas on campus. As the importance of recreation facilities on a campus is increasingly recognized as a factor related to school selection and retention, so too has the importance of facility managers increased. Campus recreation professionals also specialize in the management of their facilities so they can be used by students, faculty, staff, families, and even members of the local community. In some areas, the campus recreation facility also doubles as a community recreation center when it hosts swim meets, basketball leagues, or even softball tournaments. The significance of allowing local agencies to use a campus recreation facility is that doing so may generate revenue to offset the cost of operating the facility and aid in the town-and-gown relationship between a school and its local community. Facility managers must understand budgeting, personnel management, risk management, maintenance, scheduling, and other functions related to managing a complex organization.

Facility Management: More Than Buildings at East Carolina University

When you think of recreation facilities, you may think only of buildings. East Carolina University (ECU) is a great example of a school that is moving beyond the traditional recreation center. Its student recreation center already houses aquatic facilities, racquetball/squash courts, fitness and aerobic areas, and gymnasium areas. To expand its offerings to students, ECU developed the North Recreational Complex. Located 10 minutes from the center of campus, it includes eight multipurpose fields that can be set up for soccer, flag football, lacrosse, ultimate Frisbee, and rugby. The complex also includes a 6-acre lake for fishing and boating, a field house, and a beach area.

Passions. Budgeting, personnel management, risk management, maintenance, scheduling, complex organizations, planning, marketing.

Pay and perks. Salaries for facility managers depend upon the size and number of facilities and range from $40,000 to $60,000 for experienced managers.

Preparation. Bachelor's degree in recreation or a management-related field. Specific training and aptitude in personnel management and facility maintenance are essential. Additionally, experience managing recreation facilities is critical for management positions.

Possibilities. As the number of campus recreation centers being constructed grows, so too do the opportunities for employment in this area. Because college campuses have a variety of facilities, the opportunity to gain experience in managing other facilities such as athletic and educational facilities is excellent.

Photo Courtesy Cheryl L. Stevens

Summary of Campus Recreation, Leisure, and Intramural Career Possibilities

Career	Passions	Pay and perks	Preparations	Possibilities
Intramural and recreational sports	Recreation programming, organization, fun, creativity, teamwork, sports, communication, competition, student and community development	Entry-level salaries are typical of new grads but may rise significantly acccording to size of campus/ recreation program	Bachelor's degree in recreation or a related sports field. Experience in intramural programming and management of sport clubs is essential	Excellent opportunities for mobility as schools continue to increase their intramural and recreational sport offerings
Student activities	Working with students and faculty, organizing special events, using creativity, marking programs, working with performers and agents	Salaries tend to be average to below average for new grads; salary depends on program size and budget	Bachelor's degree in recreation, student, personnel, or higher education administration	Because this area usually partners with other campus departments as well as off-campus agencies, opportunities exist to move up into other positions in higher education and entertainment
Fitness and wellness	Fitness, health promotion, working with participants of all fitness levels, desire to improve the health of others	Typical of new grad salaries; opporutnities for private practice may also be available	Bachelor's degree in the field of recreation, exercise science/physiology, health promotion; certification through recognized organizations such as the American Council on Exercise or the American College of Sports Medicine	Increasing concerns for student wellness will provide increasing employment opportunities
Aquatics	Teaching others to swim, aquatic fitness, management of aquatic facilities, working with intercollegiate and outside swim teams	Typical of new grad salaries, but will increase or decrease depending on the size of facility and amount of revenue generated	Bachelor's degree and specific training related to aquatic facility managment and instruction	At present, somewhat limited, but higher level management opportunities are increasing as aquatic facilities are added domestically and internationally

(cont.)

Summary of Campus Recreation, Leisure, and Intramural Career Possibilities (cont.)

Career	Passions	Pay and perks	Preparations	Possibilities
Outdoor recreation	Camping, outdoor leadership, travel, climbing, mountain biking, canoeing, skiing, backpacking, sailing surfing, and other outdoor pursuits	Typically low at the entry level	High school diploma to bachelor's degree; training and certification related to an outdoor specialty is necessary as is experience in outdoor leadership	Entry-level opportunities are plentiful, as are internships; higher level management positions are limited and sought after
Facility management	Budgeting, personnel mangement, risk management, maintenance, scheduling, complex organizations, planning, marketing	Entry-level salaries are typical of new grads but may increase according to facility size and budget	Bachelor's degree and experience working within recreation facilities as well as an ability to manage multiple tasks	An ongoing increase in campus recreation facilities has created an increased demand for facility managers at all levels

Future Opportunities, Issues, and Challenges

The field of campus recreation has changed over time to meet the changing needs of college students. Although the future of campus recreation is especially bright with the increased understanding in how it aids in the recruitment, retention, and long-term growth of students, challenges exist that must be met. If you choose a career in campus recreation, expect the following seven topics to garner increasing attention.

Technology

Equipment. Technological development occurs at such a brisk pace that equipment seen as state of the art one year may be seen as old quickly.

Virtual leisure. With almost half of the U.S. population using smartphones and 66% of 18- to 29-year-olds using them, this device is ubiquitous in our world. A myriad of apps related to recreation and wellness are available free of charge.[14, 15] The technology of MP4 players have also been incorporated in recreation and leisure with the development of virtual trainers.

Hard to reach. It is well documented that as individuals moves through adolescence to young adulthood they become less active. Increased screen time on computers, personal devices, and video games is widely known as a cause for this decrease in activity. This "inactive" population can be hard to reach and is the target audience of campus recreation. Though challenging, savvy campus recreation service providers will continually keep up with technological developments and how to best use them as an advantage in reaching members of the college and university community.

Moving Over to Move Up

Working within higher education provides excellent opportunities to become involved with the work of several campus divisions. As an intramural sports director, you may work on a retention project with the admissions and residence life offices encouraging first-year students to join an intramural team as soon as they get to campus. This will help them feel a part of the community right away. This will also give you an idea of how schools operate and what other areas may interest you. It is not unusual for a career progression to look like this: Graduate Assistant → Intramural Programmer → Assistant Director of Recreational Sports → Director of Campus Recreation → Associate Dean → Dean!

Risk Management

The growth in adventure sports such as snowboarding, mountain biking, rock climbing, and white-water kayaking is occurring at a time when schools want to minimize their exposure to costly personal injury lawsuits. Campus recreation professionals will be challenged to provide exciting programs with an element of risk and to ensure the safety of their participants.

24-7

While campus recreation has never taken place strictly between the hours of 9 a.m. and 5 p.m., the need for programs early in the morning and late at night is increasing. As is true in other recreation professions, other people's leisure time is the campus recreation professional's work time. This means that evening and weekend work is often the norm.

Nontraditional-Aged Students

As the U.S. population ages, so does the age of students attending college. Many schools have seen an increasing number of students outside of the traditional 18- to 22-year-old age range. This translates to campus recreation professionals providing programs for specific age groups and creating new guidelines that encourage participation across the life span.

Innovation

Within every area of campus recreation is a never-ending stream of new products, programs, and practices. The area of fitness alone has seen the popularity of strength machinery that complements free weights explode, and now the equipment choices are staggering. A decade ago Pilates classes were unheard of. Today, they continue to grow and have evolved into Pilates Fusion, which adds the use of free weights. As innovation continues, campus recreation professionals will need to diligently keep abreast of the newest opportunities.

Obesity and Sedentary Living

The national trends are alarming. Childhood obesity and a lack of exercise have increased dramatically. With much of campus recreation focused on activity, it will be an increasing challenge to motivate participants to continue activities that may be perceived as causing some discomfort both physically and emotionally. As noted in Figure 2.1 in Chapter 2, emerging and future delivery systems are focused on hard-to-reach populations and encourage collaborative boundary-free structures. Some programs addressing sedentary lifestyles have taken advantage of virtual experiences such as MP4 player technology, virtual trainers such as yoga, and fitness center orientations.[16, 17] These offerings help reduce constraints for students who may feel self-conscious around their peers as they participate in more structured programs.[18]

Assessment

Schools are under increasing pressure to demonstrate what students are learning. Regional accrediting agencies have moved schools into an era of outcome-based assessment to document how academic and nonacademic areas of campus are functioning. For campus recreation, this means measuring not only the number of participants but also the benefits they, and the school, receive from programs. For example, Clemson University has created a partnership between its Park, Recreation, and Tourism Management program and the Campus Recreation program to assess the satisfaction and importance of programs for students. As well, measures are taken to reveal equipment usage. Both assessment efforts are designed to determine benefits to participants and needs for the future. The emphasis on assessment in higher education has provided campus recreation professionals with an opportunity to clearly portray the tremendous benefits of their work to recruitment, retention, and alumni loyalty.

Resources and Getting Involved

Professional Organizations

Association for College Unions International: www.acui.org
An organization of campus union/center and student activities professionals.

Association for Experiential Education: www.aee.org
Promotes and develops experiential education with a focus upon outdoor education.

Association for Outdoor Recreation and Education: www.aore.org
Provides networking and advocacy opportunities for both students and professionals in the field of outdoor recreation/education as it relates to not-for-profit agencies.

NIRSA: Leaders in Collegiate Recreation: www.nirsa.org
An organization of professionals and students that promotes quality intramural and recreational sport opportunities through education and networking.

National Swimming Pool Foundation: www.nspf.com
Provides research, education, and certification opportunities for aquatics professionals.

National Association for Campus Activities: www.naca.org
Assists student activities professionals through education and opportunities to discover and develop new programs.

National Association of Sports Officials: www.naso.org
The largest sports officials organization that addresses education and training of officials at all educational levels.

National Recreation and Park Association: www.nrpa.org
Dedicated to the advancement of public parks and recreation opportunities, this organization provides numerous educational and professional development opportunities.

Wheelchair Sports USA: www.wsusa.org
Assists in the development of sporting opportunities for athletes aged 7 to 21 with physical disabilities.

© Andres Rodriguez | Dreamstime.com

Certifications, Licenses

Certified Park and Recreation Professional (CPRP): www.nrpa.org/Content.aspx?id=412
The CPRP demonstrates entry-level knowledge within the broad field of parks and recreation with a focus upon programming, management, and facilities operation.

Fitness Certifications
American Council on Exercise: www.acefitness.org
National Academy of Sports Medicine: www.nasm.org
American College of Sports Medicine: www.acsm.org
There are many certifications within the area of fitness. It is important to select those from recognized agencies with a quality history. The three listed here are well-regarded.

Aquatic Facility Operator: www.nrpa.org/afo
This certification demonstrates knowledge of pool operations to include areas such as safety, risk reduction, sanitation, and overall management.

Certified Pool/SPA Operator: www.nspf.org/en/cpo.aspx
This certification also focuses upon pool operations. Online learning opportunities are available.

Wilderness First Aid: wfa.net
This certification focuses on providing first aid beyond the trailhead, and it is an excellent addition for anyone pursuing a position in outdoor recreation and trip leadership.

Continuing Education: www.nirsa.org and search for *continuing education*
This is one example of continuing education opportunities led by recognized professionals working in the field that will help you further develop skills in intramural and recreational sports.

Where to Gain Experience

The best way to get involved with campus recreation is to meet the professionals and students that work in campus recreation now. Your school may list part-time job opportunities in campus recreation in the student employment office. Another great way to become involved besides networking on your own campus is to check the excellent online resources at NIRSA: Leaders in Collegiate Recreation. Go to www.nirsa.org and click on "discover" and then "student resources" to find scholarship information, student newsletters, résumé, interview tips, and more.

Conclusion

If you like the atmosphere of the college campus; want a flexible work schedule that may alternate between frenzied and relaxed; enjoy serving students, faculty, and staff; and have a creative side that is willing to try new ideas, campus recreation may be a good career choice. Although challenges are present, the future certainly looks bright for this area, and there is every reason to believe that the start of the 21st century is seen as an era where campus recreation is valued more than ever.

For Further Investigation

For More Research

1. Check the website of three colleges or universities of similar size to your school. Now check the website of a school with more students and one with fewer students. How do their campus recreation programs and facilities compare to your school?
2. Pick one certification that would help you be better qualified for a career in campus recreation. What is required to earn that certification?
3. Go to the websites for the National Association for Campus Activities and NIRSA: Leaders in Collegiate Recreation. What events do they sponsor that will help you as you start your career in campus recreation?

Active Investigation

1. Pick a campus recreation program at your school. What benefits does it provide? What campus recreation programs are offered at your school?
2. Interview 10 students and determine the following:
   - Do they participate in campus recreation programs?
   - If so, what types of programs?
   - If not, why not?
   - What are some campus recreation programs they would like to see offered at your school?
3. Volunteer to assist with a special event offered by your student activities office. What tasks did the staff complete to provide this event?
4. Interview activity: Select a campus recreation professional at your school. Use the questions below to discover more about what they do. Refer to the informational interview instructions under Active Investigation in Chapter 2 for more information before conducting your interview.
   a. What is the title of your position?
   b. What are your responsibilities?
   c. What responsibilities do you like most and least?
   d. What type of personality is needed to be effective in campus recreation?

e. What are your work hours? Does this change during the year?

f. Does your job have a set routine or does it change frequently?

g. If you could add one campus recreation facility on your campus, what would it be and who would work there?

h. What advice do you have for someone preparing for a career in campus recreation?

Recommended Reading

Each of the following articles provides an understanding of the role of campus recreation within higher education, skills needed, programs offered, and the benefits provided.

- Becker, C. M., Johnson, H., McNeil, M. P., & Warren, K. (2006). Creating partnerships on campus to facilitate practical experiences. *College Quarterly, 9*(3), 5.
- Clarke, B. S., & Anderson, D. M. (2011). I'd be dead if I didn't have this class: The role of leisure education in college student development. *Recreational Sports Journal, 35*(1), 45–54.
- Gillies, J., & Dupuis, S. L. (2013). A framework for creating a campus culture of inclusion: A participatory action research approach. *Annals of Leisure Research, 16*(3), 193–211.
- Hall, S. L., Forrester, S., & Borsz, M. (2008). A constructivist case study examining the leadership development of undergraduate students in campus recreational sports. *Journal of College Student Development, 49*(2), 125–140.
- Huesman, R. L., Brown, A. K., Lee, G., Kellogg, J. P., & Radcliffe, P. M. (2009). Gym bags and mortarboards: Is use of campus recreation facilities related to student success? *NASPA Journal, 46*(1), 50–71.
- Lifschutz, L. (2012). Club sports: Maximizing positive outcomes and minimizing risks. *Recreational Sports Journal, 36*(2), 104–112.
- Staeger-Wilson, K., Barnett, C., Mahoney, S., & Sampson, D. H. (2012). Planning for an inclusive campus recreation facility and program. *Recreational Sports Journal, 36*(2), 37–44.
- Toperzer, L., Anderson, D. M., & Barcelona, R. J. (2011). Best practices in student development for campus recreation professionals. *Recreational Sports Journal, 35*(2), 145–156.

These websites contain recent information related to student activities and sports:

- NIRSA Know: www.nirsa.org/wcm/Discover
- *Campus Activities Programming* Magazine: issuu.com/naca/docs/novdec_2013_plus_webCampusActivitiesProgrammingMagazine.aspx

This website contains the latest job listings in campus recreation. It provides an excellent look at the knowledge, skills, and abilities employers seek.

- Current Job, Internship and Graduate Assistant Opportunities in Campus Recreation: www.bluefishjobs.com

References

[1]NIRSA: Leaders in Collegiate Recreation. (2009). NIRSA's rich history. Retrieved from http://www.nirsa.org/Content/NavigationMenu/AboutUs/History/History.htm

[2] William & Mary, Greek life, Phi Beta Kappa. (n.d.). Retrieved from http://www.wm.edu/offices/greeks/scholarship/phibetakappa/

[3]Mittelstaedt, R., Roberston, B., Russell, K., Byl, J., Temple, J., & Ogilvie, L. (2006). Unique groups. In Human Kinetics (Ed.), *Introduction to recreation and leisure* (pp. 197–228). Champaign, IL: Human Kinetics.

[4]McLean, D. D., Hurd, A. R., & Rogers, N. B. (2005). *Kraus' recreation and leisure in modern society*. Sudbury, MA: Jones and Bartlett.

[5]NIRSA: Leaders in Collegiate Recreation. (2013). Learn about collegiate recreation's rich and distinguished history. Retrieved from   http://www.nirsa.org/wcm/About_Us/History/Centennial_of_Collegiate_Recreation

[6]Tipping, E. (2012). State of the industry. *Recreation Management, 13*, 8–31.

[7]Hignite, K. (2006). Sweat equity. *Business Officer, 40*, 29–33.

[8]Tipping, 2012.

[9]Chronicle of Higher Education. (2012). Median Salaries of Senior College Administrators, 2011-12. Retrieved March 3, 2012, from http://chronicle.com/article/Median-Salaries-of-Senior-College/130897/

[10]Ibid.

[11]U.S. Census Bureau. (2012). *The 2012 atatistical abstract.* Retrieved April 2, 2013, from http://www.census.gov/compendia/statab/cats/arts_recreation_travel/recreation_and_leisure_activities.html

[12]National Sporting Goods Association. (2013). NSGA releases sporting goods market in 2011 report. Retrieved March 14, 2013, from http://www.nsga.org/i4a/pages/index.cfm?pageID=4495

[13]Harvard first-year outdoor program. (2014). Retrieved from http://fop.fas.harvard.edu/

[14]Hannan, M. (2013). Here to stay: Technology trends shaping the field of parks and recreation (and the one's that won't). *Parks and Recreation, 48*(2), 36–41.

[15]Cummiskey, M. (2011). There's an app for that: Smartphone use in health and physical education. *Journal of Physical Education, Recreation, and Dance, 82*(8), 24–29.

[16]Blunt, G. H., & King, K. M. (2011). Developing a fitness center-based, self-guided instructional program using MP4 player technology. *Recreational Sports Journal, 35*(1), 61–68.

[17]Rhea, D. J. (2011). Virtual physical education in the K–12 setting. *Journal of Physical Education, Recreation, and Dance, 82*(1), 5–6.

[18]Trammel, K. (2011). The sedentary lifestyle: How to help those who absolutely hate exercise. *Parks and Rec Business, 10*(1), 42–43.

" *Sport is the focus of what we do—but what we do is about more than just sports. We use sports to make a difference in the lives of the people we serve.*

—Kevin Cummings
Executive Director
Massachusetts Amateur Sports Foundation "

9

Sport Management and Sport Teams

Robert J. Barcelona
University of New Hampshire

Q: I love to play sports. Does that mean I would like a sport management career?

A: Students interested in sport management need to be interested in both sports and management. Loving sports is not enough. Sport management is a career that requires professional preparation and a specific set of competencies. Read the following questions and the rest of the chapter to see whether a career in sport management may appeal to you.

Q: Does the business side of sport appeal to you? Are you interested in sales, marketing, promotions, and events?

A: If the business side of sports appeals to you, you may want to seek a job on the business and sport performance side of sport management. Most entry-level positions in professional sports tend to be in sales, corporate relations, sponsorships, community relations, or marketing.

Q: Does working directly with people participating in sport activities appeal to you? Do you enjoy programming, scheduling tournaments, and policy implementation?

A: Most positions in recreational sports, interscholastic sports, and youth sports are focused on program development and leadership. If you work in this area of sport management, you will be hands on with participants and the actual sport activity.

Q: Are you okay with working long hours?

A: In professional sports and intercollegiate athletics, it is not unusual to arrive in the office at 8:00 a.m. and not leave until 11:00 p.m. or later during a home game. In recreational sports, contests often occur at nontraditional times, such as at night or during weekends, to accommodate participants. This means sport managers work while others play.

Q: Would you like change and diversity in your job?

A: Although sport management has fairly specific core competencies, most professionals are asked to wear many hats. The constant change of duties is one aspect that sport managers like about their jobs. Read the profiles below to see what professionals in the field think.

Key Terms

Sport management	Commercial sector
Sport participation	Sport business
Sport performance	Sport programming
Management skills	Resources/venues
Public sector	Athlete/player development
Nonprofit sector	Youth sports

Profile 1: Could This Be You?

Kevin Cummings is the executive director of the Massachusetts Amateur Sports Foundation (MASF). Kevin oversees two multisport festivals and five sport and educational programs. As executive director, he is responsible for all aspects of this amateur sport organization, including
- staffing,
- funding,
- marketing and promotions,
- sport and program operations, and
- policy development.

Kevin began working full time in the field of sport management in 1984. He is passionate about his job and took time to tell us what he does.

Q: Kevin, tell us what you do in your job.

A: I oversee a large sport organization, one of the largest amateur, multisport athletic events in Massachusetts. I'm ultimately responsible for staffing, funding, promotion, operations, bookkeeping, kicking the copier, dropping mail off—you name it. I can tell you that each day is different, and the end of the day usually looks different than I thought it would when the day began.

Q: That sounds exciting—but what does this have to do with sports?

A: Sport is the focus of what we do, but what we do is about more than just sports. We use sport to make a difference in the lives of the people we serve—whether that means providing opportunities to showcase talented athletes, promoting good sports through our sportsmanship program, providing fitness and physical activity opportunities, offering scholarship and education programs, or enhancing the careers of our staff and volunteers. In this job, it's good to love sports, but the job is about more than just that.

Q: What advice could you give someone thinking about a career in sport management?

A: Get experience. Start now—go out and volunteer with a sport organization, build your résumé. It's about more than just being a former athlete. You need to learn how to manage events, work with people, multitask. Do what is required to make it happen, and don't wait. It's not too early—my best interns are the ones who have volunteered for me for four years, and our interns have gone on to jobs in professional football, college athletics, minor league baseball, and amateur sport. They got where they wanted to go because they got experience working in the sport industry while they were in school.

Q: Great advice! Last question—what do you love most about your career?

A: I love telling people about what I do. When I tell them that I run the MASF/Bay State Games, their response always is, "Is that really a job? You actually get paid to do that?" People are always amazed that I am able to work in this job and make a living doing it. I like making a difference in people's lives. I'm proud of our success stories. Like one of our former baseball players who played in the Bay State Games. The exposure he received from our program got him a scholarship to play in college, and that opened up doors. He was recently drafted by the Washington Nationals. There are literally thousands of stories like that from former participants, volunteers, and interns.

Profile 2: Could This Be You?

Amber Lilyestrom is the associate athletic director for marketing and strategic initiatives in the Department of Intercollegiate Athletics at the University of New Hampshire (UNH). She is primarily responsible for the marketing and promotion of six ticketed NCAA Division I sports, as well as group sales, game-day presentation management, special events, and corporate sponsorship fulfillment. Amber works closely with students by teaching classes in sport marketing. Amber has worked professionally in intercollegiate athletics since 2004. She recently gave us the inside scoop on her job and what it takes to work in this segment of the sport industry.

Q: It sounds like you have a lot of responsibility in your job, Amber. Is that a good thing?

A: Definitely! It is what I love about this career. No two days are exactly the same, and there is always something to be excited about. In this job, I get to wear a lot of hats, and do different things, like marketing, game day promotions, and working with our alumni and corporate partners. I even sing the National Anthem before games sometimes!

Q: That is a lot of hats! Are there any challenges that come with so much responsibility?

A: It's hard to stay balanced sometimes. We work hard all year, but between September and March, I'm busy during the day, most weekends, and late at night. But I love coming to work, and this doesn't feel like a job. We're a smaller department, so we have a real family environment and a feeling of connectedness.

Q: How did you get interested in a career doing sport marketing and promotions?

A: I was a student athlete (women's soccer), and I was really active outside of my team, too. I also had a lot of writing experience with the school newspaper. I became co-president of the student athlete advisory committee (SAAC), and that leadership role allowed me to practice many of the skills that I need for this job.

Q: So there was a natural connection between your out-of-class experiences and sports marketing?

A: Absolutely. Being a student athlete was helpful, but it was my writing experience and my leadership role with SAAC that allowed me to develop the skills needed for this job.

Q: What advice would you give to prospective students who are interested in this career setting?

A: Take every opportunity to get involved, whether the opportunities are paid or unpaid. I'm looking for students who are creative, confident, and well spoken. Be able to sell yourself; if you can't sell yourself, how are you going to be able to sell a team? I like to see interns have a foundation or some experience with sports, but I also want to see students expose themselves to new and different experiences, too. I like students who have a willingness to learn.

Q: Great advice, Amber. One last question—how do you make a difference through your job?

A: By helping students have positive experiences. For example, our Cat Crew internship program helps students learn about the sport industry and gets them involved in sports marketing. But my job also helps create positive experiences for student athletes. Helping increase our attendance rate by 40% for women's hockey, for example, makes the game-day experience better for both the players and fans. Working with our corporate partners to design promotions that achieve their marketing objectives and improve the fan experience also makes a difference.

The Wide World of Sport Management

Sport is a significant component of our social fabric. Hundreds of thousands—and in many cases, millions—of people involve themselves in sport activities, either through active participation in recreational sports or through watching or following the athletic exploits of others. Sport is a multibillion-dollar industry that is global in scope. It is connected to many of our social systems, including education, the economy, public health, the media, domestic and international politics, and community development.

Consider the following statistics, and think about what is involved in providing and managing these sport experiences for the hundreds of thousands (and millions) of people who are participating in them:

- Over 17 million spectators attended a game at a National Football League stadium in 2012.[1]
- Approximately 70% of children aged 6 to 17 participate in team sports, and nearly 3 out of 4 teenagers play at least one team sport.[2]
- Over 7 million high school students participated in an interscholastic sport in the United States in 2011–2012.[3]

- More than 450,000 college students participated in an NCAA Championship sport in 2011–2012.[4]
- Over 41 million fans went to a Minor League Baseball game in 2012.[5]
- Over 500,000 Americans of all ages participate in State Games.[6]
- 51.4 million Americans held memberships in sports and fitness clubs in 2012.[7]

Imagine the Possibilities

Sport management refers to the professional career of planning, organizing, leading, and controlling sport events, programs, personnel, and facilities. Sport management is incredibly wide in scope. Consider the possibilities presented here:

- professional sports played by high-paid, talented athletes for the entertainment of spectators;
- grassroots sport programs that build interest in a particular sport;
- big-time college athletics events, such as the NCAA basketball tournament or the football Bowl Championship Series;
- after-school intramural sport programs and clubs;
- multimillion-dollar stadiums and arenas;
- community-based sport and fitness facilities;
- sports program designed to develop and showcase athletic talent;
- Sport programs designed to build confidence, increase fitness levels, and expose participants to a range of positive outcomes;
- major international sport competitions, such as the Olympics or the Pan-American Games;
- sport opportunities for athletes with disabilities, such as the Paralympics or Northeast Passage's Athlete Development Center;
- sport-related businesses that are profit focused; and
- sport programs and facilities, which are available to the widest array of participants, regardless of ability to pay.

All of these images are associated with careers in sport management. It is important to recognize that the sport industry is a wide and complex career landscape.

History of Sport Management

The roots of sport management can be traced back to the days of Roman sports. Even in ancient times, someone was responsible for planning and presenting large-scale sporting events for the entertainment of the populace. In the modern era, sport management as we know it can be traced back to England, with the popularity of thoroughbred racing and the development of governance structures designed to organize and manage the growth of the sport.[8] The staging of the modern Olympic Games, beginning in the late 19th century, the growth of professional sport leagues and tournaments around the same time, and the increasing popularity of intercollegiate athletics (particularly college football) laid the foundation for the professionalization of sport management. In addition, the growth of organized youth sports, intramural sports in colleges and universities, and a growing concern with physical fitness helped to illuminate the importance of participation-based sports. As a response to the growing need for educated sport professionals, the first academic program in sport management was started at Ohio University in 1964. Since then, the popularity of sport management as an academic discipline and as a viable profession has continued to grow.

Sport Management Today

Today, hundreds of colleges and universities offer academic preparation and degree programs in sport and/or recreation management at both the undergraduate and graduate levels. The body of knowledge in sport management draws on a variety of academic disciplines, including kinesiology and sports sciences, business and management, and recreation and leisure studies.[9] This makes sport management an interdisciplinary profession. One of the strengths of sport management is that professionals can work in a variety of career settings. The following sections will help you understand the job settings that may be most interesting to you.

Sport Management Philosophies

Chances are good that if you have read this far, you probably have a passion for sports. Having a passion for sports is important, and it is a good first step toward a career in sport management. However, it is important to carefully consider what your interests in sports are because not all sport management positions are the same.

Sport management professionals are involved in managing a range of sport programs, services, and venues. These opportunities exist along a continuum that focuses on sport participation on one end and sport performance on the other.[10] Think about your interests in sports, and consider your passions and talents. If you are interested in designing and managing sport programs for the primary purpose of encouraging active participation in sports, career settings such as youth and amateur sports, sport and fitness clubs, resorts, interscholastic sports, or intramural sports may be right for you. If, on the other hand, your interest is in managing and marketing sport opportunities primarily focused on elite athletes, or staging sporting events for the purposes of entertaining spectators, career settings such as professional sports, intercollegiate athletics, sport management and marketing agencies, or national governing bodies/national sport organizations may be a good fit (see Figure 9.1).

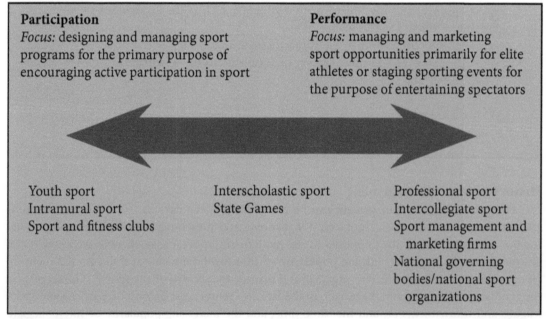

Participation
Focus: designing and managing sport programs for the primary purpose of encouraging active participation in sport

Performance
Focus: managing and marketing sport opportunities primarily for elite athletes or staging sporting events for the purpose of entertaining spectators

Youth sport
Intramural sport
Sport and fitness clubs

Interscholastic sport
State Games

Professional sport
Intercollegiate sport
Sport management and
    marketing firms
National governing
    bodies/national sport
    organizations

Figure 9.1. Particpation–performance continuum.

This continuum concept may provide sport managers with different philosophical frameworks from which to work. Providing opportunities for **sport participation** includes developing programs that encourage sport participation regardless of ability, age, sex, or other characteristics and is based on the idea that sport has the potential to yield many benefits to individual participants and their wider communities. Well-developed programs and facilities that enable wide participation in sport are justified based on their ability to improve health and well-being, reduce disease, contribute to cognitive learning, enhance social integration, and stimulate economic development, among others. In many ways, increasing opportunities for sport participation is not an end in itself, but it is a means for a sport manager to work toward achieving broader individual and societal goals.

Sport managers who are concerned with **sport performance** are generally focused on skill development and talent identification. The primary emphasis in this case is on developing skill, assembling talent, achieving elite performances, and entertaining spectators. The ends in this case may be winning championships, creating national pride, building fan loyalty, and/or enhancing revenue streams.

Regardless of where your interests lie, it is important to realize that careers in the sport industry combine both sport and management. The concept that people may gloss over is **management skills**, meaning sport managers must be passionate about the business and management-related tasks associated with staging or providing the sport experience. Although sport serves as the backdrop for the industry, we are not surprised that most of the day-to-day job responsibilities of sport managers focus on critical knowledge areas such as management, financing, event planning, marketing, legality, governance, and research, among others.[11]

Sport Management Sectors

Sport management career settings are located within all major sectors of the economy, including public, not-for-profit, and commercial sectors. Generally speaking, sport management jobs in the **public sector** refer to government-provided or -sponsored sport opportunities, such as municipal parks and recreation departments, school athletic departments, municipal sports councils, sport tourism bureaus, or armed forces sport and fitness programs in the United States. Governments may also fund or subsidize sport stadium or arena construction, maintenance, and operations (refer to Chapters 3 and 5 for details).

Sport management jobs in the **nonprofit sector** and in private sport organizations operate in the public's interest, yet do so outside the direct control of the government. Many nonprofit sport organizations exist to provide services to members or to serve particular constituencies, such as sport national governing bodies (in the United States), Ys (formerly YMCAs), grassroots youth sport organizations, or State Games (in some states; refer to Chapter 4 for more details).

The **commercial sector** consists of sport organizations that exist to make a profit for their owners or shareholders. Commercial sport enterprises can include professional sport organizations, commercial sport and fitness clubs, resorts, sporting goods manufacturers, or sport management and marketing firms. Table 9.1 shows the relationship between sport management career settings and the management sectors in which they generally fall.

Sport management jobs are varied in terms of career setting, organizational philosophy, management sector, and job emphasis. Opportunities for employment in the sport industry depend on individual interests, talents, and the realities of the job market. Sport management graduates may find employment in career settings, including the following:

- professional sport organizations
- intercollegiate or interscholastic athletic departments
- youth and amateur sports
- national governing bodies/national sports federations
- sport management and marketing companies
- school and college intramural sports
- resorts
- sport facilities and venues
- lifestyle and recreational sports
- sport councils and sport tourism
- sporting goods and merchandising
- sport and fitness clubs

Table 9.1

Selected Sport Management Opportunities by Management Sector

Public sector	Not-for-profit sector	Commercial sector
Definition:	Definition:	Definition:
Government-sponsored sport and recreation services, primarily at the federal, state/provincial, and local levels in the United States and Canada	Sport and recreation organizations that generally operate in the public's interest, but do so outside the direct control of the government	Sport organizations that exist to make a profit for their owners or shareholders
Municipal parks and recreation agencies	Private, not-for-profit community organizations	Professional sport
Armed Forces MWR programs	Local community sport organizations	Commercial sport and fitness organizations
State Games (in selected states)	State Games (in selected games)	Sport management and marketing firms
School-based intramural sports and sport clubs	National governing bodies	Sport merchandising
Intercollegiate athletics	Sport advocacy organizations	Resorts
Campus recreational sports	National/international youth sport organizations	

Sport Management: Four Major Job Emphases

The jobs that sport management graduates perform in these settings are as varied as the settings themselves. When people use the term *sport management*, it is sometimes difficult to decipher exactly to what they are referring. By saying that you want a job in sport management, not only are you suggesting a career setting (professional sports, college athletics, recreational sports, youth sports), but you are also referring to the nature of the specific job—or the job emphasis—that you are performing within the setting.

Four major job emphases exist in sport management: sport business, sport programming, resources/venues, and athlete/player development. **Sport business** refers to the business side of the sport industry. Most positions in professional sports focus on sport business. These include sales, sponsorship/corporate relations, marketing and promotions, media/communication, ticketing, financing, and athlete representation. Sport programming refers to positions that focus on the design and delivery of programs and events targeting sport participation. **Sport programming** positions include jobs in recreational sports, youth sports, or sporting event management. Resources/venues includes jobs that focus on managing the physical places where sports happen, including stadiums, arenas, multisport complexes, and sport-specific venues, such as golf courses or ski areas. Finally, **athlete/player development** refers to positions that focus specifically on talent or skill development in sports and may also refer to positions that focus on assembling sport talent. Jobs in this area include coaching, scouting, strength and conditioning, and sport operations positions within the professional sport industry.

Benefits of Sport

Sports managers are responsible for the design and delivery of sport experiences for both participants and spectators. Sport experiences are enhanced when they are directed toward some desired personal or societal outcome, or benefit. **Benefits-based sports management** (BBSM) refers to the intentional efforts sport managers undertake to ensure sport experiences yield desired benefits. The process of BBSM starts with conceptualizing the benefits that are most desired and then intentionally planning sport programs, facilities, and experiences so they have the best chance of yielding those benefits. For example, if one of the desired benefits of a major statewide sport festival is to increase economic activity in a community, festival leaders should plan to incorporate activities that would stimulate economic impact, such as marketing aggressively to out-of-town visitors, holding the event over multiple days requiring overnight stays, working closely with the local business community to provide sponsorship and marketing opportunities, and encouraging festival participants to spend money in local businesses.

Sports experiences, when intentionally designed, can yield many, if not all, of the benefit categories discussed in Chapter 1. Through their programs, facilities, and services, sport managers may improve

- personal benefits, such as increasing physical and mental health;
- social and/or cultural benefits, such as increasing community pride and identity, reducing crime, and bringing cultural groups together around shared sport experiences;
- economic benefits, such as economic growth, providing employment opportunities, and helping to create amenities that lead to a more desirable place to live, work, and retire; and
- environmental benefits, such as developing natural outdoor places to be physically active and using green technologies in the development of sport facilities.

In many parts of the world, sport is used to help achieve equity and social justice, and in fact, the United Nations has identified sport as a valuable tool for promoting development and peace. UNESCO supports many programs that attempt to bring citizens together through sports and promote peace. The organization explains this as being effective because sport "is a powerful tool to strengthen social ties and networks, and to promote ideals of peace, fraternity, solidarity, non-violence, tolerance and justice. Tackling problems...can be eased as sport has the ability to bring people together."[12] If one of your passions is to make the world a better place, sport management is a career path that may help you live out your passion through your work.

Can you imagine yourself as a sport management professional? Can you see yourself at work in a setting that provides and manages these varied experiences? If so, you may be interested in a career in sport management. The next section of this chapter covers additional details about working in the sport industry.

Careers in Sport Management

By now, you may be wondering how you can determine whether sport management is the right direction for you. Now is a good time to review the passions assignment that you completed in Chapter 2. If your list of top five passions aligns with what we have discussed so far, a sport management career may be a good fit for you, given your interests. The next step is to consider how you should best prepare for a career in the sport industry. What knowledge, skills, and abilities will you need to be competitive in the job market, and what does the overall job market for sport management careers look like? The following sections will provide answers to these questions.

"Sport...can offer the possibility of solutions where change might be needed, be it within an impoverished community or among an (at-risk) sub-population.

Through (sport development) projects, those involved might learn behaviors and values through a thoughtfully designed context, that later spur changes among membership such as in the case of a shift from violence to peace.

Sport then, may serve as a remedy to societal ills, risks, and hardships, assuming such programs are thoughtfully conceived and made available where and when they are needed to those who need them most.

—Schinke & Hanrahan[13]"

Passions

For those who truly love sport and are passionate about management, careers in the sport industry are exciting and rewarding. Remember, sport management is, first and foremost, about applying management skills in a sport-related setting. Many of the day-to-day duties have little to do with sports, per se. Sport managers are more likely to work with budgets, develop marketing ideas, or sell advertisements than they are to hobnob with professional athletes or media elites. In recreational sport settings, sport managers are likely to communicate with parents, train coaches and volunteers, develop new programs to target participation, or develop policies that govern sport contests in relative anonymity.

That said, sport settings are fun places to work. Most sport management jobs are highly sought after, and the public is generally impressed that sport management professionals make a living doing a job they truly love. Through their jobs, sport managers have the chance to impact the lives of athletes, fans, spectators, and their overall community. Think about it—in professional sports, you are usually selling a product (e.g., a team, a league, or an event) that evokes community pride and goodwill. Likewise, in recreational sport settings, you may know that you have helped young athletes develop their talents and abilities both inside and outside of sport.

Many Sport Management Jobs Have Multiple Responsibilities

Many sport management jobs have responsibilities that cut across multiple areas. For example, Mike Gamache, the program director for the Oyster River Youth Association (ORYA), an organization that provides recreational sports for youth and adolescents, has a position that is primarily sport programming, yet his responsibilities also include aspects of sport business, venue management, and athlete/player development.

OYRA's mission states that they "meet the changing needs of the children and families in our community for sports and recreational activities by acquiring and maintaining facilities, promoting volunteerism and seeking collaborative and strategic partnerships."[14]

Mike told us that, as program director, he handles a lot of things: "I'm pretty much responsible for everything that the organization does. I supervise over 100 sports programs for youth ranging in age from preschool to high school. Some of the programs require me to be very hands on. I handle budgeting and fees, player evaluation, supervision of volunteer coaches, equipment and uniforms, scheduling practices and games, coordinating meetings, communications, payroll, and organizing game officials. For other programs, I'm more hands off, as they have strong and active volunteer boards that handle most of the day-to day responsibilities."

Pay and Perks

Starting salaries in the sport industry do not differ greatly from other entry-level positions in fields such as education, general sales, marketing, or the various social sciences. In fact, they are generally similar across sport settings. It is a misconception that professional sport jobs pay significantly more than jobs in recreational sports or that jobs in the commercial sector pay more than jobs in the public sector. Variability in salary is more a function of the hiring organization and the specific sport management job than of the sector or setting. Ultimately, a good starting salary is dependent upon the individual needs and lifestyle of the job seeker.

Geography, benefits packages, and experience play a large role in starting salary. Jobs in areas with higher costs of living will often pay more to offset high living expenses. The value of fringe benefits is also important when considering total compensation. A good benefits package, including health and life insurance and retirement options may add up to 30% in value to a starting salary, making a $30,000 per year job worth close to $40,000. Opportunities to increase earning potential will grow as your sport management career advances. Top-level administrators may earn close to (or in some cases, well into) six-figure salaries with good benefits packages.

Preparation

As we mentioned before, sport management is a multidisciplinary field, meaning it draws from several academic disciplines to build its body of knowledge, including business and management, kinesiology and sport sciences, and recreation and leisure studies, among others. Jobs in the sport industry also cover many career settings, so it is important to consider both academic preparation and the development of core sport management competencies.

Students interested in careers in sport management can begin by obtaining an undergraduate degree in any number of academically related disciplines. Job seekers may find that different sport management positions require specific degrees. For example, an entry-level position as a youth sports coordinator for a local parks and recreation district may require a bachelor's degree in recreation, sport management, physical education, or a related field, whereas an event management position with a sport marketing and management firm may require a bachelor's degree in any number of fields, including marketing, advertising, business administration, or sport management.

Because career settings in sport management vary, completing an academic minor or emphasis may provide depth and direction to a sport management degree. For example, a minor in youth development or education may be useful for students who have interest in youth sports or interscholastic athletics. A minor in business administration, or a strong business foundation, including courses in accounting, economics, sport finance, sales, and marketing, may support any number of sport management careers.

Graduate degrees are usually not required for entry-level jobs in sport management. In fact, sport organizations may prefer a candidate with an undergraduate degree and relevant work (or volunteer) experience over a candidate with an advanced degree but limited experience. There are notable exceptions, however. Positions in higher education settings, such as campus recreational sports or college athletics, often require a master's degree in sport management, recreation, higher education administration, marketing, or similar fields. Sport agents often have graduate degrees in law, business, economics, or accounting. Master's or other professional-level degrees may also be helpful for career advancement.

The focus for students interested in careers in professional sports should be getting in the door. Finding opportunities for career advancement and alternative employment tracks (player development or other more competitive positions) becomes easier when working within the industry than when trying to break in from the outside.

It is important to find a university program that closely fits your desired career preference. For example, a sport management program that focuses primarily on sport business and sport marketing may not be the best program for a student who has an interest in recreational sports. Similarly, academic programs that do not offer exposure to sport business management principles may not be the best choice for students who have an interest in professional sports or other sport business settings. Before choosing a program, speak with faculty about their program's philosophy and curriculum requirements. Find out about the faculty's experience and contacts in the sport industry and the kinds of jobs their students get when they graduate. It is also a good idea to talk with students in the program to hear their perspectives.

Develop Sport Management Competencies

Sport management has a distinct body of knowledge, exemplified by its core competencies. Research on professional development in sport management has shown the following competency areas are important for sport management professionals to possess:

- business procedures
- marketing, promotions, and communications
- technology applications and computer skills
- facilities and equipment management

- governance
- legality and risk management
- management techniques
- philosophy and sport sciences
- programming and event management
- research and evaluation[15]

Although a general core set of competencies is important for sport management professionals, different career settings and jobs will emphasize specific competency areas more or less. For example, jobs in professional sports may emphasize business procedures and marketing, and jobs in recreational sports may emphasize programming and facilities management.

Also, sport management organizations can be incredibly diverse. Some professional sports front offices, intercollegiate athletics departments, or sport management and marketing firms are extremely large operations, with hundreds of employees, whereas some are much smaller. The same is true for recreational sport organizations. Generally speaking, in larger organizations, employees may have fewer job responsibilities and positions may be more focused. In smaller organizations, employees need to be more competent in more areas and job functions may be broad.[16] Aspiring sport management professionals should focus on selecting a combination of academic preparation and hands-on experiences whereby they can develop a broad base of professional competencies to better position themselves for several jobs within the sport industry.

Possibilities

A positive aspect of the sport management job market is its vast scope. Think about the job search process as if you were fishing with a net. Just like in fishing, the wider you cast your job search net, the better chance you have of landing a job in the sport industry. Consider this for a moment: Suppose you are interested in working in a sales and marketing capacity for a Major League Baseball team. There are 30 such teams, and a quick search of the employment pages on each team's website yields a small number of actual jobs. Given the popularity of Major League Baseball as an ideal employment setting, available positions often attract hundreds of applicants.

Casting your job search net a bit wider so it includes positions in the National Association of Professional Baseball Leagues (commonly known as the Minor Leagues) or in Independent Baseball will increase potential job opportunities. Hundreds of these professional baseball teams exist in the United States and Canada. However, even the most obscure professional baseball team is likely to have an extremely competitive pool of applicants for jobs they have available. Considering sales and marketing jobs with other professional sport leagues or teams outside of baseball will also increase your job search opportunities, although the same competitive employment marketplace still exists. This may sound discouraging, but it highlights the realities of a competitive job market in certain segments of the sport industry.

There is hope for potential job seekers, however. If you love sports, career positions are available in sport management. Although job opportunities in certain industry segments, such as professional sports, are limited, good jobs are available in other aspects of the industry, including recreational sports, youth sports, disabled sports, amateur sports, State Games, and venue management, among others. According to the U.S. Department of Labor, jobs in the recreation industry are expected to increase by 19% by 2020, with jobs in the fitness and physical activity industry expected to grow even more rapidly through the same time period.[17] Many of these settings are profiled in the pages that follow and are designed to give students a broader view of what the sport industry encompasses.

By now, it should be apparent that sport management is a broad and complex field encompassing many career settings and jobs. Sport management careers run the gamut from grassroots recreational sports to elite sports and athletic endeavors. The following section attempts to provide insight into some of the most popular sport management career areas. Remember, the sport industry is diverse, so it is impossible to cover many aspects of the sport management job market. Use these career possibilities to become acquainted with some sport management career options and then use the resources provided in this chapter and at www.sagamorepub.com/resources for more information.

Interested in a Career in Intercollegiate Athletics?

Seek out opportunities to do service learning, fieldwork, part-time employment, or internships with the athletic department at your college or university. Many athletic departments offer part-time job or volunteer opportunities for students in marketing and promotions, ticket sales, event management, or other areas in intercollegiate athletics. This is a good way for students to get to know the various subsets of athletic administration, get a good sense of the opportunities and skill sets required of the various jobs, and develop a network of contacts to assist with the future job search!

Interscholastic and intercollegiate athletics. School and college athletics are popular sports settings for participants, spectators, and job seekers. The unifying theme of interscholastic and intercollegiate athletics is the notion that sport participation enhances the educational experience of students and that athletics participation is an important extension of the school and college curriculum.

Passions. Leadership and supervision, budgeting, scheduling, fund-raising, marketing, policy development, networking, risk management, planning, student development.

Pay and perks. Full-time salaries are consistent with other sport management settings. Interscholastic athletic director salaries are similar to the salaries of department heads and are generally considered to be administrative-level positions. Entry-level salaries in intercollegiate athletics tend to be modest, yet strong benefits packages are often part of the total compensation package. Athletic directors at large colleges and universities are generally well paid with salaries often well into the six-figure range.

Preparation. Career paths are varied and often have different requirements for entry into the profession. Depending on the state or province, middle and high school coaches and athletic directors may be required to possess a valid teacher certification, especially in the public school system. Secondary school athletic directors should have strong coaching backgrounds, in addition to experience with league and tournament scheduling, personnel management, governance and compliance, equipment procurement, finance and budgeting, marketing and promotions, and strong leadership ability in working with parents, businesses, and other program stakeholders.

Preparation for jobs in intercollegiate athletics depends on the nature of the position. It is always wise to focus on acquiring the generally recommended sport management competencies and then to focus on the specific skills needed for particular jobs. For example, sport information directors (SIDs) must have strong writing and communication skills, a journalism background, an interest in statistics, and experience working with the media. Compliance officers usually have a strong legal background (many are law school graduates) and an interest in policy and rules enforcement. Marketing and promotions staff must be creative, have a background and interest in event planning and program design, and have the ability to sell marketing and sponsorship ideas to corporate clients. The job of the athletic director, especially at Division I institutions, is in many ways like that of a chief executive officer (CEO) in a corporation. Much of the athletic director's job is spent outside of sport. Athletic directors tend to focus on business administration principles, including fund-raising, revenue generation, governance, long-range and strategic planning, personnel management, and alumni and corporate relations.

Possibilities. Jobs in interscholastic and intercollegiate athletics are varied. In general, jobs in this setting can be found in individual schools and colleges; leagues or conferences; and state and national professional organizations, such as state high school associations, the National Federation of State High School Associations (NFHS), the National Collegiate Athletic Association (NCAA), the National Association for Intercollegiate Athletics, and the National Junior College Athletic Association (NJCAA). Besides athletic director positions, full-time jobs in interscholastic athletics in middle and high schools are available but rare. Coaching positions are generally part time. Careers in intercollegiate athletics are more varied and tend to fall into the following categories: marketing and promotions; ticket management; sport information and media relations; compliance; athletic academic affairs; fund-raising and development; facilities and event management; and athletic administration (athletic director).

Sport organizations. Sport organizations are concerned with the growth, administration, and development of particular sport activities and/or multisport events. In general, sport organizations are categorized as either sport-specific organizations, including national governing bodies and national youth sport organizations; multisport organizations; or education and advocacy organizations.

Passions. Love of a particular sport or sport-related cause and interest in the growth and development of sport and sport programs, policy development, marketing and promotions, event management, planning and organizational development, or fund-raising may help you find meaning and enjoyment with a career in sport organizations.

Pay and perks. Compensation varies by position and organization. In many cases, salaries and benefits packages are consistent with other sport management settings. In small not-for-profit organizations, jobs may be short term and tied to specific funding sources, such as grants. Many national governing bodies and national sport federations have a relatively stable number of full-time professional staff members fulfilling various jobs.

Preparation. Preparation for jobs in sport organizations is similar to other sport management settings. In most cases, an undergraduate degree in sport management, recreation management, business administration, marketing, or a related field, plus relevant work experience in the sport and recreation industry and demonstrated experience in the general sport management competencies, will help prepare a job seeker for positions in these organizations.

Possibilities. Job opportunities in this area are varied. Many sport organizations offer internships and full-time positions that focus on sport programming, event management, marketing and communications, sponsorship, and sales. These positions are generally found in the following sport organizations: (a) Sport-specific organizations focus on the growth and development of a particular sport. National governing bodies (NGBs; called national sports organizations, NSOs, in Canada) are sport-specific organizations. NGBs such as USA Hockey or NSOs such as Skate Canada are recognized as the governing organization by the sport's international federation (IF). NGBs and NSFs are charged with both grassroots and elite sports development. (b) National youth sport organizations are also generally sport specific and promote participation and development in a variety of sport activities. Examples of national youth sport organizations include Little League Baseball, Pop Warner Football, or the American Youth Soccer Organization (AYSO). In many cases, the national organization provides tools, resources, and a governance structure to guide local affiliated leagues in operating youth sport programs. (c) Multisport organizations promote both recreational and competitive opportunities in several sport activities. State Games in the United States and Provincial Games in Canada are examples of multisport organizations. (d) Education and advocacy organizations exist primarily to promote a sport-related cause or to provide education and resources related to a particular sport issue, such as coaching and parent education, character building, sportsmanship, and sport safety. Organizations such as the National Alliance for Youth Sports (NAYS), the American Sport Education Program, and the Positive Coaching Alliance (PCA) are example organizations. In some cases, sport-specific and multisport organizations also include education and advocacy as a component of their mission and goals.

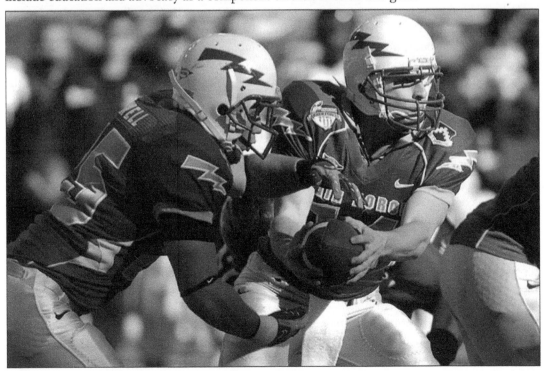

Professional sports. The popularity of professional sports is evidenced by stadium and arena attendance, television viewership, and a marriage of sports and entertainment that has led to a 24-hour media cycle of sport-related coverage, stories, and live programming. The high-profile nature of professional sports and the perceived excitement of working in this aspect of the industry have made professional sports a popular career choice for sport management graduates.

Passions. An interest in working in specific sport settings or in career paths such as sales, advertising and promotion, general marketing, operations, facility and event management, sponsorship development, media relations, community development, or corporate relations.

Pay and perks. Salaries for entry-level professional sport employees may be lower than other sport management settings, especially for positions with franchises in minor professional leagues. Some positions may be seasonal or part time. Some entry-level positions, especially sales, marketing, or corporate relations jobs, offer a base salary and commission structure. Perks include event attendance, the opportunity to affiliate with a high-profile organization, and the networking opportunities that occur through experience and becoming involved within the industry.

Preparation. Sport management students interested in professional sports should ideally complete a full-time internship with a professional sport franchise or league prior to graduation. Internships are highly sought after, usually require long hours (50 to 60 hours per week), and are mostly unpaid. Typically, internships with professional sport teams will last throughout the season—up to 6 months, in some cases. The internship experience is crucial for building a network of contacts in the industry. Networking is extremely important in all job searches, but particularly for positions in professional sports. Because jobs are so competitive, job seekers often rely on their network of contacts to help their application stand out. Many professional leagues also have their own recruiting methods. For example, attending the Winter Meetings with a résumé in hand and a list of contacts in the industry is still considered to be one of the best methods for seeking employment in professional baseball.

Possibilities. Jobs in professional sports are highly sought after. Students interested in professional sports as a career option need to work hard to find opportunities for employment. Few professional sport jobs are listed publicly, and jobs that are publicly listed, such as on a website, can attract hundreds of résumés. Most professional sport franchises are split between business and player development. The business side includes positions such as stadium operations, media relations, ticket sales, finance, corporate relations and sponsorships, and marketing and community relations. In some cases, these positions may be combined or may be labeled slightly differently. Player development positions include scouting, talent identification, coaching, equipment management, and athletic training. Almost all entry-level positions in professional sports are on the business side of the organization, typically in sales or community relations. Generally, few entry-level player development jobs are available for the typical sport management graduate. The good news is that for dedicated, hard-working, and opportunistic students, careers in professional sports are possible and available, and once in the door, career advancement and new job opportunities may become more readily available.

Sport management and marketing firms/sport agency. Sport agents represent athletes and handle contract negotiations. In addition to contract negotiations, many sport agents handle athletes' endorsement contracts, financial planning, legal services, and postcareer counseling and provide many personal care services. Full-service sport management and marketing agencies are quickly becoming the industry standard. Some sport agency firms still focus primarily on athlete representation, yet others offer a diverse array of services such as sport marketing and branding, media consultation, and event management. Some firms have even expanded their reach into the broader entertainment industry.

Passions. Your passions should fall into the areas of customer service, sales, law, negotiation and mediation, event management, or corporate relations.

Octagon, a major sport management and marketing firm, offers students the "Octagon Experience," an in-depth 10-week internship designed to provide students with experience in their "athletes and personalities" division. Another major sport management and marketing firm, IMG, offers internships in various divisions based on the organization's needs and the candidate's preference.

Pay and perks. Compensation and benefit structures will depend greatly on the size of the sport management firm, the clients that the firm represents, and the nature of the job. Sport management and marketing firms are competitive businesses. Compensation packages in the largest, best known firms can be lucrative, especially for representatives of high-profile athletes or events.

Preparation. The best way to prepare for a career in a sport management and marketing firm depends on the job you are seeking. For example, in addition to general sport management competencies, sport agents need to have significant knowledge of sport law, accounting, and financial planning. In addition to a suitable undergraduate degree with a strong business and management orientation, it is usually recommended that sport agents attend a law school that specializes in sport and entertainment law. Some sport agents pursue master's of business administration (MBA) or master's of accountancy degrees. On the other hand, event managers need to focus on concerns such as event structure, facilities, sponsorship, financing, policy development, program control, personnel, publicity, risk management, media coverage, hospitality, and event evaluation. Entry-level positions generally require a bachelor's degree in sport management, business administration, marketing, or a related field. Many full-service sport management and marketing firms, such as Octagon and IMG, offer significant internship programs designed to provide exposure to the industry.

Possibilities. Jobs with sport management and marketing firms are highly competitive. Job categories tend to focus on two major tracks: athlete representation and event management. Many sport management and marketing agencies are full-service firms that include both perspectives. Sport agents are in the business of taking care of the many needs of professional athletes. Event managers do not generally involve athlete representation, but rather they focus on planning, coordinating, and managing sporting events. These may be large-scale elite events such as the Gravity Games, or they may be large-scale grassroots events such as the NBA Hoop-It-Up.

Additional sport management career possibilities. Sport management covers such an array of career opportunities, it is not possible to go into depth on all of them. The following are three important sport management career areas discussed in more detail in other chapters.

Youth and amateur sports. Participation in organized community youth sport programs outside of school is estimated to be in the range of 30 million to 40 million in the United States and approximately 2.2 million in Canada.[18] **Youth sports** can be defined as the provision of organized sport opportunities for children and adolescents outside of the school setting. The philosophical orientation of youth sport organizations varies from primarily recreational opportunities designed to maximize participation to competitively oriented programs designed to develop and showcase athletic talent. A big challenge for youth sport administrators is articulating and enacting a positive philosophy for youth sports in an environment where goals are often different and conflicting. See Chapter 3, which covers youth development, for helpful information.

Intramural sports. The term *intramural* translates literally to "within the walls." Traditionally, intramural sport programs have been associated with school- or college-based recreational sport pursuits offered for the benefit of all students. Intramural sport programs may also be found in military settings and are offered to military personnel (and their dependents) assigned to a specific location, such as a military base. See Chapters 5 and 8 for more details on sport-related career possibilities in these settings.

Intramural sport programs differ from interscholastic or intercollegiate athletics in several ways: intramural activities are based in the school or college; activities are provided for the benefit of the students (or perhaps faculty and staff) of the school or college; they operate on a "sport for everyone" philosophy—there are usually no try-outs or cuts based on ability; and they operate with minimal or no formal coaching or supervision and are generally led by participants.

Venue management. Facilities have always been a critical component of the sport enterprise. Without access to a suitable physical space to play or perform, sport cannot occur. Similarly, as sport and entertainment have become more intertwined, designing sport facilities to accommodate the needs of both athletes and spectators has become increasingly important. With the opening of each new sport venue, new levels of athlete and spectator comfort are reached. Clearly, sport facilities and venues are critical components of the sport management industry. Refer to Chapter 10 for more details about sport venue management career possibilities.

Summary of Sport Management Career Possibilities

Career	Passions	Pay and perks	Preparations	Possibilities
Interscholastic or intercollegiate athletics	Leadership and supervision, budgeting, scheduling, fund-raising, marketing, policy development, networking, risk management, planning, student development	Consistent with other sport management settings; starting salaries may be modest, but generally have very good benefits packages; potentially high salaries for intercollegiate athletic directors	Varies with the position; demonstrated job competencies, teacher certification required for many interscholastic jobs; practical experience and academic preparation in sport management or related field	Interscholastic athletics = athletic director positions in schools; intercollegiate athletics = marketing and promotions, ticker management, sport information and media relations, compliance, athletic academic affairs, fund-raising, and development, facility and event management, athletic administration

(cont.)

Summary of Sport Management Career Possibilities (cont.)

Career	Passions	Pay and perks	Preparations	Possibilities
Sport organizations	Love of particular sport-related cause, interested in growth and development of sport and sport programs, policy and organizational development, event management	Varies by position and organization	Similar to other sport management settings, practical experience and academic preparation in sport management or related field	Jobs with sport-specific organizations (NGBs and NSFs), national youth sport organizations, multisport organizations (State/Provincial Games, Olympics), education or advocacy organizations
Professional sports	Sport-specific settings, sales, advertising and promotions, marketing, facility and event management, media and communication, corporate relations, community development	Varies by position and organization	Similar to other sport management settings, practical experience through internships and academic preparation in sport management or related field, networking is particularly important because jobs are competitive	Jobs in stadium operations, media relations, ticket sales, finance, corporate relations and sponsorships, marketing, and community relations; fewer opportunities in player development such as scouting
Sport marketing and management	Customer service, sales, law, negotiation, event management, and corporate relations	Varies by position and organization, but compensation packages with large firms may be lucrative	Focus on developing business and management competencies, sport law, accounting, financial planning, and event management; practical experience through internships and academic preparation in sport management, business, law, marketing, or related fields	Jobs in athlete representation and event mangement

Resources and Getting Involved

Perhaps by now you have a sense that a career in the sport industry is for you. You may have even identified a career setting and a job emphasis that interests you. In addition to choosing the right academic major and understanding the professional competencies necessary for a career in sport management, you should become involved in your new career in a deeper way. Consider the following sections on professional organizations, certifications, and tips for gaining experience. This information will be useful to you as you build your qualifications toward a sport management career.

Professional Organizations

In addition to finding the right academic preparation program and completing an internship, students are encouraged to seek out other professional development opportunities. Many of the subfields in sport management have professional associations that provide opportunities for knowledge dissemination and professional development for their members. For example, NIRSA; National Recreation and Park Association (NRPA); American Alliance for Health, Physical Education, Recreation, and Dance (AAHPERD); International Association of Assembly Managers (IAAM); International Health, Racquet, and Sportsclubs Association (IHRSA); Resort and Commercial Recreation Association (RCRA); Sport Marketing Association (SMA); and North American Society for Sport Management (NASSM) are professional associations that are designed to further various aspects of the sport management field. Other organizations such as Athletic Business (AB) focus on providing resources and materials for sport management professionals.

Many professional associations hold annual conferences, and most offer student membership options. A number of professional associations offer career and internship fairs, or post available jobs on their websites. Student involvement in relevant professional associations provides another pathway into the sport management field.

The following is a list of professional organizations relevant to sport management. Each of these organizations represents different facets of the sport management profession and will be more or less relevant depending on your career interests. Check them all out to see which ones appeal to you most.

American Alliance for Health, Physical Education, Recreation, and Dance (AAHPERD): www.aahperd.org

North American Society for Sport Management (NASSM): www.nassm.org

Sport Marketing Association (SMA): www.sportmarketingassociation.com

NIRSA: Leaders in Collegiate Recreation: www.nirsa.org

International Health, Racquet, and Sportsclub Association (IHRSA): www.ihrsa.org

College Sports Information Directors of America (CoSIDA): www.cosida.com

International Association of Assembly Managers (IAAM): www.iaam.org

National Collegiate Athletic Association (NCAA): www.ncaa.org

National Association for Intercollegiate Athletics (NAIA): www.naia.org

National Junior College Athletic Association (NJCAA): www.njcaa.org

National Federation of State High School Associations (NFHS): www.nfhs.org

Disabled Sports USA (DSUSA): www.dsusa.org

Women's Sports Foundation: www.womenssportsfoundation.org

U.S. Golf Association (USGA): www.usga.org

The Y (Young Men/Women's Christian Association): www.ymca.net *or* www.ywca.org

Certifications, Licenses

Many professional associations also offer the opportunity for professional certification. Some notable professional certifications in the field include the Certified Recreational Sports Specialist (CRSS), Certified Park and Recreation Professional (CPRP), Certified Youth Sports Administrator (CYSA), and Certified Facility Executive (CFE), among others. Pursuing a certification demonstrates commitment to professional development in the sport management field. In some cases, depending on the sport management career setting and particular job, professional certification is required or strongly recommended for employment. If required, you may also have to update or renew your certification, usually by attending an industry conference or taking a relevant academic class.

Where to Gain Experience

Preparing for a career in the sport industry is serious business. Although good jobs exist, most are highly sought after and competitive. Obtaining a career in sport management means more than doing well in your academic classes (although this is important, too!). It means gaining experience, building competence, demonstrating commitment, and making contacts. Consider the following tips to help you become involved and prepare for a career in the sport industry.

Enroll in an undergraduate academic program related to your career area of interest. If your college or university does not have a sport or recreation management undergraduate program, consider majoring in business administration, marketing, journalism, communications, education, or other academic programs that will help you build your competencies in the critical areas for sport management.

Get to know your professors outside the classroom. Many professors have contacts in the sport industry and can be valuable resources for helping you get started in the field. Some professors may allow undergraduates to assist with their research. These experiences build competence in critical areas (e.g., research, evaluation, and communication) and provide networking opportunities within the sport industry.

Complete an independent study. *Hksim Dreamstime Stock Photos*

If your academic program allows it, go to your professors and request to design and complete an independent study that focuses on your area of interest. Good independent studies build critical competencies in the field. Marketing and communication plans, program design, sponsorship development, or research and evaluation projects may help you show off your abilities, develop skills, and get to know your professors better outside of the classroom.

Take advantage of service and experiential learning opportunities. Many sport and recreation management programs (as well as other fields) offer classes that incorporate field-based experiences within their curriculums. Take these classes, gain experience in a range of sport settings, and put these experiences on your résumé. Be a leader, and showcase your talents when you have the opportunity. This is a great opportunity to get to know your professors.

Volunteer for part-time work in the field early and often. The experiences you gain outside the classroom are as important as what you learn inside. Start by volunteering to work in your college's athletic department or by working part time in the intramural sports office. Spend your summers working with youth in a summer sport camp or working with a professional sports organization. The more relevant work experience you have on your résumé, the better chance you will have of standing out in a competitive job market. The following is a list of settings where you may look for a part-time or volunteer opportunity:

- college/university athletic departments,
- campus recreation/intramural sports,
- community recreation programs,
- sport officiating/umpiring,
- local running or biking events,
- youth sports coaching,
- State Games,
- local professional sport franchise (major or minor league), and
- sport/recreation management major's club or association.

Join a professional organization (or two, or three!). Many areas of sport management have professional organizations that represent them. Ask your professors to which associations they belong. Register for a student membership, attend a meeting or visit the website, and see what it has to offer. Many professional organizations offer low-cost memberships to students and provide access to internship and full-time job opportunities. Some associations encourage student leadership. Take advantage of these leadership opportunities by volunteering to help at conferences, sitting on committees, or standing for office. These are great places to develop your leadership abilities and build your professional network.

Complete a full-time internship. There are a variety of internship opportunities in the sport management field. Internships provide students with real-world, practical experience. They also help to develop contacts. To rephrase the old saying, "it's what you know AND who you know" that helps open career doors in sport management. Quality sport and recreation management programs will require an internship as a component of the curriculums. Other academic programs may offer credits for internship experiences. Take advantage of these opportunities! In many cases, the internship experience is the key that unlocks the door to your first full-time job.

Develop a network of working professionals in the field. Through all your experiences, both inside and outside the classroom, continue to develop a list of professional contacts in the field. Do not be afraid to ask your contacts for career advice, information on the profession, and job search assistance. Most will be glad to help. Remember that these relationships need to be nourished. Keep in contact with your mentors even when you are not asking them for something, and always remember to follow up with a thank you!

Future Opportunities, Issues, and Challenges

As sport management continues to grow as a popular academic major, it is important that you gain exposure to the depth and breadth of the sport industry within your coursework. Sport is about more than fun, games, and entertainment. Although sport is part of our understanding of leisure, it is also a major industry segment tied to key areas of society, such as education, law, the economy, health, community development, and the media. Students of sport management must be interested in these larger systems, especially when understanding how sport fits into the fabric of a community.

As discussed in Chapter 2, the leisure service delivery system, of which sport is an integral part, is changing. For sport management, the service delivery model has flexible boundaries, is more integrated with other services, and is based on making personal connections and developing partnerships to extend the work that leisure services professionals do. Societal issues are too complex for any one profession or industry to tackle alone. For example, the solution to the obesity crisis cannot be solved by the health care industry alone. The issue requires systematic partnerships with several industry sectors, including recreation and sport management. Individuals who say they love sport but are not interested in how sport intersects with personal and community health, economic stimulus, educational outcomes, or community development demonstrate a lack of depth and limit the ability of sport management to be taken seriously as a viable academic area of study.

As you have seen, sport management is a field that encompasses much more than careers in professional sports or collegiate athletics. To have the best chance of landing a sport-related job, explore all of the potential career areas within the field and remain open-minded about the job opportunities within the sport industry. Also, keep abreast of growth areas within sport management, such as the popularity of action sports among youth; the push for active and healthy lifestyles; the development and construction of environmentally friendly "green" sport facilities; greater integration of technology into sport programs, facilities, and services; and the increasing numbers of active older adults who are interested in continuing to participate in sports. These trends, as well as future directions we cannot yet predict, represent growing opportunities for sport management professionals.

A major challenge for the field of sport management is to continue to present an integrated perspective even as the profession embraces specialized opportunities in instructional, recreational, performance-focused, and elite sport. To some extent, these divisions can be seen within academic preparation programs, as sport management is often located in various departments/academic units. Sport management may be found within business schools, kinesiology or physical education departments, or recreation and leisure studies programs. Although sport management requires a strong business and management foundation, it nevertheless remains an interdisciplinary profession. This means that sport management scholars and students need to consider sport from the perspective of a range of professional disciplines (including those listed above). In addition, those in sport management must continue to incorporate the social sciences, such as psychology, sociology, economics, history, and political science, which can all be used to frame our understanding of sport management and its place in our social systems.

Conclusion

Sport management is a demanding profession. The popularity of sport has created tremendous opportunities for careers that do not involve playing the game. Remember that sport management is both a profession and a career. Many sport management jobs demand long hours and are rarely as glamorous as they may otherwise appear. Students who are interested in sport management need to be interested in both sport and management. Being a great athlete or loving sports is not enough. Rigorous academic preparation, meaningful internship or fieldwork experiences, professional contacts, and a desire to work hard are prerequisites to an entry-level position in sport management.

For Further Investigation

The following resources have been assembled to help you find out more about careers in sport management. Websites for professional associations, relevant sport management organizations, and other information that may help you investigate sport management careers are listed here.

For More Research

1. Refer to the extensive list of professional organizations in the previous section. Choose five that seem to be the most relevant to your area of interest. Go to each website and review and report on mission, educational opportunities, upcoming conferences, educational opportunities, and job postings.

2. Below you will find organizations related to four particular areas of interest within sport management. Choose one area that interests you and go to those websites. Review and report on mission, educational opportunities, upcoming conferences, educational opportunities, and job postings.

Sport Management and Marketing Firms
Octagon: www.octagon.com
SMG: www.smgworld.com
IMG: www.imgworld.com

Olympics and Paralympics
International Olympic Committee: www.olympic.org/ioc
U.S. Olympic Committee: www.teamusa.org
International Paralympic Committee: www.paralympic.org

National Youth Sport Organizations and Advocacy
Little League Baseball: www.littleleague.org
American Youth Soccer Association: www.ayso.org
Pop Warner Football: www.popwarner.org
National Alliance for Youth Sports (NAYS): www.nays.org
American Sport Education Program (ASEP): www.asep.org

Professional Sports
Major League Baseball: www.mlb.com
Minor League Baseball: www.minorleaguebaseball.com
National Football League: www.nfl.com
National Basketball Association: www.nba.com
Women's National Basketball Association: www.wnba.com
National Hockey League: www.nhl.com
American Hockey League: www.theahl.com
East Coast Hockey League: www.echl.com
NASCAR: www.nascar.com
Indy Racing League: www.indycar.com.com
Major League Soccer: www.mlsnet.com
United Soccer Leagues: www.uslsoccer.com
Professional Golf Association: www.pga.com
Ladies Professional Golf Association: www.lpga.com

3. Examine several jobs, qualifications, and salaries in the sport management field. This particular exercise is limited to certain sport management positions, but you can do your own research and expand your search beyond the sources listed here.Check out the following websites:

- **NCAA jobs:** ncaa.thetask.com/market/jobs/browse.php
- **Sport venues and facilities jobs:** Venuestoday.com and click the "help wanted" tab or check out www.jumpinsport.com
- **Check out NIRSA's job site at** careercenter.bluefishjobs.com

Active Investigation

1. Sport Management Case Study: To gather in-depth information on a particular sport organization, conduct a short case study of an actual organization in the career setting of your choice. Collect information from websites, professional/trade associations, research journals, statistical information, personal interviews, and other relevant sources. Use a variety of sources! Research and analyze the following information:
   - Introduction of the agency/organization, including a discussion of its management sector (public, not-for-profit, commercial) and funding structure (taxes, fees, grants, fund-raising, sponsorships, some combination)
   - Organizational mission and goals
   - Description of the general range and types of services, programs, and facilities offered
   - Description of the clientele/customers/users of the service—who does the agency target or try to attract to its services/programs?
   - Description of employee positions, types of jobs, and qualifications (discuss full-time, part-time, and volunteer positions, if applicable)
   - Several issues or trends impacting the agency/organization or the wider sport management career setting
   - Additional information—include additional information related to the industry segment, information taken from personal interviews, key statistics/indicators, or other information that will enable you to obtain a better understanding of this organization and/or sport management career setting
   - Expand your search by looking at the websites of professional sport teams and leagues (major and minor) and national governing bodies/national sport federations. Look at the positions and salaries listed.
   - Gain a sense of the job types, duties, qualifications, and starting salaries for these various positions.
   - What themes do you see? Do any of these jobs or career settings interest you?

2. Revisit the list of benefits that have been attributed to leisure experiences in Chapter 1. Pick an area of sport management in which you are most interested in working, such as youth sports, professional sports, intercollegiate athletics, or State Games. Conduct research. Which of the benefits are most likely to be associated with your career area? Think about the ways that you may design, deliver, or manage a sport program, facility, or service so that it maximizes the benefits that you identified.

Recommended Reading

Martens, R. (2001). *Directing youth sports programs*. Champaign, IL: Human Kinetics.
This book offers the best collection of administrative resources available to youth sport directors. It contains a wealth of hands-on, practical information that will help you develop a sound program philosophy and compatible policies.

Masteralexis, L. P., Barr, C. A., & Hums, M. A. (2012). *Principles and practices of sport management* (3rd ed.). Sudberry, MA: Jones and Bartlett.
This text offers a comprehensive introduction to the sport management industry, and it covers a variety of sport management careers.

Mull, R. F., Bayless, K. G., & Jamieson, L. M. (2005). *Recreational sport management* (4th ed.). Champaign, IL: Human Kinetics.

This book is designed to prepare students in sport management for solid careers, and it is also a practical tool for professionals working in the field, with more than 60 forms and checklists to ensure smooth day-to-day operations.

References

[1]ESPN. (2013). NFL attendance – 2012. Retrieved from http://espn.go.com/nfl/attendance/_/year/2012

[2]Sports and Fitness Industry Association. (2011). State of team sports in America. Retrieved from http://www.sfia.org/press/369_State-of-Team-Sports-in-America

[3]National Federation of State High School Associations. (2013). Participation data. Retrieved from http://www.nfhs.org

[4]National Collegiate Athletic Association. (2012). College sports statistics and records. Retrieved from http://www.ncaa.org

[5]Minor League Baseball. (2013). MiLB attendance up in 2012 over 2011. Retrieved from www.milb.com

[6]National Congress of State Games. (2013). About us. Retrieved from http://www.stategames.org

[7]International Health, Racquet, and Sportsclub Association. (2013). About the industry. Retrieved from http://www.ihrsa.org

[8]Masteralexis, L. P., Barr, C. A., & Hums, M. A. (2012). *Principles and practices of sport management*. Sudberry, MA: Jones and Bartlett.

[9]Jamieson, L. M., & Toh, K. L. (2000). Professional preparation in sport management: A narrative meta-analysis. *NIRSA Journal, 24*(1), 31–43.

[10]Coakley, J. J. (2004). *Sport in society issues and controversies* (8th ed.). Boston, MA: McGraw-Hill.

[11]Barcelona, R. J., & Ross, C. M. (2005). An analysis of the perceived competencies of recreational sport administrators. *Journal of Park and Recreation Administration, 22*(4), 25–42.

[12]UNESCO Social and Human Sciences Sector. (n.d). Sport for peace and development. Retrieved from http://www.unesco.org/new/en/social-and-human-sciences/themes/physical-education-and-sport/sport-for-peace-and-development/

[13]Schinke, R. & Hanrahan, S. (2012). *Sport for development, peace, and social justice*. Morgantown, WV: Fitness Information Technology.

[14]Oyster River Youth Association. (n.d.). Mission statement. Retrieved from http://oryarec.org/mission-statement/

[15]Barcelona, 2005.

[16]Barcelona, R. J. (2004). Examining the importance of recreational sport management competencies based on management level, agency type, and organizational size. *Recreational Sports Journal, 28*(1), 45–63.

[17]U.S. Department of Labor. (n.d.). *Occupational outlook handbook* (2012–2013 ed.). Retrieved from http://www.bls.gov/ooh/

[18]Kremarik, F. (2000). A family affair: Children's participation in sports. *Canadian Social Trends, 58*, 20–24.

" *For as long as anyone can remember, people have celebrated. Celebration itself is perhaps the most common denominator that we have, crossing all barriers of race, religion, ethnicity, age, politics, economics, education, and geography…The need to celebrate seems inherent in everything we do and touches virtually every life on the planet.*

—Source: International Festivals and Events
website (Overview) http://www.ifea.com "

10

Event Management

Emilyn Sheffield
California State University, Chico

Polly Crabtree
California State University, Chico

Focus Questions

Q: Do you love seeing an event coming together?

A: Without a doubt, seeing results from all your efforts is one of the most gratifying aspects of becoming an event planner. Sometimes it takes a year or more to make an event happen, but you will see how all your planning and organization come together to make an event. You will be able to gauge the outcome of the event against its purpose and objectives. Successful event managers demonstrate patience, so if you are looking for instant gratification, then you may want to explore other professional options.

Q: Do you have the organizational skills to be successful as an event manager?

A: The ability to multitask is a necessity for an event manager. The successful manager needs to know where in the event management process he or she is for all events scheduled for the coming year, or sometimes even two years. Some venues, caterers, and musicians must be booked more than a year in advance, and the successful event planner will anticipate these needs and exercise appropriate advance planning. Organizational skills help the event planner deliver a great event on time and on (or hopefully under) budget.

Q: Can you deal with stressful situations?

A: Stress in the form of demanding clients, unrealistic expectations, and unanticipated problems or conditions can occur at any time. The successful event planner will use creativity and problem-solving skills to resolve challenges with minimal drama and fuss. When it is necessary to take the issue to the client, the event planner should take the problem and at least one, but preferably two, workable solutions. The most important thing for the event planner to remember is to appear calm and confident at all times. Event managers put in long hours, so stamina and consistent self-care behaviors will help them go the distance.

Q: Are you prepared to put your client in the limelight?

A: Although the potential exists for your career in event management to put you in the spotlight, the primary credit will go to your client. You have to be prepared for your client to take all the credit for your success, and you must deflect the credit your client's way. Your job as an event professional is to help your client achieve the event's objectives and make your client look good.

Key Terms

Event professional
Special event
ROI
Multitasking
Venues
Vendors
Incentive travel

Destination management company
   (DMC)
Independents
Specialized entertainment venues
Certified meeting professional (CMP)
Accepted practices exchange (APEX)
Convention and visitor bureau (CVB)

Profile 1: Could This Be You?

Sintia Morfin works for the Golden Gate National Parks Conservancy, the official nonprofit partner for one of the nation's most visited national parks. Parks for All Forever is the touchstone of the association, the largest and most successful partner association in the United States. Sintia helps plan and execute dozens of events each year for the Conservancy's members, sponsors, donors, and visitors to the Golden Gate National Recreation Area in California. She is also active in the International Special Events Society (ISES) Northern California chapter.

Sintia Morfin

Q: You studied event management as an emphasis area in your parks and recreation administration degree. How did you learn about and select event management?

A: I was talking with my academic adviser on campus and mentioned how much I enjoyed being the event planning chair for my dorm at Chico. "Did you know there was an event management program at Chico?" asked my adviser. That was all it took for me to switch majors and pursue a career in event management.

Q: You came to your current position through an internship with the National Park Service. How did first working for the federal agency help you with your position with the association?

A: I knew the regulations that govern special events in national parks, but far more important, I knew the "why" behind the rules. Most people receive a list of rules and guidelines when they stage events in national parks and other protected places, but they do not always have time to think through the reasons for the guidelines. Also, interning with the National Park Service gave me a strong sense of ownership for land and the events that occur in these special places set aside by the American people so that we all can enjoy our natural and cultural heritage.

Q: You are bilingual. How does that skill help the GGPNC fulfill its mission?

A: Being bilingual helps in lots of ways, and the recent Golden Gate Bridge 75th Anniversary celebration is a good example. The Golden Gate National Parks Conservancy, the organization I work for, and their partner agencies, the National Park Service, the Presidio Trust, and the Golden Gate Bridge Authority, work to advance the Conservancy's Parks for All Forever message. I was able to communicate with Telemundo and other Spanish language media outlets throughout the entire celebration planning process, and I understood the role and purpose of the event since I worked so closely with all the partners involved in the celebration. Being bilingual helps in other ways as well. For example, the event vendors' sales staff always speaks English, but the crews are often Spanish speakers. Since I am bilingual I can clearly communicate our needs from an event management and park protection perspective. The setup teams, in turn, feel more comfortable telling me what they need to ensure that my event is successful.

Q: What are some of your favorite Golden Gate National Parks Conservancy events?

A: I love the Trails Forever Dinner because it is our biggest and most complex event. We host nearly 500 people each year in different locations around the Golden Gate National Parks. We totally transform the location, host a fabulous fund-raiser for one of our premier programs, and then "Leave No Trace" of our event within two days. The Trails Forever Dinner has more people, more creativity, more décor…more everything.

Q: What do you like best about working with the Northern California ISES chapter?

A: Through my involvement in ISES, I get to see what's out there in other parts of the event management industry. The Bay Area has a remarkable array of associations, businesses, and organizations to support our vibrant and well-deserved reputation as one of the best places to live and work in America. I like meeting and networking with other industry professionals and learning from them. The parks are also staging areas for hundreds of large and small events, so I get to share information with my colleagues about why these marvelous parks need to be cherished by and preserved for everyone.

Q: Do you have any advice for an aspiring event planner?

A: Sure, but it's mostly the stuff that folks told me when I was in school.…Be prepared to work hard and prove yourself. Be humble but also be willing to step up to make your supervisor and sponsoring organization, association, or business succeed. Join professional organizations while you can do so affordably as a student, volunteer while you are in school, and start keeping that idea file right now.

Profile 2: Could This Be You?

Dan Vicini started his own company, Dakota Events LLC, after working for more than a decade in the incentive travel industry. His is the classic entrepreneurial strategy of finding a need and filling it well. Even better, Dakota Events LLC provides time for him to accompany corporate groups to hallmark sporting around the world. We caught up with Dan between two high-tech events, and here is what he had to say.

Q: Tell me about Dakota Events LLC. Why did you decide to create your own company?

A: Dakota Events LLC is a hospitality and event staffing company. We offer high-caliber staff to corporate meetings and incentive programs. We can provide local staff or independent contractors who travel around the country and internationally to fulfill my clients' on-site needs. On-site services include registration, food and beverage management, activities, meeting services, transportation, and executive services. Dakota Events was created because the service I was receiving from other third-party vendors was not up to standard when I was working for a former employer. Since I knew and understood what my client was looking for, I formed Dakota Events LLC to fulfill that need.

Q: Why did you set up Dakota Events as an LLC?

A: In order to do business with corporate America, you have to adhere to many laws, insurance guidelines, and company policies. When you start a company that has employees, you should always form your company as an LLC (limited liability corporation), LLP (limited liability partnership), S-Corp, or corporation. Incorporating provides an extra layer of protection if an employee, independent contractor, or company takes legal action against your firm. It also enables you to set up the mandatory insurance policies that are required to do business in any of the 50 states. Most of your clients will require that you have at least a $1 million umbrella policy that would cover anything from workers' compensation to negligence. Dakota Events is an LLC because it gives me the flexibility, tax benefits, and the legal format required by the state of Nevada. Plus that extra layer of protection for my assets should anyone take legal action against the company is really important.

Q: What do you love about your career?

A: I've had a nice run in the event and hospitality industry. I've had a chance to see the world, stay in five-star hotels around the globe, and dine in some of the best restaurants out there. Most of my friends can't believe what I do and where I go for an occupation. Most people go into an office five days a week, day in and day out. My day is different every single day. Now that I own Dakota Events, I have even more flexibility with my schedule, the jobs that I choose, and the companies I want to associate with.

Q: How does your work make a difference to your clients?

A: I would have to say that over the past 18 years of working with different clients, staff, and companies, I have developed a great sense of what my clients are looking for and the service levels that should be standard today. I can anticipate their on-site needs and make the proper recommendations enhancing their attendees' experiences. In today's market, you also have to be very budget savvy, know the clients' budgets, and always stay within their guidelines. If you can anticipate change and have the dollar amount with those changes, you will be an even greater asset to your clients.

Q: What special challenges confront you and your current company?

A: The economy runs the show in the incentive and hospitality industry. When the economy is doing well, companies spend money on meetings and incentives. The good news is that meetings have to take place, employees need to be recognized, and companies are required to invest in ideas and training.

Q: How did you get into this profession?

A: I graduated with a degree from California State University, Chico. In my opinion, resort and lodging management is one of the best programs offered there. When I graduated, it was mandatory to complete a full-time, four-month internship. Rather than taking the path in the hotel industry, I completed my internship with a meeting and incentive company in the Bay Area. When my internship was over, I was hired full time and started my career in this industry.

Q: You still find time to accompany corporate groups to big-time sporting events around the United States and in other countries. How do you swing that?

A: I've handled sporting events such as the Final Four, Super Bowl, World Series, Winter and Summer Olympics, and the PGA Tour. Honestly, these events refuel my passion for what I do. They also allow me to work closely with some of my clients in exclusive settings with their top executives. I make time for these events because they allow me to network with the decision makers and build the trust and relationships that lead to future business for Dakota Events. I also get to see some of the greatest athletic contests on earth!

Q: What career advice do you have for professionals just getting started?

A: Always treat your work or your projects like they are the most important program or event you will ever do. Do what is asked, ask questions, and take notes. Be honest and build relationships inside and outside of work. Decision makers want to know they can trust you. Trust will win business time and time again. By networking and keeping in touch with fellow students from your academic degree program, you find doors opening for you. My best advice, though, is to never burn a bridge. You never know whom you will work with next or, more important, whom you will be working for.

Pursue Your Passion for Events—and Get Paid!

Is there anyone who has not been to a special event? Professional events such as meetings and conferences, as well as social events such as festivals and concerts, permeate contemporary society. Colorful flyers capture your eye and imagination as you walk down the street. Professional associations offer conferences to help their members keep up on industry trends. Membership-based and special interest associations sponsor events to raise funds, serve members, and increase their visibility. If it seems like events are absolutely everywhere, it is because they are and the industry has expanded to include online meetings and conferences and virtual events. Participants "tweet" during sessions and post to dozens of social media sites. These same social media sites allow folks to share information quickly, and when something goes "viral," it can rapidly escalate visibility about and attendance to a gathering, often requiring last-minute adjustments to meet the demand.

A sample of recent graduates from the authors' university illustrates the range of job settings for qualified special event professionals to practice their superb skills. Each person completed an undergraduate degree in park and recreation management (gender neutral names or initials have been used here) and is now employed in the exciting world of special events:

- Taylor plans tradeshows for a large, high-tech online auction firm.
- Jamie manages a 4-day festival for a convention and visitors bureau.
- Sam coordinates international tradeshows for a software vendor.
- Alex organizes habitat restoration events volunteers at a national recreation area.
- Sun coordinates alumni events for a midsize university.
- Dana coordinates a downtown market for a business development association.
- Ryan is a trainer for a professional association.
- AJ staffs large conferences and tradeshows in convention destinations.

History and Growth of Professional Event Management

For eons, people have gathered to celebrate the seasons and cycles of nature and life. In pre-agricultural eras, groups met to trade and celebrate seasonal changes. Markets anchored celebratory and commercial activity in the agricultural era, and athletic contests increased as settlements and towns emerged. With the rising affluence that accompanied the Industrial Revolution, the stage was set for festivals, celebrations, and special events to increase in number and frequency. For years, the event planning function was embedded as part of a broader job or position, but as events grew in importance, the need for specialized professionals emerged, too.

© *Monkey Business Images | Dreamstime*

The Industrial Revolution created prosperous middle classes with the income and leisure time to support entertainment events. Ironically, this new leisure time in the form of weekends and paid vacations and holidays for the average employee led to a new industry with common professional practices, codes of ethics, and career tracks for others. Business events are still important and have evolved over time to support economic eras centered on manufacturing, services, and information.

We may be thousands of years past the early seasonal gathering of trading nomads, the athletic spectacles of early civilizations, or the first farmers' markets, but these events continue to flourish along with dozens of other business and social events. The **event manager**, or person paid to plan and implement the event, evolved with society, and now we see specialization and thousands of local, regional, state, national, and global events. Even the titles of event professionals have evolved as the complexity and importance of events have increased. Throughout this chapter, you will see the terms *planner, manager, professional* or *specialist* used in tandem with *event, festival, tradeshow, conference, convention,* and *venue*. It is an exciting time to contemplate a career as a professional in this ever-changing mix of skills, specialization, event types, and industry sectors.

Event Management Today

Most segments of the event and entertainment industry are expanding, although regional growth patterns and priorities exert an influence. A **special event** is exactly what the name suggests. *Special* refers to the nonroutine nature of the event. Although a special event may occur at the same time each year, it is special by virtue of its infrequent scheduling, its novelty, or other nonroutine feature. The term *event* suggests structure and planning. So a special event is a nonroutine but structured activity designed and implemented to achieve the sponsor's (or client's) objectives.

Meeting objectives is another way of describing the benefits of special events. Table 1.1 in Chapter 1 provides an extensive list of benefits in four categories: personal, sociocultural, economic, and environmental. Destination areas look to stellar events to draw visitors when capacity is available, to position or reposition the destination, or to add value to the visitor experience. These types of events provide individual, sociocultural, economic, and sometimes environmental benefits. Civic celebrations are back in vogue and provide individual and community benefits. Nonprofit organizations use special events to raise resources or to advance their missions generating individual, sociocultural, and economic benefits for clients and communities. Many of the sponsoring agencies, organizations, or enterprises have missions and mandates aligned with the so-importants of social and environmental justice (see

© Alphaspirit | Dreamstime.com

Chapter 1 to review these so-importants). New products are launched constantly and everyone is courting the conference and meetings market. Depending on the product or theme of the event, meeting, or conference, all four benefits can be advanced by a great event.

Special events are designed for many purposes, including the following:

- A community special event may be a seasonal or holiday event, a tournament, or a festival.
- A nonprofit organization special event may be the primary fund-raiser for the organization, a valued member service, or a way to express appreciation to volunteers, donors, and other supporters.
- A university special event may be part of a community outreach strategy or a way to encourage alumni to return to campus.

- A business special event may be part of a sales campaign or a way to draw attention to a new product, service, or location; to secure customer loyalty; or to accomplish other strategic objectives.

Trends in Event Management

Population growth and more desire for entertainment and stimulation have created an environment of bigger and bolder events. However, more people at events may result in more potential problems for the event manager. A solid understanding of societal and economic conditions will prepare you to seek opportunities in periods of change. Keeping an eye on demographic and lifestyle trends is essential to event and meeting planning and implementation. Scanning a range of sources will help you separate trends that will last from the merely trendy. When you notice the same themes in many sectors, you may have a trend on its way to becoming a basic business practice. Keep a sharp eye, and you will soon become known as a trend-spotter, or better yet, a trend*setter*, in your chosen sector of this industry.

As the new century unfolds, six things are changing the shape of the event and meeting industry, and they are likely to continue doing so for some time.

- Creativity continues to be highly prized in the event and meeting industry. Event professionals who can combine classic elements in innovative ways are always in demand. Unique and authentic events resonate strongly with sponsors and participants. Even a firm with an established portfolio of popular themes and venues can use new entertainers, new color schemes, and new lighting techniques to delight clients and guests. Social media promotion, and the opportunity for an event to go viral may have unexpected results; the event manager who can creatively implement while effectively managing social media outlets will be in high demand.

- Accountability has increased as the visibility and importance of the event and meeting industry has grown. Recession and a widespread need for transparency have created an environment of justification for events and incentive-based travel. Fiscal responsibility and **ROI (return on investment)** as well as clearly defined and measured objectives and outcomes are becoming more prevalent throughout all industry sectors. This emphasis on accountability has increased the professionalism of the industry and encouraged the growth of continuing education, professional certifications, and research and evaluation protocols.

- Sustainability has expanded to include more than just "greening" events. Environmental awareness has expanded to include social, cultural, and economic measures along with environmental measures. Wholesome, positive events and meetings now pursue triple-bottom-line goals on-site and back through the supply chain. Event invitations and materials made from recycled, reused, or repurposed materials are in high demand. With the increasing availability and accessibility of handheld technology, meetings and conferences are more consistently moving to paperless. A desire to reduce the carbon footprint of meeting, event, and conference attendance has resulted in more demand for, and consistent use of, alternate forms of transportation. Experienced professionals work to incorporate sustainability from planning to implementation.

- Inclusion has increased as event participants have become more diverse. People are living longer, a new global baby boom is underway, and societies are becoming more racially and ethnically diverse. Global economic and communication networks are bringing people from far-flung corners of the world together. Multigenerational and diverse audiences require event managers to have more sensitivity to and awareness of cultural customs and needs. The savvy planner draws from this international well to craft creative and culturally inclusive events for all. Several decades of attention to improving the physical and programmatic accessibility of public spaces, event venues, and associated infrastructure have greatly increased the ability of persons with physical, developmental, and sensory impairments to participate in civic and business life, including events, festivals, and meetings. The effective event manager will anticipate the need for even more programmatic access going forward.

- Safety and security have taken on more importance in event planning and management as the increased risk for terrorism and major catastrophic events need to be considered when large groups gather. Risk management assessments prior to an event may provide the opportunity to mitigate danger and liability. Food service requires protections to be taken against the possibility of foodborne illness. Food handlers need to be properly trained, and caterers must have the proper permits and licenses for the event jurisdiction. The Americans With Disabilities Act (ADA) requires the safe egress of all event participants. The event manager must know the locations of all exits, fire extinguishers, and emergency equipment. Pre-event evacuation drills and emergency plans can assist the event manager in controlling panicked participants. Serving alcohol at events creates other safety and security issues. Knowledgeable event planners will be well versed in the rules, regulations, and laws surrounding the service of alcohol in their jurisdiction.

- Technology has transformed all aspects of society, including the event and meeting industry. Social networking and other computer-aided communications may increase interest in events and increase communication before, during, and after the event or meeting. An increased desire for paperless meetings and conferences has given rise to new portal and cloud-based platforms. Efforts to reduce carbon footprint has created a need for event managers to know and understand virtual meeting technologies.

Sound interesting? What is the nature of the work, and how do you get started?

Careers in Event Management

Jobs for event and meeting professionals exist in every sector of society. Better yet, because event management skills are highly transferable, good professionals are able to move effortlessly between industry and organizational sectors. This skill transferability is one characteristic of the emerging and future leisure service delivery system described in Chapter 2, although you will find event planners and managers throughout the leisure service delivery system and throughout almost all industry sectors in the United States.

Skills valued in all sectors include time management, the capacity to work on multiple events with cascading deadlines (**multitasking**), the ability to remain calm when the situation is chaotic, and the resourcefulness to deliver memorable experiences and stay within the available financial and human resources. Stamina is essential. Successful event managers also possess a solid working knowledge of the fundamental concepts, current trends, and emerging issues of their chosen professional setting.

The business of events is contractual, so good planners must be able to review binding documents and work within their established parameters. No discussion is complete without mentioning the importance of fiscal responsibility and return on investment (ROI). As meeting and event management has professionalized, outcome accountability has increased. Sponsors and clients want to know that they are getting a good return on their investment in the form of visibilities, sales leads, employee skill development, or similar outcomes. On the festival and entertainment side of the industry, owners and sponsors are interested in similar accountability, albeit with different measures.

Event planning occurs months—and sometimes years—prior to the actual event and often across long distances. Consequently, written and oral communication skills and a firm grasp of business technology and software programs (e.g., smartphones and tablets, scanners, laptops, and various Web-based planning, project management, and communication devices) enable an event specialist to work seamlessly with a range of colleagues. Finally, event professionals work with and through a range of clients, coworkers, and contractors, so excellent communication skills and an ability to work with all types of talent are essential.

As with any profession, event management has a specialized language. Common terms are included in this chapter, but if you encounter unfamiliar terms in job descriptions or professional publications, you can find an extensive online glossary sponsored by the member organizations of the Convention Industry Council. Go to the well-organized CIC website (www.conventionindustry. org/StandardsPractices/APEX/glossary.aspx) for a glossary of more than 3,800 industry terms and for links to member organizations.

Passions

If you like variety, creativity, and high-energy work settings, you may find yourself drawn to a career as an event or meeting professional. If you are attentive to detail and find satisfaction from helping others achieve their business or mission objectives, this may be the career field for you. If you can remain calm and resolve problems quickly and well as events unfold, you may be successful and enjoy a long and rewarding career. Review your passions lists from Chapter 2 to align your unique strengths and interests with the world of possibilities in event management.

Preparation

Education and experience in event planning will provide a good foundation for building a career in the professional event management field. A quality education will help students learn how to function in loose, fluid team situations. Event professionals must work with employees, contractors, vendors, volunteers, and the client's representatives to design and deliver superb events for their clients.

> Regardless of their title, all meeting professionals need to have certain qualities...(such as being) resourceful, responsive, tenacious, ambitious, and principled.

The events industry values experience. Fortunately, universities tend to provide many opportunities for event management experience as part of academic programs. Recreation programming knowledge and experience provide a solid background for the organizational, communication, and management skills that a good event manager requires.

Whichever degree program you select, make sure you gain the knowledge and hands-on experience to become a proficient event management professional. Strong written and oral communication skills are required because event professionals need to communicate well with their clients, contractors, management, event audiences, and members of the media. Interpersonal skills are also an asset; successful event professionals have a knack for handling the most difficult clients and situations with apparent ease and confidence.

Possibilities

Event and meeting professionals possess a specialized skill set that transcends any single setting. Event management is widespread and growing so rapidly that you will find opportunities in all industries and sectors. As your skill set grows through experience, and your professional network expands, you may find your success and effectiveness as an event or meeting professional does not have limits.

© Photographerlondon | Dreamstime.com

Dozens of organizational schemes exist to categorize the meeting and event industry. Snodgrass[1] and Kilkenny[2] offer industry frameworks organized by work setting. Their pragmatic approach is useful for students contemplating an event management career since it shows the range of work settings. Their framework is adapted here to describe career opportunities in specialized firms, in corporate and organizational settings, and in hospitality and entertainment venues. Fortunately for you, a range of opportunities await you in the fast-growing career field.

Special event and meeting planning and management firms. Event and meeting planning and management firms exist to serve the needs of their clients. They work with a network of **venues** (e.g., facilities) and **vendors**, specialized service providers such as florists, caterers, rental companies, and entertainers, to ensure that a client's objectives for an event or meeting are met. Firm size varies to reflect the available opportunities. Some firms are national in scope with offices in most destination cities; other companies are smaller with just a few employees that focus on a single industry sector or area.

Is working in an event or meeting firm for you? It may be if you love organizing events and activities and can work as part of a team to help clients or sponsors achieve their objectives.

Passions. If you like event planning and lots of it, an event or meeting planning firm may be for you. Most firms have an operations division that organizes and implements events and meetings and a sales division that secures business for the firm.

Pay and perks. The pay ranges from hourly to career-level salaries. Perks can be creative and include travel, gift/product samples, and invitations to experience the destination, venue, or product firsthand. Many event and meeting firms are sole proprietorships or partnerships. This means with experience, you may be able to enjoy the rewards of owning your own business. A well-established firm often maintains enduring relationships with a cadre of core clients, so long-term relationships and friendships with like-minded clients are also job perks.

Preparation. In event and meeting planning, attention to detail and the ability to multitask have no substitute. Actual event experience is always a plus, and fortunately, you may gain lots of experience by planning events and activities for your social groups, clubs, and organizations. Resourcefulness and creative problem solving are valued skills to bring to the organization or firm. Many beginning positions include lots of clerical work, so good customer service etiquette, an ability to use standard office equipment, and strong computer technology skills are a plus.

Possibilities. If planning is your passion, this is the place to be. Event managers are hired for hallmark sporting and entertainment events (e.g., Olympics, Super Bowl, concert tours), well-known festivals and seasonal events, and smaller community-focused events such as farmers' markets and festivals. Add meetings and conventions and social events such as weddings and fund-raisers to this list and your options are almost limitless. Specialized event and meeting firms have evolved to include the following:

- **Incentive travel firms:** These firms create unique and memorable travel programs to reward performance in a variety of sales and technology fields. They have event planners and travel directors who accompany incentive groups to exciting destinations. Large incentive travel firms sometimes have an in-house travel agency providing more employment opportunities.
- **Destination management companies (DMCs):** These firms are experts in a single destination city or region. They typically work with incentive travel firms, conference and meeting planners, and corporate travel professionals to handle all the destination-specific details necessary to ensure a successful group gathering.
- **Independent event firms:** Independent event firms, also known as **independents**, may operate anywhere and range in size from one-person small businesses operating in a home to large full-service event and meeting firms. Depending on size and experience, an event firm may specialize in milestone celebrations such as weddings or coordinate complex national or international concert tours. Other event firms manage hallmark special events and festivals. Still others specialize in meetings and conferences. From entertainment to education, event firms handle all aspects of an event, meeting, or conference.
- **Festival management firms:** Large festivals have expanded to require full-time professional staff, especially in the areas of sponsorships and vendor relations. Even smaller festival-style events such as farmers' markets and special events in downtown entertainment districts keep a couple of folks busy planning the festivities.
- **Public relations and advertising firms:** Meeting and event management is often included in a well-conceived public relations or advertising campaign. Some public relations firms have in-house events divisions with career opportunities for event planners and other event professionals, and others partner with an event management firm to meet client needs.

Maritz Travel is a global corporation with more than 1,500 locations in 60 countries. They combine advanced technology and a vast network of suppliers to help companies achieve results through special events, incentive travel programs, and corporate meetings. The company manages more than 2,000 meetings and incentive travel programs, each serving more than 400,000 travel program participants. Go to their website (www.maritz.com) and search their wide assortment of case studies to learn how they combine industry knowledge and technology to help their clients achieve results and attain goals. Travel-related job titles with a large incentive travel company such as Maritz include travel account manager, project manager, and travel director.

Photo: Charlotte Fiorito

Event management in corporate or organizational settings. Need more ways to envision your future in event and meeting management? Do you want to combine your planning and management skills with a cause? Are you drawn to public service but cannot see yourself as a teacher or youth leader? Do you like the structure of a corporate setting? If so, you will be delighted with the opportunities that await you as an event or meeting professional in a corporate or organizational setting.

A review of the specifics related to events in corporate and organizational settings may help you determine whether this setting is for you.

Passions. Do you want to save the world or an important little part of it? Do you long to improve the human condition, support social or environmental causes, or improve society? If so, association and organizational settings provide some of your best professional opportunities. You may use your event management skills to support or improve something you care about. Working in a corporate setting showcasing innovation or training a workforce also has rewards.

Pay and perks. Pay covers a wide range and tends to be higher in corporate and government settings, but people working in the nonprofit sector often report the highest levels of job satisfaction. Job perks often include travel, hospitality-related functions, and cutting-edge industry knowledge.

Preparation. In addition to event and meeting management skills, industry knowledge is always a plus. In some sectors, experience in fund-raising and sponsor development is a valued skill. In others, a solid background in adult education or specialized content expertise is highly prized. Since many events and meetings help to raise operational funds, solid negotiation skills may distinguish you from the competition.

To learn more about event management opportunities in corporate and organizational settings, ask your campus adviser for introductions to alumni working in the sector about which you are interested in learning more. Or contact a professional association that supports your interests to see whether they can identify an affiliated professional located near you. You may also check around your hometown or campus location to see who you can "cold call" for an informational interview.

Possibilities. One of the most attractive aspects of corporate and organizational settings for meeting and event professionals is the array of opportunities available in a large, robust economy such as the United States. Professionals working in organizational, governmental, and corporate settings support every sector of society. A list of organizations where event managers are needed follows.

Corporations. Most corporations produce a product or provide a service, and this ensures they have a need to introduce that product or service to the marketplace. Tradeshows and conventions provide customers and clients with a firsthand opportunity to see new products, test services, or compare product and service features in a high-energy environment. Corporations also invest in their employees with meeting professionals attending to the training and development needed to maintain a cutting-edge workforce.

Trade and professional associations. Trade and professional associations have grown in number and importance in the past 50 years. Since many organizations rely on annual conferences and other training functions to raise operating revenue for the sponsoring organization, association staff members are often responsible for organizing these important revenue events.

© *Shannon Fagan | Dreamstime.com*

Nonprofit and nongovernmental organizations. Nonprofit organizations are devoted to member or societal benefits and enjoy a special place in society. Many nonprofit organizations hold special events to raise visibility and funding. Event professionals have a unique opportunity to design creative and entertaining events and to generate funds for the cause. Positions range depending on the size of the organization, but often the event planning duties are embedded as part of several colleagues' jobs and extensively use volunteers.

Educational. Educational institutions provide additional opportunities for event professionals. Most campuses have a full calendar of festivals, meetings, and entertainment events for community residents and campus audiences. Dozens of student clubs and organizations offer events, activities, and meetings throughout the academic year.

Governmental organizations. Many local parks and recreation departments host festivals and special events as part of a comprehensive community recreation and tourism program. In many cities and communities, governmental organizations manage some of the more important and interesting meeting and event venues. Governmental organizations also invest in workforce development and training and some maintain campuses to ensure adequate training opportunities.

Event management in hospitality and venue settings. In the past 50 years, the hospitality sector has expanded to support special events, meetings, trade shows, and conferences. From large cities to small communities, public infrastructure investments such as convention centers, sport arenas, and other specialized venues support the industry and the communities where they are located. Other private sector gathering places such as theme parks, attractions, private clubs, and cruise lines often target the meeting and event market to diversify their customer base and increase business during shoulder seasons. Check out these specifics to determine whether a career in a hospitality setting or entertainment venue may be for you.

Passions. This sector provides opportunities to plan special events and meetings within the structure of a special "built" environment. In these settings, special events and meetings are often sought to increase profitability and/or use during slower periods or shoulder seasons.

Pay and perks. Entry-level employees receive hourly wages, often without benefits. Opportunities for advancement occur early and often, especially in hotels and resorts. Mobility within a company often provides opportunities to move around the United States or to other countries. The hours are often long, but the perks are great if you love to travel. Frequent networking events provide outstanding opportunities because industry partners strive to showcase their services to impress potential clients.

Preparation. Superb organizational skills combined with a solid understanding of marketing will help you excel. Creativity and the ability to work as part of a team will ensure success.

Possibilities. You will find your best opportunities in large cities and destination areas. In smaller communities or venues, though, you may combine event planning with other job tasks. The following is a list of locations/organizations you should consider if you want to oversee events and entertainment in the hospitality sector.

Attractions. Theme parks, museums, art galleries, and similar attractions are adding meeting and event professionals to their staff rosters. Hosting events can increase the visibility of the attraction as well as support the bottom line through increased revenue.

Clubs. Country clubs, fitness facilities, and other membership-based clubs are offering more special events, often as part of the marketing and positioning strategy for the property. Generally, the event planning function is only part of someone's job. Some clubs with large food and beverage operations will have event planners on staff to assist with weddings and other similar family milestone events.

Cruise lines. Cruise lines use events to create a sense of excitement and energy on board. For general cruises, events help entertain guests. In recent years, themed cruises have become more popular; music cruises, sci-fi cruises, and wine and chocolate lovers cruises attract new passengers to cruise ships. Cruise lines have also targeted the corporate meeting and incentive market.

Hotels and resorts. Most hotels and resorts have a function space for groups and gatherings. In smaller properties, the meeting and event organizers are generally located in sales and marketing or catering. In larger properties, a convention services department provides a complete range of meeting services. See Chapter 11 for more detailed information.

Entertainment venues. Auditoriums, concert halls, and theaters are specialized entertainment venues. Professionals in these settings generally work with outside meeting and event professionals, but house managers and other venue specialists require many of the same skills to be effective, and it is a great way to pursue a special interest or to provide infrastructure that is essential to industry success.

Sport venues. Facilities have always been a critical component of the sport enterprise. Located in large or small markets with public or private financing, these facilities are primarily focused on creating environments conducive to high-quality sport experiences for athletes and spectators. The focus is primarily on sports, but construction and operating costs often require alternate uses of the venues. Chapter 9 provides more detailed information about this topic.

Convention centers. Convention centers are essential infrastructure for the event and meeting industry in larger cities and destinations. These specialized facilities are used to attract large and small meetings, conferences, and conventions to an area, along with the significant economic activity associated with these events.

Tourism organizations. Destination marketing organizations have found festivals and special events to be a great strategy to increase the visibility of the destination and position it in the competitive marketplace. Volunteers often plan these festivals and special events, but professionals are increasingly involved as contractors or employees to manage the large-scale special events sponsored by tourism organizations (See Chapter 12 for more information).

Summary of Event Managment Career Possibilities

Career	Passions	Pay and Perks	Preparations	Possibilities
Special event or meeting management firms	Lots of event planning, cause-related fund-raising, travel, entrepreneurship	Hourly to executive, creativity and solid budgeting skills help you advance quickly	Experience required, degree preferred; programming, customer service, budgeting, and strong oral and written communication skills will help you succeed	Sales or operations, coordinate event teams, plan hallmark events, own your own business or work as part of a global firm
Corporate or organization event professional	Corporate work environments, trade shows, and product launches; cause-related marketing	Hourly to executive, sector knowledge and an ability to translate event outcomes to organizational goals will help you advance	Degree preferred, sector knowledge required; experience with large events and documenting outcomes are valued skills	Positions are often located in the marketing or human resources departments
Event professional in hospitality or venue setting	On-site meetings, celebrations, sports, entertainment	Hourly to executive, hospitality or facility management experience helps you get ahead	Experience required, degree preferred; personal network or internship often gains access; supervisory experience is a plus	Catering, event/convention services; seasonal or cyclical schedules provide "break-in" opportunities if you are available

Future Opportunities, Issues, and Challenges

Event and meeting management has grown and professionalized in the past 50 or 60 years, and it appears to be poised for increased visibility and expansion. When consumer confidence is high and the economy is growing, meetings and events flourish, budgets are generous, and opportunities for professionals abound. Conversely, when the economy contracts, the event industry shifts as well. In-house event planning and management divisions become smaller or sometimes get outsourced, and the smaller independent firms often report an upswing in business during the same period. Earlier concerns about virtual events replacing place-based events has yet to occur, rather virtual technologies seem to be augmenting regular events, or expanding the number of people who can participate.

Natural disasters can negatively impact the events industry for years, adding further economic disruption to nature's first round of destruction. Seemingly unrelated scandals may have far-reaching and negative consequences as the financial sector excesses of 2008 and 2009 led to a reduction in corporate travel through all industries. Continuing scrutiny related to the cost of meeting/conference participation has further transformed the industry. Notable examples are curtailment of certain forms of travel in private and public sectors, increased attention to the benefits of face-to-face meeting participation, and accelerating the move to and investment in virtual meeting platforms.

Taking a slightly longer view, though, helps event professionals stay positive, proactive, and employed. They keep in mind that events have served human needs for thousands of years and that resourceful event professionals will always be in demand, but they also save a portion of their earnings to tide them over during the lean times.

Industry veterans are excited about the role of festivals and special events in the life of a community, regardless of how "community" is defined. Nonprofit organizations raise funds to pursue their missions through special events. Festivals and events contribute to people's happiness and enjoyment and to the host community's identity and financial viability. Planners and sponsors are delighted to showcase new talent from around the community or the world.

Similarly, conference, trade show, and business meeting professionals are excited about the growing stature of their contributions to the strategic direction of the business or association. They are pleased to be adding value through professional development and training or to be introducing new products and services to the marketplace.

Resources and Getting Involved

The Internet has become a major tool for investigating career opportunities. Key websites specifically related to parks and recreation associations and resources related to specific areas such as nonprofits, sport management, hospitality, and travel and tourism have been identified in other chapters. In addition to those resources, you should become aware of the following organizations and resources to prepare for your future career. Use the Internet for information and research, but do not forget that meeting and event management is a highly customer service–oriented endeavor that runs on personal relationships.

Professional Organizations

As the event and meeting industry has expanded and become more specialized, many organizations have emerged to support industry and professionals' needs. Several leading organizations are listed in alphabetical order, and each has its niche in the industry. The Convention Industry Council (CIC) is particularly noteworthy. This "federation of leading national and international organizations involved in meetings, conventions, and exhibitions" represents more than 30 professional organizations with more than 100,000 professionals.[3] CIC sponsors the **Certified Meeting Professional (CMP)** designation, a prestigious professional certification. CIC also sponsors APEX, the **Accepted Practices Exchange**, a collection of best industry practices. The CIC website includes links to all members' websites. In addition to the CIC website, check out websites for industry news, research, and career opportunities, including internships. Many associations have chapters located in major cities and destination areas, so check to see whether a chapter is located near you.

American Society of Association Executives (ASAE): www.asaecenter.org
ASAE and the Center for Association Leadership believe associations have the power to transform society for the better, and their passion is to help association professionals achieve previously unimaginable levels of performance.

Association for Convention Operations Management (ACOM): www.acomonline.org
ACOM members learn to be more effective service managers, gain a better understanding of the breadth of their roles, and learn about planners' expectations.

Convention Industry Council (CIC): www.conventionindustry.org/index.aspx
CIC facilitates the exchange of information, develops programs to promote professionalism within the industry (including Certified Meeting Professional, CMP, industry certification programming), and educates the public on the economic impact of the industry.

Corporate Event Marketing Association (CEMA): www.cemaonline.com
CEMA considers itself the premier community for technology event marketing professionals and an industry hub that promotes professional networking opportunities, industry education, and peer-to-peer knowledge sharing.

Hospitality Sales and Marketing Association International (HSMAI): www.hsmai.org
HSMAI is a global organization of sales and marketing professionals representing all segments of the hospitality industry and an industry leader in identifying and communicating trends in the hospitality industry.

International Association of Conference Centers (IACC): www.iacconline.com
IACC's members operate conference centers that comply with association standards to provide the most productive meeting facilities around the world.

International Association of Venue Managers (IAVM): www.iavm.org
IAVM is an organization committed to the professional operation of amphitheaters, arenas, auditoriums, convention centers/exhibit halls, performing arts venues, race tracks, stadiums, and university complexes.

International Festivals and Events Association (IFEA): www.ifea.com
IFEA's mission is to serve the needs of festival and event industry members who produce and support quality celebrations for the benefit of their respective communities.

International Special Events Society (ISES): www.ises.com
ISES provides professional development and networking so special event professionals can successfully compete in today's challenging market.

Meeting Professionals International (MPI): www.mpiweb.org/Home
MPI is a global community of meeting and event professionals that connects members to the worldwide support, industry knowledge, and business opportunities needed to be successful in the meeting planning industry.

Professional Convention Management Association (PCMA): www.pcma.org
PCMA is an organization of professionals who organize and manage meetings, conventions, exhibits, and seminars and suppliers who support the industry.

Where to Gain Experience

The key to success for event professionals is experience. Professional event management is an ever-changing and demanding field that requires upbeat and flexible creative problem solvers. For most event professionals, the ability to be a creative problem solver only comes with experience. Take advantage of the event planning opportunities presented in college: Join a social organization that holds events with other organizations; volunteer to help with student government events; or volunteer to work with campus departments that host events for students, parents, or alumni.

When you have basic event planning experience, approach the community or regional recreation department, a local nonprofit organization, or the chamber of commerce to see whether you may assist with an upcoming event. Often these investments lead to an internship, summer job opportunity, or a referral to a similar setting in another area closer to home.

So you are ready to work hard, and you had some great experiences in college. Be persistent and demonstrate your desire to succeed by your determination to find a place in this exciting world. Be resourceful and levelheaded; everyone values capable, personable, and resourceful coworkers.

Finding a Dream Job in a Dream Destination

How do you find job leads in a new area? A good starting place, when you have a geographic location in mind, is to go to the destination's convention and visitors bureau (CVB) and/or chamber website to see whether they have a member's directory online. Use keywords such as *special events, wedding planner, party planner, corporate events, destination management, incentive travel,* or *receptive operator* to find firms that are working in the geographic area. Another route is the alumni connection. Check with your campus alumni association to see whether event professionals are working in your desired geographic area. If they are, try to arrange an informational interview. A third option is to locate the local chapter of one of the professional societies to see what they can provide. Their websites are generally full of local news and contacts. Another more time intensive but tried-and-true approach is to (a) identify the elected leadership, (b) conduct background research on them and their companies/firms, (c) contact one or more for an informational interview, and (d) follow up with a letter of thanks and a résumé that you encourage them to circulate. Face time (e.g., interviewing in person) is key.

Conclusion

If you are organized, creative, patient, able to multitask, and problem solve, this may be the career for you. Reread the questions at the beginning of the chapter, and if you have negative feelings about any of them, you may want to look into a different career path. If you have positive feelings, a career as a special event professional provides a terrific way to pursue your passions. If, for example, you love organizing trips and are passionate about vintage movies, you may find a perfect career organizing consumer shows for movie buffs. If you like the idea of working in the music industry but not as a performer or music industry executive, working at an entertainment venue or in a trade association allows you to pursue your passion from a paid perspective.

Connections help you advance, and many people propel their careers by moving between companies within the same industry or geographic area or move upward within the company. But it is a small tribe in constant motion. Be honest, be ethical, and be nice to everyone; today's competitor is tomorrow's colleague. Now get out there and make your passion pay out through endless possibilities!

For Further Investigation

For Everyone

Now that you have finished this chapter, make use of what you have learned. Take action and set goals. Return to Table 1.1 in the first chapter and select a benefit. Based on your own experiences or online industry research, find a special event that furthers that benefit by increasing visibility, raising funds, or providing services to reinforce the brand.

For More Research

Select one of these four options, and be prepared to share your findings with others in your class or group:

1. **Investigate:** Research the event management field online by checking out the websites for the professional organizations listed in the chapter.
   - Research job listings for future ideas of jobs that are available in the field.
   - Look for professional development opportunities—conferences and meetings may be held close to you.
   - Search for student programming available including scholarships and internships.
   - Be creative and look at websites in a field that interests you (e.g., professional sports, music, theater, literature).

2. Contact an organization directly and conduct an informational interview with a professional in the field. Talking to a field professional may give you key insights to the field that are missed in publications and on the Web. You will most likely find that if you speak to three field professionals, you will find three different backgrounds leading to careers in event management. It will be helpful to review the informational interview instructions in Chapter 2 as you plan for your interview, and be sure to refresh your memory about the leisure services spectrum since you will find more options across the spectrum than within a single segment. Specific questions to ask include the following:
   - What is the educational background of the field professional?
   - What previous work experience do they have?
   - What recommendations do they have for breaking into the event management field?

3. Pick an area where you are interested in living. Go to their destination marketing organization (DMO) website and look for the online membership directory, where you will find listings of meeting planners, incentive travel planners, and other industry professionals. Sometimes the DMO will offer an event planner's guide. After you check out the professional opportunities in the meeting and conference area, review their special event calendar to learn about the range and scope of the festival and event scene.

4. Attend a campus or community event:
   - trade show,
   - nonprofit charity fund-raising event,
   - organized social event, or
   - large-scale concert or sporting event.

For Career Possibilities

Host your own small-scale event:
- Host a gathering for a nonprofit or cause for which you are sympathetic.
- Host a direct-sales gathering for friends and family (e.g., Mary Kay, Juice Plus, Pampered Chef).
- Host a milestone celebratory event for family and friends (e.g., anniversary, birthday, or graduation party)

After the event, ask yourself these questions:
- Can you see yourself working as an event manager?
- Which aspects of your event experience did you most enjoy?
- Which did you least enjoy?

Work with an event professional (or firm) to see whether this field may be your calling.
- Interview an event professional to get a better idea of the demands of the job.
- Job shadow an event professional during an event.

Take an active role in the event planning field.
- Volunteer to help with a university event.
- Join a campus organization that hosts events.
- Take one or more event management classes at your university.

Work in the field.
- Get an event planning internship for the summer.
- Get a part-time job in the event management field.

Recommended Reading
Trade Publications and Association Magazines
The need for planners, vendors, and suppliers to exchange information has created a strong market for trade-oriented publications. Links to online versions of some of these trade publications and association magazines enable you to find contacts, ideas, and applied information about meeting and event planning.

Convene: www.pcma.org/Convene.htm
The online version of the Professional Convention Management Association's award-winning magazine, a leading meeting industry trade publication. Past issues are archived.

Event Solutions: www.event-solutions.com
Print and online publication from Event Solutions, an events industry trade publication. Check out Event Profiles for ideas and search the Black Book for contacts.

Meetings and Conventions **Magazine:** www.meetings-conventions.com
Published since 1965, the trade publication helps planners manage events and careers. See Destinations for suppliers at various convention destinations.

One+ **Magazine:** www.mpiweb.org/Magazine/Archive
Sponsored by Meeting Professionals International, *One+* archives features, columns, and case studies. Print, online, and Spanish language versions of *One+* are available.

Special Events **Magazine:** www.specialevents.com
Print and digital versions of this publication target professionals who produce events in large-scale hospitality venues.

Successful Meetings **Magazine:** www.successfulmeetings.com
Two online publications provide meeting professionals with educational content, ideas, and resources for all types of meeting professionals.

Books on Meeting/Conference Management
Convention Industry Council. (2008). *The convention industry council manual* (8th ed.). Alexandria, VA: Author.
Comprehensive resource for managing meetings successfully with forms, lists, and industry glossary. A study reference for the CMP exam.

Craven, R. E., & Golabowski, L. J. (2006). *The complete idiot's guide to meeting and event planning* (2nd ed.). Indianapolis, IN: Alpha Books.
Part of the popular Idiot's Guide series available at most bookstores.

Fenich, G. (2007). *Meetings, expositions, events, and conventions: An introduction to the industry* (2nd ed.). Upper Saddle River, NJ: Pearson Education.
This second edition textbook has updated content and a revised chapter on technology.

McLaurin, D., & Wykes, T. (2010). *MPI's planning guide: A source for meetings and conventions* (3rd ed.). Dallas, TX: Meeting Professionals International.
Sponsored by MPI, this recently updated guide is an industry standard.

Professional Convention Management Association. (2006.) *Professional meeting management: Comprehensive strategies for meetings, conventions and events.* Dubuque, IA: Kendall Hunt.
PCMA calls PMM5 "the most complete meetings management, meeting planning and conference planning textbook in the industry" and a "life-long resource." The book is recommended reading for the CMP exam.

Books on Event and Festival Planning/Management

Allen, J. (2009). *Event planning: The ultimate guide to successful meetings, corporate events, fundraising galas, conferences, conventions, incentives, and other special events* (2nd ed.). Hoboken, NJ: John Wiley and Sons.
This book is an updated and expanded version of a popular sourcebook that expanded into a series of planning guides. Forms and checklists are included in the text with additional content at the publisher's website.

Goldblatt, J. (2007). *Special events: The roots and wings of celebrations* (5th ed.). Hoboken, NJ: John Wiley and Sons.
This text connects the growing special events industry to an "ancient human need to celebrate with ceremony and ritual" and new global opportunities. Case studies, best practices, and Web resources are included in the book.

Kilkenny, S. (2007). *The complete guide to successful event planning.* Ocala, FL: Atlantic Publishing Group.
This book provides a step-by-step guide for planning events of any size. It also includes a companion CD of additional material.

Silvers, J. R. (2004). *Professional event coordination.* Hoboken, NJ: John Wiley and Sons.
Silvers presents event planning as a production with special attention to audience and infrastructure. Additional content is available on the publisher's website.

Van Der Wagen, L., & Carlos, B. R. (2005). *Event management for tourism, cultural, business and sporting events.* Upper Saddle River, NJ: Pearson.
A resource that sets event planning within the larger context of tourism, sports, and culture and includes an emphasis on career options.

Recommended Viewing

About.com—Career Profile: Event Planner: video.about.com/careerplanning/Career-Provile-
-Event-Planner.htm

This 3-minute video captures the life of a DJ turned meeting planner. Watch his firm "turn" a room between back-to-back weddings while he describes essential attributes for success.

Education-Portal.com—Event Planning Professions Overview: education-portal.com/
videos, and search for *event planning*.

Learn about the background, aptitudes, and skills required by event planners and industry certifications and tips for gaining experience. Additional information is available on the website.

References

[1]Snodgrass, J. (2002). Become an event planner. Retrieved from www.fabjob.com/EventPlanner1.asp
[2]Kilkenny, S. (2006). *The complete guide to successful event planning*. Ocala, FL: Atlantic Publishing Group.
[3]Wallace, E., Mathai, M., Health, A., & McCann, D. (Eds.). (2008). *The Convention Industry Council manual* (8th ed.). Washington, DC: Convention Industry Council.

© *Photographerlondon | Dreamstime.com*

" *Success seems to be connected with action. Successful people keep moving. They make mistakes, but they don't quit.*

—Conrad H. Hilton
Founder of Hilton Hotel Corporation "

11

The Hospitality Industry

Morgan W. Geddie
California State University, Chico

Yao-Yi Fu
Indiana University at Indianapolis

Chang Lee
California State University, Chico

Focus Questions

Q: Do you consider yourself to be a people person?

A: Working with all kinds of personalities, and liking it, is part of a job in hospitality. Different guests have different needs, and coworkers come from all over the world. However, a hospitality job is much more than being a people person, and after working with guests on a day-to-day basis, you may find that you do not like people as much as you thought. A truly successful hospitality professional views the unhappy guest as an opportunity to serve and to improve his or her people skills.

Q: Are you okay with a job that involves a variety of activities and may involve change at any moment?

A: Anytime you are dealing with the public, you have to be ready for the unexpected. You can never say to a guest "that is not my job" even if it is not your responsibility. You must rise to the challenge to correct the situation and make the guest happy.

Q: Teamwork is usually needed in the hospitality industry. Do you really enjoy working on teams?

A: You cannot do everything on your own, or you will quickly burn out. You must learn to delegate responsibility, but to do so, you must become an excellent trainer with confidence in the abilities of your employees to make the correct decisions.

Q: Are you willing to work in the evenings, on weekends, and on holidays?

A: The hospitality industry runs 24 hours a day, 7 days a week and does not stop for holidays. You will probably work nights, weekends, and holidays. This is especially true at the beginning of your career.

Q: Are you willing to relocate?

A: A career in hospitality may take you to all parts of the world, and if you want to move up in a company, you must be willing to relocate. This is an opportunity for you to explore different parts of the United States and beyond. You may not want to leave home, but you may always make it your goal to eventually return to your hometown.

Q: Do you enjoy organizing a party or arranging an activity for your friends or family?

A: People in the hospitality industry are social. A hospitality manager must have an eye for details. You need to be able to visualize an event and be able to see it through to completion.

Key Terms

Hospitality industry
Interval ownership
Gratuities
Culinary
Lodging industry
Full-service hotels
Concierge
Restaurant industry
Certified Hotel Administrator (CHA)

Certified Lodging Manager (CLM)
Certified Food and Beverage Executive
  (CFBE)
Certified Hospitality Technology
  Professional (CHTP)
Certified Hospitality Accountant Executive
  (CHAE)
ServSafe

Profile 1: Could This Be You?

Marcia Schaefer is the event and dining room supervisor for Buca di Beppo, a restaurant in Greenwood, Indiana. She is a certified server trainer and sometimes works as a bartender at the establishment. Marcia generates new event and party business for Buca di Beppo. She negotiates contracts and guides clients through specialty ordering. She is also responsible for all front-of-house management duties including floor plans, reports, and deposits, and she often trains new servers in their duties. As one of Buca di Beppo's most valued employees, Marcia handles large groups and provides excellent service to all guests, giving a history of the restaurant and an introduction to the unique dining experience at Buca di Beppo.

Q: How do you make a difference through your work?

A: I hope that I add a little joy to the lives of the guests who visit Buca. I am reminded of a specific guest's visit that always makes me smile. It was prom night, and I was serving a table of young people who were on their way to prom. As the host brought them to their table, one of the girls snagged her dress on a piece of carpet transition strip and tore a section of the dress. She was very distraught. I got her and the others to order so they could maintain the evening's schedule. As I was talking to them, another guest at the next table announced that she had a travel sewing kit. What are the odds in this day and age? While I was doing this, I also had a table that was doing a tasting for their rehearsal dinner. The tables were fairly closely located, so I pulled up a chair and worked on the dress as I continued to describe the food and wine to the future bride and groom. I was able to repair the dress well enough to get her through the evening, and she once again was smiling and excited about the prom. I have calmed mothers of the grooms and helped with surprise birthday parties for people from eight to 80. I also have regulars that have all but adopted me into their families. I have the joy of making someone's evening a "night to remember."

Q: What challenges you about your job?

A: Every day brings new challenges of all types and levels. I have to remain calm when I deal with customer service problems. In this industry, you do not always have the privilege to deal with someone at their best. I have also gotten to a location and had to "make do" with what was on hand when things were forgotten, broken, or just different from what was promised. In this industry, "making do" also means never letting the guest know that anything is wrong or was ever wrong.

Q: How did you get into this profession?

A: I have always been the one in my family and with my friends who took care of things. I organize, construct, get donations, and just make sure everything is taken care of. I also have been accused of being a "mother hen." I have had a variety of jobs, and I always go back to the service industry where I can help to create lifelong memories.

Q: If you could give a young professional interested in this career area one piece of advice, what would it be?

A: I would tell them not to go into this industry unless they love it. It is hard work and time consuming. It takes you away from your family on weekends and holidays so that others can spend time with their families. But it can be some of the most rewarding time as well as the most frustrating times you may have.

Profile 2: Could This Be You?

Keith Johnson is the recreation manager at Marriott Desert Springs Villas in Palm Desert, California. Desert Springs Villas is a Marriott Vacation Club property.

Margo Tighe is the director of recreation at Marriott's Timber Lodge and Grand Residence Club in South Lake Tahoe, California.

Q: How do you make a difference through your work?

A: (Keith) I truly feel that what we do has a huge impact on the guest experience. If you think back on any of your own personal vacations, you probably remember fun experiences you spent with your family. It's usually centered on some kind of structured or unstructured activity. Rarely do you remember the lightbulb that wasn't working, the remote that had batteries that stopped working, or the two washcloths your room was missing. If the recreation department does its job and provides a fun way for people to spend time together, then everything else fades into the distance.

(Margo) In my personal makeup is the desire to make a difference in the lives of others and those in need, so working for a company such as Marriott with their "spirit to serve" philosophy is a natural fit. Marriott International is a corporate sponsor for Children's Miracle Network, and in my job I have had the privilege of creating and organizing a fund-raising event called "Chip In for Children," raising thousands of dollars for children's hospitals.

Q: What do you love about your career?

A: (Keith) I love the fact that I get to mix my personal enjoyment with my work enjoyment. Often I'm out doing various activities with my wife and am thinking about how I can tweak things around to make it into an activity at our resort. It also allows me to see how things work in the recreation world at various levels whether it's as a shop mechanic, someone marketing a creative idea, or being the "visionary" trying to put together a long-term recreation plan.

(Margo) I'm fortunate to be working in a career that utilizes my strengths of creativity, strategizing, and interacting with people. I come to work every day excited by the opportunity to share my enthusiasm for recreation with others. No two days are alike. I am working in an ever-changing, evolving field, and I am always challenged, changing, and growing. My job allows me to meet new people and to create, develop, and implement new programs to enhance the vacation experience for our guests. What's not to love about that?!

Q: Do you have a story about how you transformed a client's life through your services?

A: (Keith) One of my fond memories was from a Mrs. Jacobson in Park City, UT, who signed up for my mountain biking class. It was one of the first activities that I created, and it included learning how to use the gears/brakes while going down a small switchback. She hadn't been on a mountain bike before but wanted to learn so she could ride with her daughter. Mrs. Jacobson couldn't quite get it at first but was very persistent and got to the point where she could do the entire bike trail with switchbacks and all. Her excitement after we were done and debriefing with one another was infectious. All of the guests were extremely jazzed at that point. Being with someone who accomplishes something for the first time is very rewarding. Those are the moments that make everything else so worthwhile.

(Margo) I actually have many stories, but this one in particular is memorable and bittersweet. In my job, I have daily opportunities to transform lives in little ways and big ways. During one week in particular, our department was able to provide a week of happy memories for a family that included a dad, mom, and three children. A relative of this family had called our property to inform us that this particular family was on what would be their last family vacation because the mother was terminally ill and was not expected to live much beyond this final trip. My department was able to plan some extra fun activities geared toward this mom and her family, allowing them to set aside their sadness for a while and just enjoy themselves. As a staff, we had to make an effort to focus on the positive in this situation and not dwell on the fact that these children only had a short time left with their mother. It was a rewarding and challenging week.

Q: What challenges you on your job?

A: (Keith) I like trying to accomplish something that I've never done before. Learning new angles to the recreation world is always fascinating to me. Currently, I'm learning contract preparation, architecture/interior decorating for a new activities center, and stargazing. It's as if I'm trying to learn everything I can so that someday I'm ready to open "Keith's FunLand." Whether that actually happens is irrelevant. What is relevant is that I find an enjoyable way to keep that zest for life alive with my wife and my work.

Q: How did you get into this profession?

A: (Keith) I grew up snow skiing as a kid and got into mountain biking when it became popular in the late '80s. My family was always outdoorsy. We went camping and fishing to many areas on the East Coast as well as Eastern Canada. I moved out West after college and lived in many outdoorsy towns, including Lake Tahoe, CA, The Grand Canyon, AZ, Gunnison, CO, Park City, UT, as well as spent a summer in SE Alaska. I enjoy traveling and seeing what different people do in their free time for entertainment. Traveling throughout the U.S. and overseas helps you to understand what life is all about.

(Margo) In high school, I worked summers as a camp counselor. It was as a counselor that I found I loved making a difference in people's lives in a recreational setting. In college, I pursued a degree in recreation with an emphasis in therapeutic recreation and a minor in adventure travel and tourism. Following graduation, I began working for Marriott Vacation Club as a front desk agent at a Colorado property, learning firsthand about the hospitality industry. From the front desk, I moved to the activities department and eventually worked my way up to recreation manager. I transferred to South Lake Tahoe, CA, a few years ago and worked my way up to director of recreation. Along the way, Marriott has provided me with excellent management training programs. I have also had very supportive and encouraging property managers and mentors who have taken an interest in me personally and in my career development.

Q: If you could give a young professional interested in this career area one piece of advice, what would it be?

A: (Keith) Be smart, have fun, don't take yourself too seriously, laugh as much as possible, and be courteous when showing others how to do this as well!

(Margo) Know what you are good at. Do what you are good at. And do something good every day!

The Big World of Hospitality

The hospitality industry is one of the largest and fastest growing industries in the world and is expected to continue growing into the foreseeable future.[1] The hospitality industry delivers services and products to fulfill customers' expectations. The diversity of the industry makes it difficult to develop a simple industry definition, but hospitality offers great variety and opportunity. Overall, the **hospitality industry** comprises businesses such as hotels, resorts, cruise ships, theme parks, clubs, and restaurants that provide food, beverages, and accommodations to guests.

Hotels and restaurant establishments are abundant almost everywhere in the world. Therefore, the opportunity to choose where you want to work and live is great. The opportunity for career advancement in the hospitality industry is also excellent. Industry growth, faster than other industries, has allowed managers to advance more rapidly than in many other industries.

The hospitality industry provides exciting opportunities for people with a variety of backgrounds, experiences, skills, talents, and personalities. Many skills and experiences are transferable between hospitality businesses. For instance, if you have restaurant experience, you may also work for a food and beverage department or catering department in a hotel.

Hospitality Industry Origins

The hospitality industry has been around for thousands of years. In Roman times, people would open their homes to travelers in hopes that they would be given a place to stay when they traveled. The story of Joseph and Mary traveling to Bethlehem in the Bible is a perfect example of

Erwinova Dreamstime Stock Photos

early hospitality. The innkeeper had no rooms available, but he gave Joseph and Mary the use of his stable.

Over time, as travel and commerce expanded, business-minded individuals created dedicated restaurant and lodging facilities to meet the needs of growing numbers of travelers. The rapid growth of the hospitality industry can be traced in part to the many benefits that patrons derive. Individuals and groups find safe and comfortable accommodations and meals while traveling, visit establishments to celebrate milestone events and reconnect with loved ones, and visit establishments to conduct business. Growing attention to the triple bottom line of economic, social, and environmental sustainability extends positive outcomes across the entire spectrum of benefits. As noted in Chapter 1, leisure services provide many benefits. We will discuss positive social, economic, psychological, and environmental impacts the hospitality industry may make later in the chapter.

Changing economic systems led to greater industrialization, and that led to more people having more disposable income. Advances in transportation enabled the general population to travel greater distances. As people traveled more, the hospitality industry grew. The Ford Model-T made car ownership possible for average people and allowed them the luxury of travel when they wanted, where they wanted. After World War II, the interstate highway system was developed, increasing the ease of travel. The end of World War II was also the beginning of the commercial airline industry, allowing for distant travel in a short period of time.

The hospitality industry has continued to evolve and expand as states and nations have emerged. New hospitality products and new destinations continue to add adventure and excitement to this vibrant industry segment. Most hospitality firms, at least in westernized countries, are firmly in the commercial section of the leisure services delivery continuum described in Chapter 2. But new options and hybrid business models are constantly evolving. In the future, more public and nonprofit entities may provide hospitality services. One example is an innovative Head Start program in Salt Lake City, Utah. This nonprofit organization runs a Central Kitchen to provide healthy meals to preschool children, and to help cover costs, the chef and kitchen staff also cater lunches, dinners, and parties for a cost. This blending of a nonprofit agency with a hospitality service in a manner akin to a business is an example of blended or boundary service provision. If you are interested in both hospitality and the so-importants of improving quality of life, this approach may appeal to you.

Hospitality Industry Today

The hospitality industry has become a part of day-to-day life in North America. Consider your typical day—do you eat at least one meal or snack away from your apartment or home? According to the U.S. Department of Agriculture, over 40% of all meals Americans consume are eaten away from home.[2] This is mainly because many citizens work full-time jobs and often do not have time or interest in cooking a meal.

Tourist lodging is also part of the hospitality industry, and lodging is available to fit the demands of all travelers. Whether it is the budget-minded family or a top executive, a lodging option is available to satisfy. Such options continue to evolve as niche services emerge, customer demands change, or new opportunities beckon. **Interval ownership** (also known as time-sharing) is an example of how lodging has evolved. Interval ownership allows the guest to purchase a week or more at a resort for as long as the resort is in operation, and guests may even pass this interval ownership down to their children.

The cruise line industry is also growing, as only around 5% of the American population has taken a cruise. Noting this, cruise lines have expanded offerings to entice more people to cruise. These floating hotels have evolved into floating resorts with a full line of activities and excursions to fit every taste and theme. However, with this growth has come increased social responsibility to the consumer and the waters, ports, and towns on which the cruise ships rely. Social responsibility will be addressed later in this chapter.

As the hospitality industry has grown, so has consumer savvy. Today's consumers eat meals out on a regular basis, are well traveled, and have high expectations for their hospitality experiences. This means the hospitality industry must continuously evolve to meet these expectations.

Careers in the Hospitality Industry

Many hospitality jobs may look glamorous, especially positions with upscale restaurants or in luxurious resorts. Many jobs are in beautiful, clean, and comfortable settings, but a lot of behind-the-scenes work occurs that most people do not see. Whether entry-level or managerial positions, many jobs require long hours and work in the evenings, on weekends, and on holidays. The work can be stressful, hectic, and unpredictable. You may have to deal with guests who are demanding, irate, or unpleasant, or you may encounter a customer service problem that may be difficult to solve. In addition, hospitality employees are expected to provide friendly and prompt service even when they are tired or under stress. Dealing with difficult or challenging situations takes patience. However, if you have a good deal of energy, like to meet and work with people, and enjoy helping people and making them feel welcome and comfortable, this may be the right industry for you.

Before reading about the range of career options in the hospitality industry, take a moment to review your preferences and passions worksheets from Chapter 2. Evaluate each hospitality sector and position in terms of its ability to satisfy your needs.

Passions

The hospitality industry offers a variety of career options. Therefore, if you really like the idea of working in this business, you may find a position in the industry that fits your interests, talents, and personality.

The hospitality industry is a people business. Not only will you interact with different guests, but you will also work with people from different backgrounds and cultures. If you enjoy meeting and helping people, this is the right industry for you. You may even meet a few celebrities!

The work is constantly different and challenging because you help with customers who have different needs, preferences, and expectations. Anytime you deal with the public, you have to be prepared for the unexpected.

Many positions offer flexible work hours and locations that can fit your preferences. However, when beginning your career, you may not work the hours you would like. But consider the possibility of living in many wonderful places and in fabulous facilities that most people only dream of visiting! A career in hospitality can be your ticket to the world of luxury.

> Restaurant work can be stressful and demanding if you let it. The key is to not get caught up in day-to-day issues but to focus on the big picture such as workplace morale and positivity, attention to detail, and standout customer service. In terms of preparation, make a habit of constantly honing your leadership and interpersonal skills, and learn to utilize goal-setting in both the long and short term.
>
> —Nicholas Melton, 24, restaurant manager
> in Norfolk, Virginia

Pay and Perks

Salaries vary greatly in the hospitality industry because of the enormous variety of jobs. Entry-level employees frequently begin earning minimum wage. However, many increase their income with **gratuities** (tips), so the salary may not truly reflect the real income. Compensation for mid-level managers differs depending on the types, sizes, and locations of hospitality businesses. Generally, higher salaries are found in larger businesses due to more complex work responsibilities. Many upper level managers make six-figure salaries. Performance bonuses may add another 25% to the base salary.

If you love to travel, many hospitality jobs provide opportunities for traveling or living in different parts of the United States or in different countries. Some locations are more exotic than others, but all offer the opportunity to experience a different part of the country or world.

Pay and perks vary a great deal as operations range in size and location. Some hospitality businesses offer perks in addition to compensation such as free meals, lodging, use of recreation facilities, and bonus programs. Others offer employees tuition assistance. Be aware of the possible benefits so you can negotiate the best package for yourself.

Preparation

Although many jobs in the industry do not require a college degree, most of those jobs are lower paying frontline positions. If you plan to establish a long-term career in the hospitality industry, a college education or special training is needed for advancing to managerial positions. Moreover, an increasing number of hospitality businesses are hiring people with college degrees, and many companies give preference to people with a degree in hospitality management. Regardless of degree title, hospitality or recreation, a college degree may help you to advance more quickly in the industry.

Many schools in the United States offer 2-year or 4-year degrees in hospitality management or commercial recreation. The best programs combine strong leadership and management skills with excellent customer service and fiscal accountability offerings.

Many hotel, resorts, and cruise ships have recreation departments. These departments oversee the activities offered to their guests. Conference centers often have recreation departments directed more toward team-building activities. Students from commercial recreation programs often find excellent opportunities in hospitality settings where guests stay longer or conduct business on-site.

Some academic programs may focus on certain areas, such as hotel management, restaurant management, or **culinary** preparation, and other programs offer

education in all those areas. The largest programs may offer specialized coursework for those planning to work in casinos, conference facilities, golf courses, destination resorts, and cruise lines.

Many schools require an internship in the industry before graduation. The internship requirement is beneficial because it helps you gain valuable industry experience outside of the classroom. Many hospitality students are able to earn managerial positions right after graduation because of the experience they gain through an internship.

In addition to an internship, many hospitality students work part time while attending school. Hotels and restaurants offer part-time jobs such as servers, kitchen helper, front desk clerk, bellhop, and housekeeper that fit around a school schedule. Many students start building their careers in the hospitality industry with those part-time jobs, and this helps them determine whether it is the right industry for them.

The locations and settings for jobs in this industry are varied, and customers and fellow staff members will have diverse backgrounds as well. You will likely interact with customers and coworkers of different nationalities and who speak different languages. For example, 21% of all lodging sales in the United States were by international visitors.[3] In addition, many North American companies expand their businesses to different parts of the world and send employees to work in different countries. You may have the opportunity to work in a different country that speaks a language other than your own. Therefore, it would be beneficial for you to become proficient in a foreign language and, even more important, to understand and embrace different cultures.

Possibilities

As with other recreation-related careers, the hospitality industry has almost unlimited possibilities. Seek out different entry-level jobs so you learn about different aspects of operations and become a well-rounded employee. Find good mentors and good companies willing to teach and help you grow. Networking is vital in this industry. The more people you know, the more opportunities you will have for advancement. Willingness to relocate to different geographical areas is important because opportunities are often available elsewhere.

The more hospitality experience you have, the better your job possibilities will be when you graduate. Many companies offer paid summer internship programs and strongly promote students working each summer during their college career. These opportunities give students a taste of what their work will be like when they graduate and give the employer opportunities to observe

and develop potential managers. This chapter will focus on career options within the lodging and restaurant industries. If these areas interest you, cross-check information in Chapters 6, 10, 12 and 13 to locate the niches that most interest you.

Lodging industry. The **lodging industry** caters to tourists, corporate travelers who need a place to stay for a few days, and people who need extended stays due to relocation or long-term work assignments. In 2013, more than 4.9 million guest rooms were available for travelers and tourists, and the average occupancy rate for these rooms was about 61%.[4] A range of lodging properties exist from small bed and breakfast inns with only a few guest rooms to large hotels with more than 1,000 rooms. Many hotels provide basic accommodations, and full-service hotels provide restaurants, meeting rooms, exhibit halls, and ballrooms for conventions, wedding receptions, and social events. In addition, many hotels offer recreational facilities for guests to enjoy, such as tennis courts, swimming pools, spa services, fitness centers, golf courses, and planned recreational activities. As the lodging industry offers a variety of facilities and services, a range of jobs in different areas is available.

Every hotel organizes its jobs differently. Larger hotels tend to have more divisions, and jobs are more specialized. A large full-service hotel may have positions in front office, food and beverage, sales and marketing, accounting and finance, and human resources.

Although a great number of career opportunities may be found in large hotels, a small lodging business may also offer a great learning environment for essential experience in hotel operations. Consider specific areas of lodging operations to learn more.

Passions. If your interests lie in travel and luxury, consider a career in lodging. You need to enjoy finding ways to make people happy, even though you do not know and will likely never see them again. Recreation majors may find success and satisfaction in any division but most often gravitate to front-of-house positions with strong customer contact, to marketing and sales, or to employee training and development positions in human resources.

Pay and perks. The salaries vary within the lodging industry based on position, size of property, and service level. Traditionally, a larger hotel will pay more, but this is not always true. Higher end luxury hotels are usually not as large but have higher levels of service and may pay well for the right employee.

Hotels with food service on-site often provide meals to employees during their shifts. This will reduce your grocery budget significantly, giving you more discretionary income. Many lodging companies also offer free nights or reduced rates to their employees. This may be a savings when traveling and allows to experience other properties.

Preparation. Start with a job in the lodging industry! Whether during the summer or school year, you will need experience within the industry before you can advance your career. Recruiters like to see that a student has related hands-on experience. This first job may be working as a front desk clerk, bellhop, housekeeper, or server in the hotel coffee shop or restaurant. Although some of this work may not appear glamorous at first, think of it as an investment in your future.

Possibilities. Many lodging opportunities are available. From a 6,500-room casino hotel in Las Vegas, Nevada, to a four-room bed and breakfast in Buford, North Carolina, all are possible employers.

You may move up in management in a large hotel chain, as many opportunities for advancement exist. At some point, you may want to start your own small independent hotel and grow that into something large (if that is your interest). People such as Conrad Hilton and William Marriott started off with one property and built their businesses into multinational corporations.

Front office. The functions of the front office include processing reservations, registering and checking out guests, monitoring arrivals and departures, receiving and forwarding mail, providing local or other information to guests, and handling guest complaints. Since hotels are open around the clock, three work shifts are common throughout the day. Front office employees deal with guests constantly. Employees should be friendly, understanding, and willing to help everyone. For people who plan to build a career in the lodging industry, the front office is a great department in which to learn about lodging management, with a goal of advancing to a managerial position in the future.

Uniformed service. Positions in this department include bellhops, door attendants, and baggage porters. They carry bags, usher guests to their rooms, and assist guests in and out of vehicles. Many full-service hotels also have **concierges** who provide information on local attractions and events, make travel arrangements and restaurant reservations, provide concert tickets, and assist with other special requests. Some hotels cross-train uniformed personnel in front office operations in case extra help is needed at the front desk.

For an insider's look at working in the hotel industry, check out Jacob Tomsky's 2012 book *Heads in Beds: A Reckless Memoir of Hotels, Hustles, and So-Called Hospitality.* Tomsky shares humorous stories from his years working in the hotel industry and lets guests in on ways to secure top service. His anecdotes also provide insights for those who want to work in the industry. For example, he reminds would-be employees that everyone in a hotel knows everything about everyone, often

both personally and professionally, and that once a hotel opens for business, it is open 24 hours a day, with staff members always on duty.

Food and beverage. Full-service hotels provide food and beverage outlets or services such as restaurants, coffee shops, bars, banquets, and room service. Many positions in the department are similar to those in the **restaurant industry**, as are the skills required. Many hotels outsource part of their food and beverage operations to restaurant chains. Having a chain restaurant in a hotel not only promotes brand recognition for its business but also attracts more business from local residents.

Recreation programming. Many hotels and resorts offer extensive on-site recreational amenities for guests. Golf courses, aquatic facilities, recreation centers, and spas are specialized facilities often staffed by professionals from park and recreation programs. Some properties have large resort recreation divisions that operate year-round to ensure high levels of guest satisfaction.

Photo: Alisdair

Marketing and sales. Employees in this department are responsible for selling guest rooms, meeting space, or other space for weddings, banquets, and special events. The organization of this department can vary depending on the size and type of market a hotel targets. Positions may include director of marketing, sales manager, banquet manager, convention service manager, and sales representative. Sales personnel may receive bonuses in addition to salary. When a conference or special event occurs in the hotel, sales personnel need to be there with the client to ensure the event is going well. Some sales people may travel frequently to meet with clients. Therefore, work hours can be irregular and long.

Housekeeping. This department is responsible for providing a clean and comfortable environment for guests' stays. Housekeepers clean guest rooms, lobbies, halls, and other public rooms and areas in a hotel. In larger hotels, this department may include executive housekeepers, assistant housekeepers, and floor supervisors.

Accounting management. The responsibilities of this department include recording sales, preparing financial reports, and other related tasks. Accounting personnel maintain fiscal records, ensuring income and expenses are properly allocated between the cost centers, and they also respond to guest billing inquiries. Accounting employees should be detail oriented and have good written and verbal communication skills. Some hotels prefer employees with prior hotel experience.

Revenue management. Positions in revenue management are relatively new in the lodging industry. An increasing number of hotel upper managers are hiring revenue managers who help them figure out how to maximize sales. Revenue managers must have knowledge with the hotel business and be familiar with their market segments. They work closely with the front office, marketing and sales department, and catering service department to develop sales strategies that meet a hotel's revenue goals. They monitor and evaluate past pricing strategies and reservation data, analyze markets, forecast future demands, and set pricing strategies for different market segments. Thus, revenue managers must have good analytical and communication skills.

Human resources management. This department is responsible for hiring employees, employee training, employee relations, compensation and benefits administration, legal compliance, and payroll and benefits administration. Job opportunities are available for people with hotel experience or people who have a degree in human resources.

Restaurant industry. Restaurant industry jobs are found everywhere across the United States and world, in various restaurants from cafeterias, coffee shops, fast-food to casual theme or fine dining. Even in difficult financial times, today's busy lifestyles seem to necessitate that many people dine away from home. The growth of this industry is predicted to continue, and thus job opportunities are and will be abundant.

Passions. If you love food—preparing it or sharing it—the food and beverage sector is for you. You will be able to serve at one of life's most essential levels and use your specialized skills to create welcoming settings for guests and clients. For some, food and beverage is a lifelong adventure. For others, it provides a way to learn, on the job, about the importance of customer service and the role of fine dining as a tool to enable any group of people to bond over the time-honored communal table.

Service in the Sun

Desiring to provide the ultimate in customer service to guests, some hotels offer unique amenities beyond standard room service or a concierge. Dr. Shades and the Hotel Falconer Tanning Butlers are two of the more unusual positions available at high-end hotels. At the Four Seasons Resort Lanai, Hawaii, for example, Dr. Shades, is on call to clean sunglass lenses, tighten loose screws, or lend a pair of sunglasses. You may find him circulating poolside most days looking out for anyone squinting into the sun. And at the Ritz Carlton in South Beach, Florida, you may find Tanning Butlers strolling around carrying various levels of sunscreen. Finally, at a Four Seasons in Santa Barbara, California, a Hotel Falconer walks around the pool with a hawk perched on his shoulder or hand to scare away lingering seagulls. Keep your eyes open, and you may find a unique position perfect for you!

Tips on Tips

When working in the restaurant industry, you are likely to start out as waitstaff, dining room attendant, or kitchen worker before moving up. In these positions, you will rely heavily on tips, or gratuities, as your main source of income. In 2013, the federal minimum wage for tipped positions was $2.13/hour. How exactly can you—or the staff you train and manage—maximize the customer experience with hopes of earning higher tips? First, the origin of the word *tips* is debated, with some suggesting it is an acronym meaning *to insure promptness*, but most linguists contest this. Others suggest it was a phrase used by royalty, peasants, or beggars. Whatever the origins, the meaning for you is the same: Better service usually equals a bigger tip. Here are five ways to maximize the potential for earning greater tips (15% to 20% is customary in most U.S. restaurants):

- Introduce yourself by name to personalize the experience, appear friendly.
- Repeat the order back to the customer, showing similarity in thinking.
- Write "thank you" on the receipt, showing gratitude for their patronage.
- "Make the customers feel good about themselves and they will like you. The more customers like their servers, the higher the tips they are likely to leave."[5]

Pay and perks. As with most areas of hospitality, the pay range varies with the size of the operation and the position. But few other economic sectors offer such rapid opportunities for advancement. Your creativity and business acumen may be the only limits to your advancement. Perks range from complimentary meals to great industry events where professionals compete to "out-host" one another and highlight their best features.

Preparation. In addition to your campus coursework, you will need to gain industry experience. Look for opportunities to supervise others, manage some aspect of the operation, or become involved in ordering and inventory. If you want to pursue a career in food preparation, look for opportunities to attend a reputable culinary academy and broaden your expertise to include food science and costing. If beer, wine, or spirits are your forte, seek specialized expertise and knowledge in those areas as well.

Possibilities. Large or small, at home or abroad, the food and beverage sector is so varied that you will find many options to locate your niche. If you want to provide down-home community for residents of your hometown, consider a cozy café. If you want to travel the world, consider a career with a national brand seeking to increase its international presence. This sector is broad, so gain experience, finish your university degree, secure the best industry certifications (listed at the end of the chapter) and explore your opportunities.

Hosts and hostesses. Hosts and hostesses greet and seat guests, offer menus, schedule dining reservations, answer questions, and inform guests about wait times. In some restaurants, they may also work as a cashier. Hosts and hostesses are expected to make a great first and last impression on guests. Most restaurants prefer hiring people with friendly and positive attitudes.

Waiters and waitresses/servers. You are probably familiar with this position—the person who takes your order, serves food and beverages, prepares itemized checks, and accepts payments. Servers should be able to answer questions about how menu items are prepared and make recommendations based on guests' needs and likes or dislikes. They should also anticipate and react to guests' needs to provide prompt service and earn their tip. Depending on the restaurant, they may be expected to prepare salads or certain dishes at the table. Servers may also clean and set up tables and run the cash register. The work can be physically demanding as servers are on their feet most of the time, bringing hot dishes to tables and carrying heavy trays of food, dishes, and glassware. Servers also need a good memory to accurately place guests' orders. Being able to do quick arithmetic is helpful at some restaurants to total bills manually and make change.

Dining room attendants. Usually before becoming a server, a person will work as an attendant. Dining room attendants assist waiters and waitresses with removing dirty dishes and soiled linens from tables, as well as cleaning and setting tables. They also keep the dining room stocked with a supply of silverware, glasses, dishes, and linens.

Chefs, cooks, and kitchen workers. Chefs and cooks are responsible for creating menus and preparing food. Chefs usually have more skills and experience than cooks, often including specialized culinary training. Although some restaurants have standardized menus, many offer tasty and unique foods, or "specials," that provide chefs opportunities to be creative and experiment with new ideas. Some chefs are responsible for supervising kitchen operations and purchasing food supplies.

Kitchen workers daily prepare ingredients for guest meals. This may be routine and repetitive and may include measuring ingredients, cutting meat and vegetables, preparing salads and cold items, and stirring or straining soups and sauces. Kitchen workers also clean equipment, utensils, dishes, and silverware and generally assist the chefs or cooks. These employees need to be able to prepare food quickly under pressure, especially during peak dining hours. They stand on their feet for hours at a time and work near hot ovens and ranges.

Many people start their culinary careers as kitchen workers and earn their way to becoming chefs after years of training and experience. More and more people obtain training through high schools, 2- or 4-year colleges, or culinary schools.

Cruise industry. The cruise industry offers careers on land and at sea. Land-based jobs range from reservationists assisting customers with vacation planning, to purchasing agents who place orders that are loaded on ships in their homeports each week, to sales and marketing professionals who work with travel agents and meeting planners to fill the ships year-round.

Cruise ships have two components. The first is transportation, which the captain oversees with the aid of the crew, which ensures that the ship reaches each port in a timely and safe manner. The second component is lodging. A cruise ship is basically a floating resort. Cruise ships have hotel rooms called cabins, as well as restaurants, bars, shops, spas, fitness centers, theaters, child care facilities, swimming pools, and an elaborate array of recreational facilities. Positions are similar to those offered in hotels, though some may have different names.

Passions. A cruise, for many guests, is a once-in-a-lifetime adventure to celebrate a milestone event. If you like being part of a multinational group of hospitality professionals who work together to create memorable experiences for guests, this may be the sector for you. Are you intrigued by exotic ports of call? Working on a cruise ship is an excellent way to see the world.

Pay and perks. Most cruise ships are not registered as American Ships and thus are not subject to American labor laws and regulations. Consequently, pay and perks vary. Hours are long, but accommodations and meals are included, so you can save most of your pay if you are disciplined. All cruise ships have doctors and nurses on board who provide free medical care for the crew.

As a cruise employee, you will commonly work 6 or 7 days a week for 3 months. However, when you are off, you are flown home or to another destination of your choice for a month or more before returning to work on the same ship or another ship in the fleet. Most cruise ships have many services for employees, such as a dining room, bar, gym, convenience store, and even a pool. Think of it as a "village" for the local inhabitants who work on the floating resort.

Preparation. Working in a restaurant or hotel is a good way to gain experience for a job in the cruise industry. The industry does not expect you to join its crew with years of cruise experience in an entry-level position and will provide training to prepare you for a life on the seas. Cruise lines do not offer internships due to the required training before you step foot on the ship.

Possibilities. Many people work in the cruise sector for several years before moving on to more traditional hospitality careers. Career paths do exist in the cruise industry, however, for experienced and excellent personnel. The following positions are similar to those in a hotel, but have slightly different names for the cruise ship industry.

Purser. This position is similar to a front desk agent in a hotel, with the front office manager being the same as the chief purser.

Steward. This position is similar to a housekeeper in a hotel. The head of housekeeping on a cruise ship is called chief steward.

Cruise director. This position varies depending on the cruise line, but typically oversees the activities and entertainment aspect of the cruise.

Shore excursion desk agent. These employees are in charge of booking and marketing tours and activities for guests when the ship is in ports of call.

Cruise Ship Impacts

More than 10 million North Americans annually vacation on the high seas, living on a floating resort and visiting warm-weather ports. Although the industry generates billions of dollars in revenue for the United States and foreign ports-of-call, the ships may negatively impact the oceans upon which their mode of transport relies.

As global attention turns to preserving natural places and the life within it, cruise line companies are becoming more aware of and accountable for the environmental impacts of the industry. You likely remember the wreck of the Costa Concordia off the coast of Italy in the Tuscan Archipelago National Park in January 2012. The accident resulted in 32 human deaths and damage to marine life. Efforts are ongoing to relocate noble pen shells, remove and clean up diesel seeping from the ship, and reduce noise pollution underwater. The Neptune grass living below the wreckage is in danger, and its demise may impact entire ecosystems, as the grass serves as a "nursery" for the ocean, providing food and shelter for much marine life.[6]

There are more than 230 cruise ships worldwide, and most can hold up to 3,000 passengers and crew members. Acting much like a small city, each ship must find a way to dispose of its sewage, gray water, and bilge water—water that may settle in the hull and collect oil or grease—as well as food scraps and other solid garbage. The U.S. Environmental Protection Agency (EPA) has ongoing data collection to measure the amount and impact of these water discharges and is working to clarify water regulations.[7]

Environmental watch groups, including the EPA, closely monitor the impact of cruise ships on the world's oceans and are tightening down on impacts. Wanting to be part of the solution, many cruise ship operators have instated their own "green," or environmentally responsible, policies and actions. For example, some new ships are being constructed to reduce water resistance, thus increasing fuel efficiency. Others use advanced energy systems to reduce power consumption or even generate power via solar panels. These large-scale changes reduce overall ship impact.

Smaller green options—often decisions left up to the individual passenger—include options to recycle plastic and paper, reuse towels instead of daily washing, forgo laundry service, choose only sustainable seafood options, and use low-flow showerheads.

Other attempts to green ships include having tinted windows to reduce air conditioning use, recycling photo processing chemicals via specialized dealers, and having LED lightbulbs to reduce energy consumption. Finally, for the eco-conscious traveler, some cruise lines offer trips dedicated to eco-tourism. These cruise lines try to offset their carbon footprint as well as reduce it on board. Offset measures include giving a portion of the passenger ticket price to a wind farm in a developing country, supporting research on environmental practices, or providing ship space for environmental organizations. Such practices can go a long way to benefiting the environment and small communities, fulfilling several of the so-importants provided by recreation and leisure services.

Gaming/casino industry. A casino is a business operation that offers table and card games, slot operations, and other games that offer a chance to win something. Casinos also provide various entertainment activities and amenities to attract and accommodate patrons. One definition of a casino is "a building or room used for social amusements; specifically one used for gambling."[8] Prior to the late 1980s, the gaming and casino entertainment industry was restricted to Las Vegas, Nevada, and Atlantic City, New Jersey. In the late 1980s, the industry began to spread across the United States, with new casino development occurring on tribal lands, riverboats, mining towns, racinos (racetracks that offer slot machines), and dockside locations. Currently, the U.S. gaming and casino industry employs more than 350,000 workers nationwide.[9]

Native American tribal casinos refer to casinos, bingo halls, and other gambling operations on Indian reservations or other tribal lands in the United States. Riverboat casinos cruise on rivers or in harbors offering table and card games as well as slot operations, whereas dockside operations do not cruise out but offer the same games as riverboat casinos. Historic gold mining towns have been restored to their original splendor to attract tourists and offer a mix of new gambling technology and 1850s old western atmosphere. For example, South Dakota legalized gaming in the city of Deadwood, and Colorado legalized gaming in the old mining towns of Black Hawk, Central City, and Cripple Creek in the late 1980s. A racino is a combined racetrack with slot operations and table games, such as blackjack, poker, and roulette. As of 2008, 12 states have allowed racinos.[10]

The gaming industry encompasses multiple components such as casinos, including table and card games and slot/video games, horse and dog track racing, lotteries, charitable games, sport betting, and bingo halls. Casinos are just one segment of the gaming industry, yet garner much more attention from the general public and potential investors. Some people visit casinos because they like to gamble and dream of making a fortune, and others visit to seek new and different ways to enjoy their money. Senior citizens sometimes visit a casino only to seek social interaction with others, including employees. Some people visit casinos to see the building or setting, especially for casinos that have become famous landmarks. Casinos also offer various amenities to attract different people, including children, seniors, convention attendees, or those (usually high rollers) simply seeking comps (complimentary or free amenities).

The following are the major segments of the gaming industry:

- **Table games:** Tables games involve gaming where bets or wagers, usually represented by chips, are placed on a table, creating a bet between the casino and customer. Common examples of table games include blackjack, dice/craps games, roulette, the Big 6, baccarat, and poker.
- **Card games:** Unlike table games, card games do not wager between players and casino but merely offer games that players can gamble against each other with the casino providing or dealing the games. Poker is an example of a card game.
- **Slot/video games:** Slot machines feature actual spinning reels activated by the pull of a handle or push of a button, and video games feature video poker, keno, and bingo. Slots and video games have become a major source of casino revenues.
- **Bingo:** Bingo is a game in which players match numbers on cards they have purchased with numbers drawn at random.
- **Keno:** Keno is a variation of bingo in which an electronic board/screen is used to display the numbers 1 to 80. Twenty numbers are randomly selected, and players mark a keno ticket showing which numbers the player believes will be drawn.
- **Horse and dog track racing/racinos:** Many states have legalized offtrack betting, and casinos typically feature video monitors televising races at multiple tracks.
- **Lotteries:** Government-sponsored lotteries involve the lottery player preselecting numbers and determining whether they match numbers the lottery sponsor selected in a public drawing.
- **Charitable games:** Churches and nonprofit organizations offer bingo games, raffles, or set up casino-type events with all proceeds going to the nonprofit organization.

Passions. Casinos open the door for opportunities for friendly and motivated individuals full of energy and enthusiasm. When people think about employment in the gaming industry, they tend to think of the dealers and casino personnel; however, the gaming industry is more than what people see on the gaming floor. Casinos employ people who may have no experience on the casino floor. Casinos offer many employment opportunities, including food and beverage, lodging, accounting, clerical, and security, to name a few.

Pay and perks. Most casinos are open 24 hours a day, 7 days a week. Employees may work nights, weekends, and holidays. Most managers and supervisors have full-time schedules; however, many gaming dealers work part time. Like most areas of hospitality, the pay range varies with the size and location of the operation and the job position.

Preparation. If you want to pursue a career in the casino industry, you may need to look for formal management courses in colleges and universities. You may want to study hotel management or gaming management that may lead to a certificate or a degree. Individual casinos or other gaming establishments may have their own training requirements. Your company may send you to gaming schools for 4 to 8 weeks to learn casino games. Gaming and services workers must be licensed by a state regulatory agency. Applicants must pass a background check and drug test. Work experience is always helpful for casino workers. Gaming and slot supervisors usually have several years of experience working in a casino.

Possibilities. Employment in gaming services occupations is projected to grow 13% from 2010 to 2020.[11] The increasing popularity of gambling establishments such as Native American casinos and racetracks that also offer slots or table games will require more casino professionals. In general, the gaming industry has a record of investing in its employees and promoting from within. Many employees also report high satisfaction with their jobs, and the turnover rate is low.[12] The Bureau of Labor Statistics also projects an 11% increase in casino employment for the next 10 years. The casino industry is broad and diverse. It is always good for you to earn an appropriate college degree, prepare for and earn industry certifications, and explore opportunities. Those with work experience in customer service at a hotel or resort should have greater job prospects because of the importance of customer service in casinos.

Cage (cashier). All casinos have a cage, which acts as the financial hub for the casino operation. These employees issue lines of credit to customers with authorizations from credit managers. Cage cashiers also record cash coming into the cage area from various locations within the casino. Workers in the cage sell casino chips to customers for money and are often in charge of securing items from customers to be placed in safe deposit boxes. This is an entry-level position that reports to either the cage manager, supervisor, or lead cashier.

Casino hosts. Casino hosts maintain a high level of player recognition and service and establish new members. They also determine player eligibility of complimentary services and keep player information current.

Casino manager. The casino manager typically reports to the owner/general manager/CEO. Casino managers are responsible for all operations, including table and card games, slots, keno, bingo, poker, and sports and race book operations. Casino managers may need to be present in the casino at all times during table game operations. They may substitute in other positions on their breaks and in unavoidable staffing emergencies.

Dealer. Unlike slot machines, table and card games demand the attention of skilled professionals. Casinos look for dealers proficient in games such as poker, blackjack, and craps. Each game requires different rules. Dealers may deal cards, throw dice, or spin the wheels required by each particular game.

Keno writers. Keno writers report to the assistant keno manager. They conduct the keno game in a gambling establishment: receives, verifies, and records cash wagers of customers. They write keno tickets for customers in the keno lounge. They also scan winning tickets that customers present, calculate winnings, and pay customers using knowledge of rules and payoffs of the game.

Pit boss. Pit bosses generally reports to the casino shift manager, and duties include supervising and observing floor personnel to ensure compliance with game rules and internal control procedures. They also interact with players, maintain high standards of customer service, and must be aware of casino internal control procedures, state gaming laws, and bank secrecy act requirements. They are responsible for directly supervising assigned gaming activities, floor persons, and dealers.

Slot host. Slot hosts report to a director of slot operations or director of casino marketing. They solicit memberships in the slot club. They circulate the casino and solicit slot players for membership in the casino's slot club. They also work at the slot club counter to enroll new slot club members.

Additional career possibilities. Whenever or wherever people have a need to eat, drink, sleep, or sit down to rest, job opportunities exist for people with a passion for hospitality. This means you do not have to live in an urban area or resort setting to find solid career opportunities. You may find additional career possibilities in campus settings such as colleges, universities, or corporate training facilities. You may also find career options in hospitals, senior care facilities, the military, or correction centers. Some people combine a second passion, such as public service, with their hospitality training and find careers in residential camps or disaster relief. Sounds like some of the so-importants described in the early chapters of the book, does it not?

Future Opportunities, Issues, and Challenges

The hospitality industry grew rapidly in the United States during the 20th century, and although many hospitality companies are still expanding domestically, many have entered international markets to pursue continued growth. The hospitality industry is always evolving; whether it is a hot new quick-service restaurant chain with meals under $5 or an ultra-luxury resort on a secluded beach with rooms selling for $1,000 per night, the hospitality industry continues to grow.

Cruise ship sizes continue to expand, with some large enough for a park to fit in the atrium complete with trees and grass, as well as rooms on the ship's interior with balconies overlooking activities below. At the same time, much smaller ships are being built with marinas that lower off the back of the ship for water activities.

Changes in lifestyle and legislation have spawned the growth of the gaming industry. This is a heavily government-controlled industry with great potential for growth. Whether you work on the casino floor, in the hotel, or in one of the restaurants, many career opportunities are available.

A career in hospitality can involve exploring opportunities in new places to respond to the needs of adventurers and novelty seekers. An underwater resort is proposed for Dubai, and Virgin Atlantic has established itself as a pioneer in space tourism, accepting reservations for commercial space flights for a one-of-a-kind vacation experience.[13]

Affordable Housing in Hotels

During hard economic times, the number of homeless residents in the United States often increases, with homeless or emergency shelters filling up faster than usual. To address this need for housing, some cities are trying out programs that turn unused or underused hotels and motels into housing units for people in need. State lawmakers in Baltimore, Maryland, for example, created a program that, in 2013, supported nearly 1,800 families to live in city hotels or motels. The program is controversial as it costs the state close to $1 million per week, but until legislators find ways to fund additional homeless shelters or provide rental assistance funds, empty hotels and motels are a temporary solution.[14] Those who work in such a facility may have an interest in both housing/hotel management and improving quality of life for those in need.

Coffee shops, tea bars, and other small, trendy cafés continue to open at intersections, near churches, near fitness centers, near commercial retail strips, and in neighborhoods. These "third places"[15] are neat additions to livable community efforts that provide a space for regular interactions between friends and coworkers.

Finally, branded and franchise operations are finding new ways to enter new and smaller markets. Starbucks® stores are ubiquitous to the point of twin locations on opposite street corners in major metropolitan areas. At the other end of the scale, national quick-service brands and franchises are entering smaller communities with the modular and smaller scale operations that can be profitable in smaller markets while expanding the brand/franchise into new markets.

As long as people continue to travel or dine away from home, the hospitality industry will continue to evolve to meet the needs of people away from their homes. From international destinations to on-the-corner nooks, hospitality providers will find unlimited opportunities to serve guests.

Summary of Hospitality Career Possibilities

Career	Passions	Pay and perks	Preparations	Possibilities
Lodging industry	Travel and luxury	Minimum wage to executive levels	Four-year college degree in hospitality management	Front office manager, director of sales, food and beverage manager, human resources manager
Restaurant industry	Creating, preparing, and sharing food	Minimum wage to executive levels	Four-year degree in hospitality management	Owner, manager, chef
Cruise industry	Travel, guest service, and luxury	Minimum wage to executive levels	Four-year to executive levels	Sales and marketing, hotel manager, cruise director, chief purser, food and beverage manager
Casino/gaming industry	Customer service, enthusiasm	Minimum wage to executive levels	Four-year degree in hospitality or business, licenses and background checks are routine	General supervisory and managerial positions as well as other functional areas of hospitality, additional opportunities for game-related personnel

Resources and Getting Involved

Industry-specific experience has no substitute. If you think you want a career in hospitality, get job experience early and often. Look to local opportunities, your own network of contacts, and professional organizations to secure that all-important industry knowledge, expertise, and experience.

Professional Organizations

Many associations exist within the hospitality industry. These associations offer workshops, conferences, certificates, and training programs to help you learn about the industry. Many of the associations also post news articles on their websites so you can get current information about trends and industry issues. Most associations are actively seeking young professionals and offer special, deeply discounted rates for students. Joining one or more associations will provide you many networking and job-searching opportunities.

Lodging
American Hotel and Lodging Association (AHLA): www.ahla.com
American Resort Development Association (ARDA): www.arda.org

Hospitality Accounting and Technology
Hospitality Financial and Technology Professionals (HFTP): www.hftp.org

Chef
American Culinary Federation: www.acfchefs.org
International Association of Culinary Professionals (IACP): www.iacp.com

Hospitality Education
International Council on Hotel, Restaurant, and Institutional Education (ICHRIE): www.chrie.org

Restaurants, Food Service, or Catering
National Restaurant Association (NRA): www.restaurant.org
Society for Foodservice Management (SFM): www.sfm-online.org
National Association for Catering and Events: www.nace.net

Gaming Industry
American Gaming Association (AGA): www.americangaming.org
National Indian Gaming Association (NIGA): www.indiangaming.org
Gaming Standards Associations (GSA): www.gamingstandards.com
North American Gaming Regulators Associations (NAGRA): www.nagra.org

Certifications, Licenses

Some associations sponsor certification programs designed to ensure a level of professionalism and currency. Three of many certification programs available to hospitality professionals are identified here. Information interviews and online research will reveal additional certification programs for specialized aspects of the industry.

Hotel Manager Certifications
Certified Hotel Administrator (CHA) or Certified Lodging Manager (CLM)
American Hotel & Lodging Association Educational Institute: www.ahlei.org

Food and Beverage
Certified Food and Beverage Executive (CFBE)
American Hotel & Lodging Association Educational Institute: www.ahlei.org

In addition, other specialized certification programs are available for specific aspects of hospitality. Hospitality Financial and Technology Professionals, a professional association, offers two specialized certifications: Certified Hospitality Technology Professional (CHTP) and Certified Hospitality Accountant Executive (CHAE). Check with the v industry associations to learn more about their respective certification programs.

Certifications you should pursue during your college career to increase your employability include Sanitation Certification through the National Restaurant Association ServSafe Food Safety Training Program or from a state board or regulatory agency and Alcohol Safety certification, which helps servers of spirits learn how to safely provide alcoholic beverages.[16]

Where to Gain Experience

It is never too soon to begin working on your résumé, and a good place to get started is by getting involved in the hospitality associations on your own university campus. You need to be active in these clubs and become an officer. Employers like to hire graduates who have taken leadership roles.

The next step is to join national hospitality organizations and attend the regional meetings. These meetings are often held during lunch and are a perfect opportunity to network with managers. Force yourself to get out there and meet people, and before long, they will be talking to you about a summer internship or coming to work for them when you graduate!

Many national organizations also have student memberships, which means you can join for little money. You can also attend their annual conventions at a reduced price, and most have special sessions and activities for college students. Internship/career interviews are commonly scheduled during a convention, which allows you to look for a job away from home without having to travel across the country at your own expense.

Conclusion

Plenty of opportunities exist for your career development. The hospitality industry is one of the largest employers in the United States and in many other countries. Skilled and experienced managers are always needed. Many people worked their way up from bellhop or server to become top executives in the industry. Others have taken "a little restaurant" and built it into a franchise empire. Few industry sectors offer the advancement opportunities of hospitality. As long as you are willing to work hard and continue to learn, your future will be bright.

For Further Investigation

The world of hospitality is timeless and contemporary. You will find nearly limitless opportunities if you gain the requisite skills, remain flexible, and are willing to relocate. Fortunately for you, most hospitality businesses have a good online presence (after all, they exist to be found by folks who need shelter, food, and community away from home), so you will be able to find a information without leaving the comfort of your chair. Also, even the smallest communities typically have accommodations, restaurants, and nightspots, so you will be able to expand and apply your new knowledge without leaving the local area.

For More Research

1. Many job search websites are available for hospitality careers. You may explore jobs. By reading job descriptions on these websites, you will gain ideas about work activities and required skills and knowledge. Based on your particular interests—accommodations or food and beverage—select three websites and explore them thoroughly:

- **American Hotel and Lodging Association Career Center:** www.ahla.com
- **Hcareers:** www.hcareers.com
- **Hospitality Link:** www.hospitalitylink.com
- **HospitalityJobsOnline:** www.hospitalityonline.com
- **WorldJobSites:**
  www.worldjobsites.org/jobs/Jobs_by_Profession_and_Industry/Hospitality_Jobs
- **Hospitality Career Network:** www.hospitalitycareersnetwork.com
- **Hotel Job Resource:** www.hoteljobresource.com
- **Hotel Jobs Network:** www.hoteljobsnetwork.com
- **HotelJobs:** www.hoteljobs.com
- **Caterer Global Job:** www.catererglobal.com
- **Foodservice.com:** www.foodservice.com/employment/index.cfm
- **National Restaurant Association Jobs:** www.restaurant.org/Restaurant-Careers/Job-Board/Find-a-Job
- **StarChefs:** www.starchefsjobfinder.com

2. Marriott and Outback Steakhouse are two well-regarded hospitality companies well known for their employee training and development. Visit their websites and investigate the "Career" sections. Identify career opportunities that interest you within these two companies.
Marriott: marriott.com
Outback: www.outback.com

3. What is your favorite fast-food restaurant or hotel? Go to their website and find information about franchise opportunities.

Active Investigation
1. Find people who are working for hotels and/or restaurants. Complete informational interviews by asking them what they like about the job and what the challenges of their work are. See the instructions in Chapter 2 on how to conduct an informational interview.
2. Corporate properties offer mobility and jobs, but many people have pursued their entrepreneurial dreams in the hospitality sector. Ask the local convention and visitors bureau or chamber of commerce for leads to local boutique hotels/bed and breakfast inns or family-owned restaurants. Arrange an informational interview with the owners to see how they established their enterprise.
3. Keep an eye open to see when a new hotel, restaurant, or nightclub opens in your community. If possible, locate the owners and ask to meet them at the establishment. It will be a great opportunity to learn something about how the owner/entrepreneur selected the type of establishment, its location, and the proprietor's motivations in opening the business.
4. Contact the conference hotel whenever you are attending a professional meeting and ask to meet with someone at the property while you are on-site. It is one of the most cost-effective and less stressful ways to prepare for job interviews.
5. Get a part-time job in a hotel or restaurant where you are going to school or find work in a different destination resort each summer.

Recommended Reading
Hailey, A. (2000). *Hotel.* New York, NY: Berkley.
A bestselling novel about the guest and employees of an exclusive hotel.

Hilton, C. N. (1984). *Be my guest.* Upper Saddle River, NJ: Prentice Hall.
The autobiography by the founder of Hilton Hotel Corporation.

Klein, R. A. (2002). *Cruise ship blues.* Gabriola Island, Canada: New Society Publishers.
An exposé on the darker side of the cruise industry.

Kroc, R. (1992). *Grinding it out: The making of McDonald's.* New York, NY: St. Martin's Press.
An autobiography by the founder of McDonald's Corporation.

Marriott, J. W. (1995). *Marriott: The J. Willard Marriott story.* Salt Lake City, UT: Deseret Book Co.
An autobiography by the founder of Marriott Hotels Corporation.

Mitchelli, J. A. (2009). *The new gold standard: Five leadership principles for creating a legendary customer experience courtesy of the Ritz-Carlton Hotel Company.* Columbus, OH: McGraw-Hill.
A glance inside the operations of Ritz-Carlton and why the company has twice won the Malcolm Baldrige National Quality Award.

Plank, G. (2005). *Saving the St. George.* Lansing, MI: American Hotel and Lodging Institute.
A novel on the running of a boutique hotel.

Sharp, I. (2009). *Four Seasons: The story of a business philosophy.* New York, NY: Penguin.
An autobiography by the founder of Four Seasons Hotels.

References

[1]Bureau of Labor Statistics. *2006-07 career guide to industries.* Washington, DC: Author.

[2]U.S. Department of Agriculture. (2013) Food away from home. Retrieved from http://www.ers.usda.gov/topics/food-choices-health/food-consumption-demand/food-away-from-home.aspx#nutrition

[3]American Hotel and Lodging Association. (2012). 2012 lodging industry profile. Retrieved from http://www.ahla.com/content.aspx?id=34706

[4]American Hotel and Lodging Association. (2013). 2013 lodging industry profile. Retrieved from http://www.ahla.com/content.aspx?id=35603

[5]Let their words do the talking. (2007). *Psychology Today.* Retrived from http://www.psychologytoday.com/blog/six-tips-get-higher-tips

[6]Costa Concordia. (2013). *National Geographic.* Retrieved from http://news.nationalgeographic.com/news/2013/costa-concordia-seagrass-italy

[7]U.S. Environmental Protection Agency. (2012). Cruise ship discharges. Retrieved from http://water.epa.gov/polwaste/vwd/cruise_ships_index.cfm

[8]Casino. In *Merriam-Webster's online dictionary.* Retrieved from http://www.merriam-webster.com/dictionary/casino

[9]American Gaming Organization. (2009). *Facts at your fingertips: U.S. commercial casino industry.* Retrieved from http://www.americangaming.org/sites/facts_at_your_fingertipspdf

[10]Ibid.

[11]Bureau of Labor Statistic. (n.d.). Gaming services occupations. Retrieved from http://www.bls.gov/ooh/personal-care-and-service/gaming-services-occupations.htm

[12]American Gaming Organization, 2009.

[13]Virgin Galactic. (2014). Retrieved from http://www.virgingalactic.com

[14]State might put more toward hotels for homeless. (2013). *Boston Herald.* Retrieved from http://bostonherald.com/news_opinion/local_coverage/2013/08/

[15]Oldenburg, R. (1989). *The great good place: Cafes, coffee shops, community centers, beauty parlors, general stores, bars, hangouts, and how they get you through the day.* New York, NY: Paragon House.

[16]ServSafe. (2014). Retrieved from http://servsafe.com

The greatest part about my job is to hear from guests about how we have added value to others' lives. Travel positively affects people personally and socially, and our world benefits economically as well. Meeting people and connecting people from all over the world is pure joy.

—Sandy Dhuyvetter
Founder, Executive Producer, and Host
of TravelTalk MEDIA

12

Travel and Tourism

Vinod Sasidharan
San Diego State University

Greg Shaw
California State University, Sacramento

Focus Questions

When deciding whether to pursue a career in travel and tourism, consider the following questions:

Q: Do I want travel to be a regular part of my job? Am I comfortable being in new places?

A: If you have an urge to see the world and work in different locations, travel and tourism is the career area for you.

Q: Am I interested in and willing to interact regularly with new people with different viewpoints, ideas, varying knowledge levels, and diverse backgrounds?

A: As an ambassador of travel, you will extend your hand in friendship to citizens from around the world, as well as respect the environment, and celebrate the diversity of cultures while on your journeys.

Q: Do I have the passion to adopt my job and its responsibilities as my lifestyle?

A: This profession is about spending your professional time in beautifully remote or crowded rural or urban places and working with interesting colleagues who likely also want to change and better the world. It is not a career or a profession; it is a lifestyle and life.

Q: Do I have the patience to invest my time, energy, and resources in helping others, as a major part of my job, without having complete control over the final outcome of my efforts?

A: You will have to dedicate your life to tourism and guest services, to help people learn through travel and to get to know each other better, foster peace, and discover themselves once again.

Q: Are long-term personal (including social and financial) rewards more important to me than short-term monetary gains?

A: You have to be willing to invest long hours early in your career in this field, but it may not seem like work because you will be doing what you love. You cannot expect to enter this field to become rich or even paid a high salary, even though that may evolve over time.

Key Terms

Triple bottom line (TBL)
Tourism organizations
Cultural tourism
Heritage tourism
Ecotourism
Wine tourism
Tourism industry sectors

Destination management organizations
(DMOs)
Theme and amusement parks
Adventure tourism
Green travel and tourism
Sustainable tourism

Profile 1: Could This Be You?

David Williams is the deputy director for the Utah Office of Tourism (UOT). As the person in charge of market research for the office, David's responsibilities include
- gathering travel and tourism statistics,
- generating travel-related economic forecasts,
- coordinating marketing programs,
- allocating funds for destination marketing, and
- guiding political groups.

Q: What does your work involve?

A: I am in charge of the market research for the office. This includes gathering statistics—visitation at parks, the airport, welcome centers, occupancy statistics, and attractions in Utah. I also purchase visitor profiles including who is coming, demographic and psychographic information, how much people spend, and how they found out about Utah. We have around $2 million to distribute to nonprofit and destination marketing organizations in Utah for promotion.

Q: How do you make a difference through your work?

A: When I was hired, the UOT marketing budget was very small and we weren't able to get our message out to as many people as we would have liked due to lack of funding. I was able to research how other states fund their tourism offices, provided economic impact figures, and was very involved in an effort to convince the legislature to provide more marketing dollars so our office could compete in the marketplace. The legislature increased the UOT budget, so it is 10 times higher than it was previously. Now we are promoting Utah more aggressively than ever before.

Q: If you could give a young professional interested in this career area one piece of advice, what would it be?

A: I enjoy my career because I am passionate about Utah and enjoy marketing. If I didn't love living in Utah, it would be hard to come to work every day to promote it. You'll find your career much more rewarding if you believe in whatever you are doing.

Profile 2: Could This Be You?

Serge Dedina is the executive director of WiLDCOAST, an international organization that uses tourism to protect and preserve coastal ecosystems and wildlife in Latin America and the Californias. As the person who runs WiLDCOAST, Serge has an array of responsibilities, including
- raising funds for ecotourism projects,
- coordinating ecotourism projects,
- building grassroots ecotourism support,
- conducting media campaigns to promote ecotourism projects, and
- carrying out coastal conservation efforts.

Q: What do you do during the week, as part of your work?

A: We spent a week in Laguna San Ignacio, a gray whale sanctuary and UNESCO World Heritage site in Mexico, talking with ecotourism outfitters and filming a documentary with Phillipe Cousteau and Animal Planet on our efforts to protect the lagoon and gray whales and how ecotourism/ whale watching is important for conservation efforts.

Q: Provide an example illustrating how you transformed your organization (or a client) through your services.

A: One of my projects, Laguna San Ignacio Conservation Alliance, resulted in the permanent protection of a UNESCO World Heritage site that has helped build the capacity of local landowners and ecotour operators to manage complex land management projects. We helped develop a local outfitters association, get them a bank account, launched an ecoloan program to buy four-stroke engines and replace polluting two-stroke outboard engines. We worked a deal to carry out conservation easements on the land owned by the ecooutfitters, protecting 140,000 acres.

Q: What challenges you about your job?

A: The challenges include (1) working with fragile coalitions to preserve areas, (2) obtaining funding to do our work, (3) staying focused on strategic goals and not getting sidetracked, (4) focusing on business end of WiLDCOAST instead of just project management, and (5) building new programs and projects and making decisions to discard old projects.

Profile 3: Could This Be You?

Megan Smith is the commissioner of the Vermont Department of Tourism and Marketing. The agency is responsible for bringing travelers to Vermont by promoting heritage tourism, skiing, nature tourism, and other tourism activities and coordinating public–private partnerships that will sustain the authenticity and uniqueness of the Vermont experience. Megan has several responsibilities, including

- marketing partnerships between state agencies and private businesses,
- promoting all areas of Vermont tourism (groups, heritage, agritourism, outdoor recreation, culinary tourism, etc.),
- working with state legislators to pass bills related to tourism, and
- teaching hospitality and event planning courses.

Q: What would you advise a student to take most from their education?

A: Internships and hands-on learning are vital. Get as many experiences as you can in the industry. In Vermont, for example, Killington Ski Resort offers on-site dorms for interns. Their internships provide practical experience so students will learn the behind-the-scenes skills and crisis management and safety that make a resort function.

Q: What are some of the advantages of working in the tourism industry?

A: To get to my current position, I've had a long career in tourism and hospitality. I've worked both in private and public agencies and I will say that job stability is strong in the state government for her employees. All employees receive benefits and this trend is increasing in the private sector as well. Companies realize that in order to compete for the best employees they must offer competitive wages and benefit packages. A great advantage of working in the tourism industry is that there are so many types of jobs that you'll never get bored. If you don't like one aspect, you can find something else to do and still remain in tourism.

Q: What challenges you on your job?

A: I enjoy my job, and the challenges keep me motivated and excited about my work. Some of those include (1) working within the confines of state government, (2) limited budgets that restricts promotion to a drive market, (3) keeping up with new trends in tourist interest, and (4) creating new programs and experiences such as agritourism.

Q: What is a big misconception about the tourism industry?

A: That the jobs don't pay well. An enormous problem with tourism and hospitality is that all of the part-time server jobs are averaged in with salaried positions, which gives a false impression that the wages are below other industries. Server jobs are fine, but they are positions that receive lower wages with the expectation of tips. Students should know that they can make a living in tourism in a management position just as they would in another industry.

Wish You Were Here:
Going Places in Travel and Tourism

Although all tourism jobs focus on creating and providing travel products and experiences, the most unique aspect of tourism is that tourism professionals often work at the crossroads of business, environment, culture, and government. Before we go into depth about potential careers, we will review how tourism became a profession in its own right.

How Did Tourism Become a Profession?

Due to increasing interest and income among people—many U.S. citizens and citizens around the world—to travel both domestically and internationally, destinations with specialized services and products that cater to the experiential needs of the traveler/tourist have emerged and will continue to emerge around the world. In the past, travel and tourism careers were seen as jobs in private-sector hospitality services, including hotels and restaurants. Recent years have seen an upsurge in specialized forms of tourism and unique destinations, creating new tourism organizations and job opportunities across the globe. Some of these newer forms of tourism seek the **triple bottom line** that incorporates many of the so-importants of social and environmental justice described in Chapter 1.

Tourism organizations are responsible for planning and creating travel experiences for tourists. Tourism organizations consist of for-profit and nonprofit enterprises and provide specialized amenities such as recreation resources (e.g., parks and campgrounds, forests, protected areas, ski areas, beaches), sporting venues, theme parks, museums, cultural centers, historic sites, performance centers and theaters, convention centers, galleries and exhibition centers, zoos and aquariums, airlines/airports, agritourism farms, stagecoaches, railways/stations, rental cars, transit systems, cruise ships/terminals, shopping centers, wine trails, tourism information, tour companies, travel agencies, Web-based reservation systems, resorts, golf courses, hotels, and restaurants. Properly developed and delivered, tourism will yield the entire spectrum of benefits. Individuals experience new cultures and learn more about the world. Families and groups grow close and gain new insights into themselves and others. Economic and environmental benefits exist as well, but seldom without thoughtful attention to the concepts of social and environmental justice.

The significant contribution of travel and tourism to economic development, combined with the central focus on tourist satisfaction, has made it its own specialized professional area and study discipline. In addition to travel opportunities and financial rewards that tourism careers offer, professionals in the travel and tourism industry find their jobs to be exciting and fulfilling due to the variety involved in their work.

The TBL

The *triple bottom line* (or TBL) is a phrase recently introduced into business and management lingo. In 1994, a British business man named John Elkington said that all businesses should be concerned with more than financial gain or return on investment. Rather, he thought businesses should also care about impact to people and to the earth, or about social and environmental responsibility, creating the TBL of profit, people, and planet.

Profit, or the "bottom line," is measured on a standard profit and loss statement. The second part, people, means measuring or accounting for how employees and other social groups are impacted by the business, in short, being socially responsible. Finally, the third portion is planet, or being environmentally responsible. A company watching its TBL, then, would be accountable for its financial, social, and environmental behaviors over time.[1]

Travel and Tourism Today

Tourism involves the entire leisure services delivery continuum introduced in Chapter 2—and more. What makes tourism a specialized discipline and professional area is the delivery of products and services geared toward satisfying the unique needs of travelers. Today, travel and tourism consists of providing experiences that are customized based on the specific interests of tourists. For example, **cultural tourism** provides experiences to travelers who are motivated to travel for cultural enrichment purposes; **ecotourism** services provide environmental education opportunities; **agritourism** and **ag-natural** offer experiences from farms, horseback riding, and petting zoos to wine tasting and culinary-themed educational sessions for products such as cheese or olive oil; and business tourism offers products, services, and amenities to people traveling for business-related purposes. As the needs of travelers become more sophisticated, professionals in the industry continue to develop and offer innovative tourism experiences and opportunities.

The main reason the tourism industry is appealing for people with a degree in recreation, parks, and tourism is the opportunity to apply their knowledge and strengths in sectors of the tourism industry that most suit their passions. Tourism provides great careers for people who want to make a positive difference in the lives of others while enjoying the benefits of travel for themselves. **Tourism industry sectors** include hospitality establishments (hotels, restaurants), theme parks, cultural and heritage attractions, environmental attractions, nature parks, zoos/aquariums, destination management organizations, government agencies, sporting venues, specialty tour companies, and travel supply stores (also see Chapters 6, 9, and 11 for more specifics about tourism-related areas).

To be successful in the multidimensional tourism industry, tourism professionals must have an in-depth knowledge of the various components of tourism and be creative while developing new tourism opportunities for travelers. Tourism jobs may also be highly meaningful, mainly when the professional's work involves creating economic, community, and environmental benefits. The next section will help you determine whether travel and tourism should be your career choice and, if so, what options may be meaningful to you.

© Photographerlondon | Dreamstime.com

Trendy Yet Meaningful:
What Are the Career Options in Travel and Tourism?

Most tourism professionals are involved in jobs and projects that combine technological, economic, environmental, and cultural dimensions. Tourism jobs require collaborations with people from sectors such as attractions, hospitality services, transportation, visitor information, tourism marketing, governance, and nongovernmental groups. The tourism industry offers professional opportunities for individuals from almost all academic backgrounds. For example, individuals interested in business-oriented jobs may find management careers in tourism to be the best match, those interested in culture may be suitable for cultural interpretation and exhibition careers with cultural attractions, and those interested in environmental issues may find conservation-related careers with ecologically oriented tourism sectors to be most rewarding.

Creativity may also be key to being successful in the tourism industry, and this includes an ability to see the potential of current trends. The 2006 film *The Da Vinci Code* created enormous tourist interest to visit the locals featured in the film. Tourism professionals that were early to recognize this public interest created tours, trails, local partnerships, websites, and other marketing material that capitalized on the sensation the film created.[2] The economic benefits were seen not only by tourism companies but also by restaurants, hotels, and auxiliary tourist attractions. *The Da Vinci Code* phenomenon led to an unprecedented level of literary and film tourism. The surge did not last forever, and although the sites are still popular destinations, creative tourism professionals continue to examine the market for future opportunities.

Passions

As discussed earlier, travel and tourism professionals have the privilege of working at the crossroads of business, environment, culture, and government. This means that these careers may appeal to those who enjoy gathering information and keeping up current with trends. Different sectors within travel and tourism allow the person to focus more on business skills, cultural knowledge, or environmental conservation.

Before reading further, refer to your top five general preferences worksheet from Chapter 2 and your list of five aspects that matter most. How do these "life lists" align with the requirements of a tourism career? Keep in mind that the opportunity to travel as part of the job is the most significant benefit, especially for those who enjoy visiting places and meeting new people. As you consider this benefit, remember also that you need to be willing to embrace travel as a part of your work as well.

Opportunities to Travel and Work Internationally

I have had the pleasure of working in many cities in both Canada and the U.S. and have traveled extensively throughout a large part of the globe. Most importantly, I have found that the majority of people in tourism are delightful. They are people who have dedicated their lives to helping other people travel safely and enjoyably.

—John Hope-Johnstone, CEO
Corvallis Tourism

Pay and Perks

Wages and salaries for employees in the travel and tourism industry depend on academic qualifications, prior work experience, and professional certifications. Entry-level, full-time employees usually start at around the pay grade for a 4-year college graduate in an entry-level job, and advanced-level staff can earn a good executive salary.

With regard to benefits, travel and tourism professionals in the public sector tend to receive a wide range of health benefits; health coverage and insurance in the private sector tend to vary depending on level of employment and size of the organization. Travel and tourism jobs frequently come with work-related travel allowances and funded opportunities for professional development.

Preparation

Permanent positions in the travel and tourism industry have traditionally been filled by people with degrees from several academic disciplines. With the growing need for employees with specialized tourism knowledge, travel and tourism employers are increasingly seeking and hiring individuals with formal education and training in the tourism discipline.

A bachelor's degree in tourism or hospitality management or a related discipline such as recreation management is essential for acquiring a full-time, entry-level job with any reputable tourism organization. Graduates with this academic qualification, combined with 250 to 500 hours of internship and/or work experience, are seen favorably for filling permanent positions by travel and tourism employers.

Depending on an individual's specific career interests, an academic minor in business management, economics, environmental sciences, or social psychology enhances the likelihood of recruitment into the travel and tourism industry. It is typical for "new" tourism employees, especially those with bachelor's degrees, to start at entry level and then progress on to mid- and advanced-level jobs within any tourism sector. We will discuss specifics about preparation in more detail within the Possibilities section.

Broad Knowledge Yields Success

To be a success in tourism, you must have a working knowledge of its many components and how they interact. You must understand how the various sectors within the tourism industry help to move people from one place to another, not only physically but also emotionally.

TIP: Career Advancement in Travel and Tourism

Although opportunities for career advancement are plentiful within the travel and tourism industry, formal education in the tourism field, coupled with adequate professional experience, is a must for a quick and steady career progression from entry-level to advanced-level jobs.

Possibilities

Tourism is the world's largest industry. In the United States, it is among the top three industries in almost every state, thereby providing job opportunities for individuals from all academic and professional backgrounds and with varying skill levels. With growing investment in tourism development across the globe and proliferation of new, innovative tourism products and services, professional opportunities in the travel and tourism industry will continue to grow.

Organizations involved in providing tourism attractions, products, and services include those within the private sector, public sector, private–public partnerships, and nongovernmental organizations. The three major sectors that provide job opportunities within the travel and tourism industry are

- destination management organizations,
- theme and amusement parks and local attractions, and
- ecotourism and cultural tourism industries.

Tourism sectors may be created to follow the interests of a traveling public. Tourism sectors such as fitness tourism, sport tourism, agritourism, architectural tourism, heritage tourism, culinary tourism, wine tourism, literary tourism, and military tourism are just a few examples. These areas of tourism often overlap with larger tourism categories such as cultural tourism or local attractions, but many tourism promoters use them to highlight special events or sites to visitors, especially if they have regional interest.

The following portion of this chapter is intended to familiarize the reader with the functions of destination management organizations, theme and amusement parks and local attractions, and ecotourism and cultural tourism industries. This chapter will also highlight wine tourism and heritage tourism as growing tourism sectors, along with the passions, pays and perks, preparation, and job possibilities within each. You will find additional information related to travel and tourism careers in Chapters 4, 6, 10, 11, and 13.

Destination management organizations. Destination management organizations, often referred to as DMOs, may fall within the categories of local, regional, or national agencies responsible for coordinating the growth of travel and tourism within their designated areas. Examples of DMOs include national and state tourism offices, convention and visitors bureaus, chambers of commerce, economic development corporations, tourism information bureaus, visitor information offices, and port authorities. Although organizations represent the tourism needs and interests of both public- and private-sector businesses and are membership based, they are usually funded by the government, and individuals working in DMOs are government employees. The functions of DMOs and mission will vary depending on the economic significance of tourism for the area. DMOs are usually involved in marketing the destination to tourists and media campaigns; providing information regarding travel opportunities, tourism attractions, and businesses in the area; coordinating the services of tourism enterprises at the destination; conducting tourism research and compiling travel statistics; providing technical know-how to tourism enterprises; facilitating the creation of new tourism opportunities; assisting in tourism policy making; and creating a general appreciation for tourism.

Passions. Tourism marketing, tourism economics, travel trends analysis, travel research, travel and tourism innovation, coalition-building among diverse groups and partnerships, working with people, and work-related travel.

Pay and perks. Entry-level, full-time employees usually start at around the pay grade for a 4-year college graduate in an entry-level job, and advanced-level staff may earn a good executive salary. Being government employees, DMO staff tend to receive benefits including full medical, dental, vision, and prescription drug coverage, along with a minimum of 2-weeks paid vacation time, life insurance, disability compensation, and 401(k) plans. DMOs also offer professional development opportunities, which may include tuition reimbursement and funding for continuing education and conference attendance.

Preparation. A bachelor's degree in tourism or hospitality management or a closely related discipline such as recreation management, coupled with adequate professional experience, is a must for a quick and steady career progression from entry-level to advanced-level jobs. DMO employers also high favor individuals with a master's degree in tourism, hospitality, or related areas and meeting and convention industry professional certifications.

Possibilities. Examples of job titles for positions with DMOs are director of convention and visitors bureau, convention services manager, sales and services coordinator, sales manager, tourism manager, destination management specialist, and visitor information officer. Refer to the chapters on recreation in nonprofits and community-based recreation for information to complement travel and tourism jobs in these settings.

For example, tourism managers at a county tourism office would be responsible for assembling informative news releases, pamphlets, and brochures; coordinating a multitude of activities at one time; and establishing and maintaining effective working relationships with a tourist development council, county staff, and outside agencies. They need a bachelor's degree in marketing, public relations, journalism, communications, business or public administration, or hospitality management and 5 years of progressively responsible experience in advertising or marketing in a public or quasi-public agency. They also need extensive knowledge of the principles, practices, and procedures of marketing and public relations.

Theme and amusement parks and local attractions. Theme and amusement parks and local attractions vary in scope from being significant at the local, regional, or national level, or even international level. Examples of national attractions include SeaWorld, the Walt Disney Company, Six Flags, and Universal Studios. Attractions of regional/local significance include Lego Land, California; Idlewild, Pennsylvania; Kennywood, Pennsylvania; and Cedar Point, Ohio. Art, science, and natural history museums; performing centers and opera houses; and aquariums, zoos, and zoological gardens are also tourism attractions. Events, festivals, and fairs showcasing arts, film, music and dance, comedy, and technology are increasingly becoming vital attractions drawing large numbers of tourists to destinations. Although theme parks and local attractions differ greatly in their respective functions and operations, the central goal of these tourism enterprises is to create entertaining experiences that have significant potential to attract and host visitors. The success of these enterprises depends on strategic partnerships with other sectors such as transportation, travel agencies, tour operators, DMOs, and hospitality services.

Passions. Working with people, guest services, guest entertainment, service innovation, new technology, partnerships, marketing, and economics are passions specific to this area.

Pay and perks. Although these tourism enterprises rely heavily on part-time or seasonal employees hired at minimum wage and higher, entry-level, full-time employees usually start at around the pay grade for a 4-year college graduate in an entry-level job. Advanced-level staff may earn a good executive salary. Employees may receive a multitude of benefits, including medical, prescription, vision, dental, life and disability insurance, 401(k) and Section 529 plan, performance bonuses, profit sharing, flexible job hours, paid time off/personal/holidays, and opportunities to earn awards.

Preparation. A high school diploma is adequate for most part-time or seasonal jobs in theme parks, attractions, and events. Most full-time jobs require a bachelor's degree in tourism or hospitality management or a related discipline such as recreation management, coupled with adequate professional experience.

Possibilities. Examples of job titles available in theme parks and working with local attractions include event manager, visitor information officer, rides manager, operations manager, media relations manager, project manager, promotions manager, and hospitality manager. Refer to the Chapter 10 for more information about careers in this specific area.

For example, event managers at amusements parks direct the concept, development, and implementation of internal and external events supporting marketing, sales, recruiting, and/or synergy efforts through creativity, communication, collaboration, and commitment; negotiate and manage all logistics associated with outside vendors; interface with all levels of management and business units to ensure project objectives are achieved; manage internal and external creative resources to develop creative content; ensure high quality throughout the preplanning and on-site stages by overseeing (as applicable) accommodations, food and beverage, branding, audiovisual, lighting, entertainment, and staffing; maintain strong working knowledge of event-day logistics and operations to ensure a high level of guest satisfaction; anticipate issues of concern and develop thorough contingency plans; manage event budgets; and manage and prioritize multiple projects. They should have a bachelor's in hospitality, communications, or a related field; 2 to 5 years event and meeting planning; cross-platform knowledge (MAC and PC); ability to travel; ability to communicate effectively and efficiently across all departments/business units; strong relationship-building skills; and proven ability to work in a demanding environment. They must also be self-starters.

Ecotourism and cultural tourism industries. Ecotourism and cultural tourism industries are based on the principle of **sustainable tourism**, whereby the ecological and cultural resources of destinations are conserved, protected, and enhanced; tourism and other business opportunities are created to generate jobs for the local population; and low-impact forms of tourism are adopted. Ecotourism and cultural tourism, together referred to as sustainable tourism, promote experiential education for visitors by integrating and interpreting natural, social, and cultural themes at the destination. The enterprises that offer sustainable tourism products and services promote conservation through socially responsible (corporate social responsibility) and ecologically sound (environmentally friendly) business practices. Although some DMOs and theme parks, attractions, and events may adopt sustainable tourism as their business model, other sectors that offer ecotourism and cultural tourism products and services include tour operations and expeditions, **adventure tourism**, nature parks and centers, cultural/heritage centers and museums, conservation organizations, resorts and hotels, restaurants, and transportation.

Passions. Conservation, environmental ethics, social ethics, cultural diversity, biodiversity, languages, economics, business, fund-raising, technology, innovations, education, training, working with people, regular travel as a major part of work, collaborating with other professionals.

Pay and perks. Salaries will be based on skills and experience, ranging from entry level to full time. Employees usually start at around the pay grade for a 4-year college graduate in an entry-level job, and advanced-level staff may earn a good executive salary. Comprehensive benefits plans are usually provided, including health insurance, tax-deferred retirement plan, vacation leave, and holiday leave. Compensatory time is often awarded for weekend work.

Preparation. Most full-time jobs require a bachelor's degree in natural resources or sustainable tourism management or a related discipline such as outdoor recreation management. A minor in environmental sciences or related disciplines such as geography is highly recommended, along with adequate professional field experience.

Possibilities. Some of the jobs available in the ecotourism and cultural tourism industries are cultural interpretation specialist, environmental interpretation specialist, conservation manager, museums and historical/cultural sites exhibit developer, museum director, tour and tourism director, zoos and aquariums exhibit developer, nature tourism coordinator, and environment and culture program coordinator. Refer to Chapters 6 and 13 for more details on travel and tourism careers that overlap with these areas.

Photo courtesy Paige Viren

For example, a project coordinator for an international environment and culture program will report directly to project managers and be located within the program. The responsibilities may include developing and managing annual budgets and revising budgets quarterly; supporting the development and assembly of project funding proposals; composing and coordinating funder reports; establishing and managing contracts with partner organizations, consultants, and researchers; planning and organizing workshop and conference logistics; updating websites and developing new outreach materials; and supporting staff in annual project planning, meeting institutional deadlines, and completing general administrative tasks. Successful applicants must have a bachelor's degree in a related field (political science, environmental science, international development, etc.) and be passionately committed to issues of environment and development. This position requires a highly motivated individual with exceptional organizational, communication, and interpersonal skills as well as the ability to handle and prioritize competing demands. This position is full time. Knowledge of another language is a plus.

Wine tourism. Wine tourism is a multifaceted industry that involves several activities that occur at wineries and in wine regions. In addition to the most common activities of wine tasting and wine purchasing, people visit wine regions for the scenery, for restaurants, for events at wineries (for wine club members and the general public), for weddings, for educational seminars, and for auxiliary activities such as shopping. Some of the more popular wine regions such as Bordeaux in western France, Tuscany in central Italy, and Napa Valley in central California, attract more than 5 million visitors annually, making wine tourism a significant player in the overall tourism numbers for those countries.

Wine tourism has grown significantly in the last decade in several countries, including the United States, France, Spain, and Argentina. In the United States, as of 2003, all 50 states now have at least one bonded winery and at least one winery open for wine tasting.[3] California contains half of the 7,000 wineries in the United States and produces 90% of U.S. wine.[4] Washington, Oregon, and New York are the next three states in terms of number of wineries and production, and wine tourism has been increasing annually in these locations. France, at the time of publication, is listed as the world's top wine producer (although Italy could retake the title in the near future). The country's most famous region, Bordeaux, began a transformation in 2007 to attract more wine tourists by increasing the number of hotel rooms in the region, by creating a Bordeaux Wine Festival, and most significantly by beginning construction on the Wine and Cultural Center to open in 2014.[5] Spain is also moving aggressively to attract more wine tourists. The country's most important region is Rioja, yet not much literature existed on Rioja as compared to famous wine regions in France, Italy, the United States, and even Germany. In 2012, perhaps the first significant guide/history to Spain's Rioja region was released (*The Wine Region of Rioja* by Ana Fabiano), and since 2005, several new wineries and hotels designed by world-famous "starchitects" such as Frank Gehry, Zaha Hadid, and Santiago Calatrava have been built in Rioja. The starchitecture has purposely expanded the **architectural tourism** "Bilbao Effect" created after the opening of Frank Gehry's Guggenheim Bilbao in 1997 onto the Rioja wine region, which is a close drive from the city of Bilbao for travelers.

Another New World example of an increasing focus on wine tourism is in Argentina. Argentina's Mendoza Valley has become increasingly famous for its malbec wines, and in the last several years, new wineries have been designed to serve as premier showplaces for tourists. Although wine tours are challenging due to the wine region's location near the Andes (and the relatively long distances between wineries as compared to Bordeaux or Napa Valley), Argentina has worked aggressively to design tours to the Uco and Mendoza valleys. Similar developments have been occurring in South Africa, Australia, and Chile.

Wine tourism is not only being promoted by the major wine-producing countries. Mexico's Valle de Guadalupe, Arizona's Verde Valley, Israel's Galil, and Japan's Okushiri Island have recently moved to open new wineries, tasting rooms, wine centers, and supporting infrastructure related to wine tourism.

Why the interest in wine? Wine consumption has increased steadily in the United States for the past three decades, and in 2010, the United States became the world's largest consumer of wine. Although wine consumption has increased in the United States for all age groups and ethnicities, Millennials have been surprisingly assertive in their wine interests, showing a typical knowledge and interest in wine that was, until recently, identified with Americans in their late 40s and early 50s. Millennials are then positioned to be important participants in tourism (both as guests and as winery employees). Finally, wine tourists are also seen as "good tourists" in that they tend to spend more on other aspects of a vacation such as dining, shopping, and hotel rooms. This may make wine tourism appealing for regions that produce wine.

Great Time to Be in Wine

Lodi has a rich history, but it's still a new region in the world scene. Wine regions are still being discovered, and it's a great time for Lodi. All hospitality has its own area of coverage, and the wine industry is thriving. Even in this economy, the industry is still growing. There are always new wine drinkers.

— Jeremy Bowe, Manager
Lodi Wine and Visitor Center

Copyright 2014 Karen Burleson

Passions. Making people happy, creating unity in the workplace, understanding policy, resolving visitor complaints, organization, implementing new technology and social networking, maintaining partnerships, marketing, learning about wine and viticulture, and making wine a part of everyday life for visitors.

Pay and perks. Wine industry jobs often grow out of careers in hospitality. New employees may begin working in tasting rooms, but as with other frontline hospitality jobs, promotions may occur rapidly. Support and benefits vary per location for part-time employees, but most locations offer discounts on wine and opportunities to participate in wine events. Full-time employment offers standard medical benefits, opportunities to travel, and opportunities for continuing education.

Preparation. To serve wine in a winery tasting room, you must be of legal drinking age in your state. However, most states allow those under the age to work in the tasting room performing all duties except serving. Full- and part-time employment require a basic knowledge of wine that may be learned while on the job, although you should prepare by reading a few basic texts on wine before applying (such as Kevin Zraly's *Complete Wine Course* or Karen MacNeil's *The Wine Bible*).

Most full-time jobs at a winery require a bachelor's degree. These jobs often relate to tasting room management, event management, or winery marketing. Depending on a your interest, a bachelor's degree can be supplemented with certifications. For example, if you want to work as a sommelier (an expert at pairing wine with food), you should begin courses toward certification. This process may take several years, although you may be able to be employed as a sommelier (rather than a Master Sommelier) before finishing the certification. Another option is to become a Certified Wine Educator (CWE) through the Society of Wine Educators. If you consider yourself more of a beer connoisseur, you may become a trained cicerone, or beer expert. A private program will train you in storing and serving beer, beer styles, flavoring and tasting, the brewing process, and beer–food pairing. By passing a course or two, you will become either a Certified or Master Cicerone.[6]

Copyright 2014 Karen Burleson

The other area of tourism for which you will need additional education is winemaking. Numerous programs exist in viticulture (the growing of wine grapes) and enology (the science of winemaking) at community colleges, at 4-year universities, and at the graduate level. The most famous programs in the United States are at the University of California, Davis, and California State University, Fresno. A new minor at California Polytechnic State University, San Luis Obispo, called Wine and Viticulture seeks to educate students about winemaking, viticulture, enology, and marketing as related to winemaking.

Possibilities. Jobs related to wine tourism exist at wineries, with destination marketing, and in resorts and restaurants. Some of the jobs are tasting room manager, event coordinator, winery tour leader, wine region tour leader, wine club manager, sommelier (with additional education), winemaker (with additional education), wine region promoter, social marketing specialist, and Certified Wine Educator (with additional education).

Tasting rooms. For students interested in hospitality and tourism, wineries offer many employment options. Most wineries are not connected to large grocery store chains or restaurants to sell their wine. They rely on face-to-face sales in their winery tasting rooms. For this reason, winery tasting rooms are first and foremost hospitality centers. All of the skills students learn in relation to customer service for any hospitality position that involves direct contact with the public will apply at a winery tasting room. In addition, wineries are event centers. The largest profit margin for a winery is the selling of wine club memberships, and one of the perks of being a wine club member is being able to attend regular events at the winery. People who are not club members may also attend events, and wineries often host additional events (e.g., wine and chocolate weekend near Valentine's Day or a crush festival in November) that are open to the public for a charge.

Tours. On-site at wineries, you may also conduct tours of the facility. This follows skills you may learn in recreation and tourism interpretation courses. Vineyards and the winemaking process/ facilities are highly interesting to wine tourists, and although these areas are complex and scientific, the tour director must make them understandable to the average traveler.

Weddings. Many hospitality, tourism, and event planning students are also interested in wedding planning. Wine regions have varying rules on hosting weddings at wineries, but in the regions that allow them, they are a thriving business. Vineyards make an excellent romantic backdrop for wedding ceremonies and receptions, and the winery will also benefit by providing the alcohol consumed during the event.

Social networking. Students in the related fields of tourism, hospitality, and event planning may also find job/internship opportunities at wineries related to social networking. Twitter, Facebook, and blogging sites are now being used extensively by wineries, and they are looking for Generation Y to help them move more aggressively into this type of marketing.

Region tours. Wine region tours are popular, and you may find employment organizing and conducting tours either directly as a tour leader or as a manager of a tour company. One such company, Sacramento Day Trippers, conducts wine tours throughout California that incorporate wine, food, and music. The Napa Valley Wine Train is a unique touring option that gives guests access to wineries, food, and pristine views of Napa Valley vineyards.

Restaurants. Students looking to work in any location that has a restaurant will appreciate a knowledge of wine, wine lists, and wine pairing. The title of sommelier is used to describe someone at a restaurant who is in charge of wine and food pairings. The sommelier is responsible for preparing the wine list to complement the chef's entrées, properly storing and cataloging the wine, and assisting guests with making wine choices.

Manager and wine club director. The manager and wine club director at a wine region visitor center must have the ability to direct tourist traffic to the wine center and the wine region. In this position, you are the go-between between wineries and visitors. You will be responsible for arranging wine education and wine pairing education, understanding the guests and selecting wineries for them to visit, creating and organizing wine region events, creating marketing concepts for the wine region, offsetting negative guest experiences, understanding nonprofit management and legal status, hiring, promoting and disciplining employees, maintaining contacts with winery owners in the region, and creating sales through the wine club. The wine club may be the primary source of income for a facility, and this requires attracting new members, maintaining existing members, creating special events for wine club members, coordinating shipping and payments, planning wine club shipments, and communicating with other wineries. This position requires a bachelor's degree in hospitality, communications, or related field; 5 years experience in hospitality or event management with strong emphasis on organization, communication skills, customer service, and social networking; strong skills in creativity, self-starting, and desire for continued industry-related education; financial skills related to wine club management and profitability; regional knowledge related to industry; and ability to create and maintain business partnerships and relationships.

Heritage tourism. *Heritage tourism* is a broad umbrella term for an expanding area of tourism that may encompass aspects of DMOs, theme parks, local attractions, sustainable and cultural tourism, and other areas. In the United States, for example, heritage tourism ranges from the 600-mile long California Mission Trail to the nearly 450-year-old Saint Augustine, Florida. Heritage tourism includes Civil War reenactments on national park lands to jazz festivals in city parks. But it may be more complex than simply looking at history. Karen Peterson's 1994 article on heritage tourism indicated that many tourists will consider visiting Epcot Center with its cultural pavilions, an example of heritage tourism.[5] The range of attractions and experiences may make defining heritage tourism difficult from marketing occupational perspectives. A good working definition, however, puts heritage tourism at the crossroads of cultural tourism and historic tourism, allowing heritage tourism to bring living culture to the historic past.

Tourists invariably want to learn their own heritage or the heritage of others. Students interested in heritage tourism will discover that not only is the public interested, but also many governments (at local, state, and federal levels) are apt to provide funding incentives to preserve historic attractions and tourism related to heritage visitation. Other agencies also provide support for preserving and promoting heritage tourism. In the United States, for example, the National Trust for Historic Preservation provides a Heritage Tourism Toolkit that can be followed and adapted to any location.

In the United States, tourism directors will find several online resources related to promoting heritage tourism in their region. Students interested in heritage tourism should review the online Cultural Heritage Toolkit created by the Vermont Arts Council. Vermont has been successful in their efforts to "keep Vermont, Vermont." For example, it was learned that one of the favorite activities of tourists was driving Vermont's two-lane highways. The Department of Tourism and Marketing worked with state legislators to ban billboards and flashing signs in the state. This has helped preserve the pleasing rural and natural aspects of Vermont that attract heritage tourists.

Passions. Historic preservation, traveling with work, research, hosting/event planning, history, culture, educating, training, working with the public, presenting, fund-raising, working with professionals from various disciplines and fields, relationship building.

Pay and perks. Management-level jobs in heritage tourism offer competitive rates for college graduates, although students typically begin working at a lower supervisory level. Benefits vary depending on how the tourism agency is funded. If it is part of a state agency, employees receive the standard health, retirement, and financial planning benefits that all state employees receive. Some heritage tourism agencies operate outside of the government as nonprofits or for-profits. In these cases, benefits will vary depending on employee rank and the agency's own benefits package.

Preparation. Most full-time jobs require a bachelor's degree, and because of the multidisciplinary nature of heritage tourism, a degree in recreation, tourism, or hospitality management should be accompanied by a minor in public history or historic preservation. (This can work in reverse as well, with public history or historic preservation majors also obtaining a minor in tourism or hospitality.) Students more interested in the cultural aspects of heritage tourism should focus on a minor in cultural anthropology. Minors in architectural history, cultural geography, governments, or other fields related to aspects of heritage may also be helpful to students. However, a keen interest in heritage tourism is essential, and enthusiastic job applicants may be as competitive without supporting minor degrees.

Passion for Innovations

I love my work since the travel and tourism industry is nearly always on the cutting edge. Today, you'll find hotels offering cutting-edge business tools, plus your favorite selection of tunes to be downloaded to your iPod. You'll sleep on the latest memory foam mattresses from a hotel that will even sell you the product. Your aircraft is a miracle of modern technology, more glue than rivets and the miracle of the modern Global Distribution System (GDS) allows you to make the airline and all other reservations easily and safely. The cruise ships of today offer amenities never dreamt of ten years ago, and all of these things are brought together by a network of amazing technologies.

—John Hope-Johnstone, CEO,
Corvallis Tourism

Master's degrees may be extremely helpful in this area with a focus on a particular aspect of heritage interpretation, the history/culture of a particular region or time period, combined with advanced studies in marketing, fund-raising, and preservation.

Possibilities. In heritage tourism, jobs range from tour guide and docent work, to event planning and management, to director positions with state governments. Opportunities for students may happen at a heritage tourism site or within the government structure. Recreation students should pay attention to their coursework in management that covers government agencies.

For example, the commissioner of a department of tourism is responsible for budgeting, fund-raising, creating long-range goals and strategic plans, marketing partnerships, concept development, managing media coverage, lobbying, working with legislators, managing a diverse set of employees, promoting many tourism types, working with tourism directors in other states, traveling to other states/countries, maintaining the authentic tourism experience, creating tourism policy, multitasking, managing events, managing sales, creating relationships within the local tourism and hospitality agencies, social networking, and working with travel partners. This position requires a bachelor's degree in recreation or hospitality; several years experience in event management, budgeting, marketing personnel management, presenting/communication; and a strong background in government proceedings and government funding. This person must have strong people skills, have the ability to be firm but supportive, and be able to be a creative thinker in terms of developing concepts and finding public–private partnerships.

Future Opportunities, Issues, and Challenges

Considering the growing global economic significance of tourism and the widespread prevalence of tourism resources, several new employment opportunities have become available as a result of technological innovations, integrated travel infrastructure, new tourism products and services, and increasing traveler interest in the travel and tourism industry. With these new technologies and resources, contemporary tourism professionals are able to effectively align their efforts and strategies to address ecological (environmental) concerns in response to changing/evolving societal priorities and awareness. Social concern for responsible practices has resulted in a plethora of **green travel and tourism** products, industry alliances, and organizations, which attempt to make a difference in the industry by encouraging positive environmental changes in the business landscape.

Summary of Hospitality Career Possibilities

Career	Passions	Pay and perks	Preparations	Opportunities
Destination management organizations	Marketing, tourism, economics, travel trends analysis	Entry-level salaries will be those of a typical 4-year college grad up to executive levels	Bachelor's degree in tourism or hospitality management	Director, manager, coordinator, officer, seasonal jobs
Theme and amusement parks and local attractions	Service, guest entertainment, service innovation, new technology partnerships, marketing, economics	Entry-level salaries will be those of a typical 4-year college grad up to executive levels	High school diploma to 4-year college degree	Director, manager, officer, seasonal jobs
Ecotourism and cultural tourism industries	Conservation, environmental ethics, cultural diversity, biodiversity	Entry-level salaries will be those of a typical 4-year college grad up to executive levels	Bachelor's degree in natural resources or sustainable tourism management, minor in environmental sciences	Interpretation specialist, conservation exhibit developer, director, coordinator, seasonal jobs

Tourism is a business and a community development tool with significant economic, environmental, sociocultural, and political ramifications. Tourism businesses face the growing challenge of balancing profitability with quality of life in host communities. Issues at the intersection of the tourism industry and communities include transportation, migration, communication, unemployment, education, natural resources, and economic development. In this wider sense, sustainable tourism management is a comprehensive and inclusive approach and an ongoing process. Sustainable tourism management underlines the interdependence of the environment with economy and society—the triple bottom line. The triple bottom line framework encompasses a broad spectrum of issues including natural, economic, social, and cultural diversity; equity and human rights; corporate and individual responsibility and citizenship; globalization; and localization issues in travel and tourism.

Resources and Getting Involved

The information presented in the following sections is intended to provide you with a starting point to get acquainted with various key for-profit and nonprofit organizations in the travel and tourism industry, including their respective functions. Additionally, the main professional certifications and licenses recommended for those pursuing entry-level and advanced careers in the travel and tourism field have been listed for your perusal.

Professional Organizations
Association of Destination Management Executives (ADME): www.adme.org
ADME is a global nonprofit association dedicated to increasing the professionalism and effectiveness of destination management through education, promotion of ethical practices, and

availability of information to the meetings, convention, and incentive travel industries, as well as the general public.

Cultural Heritage Tourism: www.culturalheritagetourism.org
This electronic clearinghouse includes information provided by many members of Partners in Tourism, a coalition of the national organizations and agencies with an interest in cultural heritage tourism. This site is a resource for organizations and individuals who are developing, marketing, or managing cultural heritage tourism attractions or programs. For those just getting started, the website has guiding principles and how-to steps for launching a new effort. The website features success stories and the resources section includes key contacts in virtually every state as well as national resources for funding, technical assistance, and other programs.

Destination Marketing Association International (DMAI): www.iacvb.org
As the world's largest and most reliable resource for official destination marketing organizations, DMAI is dedicated to improving the effectiveness of over 1,300 professionals from 600-plus destination marketing organizations in more than 25 countries. DMAI provides members—professionals, industry partners, students, and educators—the most cutting-edge educational resources, networking opportunities, and marketing benefits available worldwide.

Ecotourism at Conservation International (ECOTOUR at CI): www.conservation.org/learn/culture/ecotourism/pages/ecotourism.aspx
CI is a United States–based international nonprofit organization that applies innovations in science, economics, policy, and community participation to protect the Earth's richest regions of plant and animal diversity in biodiversity hot spots, high-biodiversity wilderness areas, and important marine regions around the globe. CI has supported the development of exemplary ecotourism products by providing technical assistance, capacity building, and funding to communities, entrepreneurs, and partners by developing viable ecotourism products and services; improving business management skills; designing marketing strategies and creating market links; and developing associations, networks, and clusters that strengthen destinations.

International Association of Amusement Parks and Attractions (IAAPA): www.iaapa.org
IAAPA is a nonprofit association that works behind the scenes to help attraction owners run their business smoothly and profitably. From increasing earnings and discovering new sources of revenue to improving operations and employee performance, IAAPA resources and programs are designed to ensure that attractions succeed.

National Trust for Historic Preservation: www.preservationnation.org/information-center/economics-of-revitalization/heritage-tourism/
The National Trust for Historic Preservation was officially established by President Truman in 1949. The National Trust supports and funds grassroots preservation efforts around the United States. This preservation involves a range of projects from protecting small businesses and local main streets, to setting architectural standards for preserving and renovating historic plantations, to providing staff to support local heritage tourism.

Pacific Asia Travel Association (PATA): www.pata.org
PATA's advantage is that it continues to influence the direction the industry takes through its unique membership structure of public-sector tourism organizations; air, land, and sea carriers; and organizations engaged in the production, distribution, financing, consulting, educating, and other technical aspects of the travel industry.

The International Ecotourism Society (TIES): www.ecotourism.org
TIES promotes responsible travel to natural areas that conserves the environment and improves the well-being of local people by creating an international network of individuals, institutions, and the tourism industry; educating tourists and tourism professionals; and influencing the tourism industry, public institutions, and donors to integrate the principles of ecotourism into their operations and policies.

World Tourism Organization (UNWTO): www.unwto.org
The UNWTO, a specialized agency of the United Nations, is the leading international organization in the field of tourism. It serves as a global forum for tourism policy issues and practical source of tourism know-how. The UNWTO plays a central role in promoting the development of responsible, sustainable, and universally accessible tourism, with the aim of contributing to economic development, international understanding, peace, prosperity, and universal respect for human rights and fundamental freedoms. In pursuing this aim, the UNWTO pays particular attention to the tourism interests of developing countries.

United States Tour Operators Association (USTOA): www.ustoa.com
USTOA is a professional association representing the tour operator industry. The organization comprises companies whose tours and packages span the globe and who conduct business in the United States. The association has established some of the highest standards in the industry, including the principle of ethical conduct as determined by a set of professional standards. Additionally, members must represent all facts, conditions, and requirements relating to tours and vacation packages truthfully and accurately.

World Association of Zoos and Aquariums (WAZA): www.waza.org
WAZA's mission is to guide, encourage, and support the zoos, aquariums, and like-minded organizations of the world in animal care and welfare, environmental education, and global conservation. WAZA is the umbrella organization for the world zoo and aquarium community. Its members include leading zoos and aquariums and regional and national associations of zoos and aquariums, as well as affiliate organizations, such as zoo veterinarians and zoo educators.

Wine Institute: www.discovercaliforniawines.com
The Wine Institute is an association of 1,000 California wineries and related wine businesses. The organization's goals include marketing California wine, advocating for public policy that supports responsible wine production and consumption, and creating an environmentally friendly and sustainable wine industry. The organization is involved in wine tourism to the state and provides extensive visitor information on California wineries, wine regions, wine events, and restaurants.

World Travel and Tourism Council (WTTC): www.wttc.org
Raising awareness of the importance of travel and tourism, promoting synergies between the public and private sector, generating profit, and protecting natural, social, and cultural environment are the fundamental components of WTTC's mission. The WTTC is the forum for business leaders in the travel and tourism industry. With chief executives of some 100 of the world's leading travel and tourism companies as its members, WTTC has a unique mandate and overview on all matters related to travel and tourism.

Certifications/Licenses

Professional certification/licenses are increasingly popular among working professionals interested in fast-tracking their career progression.

Destination Management and Marketing Industry Certification
Professional in Destination Management: www.destinationmarketing.org
Certified Destination Management Executive: www.destinationmarketing.org
Destination Management Certified Professional: www.adme.org

Ecotourism and Sustainable Tourism Certification
University Consortium Field Certificate (UCFC) in Sustainable Tourism:
www.ecotourism.org

Tour Operators and Wholesalers Certification
Travel Trade Supplier Certification: www.traveltradesmart.com

Cruise Industry Certification
Cruise Lines International Association: www.cruising.org
Cruise line industry certification comes in many types including Accredited Cruise Counsellor, Master or Elite Cruise Counsellor, Counsellor Scholar, or Luxury Cruise Specialist.

Cultural and Environmental Attractions Certification
National Association for Interpretation: www.interpnet.com
Cultural and environmental attractions industry certification for many specialties such as Interpretive Manager, Interpretive Planning, Heritage Interpreter, and interpretive trainer, guide, or host.

Wine Education Certification
Certified Wine Educator: www.societyofwineeducators.org/education-certification/cwe

Where to Gain Experience

Travel and tourism organizations are increasingly seeking and hiring individuals with formal education and training in the tourism discipline. For acquiring an entry-level, full-time job with any reputable tourism organization, it is essential to have between 250 to 500 hours of volunteering, internship, and/or work experience, in addition to a formal degree in tourism or hospitality management, or a related discipline such a recreation management. While in college, students may find internship and volunteer opportunities at local convention and visitor bureaus, theme parks, cultural and environmental attractions, tour companies, and so forth. Some ecotourism and cultural tourism work opportunities may even be available through intramural programs at local colleges and universities.

For More Information

Jobs in food, hospitality, and travel: www.quintcareers.com/hospitality_jobs.ht
Hospitality, recreation, and tourism career guide: www.khake.com/page61.html
Ecotourism Job Center: www.ecoclub.com/jobs/
Tourism jobs: www.smarthunt.com/Smart-jobs.cfm?CatID=28

Travel and Tourism Professionals

The travel and tourism industry is dynamic and trend-oriented. The industry is unique in that it offers careers for those with all skill levels and academic backgrounds. The travel and tourism professional has

- varying knowledge levels and passion to adopt the job (and its responsibilities) as a lifestyle;
- patience to invest time, energy, and resources in helping others, as a major part of the job, without having complete control over the final outcome of efforts (if you want to work in this profession, you need to be able to prioritize long-term personal, including social and financial, over short-term gains); and
- commitment to broaden his or her knowledge every day regarding how other sectors within the tourism industry function and operate.

If these factors are compatible with your job expectations, a career in the travel and tourism industry is likely to be highly satisfying and personally meaningful.

Conclusion

If you aspire for entry-, mid-, and advanced-level careers within the travel and tourism industry, to be successful in this field, you will need to incorporate travel as a routine part of the job and regularly interact with new people with different viewpoints/ideas.

For Further Investigation

For More Research

1. **Career Exploration:** Visit the websites of any five professional organizations from the previous section. From each website, identify a job/career that suits your professional goals and aspirations in travel and tourism.
2. **Occupational Certification:** From the list of professional certifications/licenses, identify two certifications/licenses that would help you move toward an advanced-level career in travel and tourism. Create an action plan with a timeline for the steps you could take to earn these certificates.

Active Investigation

1. **Informational Interviews:** Contact a travel and tourism professional and set up an interview. During the interview, ask questions regarding qualifications, competencies, and experiences required to be a successful leader in the field. Review the informational interview instructions in Chapter 2 as you are planning your interview.
2. **Field Observations:** Take a break and be a tourist for a week in your hometown. What are your needs? Which of your needs were fulfilled? Which were not? Why? How can your hometown make changes to satisfy the tourist?
3. **Journal Logs:** Maintain a journal for a month. In the journal, record what the media has to say about tourism, locally, nationally, and internationally. In your entries, examine whether any of the international tourism trends are likely to change the way in which travel and tourism is being managed at local and national levels.

4. **Local Action:** Write a letter or publication piece to your local newspaper, radio station, or website about the positives and negatives of tourism in your area. What can be done to improve visitor knowledge about your area? How will your ideas help the area economically, environmentally, and socially?

Recommended Reading

Biederman, P. S. (2008). *Travel and tourism: An industry primer.* Upper Saddle River, NJ: Prentice Hall. Written by a former chief economist at Trans World Airlines, this book explores travel and tourism comprehensively, including travel sectors, promotional strategies, economic influences, and business principles that govern the industry.

Boniface, B., & Cooper, C. (2009). *Worldwide destinations: The geography of travel and tourism* (5th ed.). Oxford, United Kingdom: Butterworth-Heinemann.
This unique text provides an up-to-date global perspective that explores the demand, supply, organizational aspects and resources of every tourism destination in the world. Current issues such as climate change, economic capacity, "grey" tourism, and social impacts are discussed.

Cook, R. A., Yale, L. J., & Marqua, J. J. (2010). *Tourism: The business of travel* (4th ed.). Upper Saddle River, NJ: Prentice Hall.
This text presents an integrated model of tourism and addresses consumer behavior, service quality, and personal selling. The authors cover the industry from a business perspective, including management, marketing, and finance.

Eberts, M., Brothers, L., & Gisler, A. (2006). *Careers in travel, tourism, and hospitality* (2nd ed.). New York, NY: McGraw-Hill.
If you think a career in travel and tourism is your thing, read this book, and the authors will help you hone in on the specialty area most suited to your passions, interests, and abilities.

Goeldner, C. R., & Ritchie, J. R. (2009). *Tourism: Principles, practices, philosophies.* Hoboken, NJ: John Wiley and Sons.
This book, written by well-known consultants in the travel industry, provides useful information and guidance for tourism promotion and development organizations, chambers of commerce, and other organizations involved in the travel and tourism business.

References

[1]Triple bottom line: It consists of three Ps—Profit, people and planet. (2009, November 17). *The Economist.* Retrieved from http://www.economist.com/node/14301663

[2]Leeman, S. (2006, May 23). Da Vinci Code tourists flock to Scottish chapel. Retrieved from NBC News website: http://www.nbcnews.com/id/12940481/

[3]Shriver, J. (2003, September 22). A very good year for vintners. *USA Today.* Retrieved from http://usatoday30.usatoday.com/travel/vacations/destinations/ 2002/2002-06-28-wine-main.htm

[4]Wine Institute. (2013, February 19). US/California wine production. Retrieved from http://www.wineinstitute.org/resources/statistics/article83

[5]Voss, R. (2010, December 15). Innovator of the year: Alain Juppé. *Wine Enthusiast, 23*(13), 60.

[6]Cicerone Certification Program. (n.d.). About. Retrieved from http://cicerone.org/content/about

“ *There are two major reasons I love doing what I do: First, there is the satifaction of seeing our guests have a really great time and feeling the enrichment they are receiving from the experience. The second is being a part of helping our community economically, socially, and environmentally by bringing in visitors who are eco-sensitive, and sharing the beauty and wonder of this wilderness area with them. We do all this while creating jobs and tourist revenue that supports the community.*

—Matt Polstein
New England Outdoor Center ”

13

Commercial Recreation and Leisure Businesses

Paige P. Viren
East Carolina University

Jim Greiner
*Wildwater Ltd. Rafting and
Starfish Exuma Adventures in the Bahamas*

Focus Questions

Q: As many jobs in commercial recreation are seasonal in nature, are salaries also seasonal? How can I compensate for off-season unemployment?

A: Many jobs in this field are seasonal in nature, so it is important that you develop skills that will make you indispensable in the off-season. For instance, the kayak instructor who develops skills in repairing kayaks and kayaking gear may stay employed for most of the off-season getting gear ready for next season. Another example is the ski instructor who leads hiking trips during the summer or takes employment with a rafting outfitter. Also, almost all commercial recreation businesses have a core of one or more key people who work for all or most of the year. Your goal should be to grow yourself into becoming that indispensable person.

Q: After I graduate, I want to take some personal time to enjoy traveling and experiencing different cultures before I settle down. Is this possible?

A: Those who live frugally may enjoy an outdoor adventure life where each year brings new experiences and different challenges and may enjoy traveling and new experiences until they decide to settle down. Opportunities for seasonal jobs abound in the leisure industry. Use this time to build your résumé and experiences by taking jobs that will prepare you for the future.

Q: What qualities do I need to possess to operate my own business successfully?

A: A great starting place includes good people skills, an entrepreneurial spirit, a good work ethic, and adequate working capital.

Q: How can I get the working knowledge necessary to operate a successful recreation business?

A. The best way to learn a business is to be involved with an existing successful business. Find a part-time or summer job with a reputable company while you are in school. Do this at several companies over the 4 to 5 years you are in college, and you will learn how to make your business a success.

Q: What academic courses would help me succeed in a private recreation business?

A: Courses such as economics, accounting, business, marketing, finance, group dynamics, computer skills, and public speaking are important subjects to supplement your recreation career courses.

Key Terms

Leisure entrepreneur	Expenses
Enterprises	Profit
Income	Commercial recreation and leisure business

Profile 1: Could This Be You?

Jack Wise is the CEO of Wildwater Rafting, an outdoor adventure firm located in the southeastern United States. He has been with the company for more than 30 years, starting as a river guide, then becoming a river manager, and finally serving as the chief executive officer of the $5 million company that takes over 80,000 people down white-water rivers and through the trees on Canopy Tours annually. During his tenure, the company has grown to five times its initial size. Since he arrived, the company has operated a sailing and kayaking operation in the Bahamas and has added five Canopy Tours, lodging, food service, and ropes courses. Jack is the perfect example of a person who started at an entry-level position and worked his way up to the company's most important position through hard work and experience. He built his skill set along the way. His responsibilities include

- supervising the operation of five activity centers;
- overseeing the hiring and training of more than 350 employees annually;
- managing budgets and spending as well as keeping accurate records;
- coordinating logistics, staffing, and equipment use between locations;
- overseeing relationships with government agencies that administer business permits; and
- managing the business office and trip reservations.

In an interview with Jack, we asked him about his career in the private sector of the recreation industry.

Q: What are the most rewarding aspects of your job?

A: There are a lot of exciting things, but I would have to say that the most rewarding is providing people with the opportunity to try new and exciting experiences in a special environment. It's also a bonus to be involved in all these fun experiences myself.

Q: There must be some parts of your job that are difficult or frustrating. What are some of those areas?

A: In a phrase: human resources. My main challenge is finding highly motivated employees and then training and keeping them. Since we are a seasonal business, we can rely somewhat on students and teachers to do the face-to-face leadership of operating trips, and separating those who see it as a working vacation from those who are looking for a career opportunity is often difficult.

Q: What personal characteristics do you look for when you are hiring new employees in the adventure business?

A: Key qualities I look for are integrity, an interest in quality standards, good communication skills, a positive first impression, a willingness to learn, and reliability. The willingness to go the extra mile when needed is a critical asset. When hiring, it is important to realize that as an organization we are an integrated team, so you need to make sure you hire quality people.

Q: What advice would you give someone who wants to pursue a career in an outdoor adventure business?

A: A college education is important to give you the basis from which to operate, plus personal experience and the willingness to attempt anything and everything. In short, an entrepreneurial profile. Since a career-oriented person will necessarily need to have business skills to advance to a management position, I would recommend a minor in business, marketing, or economics. Strong computer skills are also very helpful. If you can't get the minor, at least take some courses to learn how to operate a successful business.

Q: What misconceptions do you find new employees have about the adventure business?

A: Some people come into this business thinking it's all fun with no work or responsibility. They have unrealistic expectations. Most entry-level positions are seasonal, and the more skills you bring or develop, the faster you will get a year-round position.

Profile 2: Could This Be You?

Garrett Graham, manager of Camp Ton-A-Wandah, is a young man on a mission. He is the director of one of the most prestigious and successful girl's camps in the Great Smoky Mountain area of North Carolina. The camp started in 1933 and accommodates three sessions each summer of over 200 campers. This area has over 60 other summer camps competing against one another for the camping dollar. Each summer, campers flock to Ton-A-Wandah (Cherokee for "Where the Waters Fall,"), and Garrett's job is to operate the program and please the campers and their parents. It is also his job to recruit campers to choose Ton-A-Wandah over other camps.

In his eighth year as director, Garrett oversees maintenance, recruits staff, and operates three sessions of more than 200 campers each during the summer. To generate additional revenues, the camp also rents its facilities to church groups, family reunions, and weddings during the off-season. He supervises a full-time staff of seven. In a conversation with Garrett, we probed his mind about this job.

Q: What are the most rewarding aspects of your job?

A: Relationships with staff, families, and clients. We build relationships with families based on trust, and we are, in fact, the parents of each camper during the three weeks they are at camp. Every day is different. The job requires a great deal of flexibility, so I need to be good at a number of things. Other pluses are I don't have to wear a tie and I'm being paid for something I love to do.

Q: Some parts of your job must be difficult or frustrating. What are some of those areas?

A: When things don't go as planned, like dealing with the H1N1 virus. We have to have almost instant alternatives for each problem as it occurs. Also, I am on the road a lot and away from my family. Each winter, I spend many days on the road recruiting campers and interviewing potential staff members. It can get old very quickly.

Q: What personal characteristics do you look for when hiring new employees in the adventure business?

A: I hire staff that are willing to work in a group, self-starters, people that take personal pride in their job, and people who value personal integrity.

Q: What advice would you give to someone who wants to pursue a career in the private camp business?

A: Be flexible, be willing to work hard without complaining, and hone personal relationship skills. Get a job in summer working at a camp, and then work for another camp. Get involved in as many different perspectives as possible. Join the American Camp Association and the Association of Experiential Education. (See professional organizations at the end of this chapter.)

Q: What misconceptions do you find new employees have about the summer camp business?

A: They don't understand how long the day can be, they think it is all fun and excitement, and they forget that you don't go home at the end of the day. This is a 24-hour-a-day commitment, with only 24 hours off every three weeks.

Q: What should a new staff member expect in the way of salary and benefits?

A: The salary for a summer camp counselor is only $200–$300 per week plus room and board. Year-round program staff and management make a salary equivalent to teachers and other entry-level social workers. The salary range for camp directors varies, but it's closer to what a school administrator makes.

Q: In retrospect, what are some of the things you wish you had known but didn't when you first joined Camp Ton-A-Wandah?

A: I wish I had experienced more of budgeting, selling, and record keeping. But mostly, I wish I had known how much fun and rewarding this work could be earlier in my career. I would have saved myself a lot of time and trouble searching for the perfect job.

What You Should Know About Commercial Recreation as a Profession

Traditionally, people tend to think of recreation, parks, and leisure services as a public service. If you ask the general public to describe the profession, they normally speak of national parks, Little League baseball, local tennis courts, neighborhood parks and open space, or morning fitness classes. As highlighted in the leisure service delivery system in Chapter 2, commercial enterprises are at the opposite end of the public nonprofit sector. However, the blurred boundary between public and private sectors is evident as commercial leisure and recreation activities may occur in public settings. For instance, a commercial hiking or rafting trip may occur in a national park. This example emphasizes the blending of sectors and underlines the necessity for partnerships and collaboration.

> A career in recreation and leisure may be viewed as a 'lifestyle' business in which owners typically prioritize their passion for recreation and exploration over maximizing revenues in business.

But if people voted with their pocketbooks, an entirely different picture would emerge because the public's actual consumption of leisure services tends to validate private for-profit recreation activities as the leader of the pack. Expenditures for professional athletics, movies, concerts, entertainment, amusement parks, outdoor and adventure recreation and travel, and hundreds of hobbies, crafts, and cultural pursuits easily outspend the public sector. Although other chapters in this book cover many of these for-profit recreation pursuits, this chapter will concentrate on opportunities for leisure entrepreneurs, particularly in the outdoor adventure and retail recreation areas. The **leisure entrepreneur** is willing to take the chance that he or she can generate enough revenue from the leisure activity to sustain financial existence and support the quality of life or lifestyle he or she desires.

Background of Leisure Entrepreneurship in the United States

In a country whose national philosophy is based upon a market economy and free enterprise as well as individual initiative, it is no surprise that recreational enterprises have flourished here. **Enterprises** can be described as businesses that generate income from their clients that is adequate to pay for all expenses and still produce a profit. **Income** is the total dollar amount the business generates, **expenses** are the total dollar amount of all payments made to support the business, and **profit** is the amount by which income generated exceeds all expenses of the business.

Early in U.S. history, much leisure enterprise was fostered by the extravagant pastimes of the ultra wealthy, such as hunting clubs, country clubs, horseback stables, and the "life." But as the middle class expanded, they too wanted outlets for their leisure, so activity and interest-based clubs began to flourish. Theodore Roosevelt opened the door to recreation for the general population by championing national parks and monuments and by encouraging the general population to visit them and participate in outdoor activities. Guides and outdoorsmen (and later women) provided much of the expertise and equipment for the general public to enjoy these pursuits. Of course, guides charged for their services, and the private sector of recreation services was born.

Even today, the lodges, restaurants, and activities at national parks are still typically provided by the private sector (see Chapter 6 for more information). In the meantime, the United States has embraced the private provision of recreation services to supplement what the public sector provides.

Ups and Downs of Commercial Recreation Businesses

Although the for-profit segment of the leisure profession is arguably one of the fastest growing categories in the field, it may also be one of the most transient and unstable. New business starts in the recreation and leisure area fail more than 60% of the time for several reasons. First, specific activities may peak and slump quickly. Some leisure activities fall in the category of fads and may produce a great short-term gain, but fade quickly as time goes on. For example, slot car racing, indoor tennis centers, and drive-in movies are mostly activities of the past. A major ski area has not been built in the United States for more than 20 years. Tennis peaked in the 1980s, as did tent camping. Do not confine your recreation enterprise to a single activity area that may be only a fad and fade away as quickly as it appeared.

Another reason many recreation businesses may fail is because those who choose this type of business do so because they have a personal interest for a particular activity or pastime, but they often lack the knowledge and requisite dedication, skills, or experience necessary to turn it into a desirable, sustainable business. A big difference exists between loving to hunt and fish and supporting yourself (and maybe your family) as a professional hunting or fishing guide.

On the other hand, a career in recreation and leisure may be viewed as a "lifestyle" business in which owners typically prioritize their passion for recreation and exploration over maximizing revenues in business. Individuals usually start up an activity-based business with minimum capital, and the seasonality of many leisure businesses allows entrepreneurs to work another job either part time or seasonally to support the recreation business until it grows enough to support them full time. In the past, lifestyle business owners were viewed as less significant or serious than companies whose primary goal was to increase shareholder value and generate ever-increasing profits, the general aim of commercial recreation in today's business climate that emphasizes triple bottom line success and sustainability.

As you can see from the interviews at the start of this chapter, it is great to be in a job that allows you to follow your personal interests and make a living doing what you really enjoy. For some, this personal joy is enough, and many highly educated persons cherish their lifestyles so much that they are willing to eat peanut butter and share a small apartment with three friends in the off-season to enjoy the benefits of doing what they love.

Careers in Commercial Recreation and Leisure Businesses

For this chapter, the phrases *commercial recreation* and *leisure business* are somewhat narrowly defined. Although we could include movie theaters, game arcades, resorts, cruise ships, and many commercial sports, fitness, and cultural activities as commercial recreation, we will restrict our definition to privately funded businesses that offer instruction and participation in outdoor adventure and other recreational activities. For the purpose of organization, we have grouped commercial recreation and leisure businesses into four categories: campgrounds and camps, water-related businesses, specialty recreation activities, and retail and hobbies. When selecting a career path, you must consider many aspects in terms of passions, pay and perks, preparation, and possibilities.

Passions

Passions are the intrinsic values of the work experience that complement your personal values and life goals. For many in the commercial recreation field, their career path began with recognizing a problem or unmet need they themselves experienced. For people interested in entering the commercial recreation and leisure industry, the opportunity to create experiences or products they wish they could have had or bought always exists. Personal excitement for the major activity (or activities) involved, love of learning and doing, risk taking, entrepreneurship, physical challenges, analysis, love of teaching, problem solving, personal relationships, and communication are prerequisites for success in this challenging (but enjoyable) vocation. (Refer to the passions you listed in Chapter 2 and consider whether this career area may be a good fit for you.)

As a matter of fact, the opportunity to do well financially in the private sector is significantly better than in the public sector, where job security and a highly structured bureaucratic environment are the norm. People who crave great creative freedom and flexibility and are risk takers tend to thrive in private enterprise. On the other hand, these same folks must have discipline, organization, a nose for business, and strong people skills to ultimately be financially successful. A bit of luck also may help, or you can make your own luck by analyzing the situation thoroughly before making a commitment. Let us offer a personal story to illustrate this point:

In 1970, the second author was invited by a friend to canoe the Chattooga River on a trip sponsored by Clemson University and the Sierra Club. I was awed by the beauty and wildness of the river and that it was totally undeveloped and government owned. I had previously rafted the Youghiogheny River in Pennsylvania with a private outfitter and had a blast. It occurred to me that the Chattooga River had the potential to match or even surpass that fine river. I started researching the Chattooga, its launch and retrieval points, its rapids, and whether I could convince the Forest Service to grant me a permit to operate guided trips.

On one of my research trips, I crossed the river on a highway bridge and noticed a group of rafters preparing to launch. On a whim, my wife and I decided to chat with the group. Imagine our surprise when we discovered that the group was from Warner Brothers, and they were there filming scenes for the movie *Deliverance*, which was to debut the next winter.

On the spot, we decided we would start our business here. With the help of a friend who was the local bank president, and all the cash value of my life insurance policy, we bought six rafts, wooden paddles, and kapok life jackets; rented an abandoned schoolhouse; and founded Wildwater Ltd. Today, Wildwater is more than a $3 million enterprise with 200 employees and almost 60,000 river trips each year. In addition to rafting, Wildwater conducts kayak and canoe clinics and trips, operates Jeep tours and canopy zip line courses, conducts corporate retreats, provides lodging and food service, and operates four stores.

We often think, "What would have happened if we had been at the bridge 30 minutes earlier or 30 minutes later and had missed the film crew. Would we have still taken the chance?" We will never know, but the story illustrates the need for luck or divine intervention in becoming an entrepreneur.

Recreation businesses are not for the fainthearted because recreation business failures are common. Successful business operators must be willing to work long hours at odd times, sometimes for little evident immediate reward. They must be willing and able to take risks, accept the consequences of their successes and failures, and be willing and able to get up again each time they are knocked down. If you enter this area of the profession, go into it knowing that the percentage of failures in private business ventures is much greater than in other sectors and that job security is not assured. It can be a great ride, but it is not for the timid or lazy.

Although risks are involved, the potential rewards of financial and personal satisfaction are significant. Something about making your living doing the things you most enjoy transcends the profit motive. Loving what you do and doing what you love more than makes up in satisfaction and contentment for smaller financial rewards. Living your particular lifestyle and the freedom to make your own decisions and guide your own destiny are in themselves reward enough for experience-oriented individuals.

Pay and Perks

Monetary compensation varies tremendously in this segment of the leisure job market. Beginning pay starts at minimum wage and increases with experience and skill level. Full-time professionals in this area earn the equivalent of teachers and others in the human services field. Many jobs in this field include discounts or free use of personal equipment and gear and opportunities to live in areas of great scenic or recreational opportunities, and sometimes lodging and meals are included as well. Mostly, guides and instructors start at minimum wage, and that amount may double with experience and tips. Often, particularly in wilderness areas, employees also receive room and board.

Those owning their own successful business may become financially independent or they may lose everything, depending on their business acumen, willingness to work, knowledge, and ability to relate to others and solve problems. A commercial leisure and recreation business may be viewed as a lifestyle in which individuals prioritize their passion for recreation over maximizing revenues. A career in this area also allows you to connect your work to causes about which you are passionate such as the environment or supporting your local community. Developing or working for a business whose focus is to protect the local culture, conserve the environment, and at the same time be economically sustainable, embodies the triple bottom line illustrated in the introduction to this text.

An excellent example of the concept of the triple bottom line is country singer Dolly Parton. She took a broken-down amusement park in her native Sevier County, Tennessee, and through innovation, cultural education, music, and good business practices turned it into Dollywood, the area's largest employer and a solid moneymaker with gross revenues of more than $100 million annually. In addition, she provided training and employment to many locals living on low incomes, who otherwise may have been destitute. Her efforts also helped to preserve many classic mountain crafts, music, and other unique cultural components.

Among the perks of working for or operating a for-profit recreation business is the joy of being able to participate in your favorite pastimes and getting paid for it. Most employers have free or reduced prices for family, and in the industry, companies commonly have reciprocal agreements allowing employees to enjoy free or reduced prices at similar enterprises. For instance, Wildwater Rafting provides complimentary raft trips for Dollywood, the Biltmore house, and the Great Smoky Mountain Railway employees, and in return, these attractions provide complimentary tickets to Wildwater employees. Wildwater also has a co-op program with manufacturers of outdoor gear and clothing so employees receive discounted or free merchandise. These manufacturers believe that guests seeing guides wearing a particular style or brand of clothing or gear will influence the guest to purchase that brand, and they are willing to provide free or wholesale goods to the outfitter and its staff for that benefit. Finally, through trade associations and industry groups, employees and owners get to meet and know others in their particular field from across the country, which often results in complimentary reciprocal experiences and job opportunities for both employees and business owners.

Preparation

If you want to work in, or someday own, a recreation business, you will need to prepare yourself and gain the education and experiences necessary in the specific industry you are considering. First, you will want a college degree in a professional discipline such as leisure services or recreation management or in a parks, recreation, and tourism curricula. Many of the classes you take will include hands-on projects to help you gain necessary skills. In addition, plan to take courses or a minor in business and/or marketing. While you are in school, you will want to build your résumé by getting quality work experiences during the summer with successful companies in your chosen field.

The recreation businesses discussed in the next section have summer and part-time job opportunities you should consider while attending college. These summer (or part-time positions) give you an advantage when looking for a good internship or searching for your first full-time job.

The smart student will begin summer and/or part-time work at the end of the freshman year of college. Some will choose to experience different jobs each summer until they find the one that offers them the opportunities and experiences they wish to pursue on a career basis. Supervisory-level hiring in the for-profit sector is often done in-house or from competing companies. Therefore, if you find a good fit during summers or internships at a good company, you may wish to explore job options with that employer for postgraduation full-time employment.

Some companies have guide schools or training sessions for potential employees. This is an important consideration if you are trying to choose between job offers. Attending these workshops or schools will increase your job placement opportunities significantly. If the management staff of a company gets to know you and your abilities through their school or training sessions, they will be more likely to select you when jobs are available.

Once you have the job, tell the boss that you have prepared for a career in this type of business and are interested in learning as much as you can about how it works and the opportunities for advancement available in the company. Front-line employees in this type of job typically take a short-term look at their employment, or concentrate on the experience itself rather than the analysis of what makes the business successful. Let the boss know that your education prepares you for management and responsibility, and he or she will likely develop a new respect for you and open the gate to experiences that will lead to future advancement.

Possibilities

Multitudes of opportunities are available in commercial recreation with potential for great personal rewards. Some people may even find fortune and fame. Although the seasonal nature of most for-profit recreation enterprises makes becoming a millionaire less likely than other pursuits, you have only to look around your home community or favorite vacation area to see hundreds of people who have made significant business successes by building on their personal talents and passions. As stated earlier, the businesses we discuss will be restricted to privately funded businesses that offer instruction and participation in outdoor adventure and other recreation activities, including some of the retail aspects of those businesses. For your convenience, we have grouped commercial recreation possibilities into four categories:

- campgrounds and camps
- water-related businesses
- specialty recreation activities
- recreation retail and hobbies

Although hundreds of categories of private leisure businesses exist, we will summarize most of these into the four major areas listed below.

Making a Living and Loving Your Life

Most for-profit recreation ventures start out small, and many remain small. The wilderness areas of the American west are heavily populated with fishing, hunting, and backpacking guides who run one- or two-person family businesses. To many of these entrepreneurs, having their desired lifestyle is their most important value. Many of these businesses are passed down from father and mother to son and daughter for generations.

For these folks, lifestyle, nature, and simplicity are values to be treasured. Many sailboat charter captains live by the same creed. By and large, these people care little about amassing fortunes and possessing material items. Their idea of paradise is living life simply, enjoying the sharing of a special place or experience with others, and having their "hobby" provide enough cash to provide for the basics.

Significantly less than half of the 20-plus white-water rafting companies on Tennessee's Ocoee River operate under the same ownership as when the river first granted permits for rafting some 25 years ago. The Ocoee is a dam-controlled river, so operators can only count on about 100 days a year when the Tennessee Valley Authority releases enough water from the dam to allow rafting. Many have found making a living in those circumstances to be difficult at best, impossible at worst.

One of the inevitable pitfalls of the commercial sector is the seasonality of many businesses. Snow skiing, rafting, sailing, and most watersports operate in restricted time frames when the weather allows participants to comfortably participate. Unless you are located in Florida, southern California, or other temperate areas, leisure businesses are required to earn their profits over a short period. As a result, many jobs with these firms do not provide year-round employment. This presents a challenge for the business owner and his or her employees, and it presents a challenge for business owners who never know whether the employees they trained this year will be back the next year. The other issue brought about by a restricted season is that employees typically work long, hard hours during peak season. But the experience of making a living through personally meaningful and fulfilling work is often more than enough to sustain employees through long hours, physically demanding labor, or extreme weather conditions.

Campgrounds and camps. Campgrounds and camps share many similarities. Both involve an outdoor or wilderness experience, but private campgrounds cater to couples and families who occupy tents, tent campers, trailers, and motorized recreational vehicles (RVs), and most private camps offer supervised programs in an outdoor setting primarily for youth. Private camps operate mainly during the summer months.

Passions. This is an area where it is easy to fall in love with the job. Those who glory in the out-of-doors and natural environment will find much to attract them to this area. Both the campground environment and summer camp program have an abundance of contact with adults having fun and children playing. The opportunity exists to educate and create an environment full of fun, learning, and fulfillment.

Pay and perks. Both campgrounds and camps are seasonal in nature, which limits their ability to provide high compensation. For the few who are management-level and full-time employees, compensation is similar to teaching and social work salaries. Those who own successful camps that attract a year-round affluent clientele do much better, but the real perks are in the lifestyle and low-key off-season, which allows freedom. Frequently, camp management personnel are offered lodging free or housing at a low rate.

Preparation. A degree in parks and recreation management, leisure services, education, or outdoor education is a good start. Courses in child development, natural sciences, and personal skills are helpful. The best preparation may come from the experience of actually camping or serving as a camp counselor while attending college. The American Camp Association (ACA) holds conferences and workshops for camp staff and management.

Possibilities. Most camps and campgrounds are family owned and operate with a small year-round staff. Most summer camps raise their own staff from counselors. The industry is experiencing little growth, so staff positions are rare. Also, campgrounds are experiencing little or no growth, so opportunities are limited.

Campground operations. Although governmental agencies (national parks and forests, Bureau of Land Management, Corps of Engineers, state, county, and municipal government) own and operate a large number of the country's more than 20,000 campgrounds, over 3,900 campgrounds are operated as private enterprises, including a few located in public parks but managed by private companies.

Privately owned campgrounds are located in every state and range in size from less than 10 campsites to over 1,000 in a single business. Typically, they are open when weather and demand permit, which means some are year-round and others operate for only a few peak months.

Private resident camps. Many summer camps are operated by nonprofit organizations such as YMCAs or Boy Scouts/Girl Scouts, but the overwhelming number of resident camps are privately owned and operated as private for-profit enterprises.

Although most camps operate in a limited 10- to 12-week period over the summer months, key staff and management have a full-time responsibility to recruit campers, maintain and improve facilities, and recruit and train staff year-round. Many camps recruit summer staff from former campers and full-time staff from the summer paid staff. Request a listing of camps near you from the ACA, which certifies and evaluates resident camps. The ACA lists over 2,400 accredited camps operating in the United States. The ACA inspects these camps on over 300 standards involving health, safety, and program quality. The ACA has 24 regional offices in the United States. Camps hire counselors, waterfront directors, sport and activity directors, and specialty activity directors. (Many camps specialize in certain activities.)

Water-related businesses. Everybody loves the water. If you do not live on a lake, river, or sea, you probably want to vacation there. From this primal instinct to be on or near the water, many marine-based businesses have developed. Technology has added to the list of activities with the invention of sport kayaks, jet skis, kiteboarding, and motorized scuba scooters.

This is a job area with a sustained growth pattern, but the boat and motor area is profoundly affected by economic downturns. However, the remainder of the market continues to enjoy good growth, and a number of opportunities for expansion are available.

© *Photographerlondon | Dreamstime.com*

Passions. Watersports-based activities have an almost automatic appeal to most people. Just look at the crowded beaches, fast boats, and multitudes of cars carrying canoes, fishing gear, and trailered boats. Everyone seeks the water. In spite of warnings to the contrary, check out the number (and severity) of suntans as you walk along almost any street in the United states. We are a culture of sun worshippers and water spirits. If this aquatic wanderlust haunts you daily, you are a prime candidate for a job in this sector.

Pay and perks. This axiom applies: If your goal is to spend personal time surfing or fishing, you had best resign yourself to the title of beach bum or surfer dude. To find financial success in this area, you need to either be the best at your trade or start with a goal to one day own your own company. Starting pay ranges from tips only to minimum wage. Many jobs are seasonal, but this is definitely a growth environment.

Preparation. As per most of these career areas, personal participation in watersports is the first introduction to the specific activities in this category. The local YMCA, boating clubs, canoe clubs, scuba dealers, colleges, and private businesses may advance your skill levels in these activities. The Red Cross, American Canoe Association, and the Professional Association of Diving Instructors offer advanced skills courses.

Courses will provide you with the basic skill set but will not provide the background you will need to operate the business successfully. A college degree in recreation management or business administration with courses in public relations, marketing, business, and finance will round out your preparation. Part-time and seasonal employment and participation in professional organizations are essential to your continued success.

Possibilities. Water-based activities seem to grow bigger and better from year to year. Although economic conditions may temporarily hold down sales of costly equipment (boats, gear, canoes), the demand for learning and participating in water-based recreation moves up steadily.

This is an area where weather may make a significant difference in the season and consequently in the profitability of the business. A number of innovative companies have paired warm-weather activities with winter activities or indoor sports. For instance, several ski and canoe shops continue to produce business year-round.

Boating. This industry is booming and brings with it loads of opportunities for career employment. According North America's leading association representing the recreational boating industry, the National Marine Manufacturers Association (NMMA), boating is an important contributor to the U.S. economy, generating $35.6 billion in direct sales of products and services in 2012, a 10% increase from 2011. Data from NMMA's annual Recreational Boating Statistical Abstract signals the beginning of a recovery for the U.S. recreational boating industry. "Pent up demand for boast following years of diminished willingness to spend by consumers, improved credit availability for buyers and boating businesses, positive shifts in consumer confidence and an overall interest in the benefits of the boating lifestyle are steering the industry toward recovery" as noted by NMMA president, Thom Dammich. Mr. Dammich went on to say, "Americans' passion for enjoying the boating lifestyle is taking precedent as they put aside concerns about the economy in favor of creating lifelong memories with loved ones."[1]

Of the 232.3 million adults living in the United States in 2012, 88 million people (37.8%) participated in recreational boating, a 6% increase from 2011 (2012 NMMA Recreational Boating Statistical Abstract).[2] Marinas, pleasure cruises, sailing schools, resort rentals, and charter boats are examples of the companies that need people to assist them in this fast-growing market. In virtually every city, town, or tourist spot with a water source nearby, from one to dozens of private companies offer the public sightseeing, naturalist, historical, or action boat tours.

For example, a Chicago tourism publication listed 17 companies offering services for the public based from a boat. For a good list of marine, fishing, watersports, and boat organizations, check out the website for Marine Way Points, a company that shares news and resources with the boating community, as well as manages a directory of additional websites for information on diving, fishing, sailing, and weather.

Dive and snorkel shops. One of the best opportunities in the commercial recreation field is the area of diving and snorkeling—recreation under the surface of the ocean. This fascinating activity introduces participants to the many wonders of marine life, fanciful coral formations, colorful tropical fish, and the company of sea predators such as sharks, barracuda, and rays.

Extensive in-service training is required to instruct in this potentially dangerous field. Most of this training is done through the Professional Association of Diving Instructors (PADI). According to the PADI website, more than 6,200 dive shops and resorts are located around the world, and the association certified more than 900,000 divers in 2013.[3] For more information, visit the PADI website (www.padi.com/scuba). Almost all dive or snorkel businesses are privately owned and operated.

Most resorts and water-based hotels have dive and snorkel programs for their guests and the public. Although some of the larger and more specialized lodging establishments operate their own programs, the vast majority of dive and snorkel programs at resorts and hotels are concessions, meaning they are owned by individuals.

We recommend you avoid one segment of this industry—cave diving. This has been one of the most dangerous activities of our time, and it is difficult, if not impossible, to get liability insurance. The death rate is among the highest of all sports.

Canoe and kayak liveries and guided trips. The popularity of sea kayaking as a recreational activity has expanded this area of recreation businesses greatly in recent years. Sales of recreational kayaks has increased fourfold over the last decade. Many companies offer instruction in sea kayaking, day trips, and multiday expeditions. These enterprises supplement the traditional canoe rental and instructional business and make this area one of the fastest growing segments in America. Canoe, kayak, and paddlesports liveries (rentals) and instructional programs operate in every state and in almost every country in the world. This sport has been particularly popular with baby boomers, those currently 40- to 60-years-old, and early seniors likely due to its low-impact nature and is in a strong growth position due to the age diversity of the population upon which it draws.

An area of particular interest to entrepreneurs is the overseas kayak expedition business. Kayak owners are older and more affluent and find the excursion to exotic locations attractive. These excursions usually cost from $1,000 to $4,000 per person, and the high ticket price makes this area attractive to those who offer these trips. Many current kayak businesses offer trips worldwide to exotic destinations such as Costa Rica, Belize, Turkey, and Ireland.

In most areas, these businesses are seasonal in nature. (Try Florida, California, Arizona, or the Caribbean if you are looking for year-round employment.) Many active persons combine a summer sport (canoe guide) with a winter sport (ski instructor) for year-round employment.

The Paddlesports Industry Association (PIA) is the trade organization for the growing business of canoeing, kayaking, and human-powered watersports. Their 1,000-plus members are prime employers for those with a serious interest in the watersports business.

White-water rafting and kayaking. The white-water industry is a dynamic portion of the adventure travel business, with white-water rivers located in more than 30 states and an estimated 12.4 million persons participating in this activity annually. Many of the industry leaders in this field began as raft guides while in college and are now owners or managers for the more than 500 firms now offering white-water adventures in the United States.

Specialty commercial recreation activities. Name an interest area where people spend their leisure time, and you will come up with a new and extensive list of opportunities for private recreation businesses. Whether it is running, exercise, model railroading, sewing, motorcycle riding, or cultural arts, a potential market exists for someone to make a living supporting that industry. Whether it is retailing items enthusiasts need to do the job or offering instruction in how to do it properly, money may be made servicing people's leisure needs.

Go Fly a Kite!

Kitty Hawk Kites started out in 1974 teaching a few people how to hang glide off the same sand dunes where the Wright brothers conducted the first successful airplane flight. Now they have 13 stores all over the North Carolina Outer Banks offering kayaking, eco-tours, jet boat tours, hiking trips, kiteboarding, parasailing, and a never-ending variety of outdoor activities. Their 200-plus seasonal employees provide activities for over 15,000 people annually, but time has proven that their retail stores with outdoor apparel, kites to fly, and recreation gear are the main revenue producers for this unique recreational enterprise.

Passions. This is an area where personal interests may meld into business success. If you have a particular sport, interest, or hobby you love, you may be able to fulfill your personal dreams and your financial dreams all at once if you have an entrepreneurial spirit. Doing a job you love and for which you have a personal passion immeasurably increases your chances of success. Thousands of small businesses exist today based upon serving the needs of leisure enthusiasts.

Pay and perks. It all depends on you and that YOU can make the choices that ultimately will determine its success or failure. Working at an existing business to learn it may mean a minimum wage or slightly more. As you progress, you could become the manager of a local franchise and earn a comfortable living. Eventually, when you own and operate your own business, you could live comfortably on the profits. Owning your own business also has its perks. You may legally charge many expenses to your business. You may also take perks that relate to the business instead of having to pay for them out of pocket. So, ownership has its privileges (along with some tax benefits).

Preparation. The same basic educational requirements of a bachelor's degree with an emphasis on recreation and business will set the stage for success. A number of college entrepreneurship programs are available that can hone your business senses. If you have another major, take advantage of some of their classes as a minor. Ultimately, your best preparation for these areas is actual work experience, along with programs presented by industry-related professional organizations.

Possibilities. People with a personal interest, talent, and strong passion for a specialty commercial recreation business may find their lifelong dream and the land of opportunity here. Remember, it takes an entrepreneurial spirit, good business sense, and access to paying clients to make your career choice in this area become a reality. Your choices are as diverse and abundant in the specialty commercial recreation activities area, and what follows are descriptions of four popular commercial recreation specialty business ideas.

Horseback riding and dude ranches. Riding stables and other recreational activities with horses are increasingly popular across America. Ellen Hargrove, past president of the Colorado Dude Ranchers Association (www.duderanching.org), indicates that more than 2,400 permits are currently in effect for commercial horseback riding on government lands, and that does not include all of the businesses who use only private land for their rides and trips. For further information on this industry, try the American Horse Council (www.horsecouncil.org) or the American Quarter Horse Association (aqha.com).

Fishing, hunting, and backpacking guides. Perhaps the ultimate job for a person who loves to fish, hunt, or hike is to be a wilderness guide. It is a profession a person may more easily be born into than trained for. Skilled fishing guides who know where the fish are or backpacking guides who lead the youth group into unknown territory and away from danger gain their expertise from doing and seeing rather than from formal education.

But turning that interest into a successful business requires skills such as bookkeeping, marketing, social skills, computer skills, and more. In a world where supply is plenty and demand is limited, the guide with a college education stands an excellent chance of making it in a difficult profession.

In many ways, the wilderness fishing or hunting guide has a fairly easy time starting his or her own business. The cost of a guiding business may be as little as several thousand dollars and a phone line and website. Some connections and insurance may be all an entrepreneur needs to start a business. Be aware, though, that a single-person business depends fully upon the full commitment of the founder and the successes and failures in this area. In most areas, both permits and certification are required, so do your homework.

Snow skiing, snowmobiling, and winter sports. If you live in (or want to live in) one of the snow belt areas of this country, or in Canada, you may want to look into winter sports. However, most companies who have businesses in the for-profit recreation field use this as a supplement for other summer or year-round businesses. For instance, a Colorado couple rents skis and organizes ski trips for youth groups in their area as winter revenue. In the summers, they earn a living taking photos of families riding a commercial vintage steam train. The two businesses dovetail to provide a steady stream of income, which sustains them year-round. Also, do not forget ice skating (and hockey), which can be operated year-round.

Bicycles and motorcycles. In 2012, bike sales actually overtook car sales in 23 of the 27 European Union member states. In Italy, bikes outsold cars for the first time since World War II, and in Spain, bike sales topped the transportation charts for the first time ever.[4] The U.S. Bicycle Market report reported 2012 as a solid year for the U.S. bicycle industry, with direct effect sales of $6.1 billion, including retail sales of bicycles, related parts and accessories, through all channels of distribution.[5]

The Motorcycle Industry Council (MIC) reported a small increase in U.S. motorcycle sales in 2013 with street motorcycles and adventure motorcycles showing the biggest growth over 2012. For 2013, MIC reported that there were 465,783 motorcycle sales in the United States, an increase of just 1.4% over the 2012 numbers.[6]

Recreation retail and hobbies. Hobbies and their associated retail shops provide a fascinating and wide-open area where small business opportunities abound. Those with personal interests may turn those interests into a lifetime vocation. One of the most obvious successful examples of a hobby business is Build-a-Bear Workshop.

The Bear That Built an Empire

In 1997, Maxine Clark had an idea. It certainly would be fun and maybe she could even make a little profit if she opened a store that allowed children to stuff and dress their own teddy bears. In 2013, Build-A-Bear Workshop® was named one of the FORTUNE Best Companies to Work For® list for the fifth year in a row. Clark lived out her dream and served as the Chief Executive Bear until June 2013. Today, more than 400 such stores are located worldwide, including company-owned stores in the United States, Puerto Rico, Canada, Ireland, the United Kingdom and franchise stores in countries around the world. Clark is one of the true innovators in the leisure-related retail industry. She is one of many Americans who took an idea based on a personal hobby and turned it into a huge success.

Passions. Nothing is like doing exactly what you enjoy most and making a living doing it!

Pay and perks. Look through the list. It is as diverse as this country. There is something for everyone and everything for someone. In this environment, salaries or income is difficult to anticipate. But the perks of owning your own business to support your participation in it and to share it with others is a great perk!

Preparation. To be honest, the best preparation is learning by doing. You may increase your business sense by having basic math, economics, bookkeeping, and marketing courses and by learning from experts in your field, but most of your education will be at the school of hard knocks!

Possibilities. Consult the individual activity descriptions for a list of pertinent professional associations and organizations in your specialty area. Active membership and attendance at professional conferences and training events will gain you good friends, better tips on how to succeed, and a wealth of information you will need to stay competitive.

Areas where hobbies have led to gainful employment and/or business ownership include the following:

- ceramics shops
- shooting galleries and target ranges
- pet salons and pet training facilities
- quilting and sewing classes and stores
- miniature golf courses and driving ranges
- sport instruction clinics
- model train, car, and military diorama stores and clubs
- video game parlors, competitions, and programming
- musical instruction, performance, and sales
- travel clubs and organized tours
- fitness clubs, gyms, and physical fitness trainers

The list goes on and on. Think of any hobby or leisure activity, and you will begin to see needs in that particular area where private enterprise could provide goods and services to satisfy demand. This list of for-profit (or commercial) recreation can be expanded to hundreds of interest areas, including hobby shops, ceramics and crafts, and exotic activities such as adventure racing, skateparks, go carts, game arcades, and virtually any leisure activity you can imagine that can support commercial partnerships. Many astute operators began profitable businesses as a result of their own personal interests and hobbies.

Summary of Commercial Recreation and Leisure Business Career Possibilities

Career	Passions	Pay and perks	Preparations	Possibilities
Campgrounds and camps	Being in the outdoors and natural environment, fun, learning, fulfillment	Compensation similar to teaching and social work salaries	Bachelor's degree in parks and recreation management, leisure services, education, or outdoor education	Seasonal, camp staff positions are limited, little or no growth trend in campgrounds, opportunities limited
Water-related business	Automatic appeal to most people who have a strong desire to be near water	Starting pay ranges from tips only to minimum wage; many jobs are seasonal, but this a growth environment; start your own successful business and the sky is the limit	Personal participation in watersports is the first introduction to the specific activities in this category; American Canoe Association and PADI offer advanced skills courses; college degree in recreation management, with courses in public relations, marketing, business, and finance	Water-based activities seem to grow bigger and better from year to year; although economic conditions may temporarily hold down sales of costly equipment (boats, gear, canoes), the demand for learning and participating in water-based recreation moves steadily up
Specialty commercial activities	Special interests can blend with business success when you are doing a job you love and for which you have a personal passion, this increases your chance of ultimate success	Working at an existing business to learn it may mean earning around minimum wage; as you progress, you could become the manager and earn a comfortable living	Bachelor's degree with an emphasis on recreation, college entrepreneurship programs to hone business sense; best preparation is work experience, along with programs presented by industry-related professional organizations	Personal interest, stong passion, and entrepreneurial spirit make choices diverse and abundant in the specialty commercial recreation activities area

(cont.)

Summary of Commercial Recreation and Leisure Business Career Possibilities (cont.)

Career	Passions	Pay and perks	Preparations	Possibilities
Recreation and retail hobbies	Nothing is like doing exactly what you enjoy most and making a living doing it	Difficult to anticipate salary or income, perks of owning your own business to support your participation in it and to share it with others is a great perk	Best preparation is learning by doing; you can increase your business sense by having basic math, economics, bookkeeping, and marketing courses and learn from experts in your field by doing, but most of this education will be the school of hard knocks	Consult the individual activity descriptions for a list of pertinent associations and organizations in your specialty area. Active membership and attendance at professional conferences and training events will gain you good friends, better tips on how to succeed, and a wealth of information you may need to stay competitive

Future Opportunities, Issues, and Challenges

The commercial recreation field is broad and diverse, so pinpointing opportunities, issues, and challenges is difficult. Suffice it to say that millions of people are employed today in positions that allow them to work and earn money while pursuing a personal pastime. In times of economic downturn, people will vacation closer to home, so local commercial enterprises may do better. In times when the economy is better, people will travel farther and spend more. Thus, do your research, stay on top of trends, and consider short- and long-term patterns to capitalize on opportunities. Plan accordingly. In short, plan your business and work your plan.

As America's leisure appetite expands to new activities and pursuits, numerous job opportunities become available, and persons with the proper skills and experience are in a good position to take advantage of this and be promoted to higher positions quickly. A good example of this is the amusement park field, where over 80% of supervisors holding top positions in parks such as Disney World, Great Adventures, and Busch Gardens have worked their way up the ladder quickly, and the average age of year-round supervisors is late 20s or 30s. Compare that to other fields where managers tend to be in their 50s and 60s.

If you have a passion for commercial recreation enterprises, look for opportunities to integrate your interests with your need for employment. Then after you learn the trade, attempt to make it your own through ownership or management opportunities.

Resources and Getting Involved

The key point is, your own specific interests develop as you learn more about your field of interest through part-time and seasonal work opportunities. Hands-on experience will be your greatest resource in this all-encompassing, generic segment of the leisure industry.

Professional Organizations

Every segment of the recreation business market has its national, regional, and local professional or interest organizations, as well as participant organizations. Google your activity area and/or use your yellow pages to start the search. Better yet, consult someone you know who has interest and knowledge in your specific interest area. The following organizations will get you started.

Adventure Travel Trade Association (ATTA): www.adventuretravel.biz
ATTA is a global membership organization and home to a thriving community of more than 800 responsible, profitable businesses, destinations, and media that transform customers and businesses alike into advocates for sustainability and justice worldwide. Members include tour operators, tourism boards, specialty travel agents, guides, accommodations, media, and service providers.

Resort and Commercial Recreation Association (RCRA): www.rcra.org
The RCRA is an international nonprofit, nonregulatory organization comprising professionals, educators, and students in resort and commercial-related industries. The mission of RCRA is to serve as a vehicle to communicate, educate, and promote standards of professionalism within the industry and to provide opportunities for continuing education, networking, and awareness of industry trends.

American Camp Association (ACA): www.acacamps.org
The ACA (formerly known as the American Camping Association) is a community of camp professionals who, for 100 years, have joined together to share knowledge and experience and to ensure the quality of camp programs.

National Association of RV Parks and Campgrounds (ARVC): www.arvc.org
ARVC is the only national association that exclusively represents the interests of all commercial RV parks and campgrounds in the United States. Membership includes RV parks and campgrounds, cabin and lodge resorts, membership campgrounds and resorts, industry suppliers, and park developers.

Professional Paddlesports Association (PPSA): www.paddlesportsindustry.org
PPSA is the premier trade association fostering paddlesports business. This organization's mission is to provide information on safety, paddling locations, and paddling basics to enhance participants' paddling experiences. Another goal is to increase the number of people who participate in paddlesports and how often they go paddling.

Outdoor Industry Association (OIA): www.outdoorindustry.org
The OIA is the premier trade association for companies in the active outdoor recreation business. OIA provides trade services for over 4,000 manufacturers, distributors, suppliers, sales representatives, and retailers in the outdoor industry. The OIA seeks to ensure a healthy and diverse specialty retail and supply chain based on quality, innovation, and service.

Colorado Dude and Guest Ranch Association: www.coloradoranch.com
Membership in the Colorado Dude and Guest Ranch Association offers many benefits besides just the credibility of being a part of a reputable trade association. These perks will not only enhance your knowledge as a rancher but also improve your business.

National Ski Area Association (NSAA): www.nsaa.org
The National Ski Area Association is the trade association for ski area owners and operators. It represents 329 Alpine resorts that account for more than 90% of the skier/snowboarder visits nationwide. Additionally, it has over 400 supplier members who provide equipment, goods, and services to the mountain resort industry.

Certifications and Licenses

Most recreation and leisure jobs offering skills instruction or having an element of adventure require certification and training. Maine, Montana, New York, California, Idaho, and many other states license guides. In addition to college and university programs, the National Outdoor Leadership School (NOLS) provides training for outdoor leaders. Since many leisure activities are held on national and state parks and recreation area, permits for outside vendors are usually required, and that state or federal agency will regulate vendors. In most other activities, professional organizations such as the ACA and PADI provide the appropriate certification.

Remember, if you do not have all the credentials and permits you are required to hold, you are not a professional, so never put yourself in that position. If you do, you put your self at risk of being sued and the loss of your business and your home. You should also have adequate liability insurance to cover yourself and your guests.

American Canoe Association (ACA): www.americancanoe.org
The ACA offers skills courses and certification courses to paddlers of all skill levels in multiple disciplines. These courses represent a body of knowledge, sets of skills, safety procedures, and other materials deemed appropriate for the particular environments of the disciplines.

Maine Guides Online: www.maineguides.com
Maine Guides Online is a one-stop resource that provides easy searches for Licensed Professional Maine Guides throughout the state or for any Maine recreational sport from bird-watching to white-water rafting.

New York State Licensed Guide Certification: www.dec.ny.gov/permits/30969.html
The licensing of outdoor guides is regulated by the New York State Forest Rangers. In general, a guide is a person, at least 18 years of age, who offers services for hire, part or all of which include directing, instructing, or aiding another in fishing, hunting, camping, hiking, white-water rafting/canoeing/kayaking, or rock and ice climbing.

National Outdoor Leadership School (NOLS): www.nols.edu
NOLS is a 501(c)(3) not-for-profit educational institution that takes people of all ages on remote wilderness expeditions and teaches technical outdoor skills, leadership, and environmental ethics.

SCUBA Organizations and Certification
Professional Association of Dive Instructors (PADI): www.padi.com
PADI is one of the world's leading scuba diving training organizations.

National Association of Underwater Instructors (NAUI): www.naui.org
NAUI Worldwide is one of the world's most respected, largest nonprofit diver training organizations. It was established in 1959 as a membership association and organized solely to support and promote dive safety.

Scuba Diving International (SDI): www.tdisdi.com
SDI was created in 1999 and grew out of the success of its sister company, TD, which specializes in the more advanced disciplines of dive training. They have streamlined course materials to let students study the essential academics with an emphasis on practical diving skills learned in the pool and open water environments.

Technical Diving International (TDI): www.tdisdi.com
TDI is the largest technical certification agency in the world. As one of the first agencies to provide training in mixed gas diving and rebreathers, TDI is seen as an innovator of new diving techniques and programs, which previously were not available to the general public.

Handicap Scuba Association (HSA): www.hsascuba.com
HSA was founded in 1981 and is now the world's leading authority on recreational diving for people with disabilities. Headquartered in California, HSA International extends its underwater educational programs worldwide.

Where to Gain Experience

In an effort to make a living doing something they really enjoy or for which they have a personal passion, graduates may enter these areas without a good business plan or adequate capital and may quickly fall by the wayside when the business does not attract enough revenue to become viable.

To increase your chance of success in this field, plan to take a position in a currently successful leisure business for several years. Work your way up the ladder of responsibility until you know enough about the business aspects of the company to start your own company. At this point, you will have a much better chance of success in starting your own business. You may also be chosen for a position with more responsibility in the company where you work or in a similar company. One of the best ways to prepare yourself for advancement is to learn all aspects of the business, from accounting to reservations, from ordering equipment and supplies to maintenance routines. In doing so, you will make yourself more valuable to your current company and increase your capability to successfully start your own company.

Do not hesitate to let the business owner or manager know of your desire to learn the business and to make it a career. Personal communication of your goals to the management will provide you with opportunities to learn the business internally and will alert management of your desire to be a career player.

Additional Online Resources

Explore job opportunities in the outdoor recreation and adventure industry at the sites below. Note that many of the professional associations listed previously also have career information and/or job bulletin links on their main sites.

CoolWorks.com: www.coolworks.com
CoolWorks.com can help you finding a seasonal job or career in some of the greatest places on Earth. Get a summer job in Yellowstone, Yosemite, or another national park. Find a summer job as a camp counselor. Ski resorts, ranches, theme parks, tour companies, and more are waiting for you. Let CoolWorks.com show you the way to live out your own amazing adventure!

OutdoorIndustryJobs.com: www.outdoorindustryjobs.com

OutdoorIndustryJobs.com enables outdoor, bicycle, winter and snow sports, action sports, fishing, and hunting industry job seekers and employers to network and connect. In these particular industries, a passion for the outdoors is the common denominator between the job seeker and the employer. Its mission is to provide the platform where "the passion can happen" for both job seekers and employers alike so they may form mutually beneficial life and business relationships.

MarineWaypoints.com: www.marinewaypoints.com

MarineWaypoints.com is a marine-related site dedicated to learning resources, a boating community, news, and more. It is also a directory of marine-related websites, including boating, diving, fishing, gear, sailing, weather, and much more.

America Outdoors, Information Services for Outdoor Recreation Enthusiasts: www.americaoutdoors.com

America Outdoors is an outdoor information center and gathering area for outdoor recreationists who enjoy the great outdoors. America Outdoors offers numerous resources.

Fun Jobs: www.funjobs.com

Fun Jobs is dedicated to bringing together people who love their work and employers who love their people.

Mountain Resort Community Employment Connection: www.mountainjobs.com

Mountain Jobs is a connection to ski jobs, summer jobs, and seasonal and full-time professional careers.

Conclusion

Success is sweet and satisfying, especially for those who choose carefully and enter the commercial recreation field with adequate preparation. Even with knowledge of the limitations and obstacles, this calling has many benefits.

Doing something you personally enjoy and sharing that experience with others is gratifying. For many, having the off-season open to pursue personal goals or another job opportunity is a positive. A common application of this is beach lifeguards spending the winter on snow ski patrol or instructing skiing or schoolteachers organizing hiking trips over the summer.

However, be cognizant that as your responsibility level increases in a company, the amount of off-season leisure time will probably decrease, and if you become the proprietor of a successful enterprise, the free time will likely disappear.

America loves its leisure. Even in times of recession, folks are likely to give up almost everything but their vacations and their leisure activities. This sector is growing by leaps and bounds. What better place to be than in the center of the fray enjoying what you do while helping others have fun!

For Further Investigation

Active Investigation

1. Research and visit a local site. Search the Internet for the activity or interest of your choice. Enter your local city or state along with the activity to find nearby service providers. After checking out the websites to determine whether they do the activities in which you are interested, give the best of them a call or stop by for a visit to see for yourself.

2. Conduct an informational interview. After you have satisfied yourself of the validity of the business, contact the owner or manager and ask whether you may stop by for a visit. Explain that you are pursuing a degree in recreation management and are interested in learning more about their specialty. Use the informational interview instructions in Chapter 2 to prepare for your interview. Whether this leads to future employment or an internship, or simply provides you with a future contact or additional information, you will find this direct and personal method produces great results.

For More Research

1. Consult your curriculum adviser, someone working in the field, your school's career center, the library, or and the Internet to learn more about career opportunities in your area of interest. See what minors are available at your school to complement your major and interest in commercial recreation (e.g., business, marketing, public relations).

2. Choose one area of interest in commercial recreation and determine what certifications and licenses would be an asset. Use the Internet to prepare a report detailing the type of training and experience needed to acquire the certification(s). Make sure your report includes a budget so you can determine how much it may cost you to pursue each certification.

3. Visit the website for the Resort and Commercial Recreation Association (RCRA), the professional organization of commercial recreation field, with a strong emphasis on the resort and tourism sector (www.rcra.org). See how much it costs to join as a student and make a list of the benefits you would receive from this membership. Also, check out the next conference and see whether your school will support you and other students to attend.

4. Investigate potential jobs and salaries. Go to www.coolworks.com and www.outdoorindustryjobs.com and locate at least five current job postings that interest you. Report on qualifications, salary range, and application requirements. Apply for one or more jobs for next summer.

Recommended Reading

Crossley, J., Jamieson, L., & Brayley, R. (2007). *Introduction to commercial recreation and tourism: An entrepreneurial approach* (5th ed.). Champaign, IL: Sagamore.
This book is a stepping-stone to understanding the scope, characteristics, entrepreneurial strategies, and management aspects of commercial recreation and tourism.

Goeldner, C. R., & Ritchie, J. R. B. (2009). *Tourism: Principles, practices, philosophies* (11th ed.). Hoboken, NJ: John Wiley and Sons.
This book examines how different components of the industry work together to create a unified, successful travel experience.

Bolton, W. K., & Thompson, J. L. (2000). *Entrepreneurs: Talent, temperament, technique.* Oxford, United Kingdom: Butterworth-Heinemann.
This book is the most comprehensive treatment of the entrepreneur on the market.

Bolton, W. K., & Thompson, J. L. (2003). *The entrepreneur in focus: Achieve your potential.* London, England: Thomson.
This book is about identifying and releasing entrepreneurial potential. Using the idea of character themes, it defines the entrepreneur in terms of six key themes and provides readers with the opportunity to assess themselves in these areas.

References

[1] National Marine Manufacturers Association. (2013). Recreational Boating Statistical Abstract. Retrieved from http://www.nmma.org/statistics/publications/statisticalabstract.aspx

[2] Ibid.

[3] PADI. (2013). About Padi. Retrieved from http://www.padi.com/scuba/about-padi/default.aspx

[4] European Automobile Manufacturers Association. (2014). Statistics. Retrieved from http://www.acea.be/statistics

[5] Edmondson, B. (2013). The U.S. bicycle market: A trend overview. Retrieved from Gluskin Townley Group website: http://www.gluskintownleygroup.com/

[6] Motorcycle Industry Council. (2014). Retrieved from www.mic.org

“ *Choose a job you love, and you will never have to work a day in your life.*

—**Confucius** ”

14

Preparing for a Career in Recreation

Craig M. Ross
Indiana University

Focus Questions

Q: How do I learn more about a career in recreation, park, and leisure services?

A: Read, ask questions, and try it! Reading is the simplest way to learn about career opportunities. Read the resources available to you, including those at the end of each chapter. Visit with your university campus career services department for specific career resources, manuals, and guides or use the university/public library careers section. The Internet is also an excellent way to discover and research career opportunities. Once you have read the literature, ask professionals in the field for their perspective on these careers. The informational interview technique is a great way to speak with experts in the field. Also, job shadowing with current practitioners will give you a better understanding of what occurs behind the scenes. One way to determine whether a certain career in recreation, park, and leisure services is best for you is to experience practical hands-on opportunities in typical jobs associated with your career choice while you are in college. Working part time or volunteering during the school year, being employed in a summer job, or completing an internship for academic credit are excellent ways to see whether you would enjoy the work and the environment.

Q: How do I know what is the "perfect" career choice for me?

A: To make good career choices and decisions, you must "know yourself." Self-assessment involves an honest, personal self-exploration in which you identify and prioritize your values, interests, skills, personality, and lifestyle. The more accurate and honest you are during this phase, the better the chances of making good career decisions.

Q: What if I do not know anyone working in this field? Will I still be able to find a job?

A: Absolutely! Since many jobs are never publicly advertised (known as the "hidden job market"), you must actively seek out contacts in the field. Establishing and maintaining these contacts is called networking, which we will discuss in further detail in this chapter. Networking relates to the old adage, "It's not what you know, but who you know," and is certainly true in preparing for a career and the subsequent job search process. Developing a strong network of contacts early in your college education helps you become known to people in the field who may be hiring or may be in a position to refer you to someone who is hiring. Being an active member in student or professional associations is an excellent way to start making contacts, too.

Key Terms

Career planning

Career exploration

Values

Interests

Skills

Personality

Lifestyle

Informational interview

Campus career services

Technology

Student or professional organization

Networking

Job shadowing

Part-time work

Summer job

Volunteering

Internship

Certifications and licenses

Job search

Portfolio

Résumé

Cover letters

Job interview

Testimonial Letter

"Hello there! I hope you are doing well! Things are going great for me, which is why I'm writing you. I feel that my education and experiences paved the road to success. I have many suggestions and experiences that would be helpful to any upcoming graduate, or even someone who has graduated, but cannot seem to find their path.

Upon completion of an internship with a Tour company in Florida and graduation, I made my official move to Orlando, FL. My first position was a Sales Representative for a Tour company. I dealt with other tour operators who were bringing groups to Orlando yet needed a resource for hotels, attractions tickets, meal functions, etc. It was a great way to break into the travel/tourism industry.

A year later, I was brought on board by another, yet very different tour company. I became a Sales Manager, in charge of working with schools and groups directly. I provided tour packages for student groups to any destination throughout the country, our top markets being Orlando, NYC, Chicago, Washington D.C., New Orleans, Boston, etc. This gave me managerial experience, not to mention the freedom to manage my own accounts.

Next week, I am making another move to the Arizona area. I am the new Sales Manager for the Hard Rock Café! My responsibilities will include bringing large parties from various markets into the restaurant. I will also take part in promotions and community events. I am very excited about this position and the opportunities that exist in Arizona. The Hard Rock corporation is known throughout and has an outstanding reputation.

Throughout my short career, I have been employed by Disney. When I decided to make the move to Orlando, I knew that I was doing it all alone, so before I even moved here, I got a job as a server at Walt Disney World. This has been an invaluable experience, has taught me many lessons, and proved a network of friends. This weekend job also gave me the extra income, allowing me to live by myself. It has not always been easy. I work a 40+ work week, then go to work at 7:00 a.m. on Saturday and Sunday. However, it has all been worth it! I cannot stress enough how invaluable it is to hold a part-time job while also having a career. It forces you to be responsible and use your time wisely.

My point in sharing all this with you is that I am an example of how hard work and dedication truly pay off. Each position I have attained has been a promotion and a significant pay raise. However, I really put myself out there and did everything I could do to get the job/career that I desired. I witness other 24- to 30-year-olds and their quest to find a job. It seems to me that people truly do not know how to best look for a job. They simply send out a few resumes and claim they are unable to find a job. I found a job in Phoenix, while living in Orlando. Anything is possible! I encourage young people to send their resumes EVERYWHERE! Someone will pass it one to someone else, and so on. Post your info and resume on CareerBuilder and Monster. Go to Job Fairs. Do extensive research on CVB websites. Looking for a job is a job within itself.

Have a GREAT DAY!

(letter from a former student)

Discover a Professional Career

Career planning is an individual journey of self-exploration in which you take responsibility and control for your future as a professional. Career planning is not to be confused with job searching. Job searching, although extremely important, is just one aspect of career planning. Career planning is an ongoing lifelong process that incorporates short-term and long-term career goals and objectives and has many rewards and challenges. Career decisions you make in college today will provide the foundation for your future life and career choices.

Although some students know exactly what professional career they want after graduation, most explore several options while in college before deciding on the right career path. This **career exploration** process is a combination of learning about yourself and discovering the potential work environments that may interest to you. In many cases, career exploration is a systematic process of elimination, that is, eliminating career options that are not well suited to you!

Thus, career planning is an individual process, or way of thinking, about how to make informed decisions regarding the career options through your college years and beyond. Remember the old adage, "If you don't know where you're going, any road will take you there." Every journey begins with the first step, but do not travel down just any road. Be focused and make informed decisions.

Your first step begins with an honest self-assessment. Socrates referred to this as "know thyself." Knowing who you are, your strengths and weaknesses, your personal and career interests, what you value most, and your desired lifestyle will help you determine career pathways. Also, understand that the self-assessment and career exploration steps are ongoing processes that are never really complete.

Assess Your Values, Interests, Skills, Personality, and Lifestyle

As discussed in greater detail in Chapter 2, conducting and gathering as much information about yourself as possible to make good career decisions is important. This is the initial step in the career planning process and typically involves a personal self-exploration or self-assessment inventory of your values, interests, personality, skills, and lifestyles.

- **Values** are the principles and beliefs that you use when making important decisions in your life. You probably already have a core set of values that you developed as a youth and ones that you strongly believe are important.
- **Interests** are activities or experiences that you like to do and find rewarding and enjoyable. What are your interests in the classroom? Beyond the classroom? At work?
- **Skills** are those items that you may have learned from previous full- or part-time jobs, volunteer experiences, sport participation, or other school and social activities.

- **Personality** describes an individual's pattern of behavior, thoughts, feelings, and motivation. Since each of us has our own personality traits, it is important to find a career path that complements these personality characteristics, not conflicts with them.
- **Lifestyle** represents personal values of where and how you live, work, and play both now and how you see yourself in years to come. In most cases, your career choice will significantly impact your lifestyle!

Devote quality time and attention to the self-assessment phase of career planning. By being honest and sincere in your self-assessment, you become more aware of your existing skills and abilities and may learn and discover your strengths (as well as weaknesses!) and interests. Once this inventory process is complete, you may then begin to identify the recreation settings, organizations, and agencies that are a good fit with these qualities and make the best of your skills and abilities. In this career planning phase, finding the ideal job that perfectly matches all of your values, interests, skills, personality, and lifestyle is not necessary. Rather, your goal should be to begin to prioritize your values, needs, and wants and to make a more informed decision on a career path that is best for you. The more accurate your self-reflection is, the better the fit will be for a successful career choice.

Also, understand that no career choice is set in stone. You will soon find that the real world of work is constantly changing and evolving. What is a common practice in a career setting today may be obsolete by the time you graduate. On the other hand, your personal life, lifestyles, and relationships will change, too. The importance and priority that you place on some values today as an undergraduate may be different a few years from now as you continue to grow and mature. Subsequently, your career options will change because you will change. Although it is important for you to focus on one career direction for now, the Bureau of Labor Statistics reported that "individuals held an average of 11.3 jobs from ages 18 to 46, with nearly half of these jobs being held before age 25."[1]

Career Exploration:
Research and Explore the Occupations in Recreation

Researching specific careers allows you to make an informed decision about your career goals. During this phase of career exploration and development, research, gather, and learn as much information as possible about what occupations will maximize your strengths and match your interests, values, lifestyle, and personality traits. Most career information can be found by observing and interacting with professionals in the field and reading publications (books, newsletters, booklets, pamphlets, etc.) written by professionals and professional associations. The Internet is also an excellent resource, as are public and university libraries and college placement offices or career development centers. Other sources that have information about occupations include current newspapers, trade journals, professional magazines, and agency annual reports.

During this information-gathering phase, the systematic process of collecting and evaluating information ultimately results in making decisions on career choices. Depending on the individual and circumstances, this process could be condensed into a matter of a few weeks (not recommended!) or expanded to several years. A number of sources are available for you to gather information. The easiest approach is to obtain information directly from the company or agency. Most will provide you with their most recent annual report, job descriptions, flowcharts, program policies, mission statements, and various public relations documents. Another source is to talk with your friends, colleagues, career advisers, faculty mentors, and alumni. The following is a list of Internet resources:

Better Business Bureau (BBB): www.bbb.org/search
The BBB gathers and reports information on fair and effective businesses and business practices across the United States.

Annual Reports: www.annualreports.com
This is a free Internet source that provides users with one of the most complete and up-to-date sites of annual reports from various companies.

NewsLink: newslink.org
U.S. Newspapers is a comprehensive gateway to newspapers, magazines, and radio/TV resources.

U.S. Newspapers: www.usnpl.com
U.S. Newspapers is a comprehensive gateway to newspaper websites around the world and provides local community information, news, and classified sections.

GuideStar: www.guidestar.org
GuideStar is an excellent source of data and information for over 1.7 million nonprofit organizations.

Yellowbook: www.yellowbook.com
Yellowbook is the largest independent publisher of yellow pages, which provides users with the most complete source of local buying information in print and online.

No matter what career path you finally choose, enjoy exploring and learning about the career options during your undergraduate education. Gain practical experience and valuable networking opportunities along the way. Get involved in student and professional organizations and other extracurricular activities. Attend professional association conferences. Solicit the help of a faculty mentor. By taking advantage of these diverse experiences and making networking connections with professionals in the field, you will become more marketable when you begin the job search process.

Informational Interview

One of the most effective ways of obtaining background information about a particular career in recreation, park, and leisure services is to conduct an **informational interview** with people who work in a job you may be interested in pursuing. They are an invaluable resource for insider information regarding an occupation. The purpose of the informational interview is to talk to people in a career that you are considering and gain or discover as much information as possible about what the career is really like! It is not designed as a job interview for a specific job! If conducted properly, informational interviews will allow you to expand your professional network of colleagues, keep up-to-date on career information, and build confidence in your interviewing skills. Refer to Chapter 2 for more details regarding the process and questions that may be asked in an informational interview.

Make the Most of Your Formal Education

Brainstorm as many college majors and career options as possible as you begin your educational pursuits. You may choose from several majors and careers in recreation, park, tourism, and leisure services. Formal education, in conjunction with practical experience, provides the knowledge, skills, and abilities necessary to work in this field. Making an informed decision on a major and/or career must align with your values, skills, interests, personality, and desired lifestyle that you identified in your self-assessment process.

Selecting a College and Major

Once you have identified potential college majors and career options, you need to learn more about them. Good career decisions require careful thought about all aspects of your choices. Gather as much specific information as possible, such as academic departments, typical academic courses, faculty, degree requirements, sample job descriptions, potential salary ranges for selected occupations, and employment outlook overviews, for each career area you are considering. This will increase your chances of making good decisions.

The academic curriculum you choose should be related to the job that you desire. Having subject matter expertise in a particular discipline is a requirement for most jobs in this field. For example, if you are planning a career in the tourism industry, you should orient your curriculum choices toward building fundamental skills in customer service, event planning, and managing businesses such as hotels, resorts, cruises, and casinos. However, many skills are generalizable and transferable across content areas, and mastery of these skills is key to having flexibility in your career.

Use Campus Career Services

Most colleges and universities provide free career development services by offering career programs, resources, and staff assistance to help you assess your career interests and assist in the job search process. **Campus career services** departments provide career advising, career-related job fairs and workshops, mock interview practice sessions, library and Internet resources, job listings, résumé and cover letter preparation, and in some cases, alumni mentorship and networking services.

Putting Your Best Face Forward

A virtual presence is almost impossible to avoid in this day and age. Although you may find posting party pictures or 'witty' comments on your social media sites fun, sometimes hiring managers see those comments, and this could cost you the job. The following are tips for using your Facebook, Twitter, Myspace, or other social media to your advantage:

- Consider your site an extension of your résumé. Use social media to show your activities that contribute to the community.
- Post a great profile picture. Make sure your head shot allows for eye contact with the viewer. This personalizes your profile.
- Make connections. If you are looking for information about a particular industry or company, post that as your status and see what your connections bring to you.
- Mention your Facebook page. Yes, go ahead. Talk about your Web presence. It lets employers know you are tech savvy.[3]
- Go deeper. Create your profile based on the "big five" personality traits: conscientiousness, emotional stability, agreeableness, extraversion, and openness to experience.
- Build your professional network. Be sure to "like" any pages that have to do with your field. This will get you noticed.

Technology and Career Preparation

Significant technological changes are occurring in society; in the recreation, parks, tourism, and leisure services fields; and in career preparation. **Technology** is changing not only the way we work but also the way we get jobs. Advancing technology and the popularity and growth of the Internet have created a new dimension in the job search process and the use of technology is now an essential resource in career preparation and job searching. With the introduction of the second generation of the World Wide Web in the past several years, social networking and dynamic websites are now replacing first-generation static websites. Social networking technologies and tools available today are completely unique and have expanded to include not only the Internet but also mobile phone technology:

> The tools of the networking trade are changing and moving online, where e-mail, IM, and social-networking websites such as LinkedIn, Facebook, and some specific to industry and careers are the means to make new contacts and interact with current ones.[2]

LinkedIn is a social networking website used mainly for professional networking in which members are allowed to maintain a list of contacts (contact network) whom they have invited to become a "connection." Users may search a specific company in hopes of finding individuals who are connected to other individuals they know. LinkedIn users may also upload their résumés and profiles as well as post their own photos to potential employers.

Although social networking may be an asset in your job search process, you must be careful and discreet in deciding what to post. A growing number of employers search potential candidates' social media sites to get a better glimpse of the individual. Protect your image and character by not posting anything on your site you would not want a prospective employer to see (i.e., derogatory comments, revealing photos, etc.).

Getting Involved:
Student and Professional Organizations

Being a member of a **student or professional organization or association** may be an important factor in the success and enjoyment of your college experience and later years as a professional in the field. Such bodies represent and promote the needs and interests of professional practitioners in a particular field or industry. In addition, they provide opportunities to their members for professional education and development, professional certification, and standards. The large number of professional associations for recreation and leisure services providers helps members understand and promote their profession and facilitates career development.

Although academic learning of theories and concepts is the primary goal of a college education, extracurricular activities associated with student and professional organizations help you learn, develop, and grow beyond the walls of the classroom. They may provide you with hands-on training and encourage continuing educational and professional development opportunities to better prepare you for your future career. Student and professional organizations also provide leadership opportunities. Being involved as an officer, committee member, presenter, or attendee at a local, state, or national conference, or just being an active member, may earn you acknowledgment from colleagues and professionals and give you the chance to gain leadership experience and distinguish yourself from the average student who only attends classes.

You may gain much from becoming a member of a student and professional organization. It looks impressive on your résumé, but far more valuable reasons exist for becoming actively involved while in college, which are discussed in the following sections.

Marketplace Resources

When it is time to start the job search process, you will have valuable job hunting resources available through professional organizations. Most organizations' websites provide marketplace resources such as job announcements and job alerts, résumé posting services, salary survey data, and other career and job resource tools.

Networking and Continuing Education

Student and professional organizations host meetings, seminars, regional and national conferences, and other events where you can interact with leaders and other professionals in the field. Most organizations provide a membership directory (either hard copy or Web version) that provides contact information for professionals in the association so that you can connect with peers in the association community and have them become a part of your professional network.

Updated Professional Information

Most associations provide journals, magazines, newsletters, or electronic mailing lists that offer up-to-date information on important trends and issues facing the field. Professional organizations give you firsthand access to great resources on the current state of your field.

Networking: Connecting With the Right People at the Right Time

Career planning is about making contacts and relationships. *Networking* is the formal term used to describe this process with people in the profession. It is a critical part of the career preparation and job search process and one of the most effective tools used in job hunting. "Approximately 80% of all job positions are filled without employer advertising."[4] These positions are filled by word of mouth, personal contacts, and referrals. Networking, then, is the key to tapping into jobs in the hidden job market. Trying to find a job without networking is difficult and frustrating. Start building relationships and a network as early as possible in your career planning process and academic program.

Getting involved with organizations and people who share your career interests may advance networking. It is never too late to start! Proper networking will help you achieve your personal and professional career goals by opening up new avenues for you to pursue. Take the time to brainstorm possible networking sources, and follow up on this list. Do not limit yourself geographically or be hesitant to talk to others about your skills and talents. Inform everyone you know that you are looking for employment (parents' friends, former high school and college classmates, religious leaders, your dentist and physician, neighbors, part-time work colleagues, professional acquaintances, etc.). Have confidence in yourself and your abilities to be a great professional in the field of recreation, park, and leisure services. Remember, networking is a lifelong process of building relationships to help you succeed in reaching your goals. The following resources will help you learn more about this important process:

Hansen, R. S. (n.d.). Networking your way to a new job. *Quintessential Careers*. Retrieved from http://www.quintcareers.com/networking_guide.html
This great article describes the various steps to successful networking in the job search process.

Admin. (2010, June 16). Networking techniques for job hunters. Retrieved from Distinctive Documents website: http://www.distinctiveweb.com/top.htm
This article outlines basic networking strategies to gain access to the hidden job market.

Doyle, A. (n.d.). Successful job search networking. Retrieved from About.com website: http://jobsearch.about.com/cs/networking/a/networking.htm
This article provides sample job search networking letters and other networking tips and provides ideas on how to approach networking contacts.

Hands-On Experience

Career-related opportunities provide hands-on experience to acquaint and familiarize you with the options in the recreation and leisure services field. In many cases, they offer a starting point for locating career and job opportunities. These hands-on opportunities allow you to contribute and excel outside of the formal classroom. Job shadowing, part-time work, summer jobs, volunteering, and internships build self-confidence and maturity and equip you with specialized skills, as well as transferable skills, that are important in today's workplace. These opportunities tremendously impact your career direction and the job search process when you complete your academic degree. Informational interviews and job shadowing generally only take from 30 minutes to a few days. Part-time jobs, career-related volunteering, and internships may last a summer, several semesters, or even longer. Prospective employers are focusing more on work experiences (both paid and volunteer) as a way to screen and assess candidates' skills and abilities before they consider them for a position.

Job Shadowing

Job shadowing is a career exploration strategy that is great for high school and college students. Many colleges have formal job shadowing programs that involve spending a period of time with an expert in the field, observing firsthand what that professional does on a daily basis, what the working environment is like, and with whom (customers, clients, participants, etc.) he or she daily interacts. By taking advantage of job shadowing opportunities, you will observe the workplace culture and environment and obtain a behind-the-scenes look at the day-to-day operations. This information and experience may help you immensely to decide upon a first career.

Part-Time Work

Part-time work during college is valuable for several reasons. First, and most obvious, with the cost of college education increasing every year, additional financial support is always welcome! In addition to earning extra money, you will learn responsibility, work ethic, and lessons about the real world. These experiences may be beneficial in acquiring job skills, self-management skills, and transferable skills (i.e., budgeting, meeting deadlines, project planning, supervision, leadership, people skills, etc.) that can be transferred from one job, or even one career, to another. Being able to include these on your résumé or discuss them during a job interview will enhance your position in the job search process.

Summer Jobs

Working at a **summer job** is an excellent opportunity to pursue an area of career interest and to learn and experience the daily operation of a particular organization or agency, not to mention a chance to earn extra money for school! A number of summer jobs in recreation and leisure services exist at national, state, and local levels in parks, hotels/resorts, camps, YMCA/YWCA, theme parks, health and fitness centers, local pools and regional theme water parks, and commercial recreation venues, to mention a few.

Volunteer Opportunities

Volunteering your time and service is a great way to gain experience and learn more specifics about a particular career field or interest that you may want to pursue. It also demonstrates your enthusiasm and potential leadership skills for the field. Serving as a volunteer provides exposure to a work setting and the people and job tasks that are associated with this career setting. In addition, the knowledge, skills, and experience that you acquire as a volunteer will enhance your résumé and marketability when you pursue full-time employment. Involvement with organizations outside of the classroom and paid work responsibilities provide insight into potential employers of the type of person you are and how you may contribute to their organization in the future. Volunteering at events is an excellent way to network with industry professionals while gaining practical experience.

Internships

An **internship** as defined by the National Association of Colleges and Employers is

a form of experiential learning that integrates knowledge and theory learned in the classroom with practical application and skills development in a professional setting. Internships give students the opportunity to gain valuable applied experience and make connections in professional fields they are considering for career paths; and give employers the opportunity to guide and evaluate talent.[5]

It is a capstone hands-on experience, usually completed in the senior year of college, where a student has the opportunity to apply theories and concepts learned in the classroom to real-world work situations to gain and develop career-specific skills and experience.

Internships vary greatly from one agency or organization to the next. Traditionally, a sponsoring recreation, park, and leisure services agency works with the student to meet specific learning goals and outcomes that the student and his or her university faculty adviser have developed and provides special mentoring or contact/networking opportunities. In exchange, the student intern agrees to assist the employer in meeting the specific department or programming needs in a variety of roles and responsibilities. Internships may be paid or unpaid, with or without academic credit, and completed in 1 semester, 2 semesters, a 14-week summer session, 1 year, and so forth. Having completed an internship experience prior to graduation gives you an edge over other candidates in a competitive job market. In many cases, organizations offer a full-time position to a successful intern.

Selecting Your Internship

The best way to approach the selection process is to treat the internship as if it were a full-time position. Research, preparation, and follow-through, essential in the job search process, are also important elements that may make the difference in having a successful and enjoyable internship experience.

Once you have researched and identified the career setting that you are interested in pursuing, you should be ready to write specific internship objectives that will guide you through the search and selection process. You will notice that the possibilities are numerous and vary in degree of duties and responsibilities, so you want to examine these carefully to have a meaningful internship experience that meets your needs and wants.

In researching possible internship agencies, your faculty internship coordinator will play a significant role in the selection process and may provide valuable information about agencies that have hosted quality internships in the past. Collect as much information as possible about agencies that may host interns to see whether that agency fits your particular needs. Seek leads from faculty, friends, family, alumni, and students just completing their internship. Contact employers in your field of study to see whether they have an existing internship program or inquire whether they would be willing to discuss the possibility of an internship. Review your informational interviews to see whether they have any suggestions or leads.

> "
> Millennials may care a lot more about a satisfying job experience, inspiring culture and quality relationships than rewards-based motivation.
> —*Forbes*[6]
> "

After you have collected your agency information and before making a decision to apply for an internship, ask yourself specific questions regarding the internship experience. Example questions include the following:

- When do you want to intern? Fall, spring, or summer semester?
- Where do you want to work? What city, state, region of the country?
- Do you need to live at home or in close proximity, or do you have family or friends in other parts of the country with whom you may live?
- How much money do you need to make during the internship? Would the agency or university allow you to combine an unpaid internship with a part-time job?
- What are the specific duties and responsibilities of the internship?
- What is the probability that the agency will offer you a position upon completing the internship?

Certifications and Licenses

Professional associations grant credentials such as **certifications and licenses** to individuals who can demonstrate knowledge, problem-solving abilities, willingness to learn, and expertise in any given field. Certifications and licenses ensure that professionals are qualified and can meet approved standards of performance. During the certification process, an individual voluntarily submits his or her credentials to a board for review of competencies, criteria, or standards that the certifying agency has identified. Some careers (i.e., therapeutic recreation) will require individuals to possess a particular certification before employment.

The National Recreation and Park Association suggests the following reasons to become a certified professional:

- greater career opportunities and advancement
- demonstration of your commitment to the park and recreation profession
- enhanced quality of park and recreation services nationwide
- recognition of your accomplishments and ability to meet national standards
- expansion of your skills and knowledge through continuing professional development[7]

One of the leading and most recognized recreation certification programs in recreation, park, and leisure services for beginning to mid-level professionals is the Certified Park and Recreation Professional (CPRP) credential, administered by the National Recreation and Park Association and governed by the National Certification Board. The National Recreation and Park Association also offers the Aquatic Facility Operator (AFO) certification for pool operators and aquatic facility managers and the Certified Playground Safety Inspector (CPSI) for individuals who inspect playgrounds for safety-related issues. The National Council for Therapeutic Recreation Certification provides an independent certification, the Certified Therapeutic Recreation Specialist (CTRS), for professionals who work with people with mental and physical disabilities as well as the elderly. Many other specialty certifications are available in recreation, park, and leisure services.

Earning certification credentials alerts prospective employers that, in addition to earning your academic degree, you have been tested by a national certification board on related professional topics and have shown your dedication to your chosen profession through voluntary certification. Increasingly, employers are including certifications as a desirable (in some cases, a must-have) part of candidates' career portfolios. Regardless of what your particular area of career interest, speak with your academic faculty and practitioners in the field to determine what credentials are necessary and advantageous for you to possess, and get them.

Job Search Strategies

The **job search** is the culmination of integrating and applying all that you learned during the career planning and exploration phases. It involves a systematic plan that consists of portfolios, résumés, cover letters, interviews, and job offers. Organizing your portfolio, creating your résumé, developing a well-written cover letter, and practicing for job interviews are necessary for you to succeed in the job search process.

Portfolios/Electronic Portfolios

A career **portfolio** is an excellent job search tool that is used to capture your skills, abilities, and accomplishments. "A portfolio goes well beyond a cover letter and the traditional résumé. It is a portable means of storing, tracking, and presenting samples (known as artifacts) illustrating candidates' skills and achievements."[8] The portfolio is an honest self-reflection of your current knowledge, skills, abilities, and experiences and is accomplished by gathering examples of your work and other documents that would support these accomplishments. Portfolios generally include the following sections or categories:

- education
- résumé
- reference letters
- professional training including proof of all training certificates, licenses, certifications, workshops/seminars, or specific courses such as first aid, CPR, WSI, and so forth
- conferences you have attended
- thank-you letters from an association, customer, and/or participant that appreciated your assistance
- letters of recommendation or testimonials

- articles/publications/presentations you have written for a professional publication
- in-house publications (i.e., health tips, etc.) or news releases related to a program or special event that you coordinated or hosted
- past or current job descriptions that outline duties and levels of responsibility
- performance appraisals
- academic projects or other samples of work that you completed while in college that showcase your talents and/or competence

> The 9 to 5 job may soon be a relic of the past, if Millennials have their way. A slow climb in a company was once the accepted career path. However, today the experiences of men and women starting their careers are closer to juggling multiple positions than steady growth.
>
> Freelancing and self-employment are on the rise. Meanwhile, 60% of Millennials are leaving their companies in less than three years. Reports indicate three roots to Millennials' discontent: the drives for flexibility, purposeful labor and economic security.
>
> —*Forbes*[10]

Although the portfolio is a collection of your documents, or artifacts, the electronic portfolio (also known as an ePortfolio, e-portfolio, efolio, digital portfolio, or webfolio) is basically an electronic version of a paper-based portfolio.

An ePortfolio (electronic portfolio) is an electronic collection of evidence that shows your learning journey over time....Evidence may include writing samples, photos, videos, research projects, observations by mentors and peers, and/or reflective thinking. The key aspect of an ePortfolio is your reflection on the evidence, such as why it was chosen and what you learned from the process of developing your ePortfolio.[9]

Résumés

A **résumé** is a summary of your professional and personal experiences that introduces you to a potential employer. The main purpose of the résumé is to get your foot in the door of an agency so that they will be interested in personally interviewing you for the job. In most cases, the résumé does not get you the job; it is at the interview that the job is won. However, the résumé is usually the first impression that an employer has of you. It may be a deciding factor on whether you remain in the pool of qualified applicants, so create, design, and organize your résumé in a professional manner. Most important, résumés should be skills-based and clearly reflect your particular skills and accomplishments and how you have excelled and mastered these skills.

The common résumé formats are chronological, functional, and combination. The chronological format is the most popular format and is a chronological listing of employment and employment-related experiences including specific employer names, locations, and dates of employment. The functional format highlights skills, experience, and accomplishments and is organized by functions or skills and qualifications rather than by employer and dates of employment. The last format is the combination format, which features a combination of functional attributes and includes a chronological listing of employment, education, and related experiences. Choose the format that best displays and showcases your strengths and accomplishments.

Regardless of the résumé format that you choose, you should be using a number of basic principles to write your résumé, including the following:

- Be brief but targeted. One to three pages is an acceptable length of a résumé, especially for undergraduate students.
- Include basic content such as name, current and/or permanent address, telephone number (both landline and cell), and e-mail address.
- More specific required content includes education, professional employment experiences (both paid and volunteer), honors, awards, licenses and certifications, and professional memberships.
- Optional content includes job objective, presentations and publications, community activities, references, and special skills, hobbies, and interests.
- Use measurable outcomes and numerical values that may enhance your qualifications and accomplishments.
- Use carefully selected and appropriate action verbs when describing your work experience and job responsibilities.

Your résumé should always be consistent with expectations of professionals in the field, free of spelling and grammatical errors, and above all, honest. Last, your résumé should always be up to date and mirror your personal and professional development. As you grow professionally by gaining skills and experiences, so should your résumé.

Cover Letters

Cover letters are a great way to introduce and personalize your résumé and target your skills. They provide an opportunity for the employer to gain more insight into your interest in their position and for you to highlight and explain specific experiences and accomplishments that reinforce your strengths for the position that may not be evident in your résumé. A cover letter, as with the résumé, should be free of spelling and grammatical errors and usually is only one page in length. Your cover letter should be addressed to a specific person that is responsible for conducting the review process for this position. If you do not know the specific name of the person to receive your application material, search the Web for the agency or call the agency for further clarification.

The cover letter gives you an opportunity to direct the reader to your specific qualifications that meet their needs and to explain why you are interested in this particular job and agency. The content of the letter should include

- a brief introductory paragraph of who you are, how you learned of the position opening, and why you are writing;
- a second paragraph highlighting your experience and education that makes you an ideal candidate for the position;
- a third paragraph explaining in more detail your interests and motivation as to why you are interested in the position and agency and how your credentials meet their specific needs; and
- a final paragraph to be proactive and structure future follow-up steps on your part.

Interviewing

Although a well-written résumé and cover letter are essential in the job search process, the **job interview** is what will make or break your chance of being selected for the position. Employers use a number of job interview types, such as telephone screening, in-person screening, peer group interviews, luncheon interviews, stress interviews, and video conferencing. Regardless of the interview type that you may experience, employers are looking for your communication skills, confidence, personality, accomplishments, and knowledge about the field and their particular organization. On the other hand, remember that the interview is a two-way street. It is also your opportunity to learn more about the organization and how you may fit in this work environment.

The following are general pointers that may help you succeed at the interview:

- Be prepared. Research the organization prior to the interview.
- Always be on time by arriving 10 to 15 minutes prior to your scheduled interview.
- Dress appropriately by selecting clothing appropriate to the job for which you are applying.
- Communicate your best image by highlighting your experiences and accomplishments.
- Demonstrate your enthusiasm, excitement, and positive attitude for the position for which you are interviewing as well as the field.
- Handle difficult questions by giving direct and honest answers.
- Follow up in writing by sending a thank-you letter or note to each person with whom you interviewed.

Conclusion

The career planning process suggested in this chapter is exciting and interesting, and it will require a substantial amount of work for you to succeed. Although no single path exists to securing a job, you must know how to present yourself to potential employers in a positive light. The first step in the process is to complete an honest self-assessment (both personally and professionally) so that you can identify and match your skills and interests with occupations in the field. Once this is done, investigating student and professional organizations is a good place to begin developing a professional network. Acquiring practical hands-on opportunities is essential in familiarizing and gaining experience with the occupations in recreation, park, and leisure services. Job shadowing, part-time work, summer jobs, volunteering, and internships build your self-confidence and establish your credentials. Last, the job search is the culmination of the entire career planning process and consists of developing and maintaining your portfolio, creating a résumé, writing personalized cover letters, interviewing with potential employers, and then receiving the ultimate prize—a job offer!

Further Investigation

For More Research

1. Develop a career action plan for the remainder of your undergraduate academic career. As a part of this plan, describe your overall career goals, develop a realistic timeline for meeting these goals, and reflect on how internships, part-time jobs, or volunteer work may help you in your action plan. In addition, list the agencies or organizations for which you may work as well as the resources that you will need to reach your goals.
2. Write a reflective essay on the career setting in the recreation, park, and leisure services industry for which you may be interested in working (municipal parks and recreation, military MWR, campus recreation, YMCA/YWCA, etc.). Describe your current leadership style and reflect on how this style may be beneficial for this particular setting. Explore additional qualifications that are needed to be a successful leader or employee in this setting. Describe the steps that you would take to ensure that you are meeting these qualifications.
3. Describe how you will establish a professional network as you begin the job search process.
4. Create an overall career timeline for the next 5 to 10 years and strategies to keep you on track during this timeframe.

Active Investigation

1. Research professional organizations and associations that are prominent in your chosen career. Obtain and complete a membership application form for one or two of these professional associations. You are not required to apply for membership in the association but are strongly encouraged to do so.

2. Create a "One-Minute Career Elevator Pitch." Imagine yourself in an elevator where you meet a potential employer. The employer introduces himself or herself to you and asks you the proverbial question: "So tell me a little about yourself." You have approximately 60 seconds to tell your story! In completing this assignment, write down answers to the following questions:

   a. Who are you? Include your name, university attending, major, etc.
   b. What are you really good at, and why are you so are passionate about your career or job opportunity at this agency?
   c. What are the strengths that you could bring to this potential employer.
   d. Close with a hook or memorable tagline that will stay with the employer when he or she leaves the elevator.

3. Design and create your personal résumé. After you write your résumé, write a sample cover letter that you would send with your résumé in response to a newspaper ad or an online announcement of a job in which you are interested, a cold call cover letter to an employer, a networking letter, and a follow-up interview thank-you letter.

4. Research two agencies or organizations that you would be interested in pursuing as a career opportunity. Gather as much information about the agency or organization that you think would be relevant in determining whether they would fit with your career aspirations. Develop three to five questions to ask during an interview with them.

Recommended Reading

Bolles, R. N. (2013). *What color is your parachute?* Berkeley, CA: Ten Speed Press.
A practical manual for job hunters and career changers that has been annually updated for the past 40 years and is still considered one of the bestselling job hunting and career planning books with its step-by-step plan and guide in mastering the career planning process.

Bolles, M. E., & Bolles, R. N. (2011). *What color is your parachute? Guide to job-hunting online: Career sites, cover letters, gateways, getting interviews, job search engines, mobile apps, networking, niche sites, posting resumes, research sites, and more* (6th ed.). Berkeley, CA: Ten Speed Press.
A desktop guide that helps job seekers navigate the overwhelming amount of information available on the Internet to find the most useful sites and avoid common pitfalls. In addition, the book includes hundreds of annotated website recommendations geared to the job search process.

Bureau of Labor Statistics. (2013). Occupational outlook handbook, 2012–2013. Retrieved from http://www.bls.gov/OCO/
This website provides excellent job search tips, links to information about the job market in each state, as well as the training and education needed, earnings, expected job prospects, what workers do on the job, and working conditions for hundreds of jobs.

Kessler, R. (2012). *Competency-based interviews: How to master the tough interview style used by the Fortune 500s.* Pompton Plains, NJ: Career Press.
Clear and easy-to-use information and methods are shared to help job interviewers feel comfortable prior to and during an actual interview. A useful book that provides insights into today's world of job interviewing.

Labovich, L. M., & Salpeter, M. (2012). *100 conversations for career success: Learn to network, cold call, and tweet your way to your dream job!* New York, NY: LearningExpress.
Another book that is full of practical, effective, and easy-to-follow examples for career success. Provides an excellent chapter on how to make connections on LinkedIn.

Levinson, J. C., & Perry, D. E. (2011). *Guerrilla marketing for job hunters 3.0: How to stand out from the crowd and tap into the hidden job market using social media and 999 other tactics today*. Hoboken, NJ: John Wiley and Sons.
This book is filled with many practical ideas, tips, and insights into the job search process. Innovative and up-to-date information is provided on how to be proactive and assertive in the process.

Pollack, L. (2012). *Getting from college to career*. New York, NY: HarperCollins.
Good information on how to get your foot in the door and how to stand apart from other job seekers.

Reeves, E. G. (2009). *Can I wear my nose ring to the interview?* New York, NY: Workman.
Written in an upbeat, positive, and nonintimidating style, this book serves as a good starting point that offers numerous practical suggestions and advice for new job hunters or college grads in the job search process from start to finish.

Ross, C. M., Beggs, B. A., & Young, S. J. (2010). *Mastering the job search process in recreation and leisure services* (2nd ed.). Sudbury, MA: Jones and Bartlett.
This book guides readers just starting out in the field of recreation and leisure services through each step of the job search process, from both an employer's and applicant's point of view. Chapters cover researching an organization, portfolios, cover letters and résumés, interviews, internships, and navigating the transition from college to professional life.

Salvador, E. U. (2011). *Step-by-step resumes: Build an outstanding resume in 10 easy steps!* (2nd ed.) Indianapolis, IN: JIST Publishing.
This book provides an excellent and comprehensive step-by-step method in creating a résumé and provides a number of practical and strategic tips.

Yate, M. (2013). *Knock 'em dead secrets & strategies for first-time job seekers*. Avon, MA: Adams Media.
Practical methods and strategies for finding a new job or new career and a must book for undergraduate students who want to achieve success in the job search process.

Recommended Career and Job Search Websites

CareerBuilder: www.careerbuilder.com
CareerBuilder offers both online and print networks to help job seekers connect with 9,000 employer career websites including 140 newspapers.

CollegeGrad: www.collegegrad.com
This career website provides information on résumé writing, networking, job searching, and so forth for entry-level job searches conducted by college students and recent grads.

JobInterview.net: www.jobinterview.net
This excellent site provides interview questions and answers, job interview tips, various interview techniques, and sample questions to ask the employer during a job interview.

JobStar Central: jobstar.org
JobStar is a public library–sponsored guide for job seekers including résumés, cover letters, salary surveys, and career selection.

Monster: www.monster.com
Monster is one of the largest employment websites in the world and is the largest global job search engine with over 1 million job postings at any given time.

National Association of Colleges and Employers: www.naceweb.org
This site offers career and job search advice for new college graduates as well as updated salary surveys for new graduates.

Quintessential Careers: www.quintcareers.com
Various job search tools are provided, including expert advice, career articles, and some of the best job sites on the Web.

Riley Guide: rileyguide.com
This site is one of the oldest and most comprehensive directories of career and employment resources available online and provides a guide to the best the Internet has to offer for job search and career information.

USAJobs: www.usajobs.gov
This is the official job site of the U.S. federal government and a one-stop source for federal jobs and employment information.

WetFeet: wetfeet.com
WetFeet provides insightful profiles of companies, careers, and industries to guide job seekers toward finding the right career and the right job.

References

[1]Bureau of Labor Statistics. (2012, July 25). Number of jobs held, labor market activity, and earnings growth among the youngest baby boomers: Results from a longitudinal survey [News release]. Retrieved from http://www.bls.gov/news.release/nlsoy.nr0.htm

[2]Fogarty, K. (2009). Can you Facebook your way to a new job? Retrieved on March 5, 2013, from The Ladders website: https://cdn.theladders.net/static/pdf/socialnetworkingThree.pdf

[3]Levin-Epstein, A. (2011, March). Facebook & your job: 5 ways to get hired. *CBS News*. Retrieved from http://www.cbsnews.com/news/facebook-your-job-5-ways-to-get-hired/

[4]JobStar Central. (2013). Hidden job market - What is it? Retrieved March 2, 2013, from http://jobstar.org/hidden/hidden.php

[5]National Association of Colleges and Employer. (2012). NACE position statement on U.S. internships: A definition and criteria to assess opportunities and determine the implications for compensations. Retrieved March 2, 2013, from http://www.naceweb.org/connections/advocacy/internship_position_paper

[6]Strauss, K. (2013, September). Do millennials think differently about money and career? *Forbes*. Retrieved from http://www.forbes.com/sites/karstenstrauss/2013/09/17/do-millennials-think-differently-about-money-and career/

[7]National Recreation and Park Association. (2013). Certification programs. Retrieved February 26, 2013, from http://www.nrpa.org/certification/

[8]Ross, C. M., Beggs, B. A., & Young, S. J. (2010). *Mastering the job search process in recreation and leisure services* (2nd ed.). Sudbury, MA: Jones and Bartlett.

[9]Barrett, H. C. (2011). Balancing the two faces of eportfolios. In S. Hirtz & K. Kelly (Eds.), *Education for a digital world 2.0: Innovations in education* (2nd ed.). British Columbia, Canada: BC Ministry of Education and OpenSchool BC.

[10]Taylor, K. (2013, August). Why millennials are ending the 9 to 5. *Forbes*. Retrieved from http://www.forbes.com/sites/katetaylor/2013/08/23/why-millennials-are-ending the 9-to-5/

" *Students are entering a vastly different world now from that even just 10 or 15 years ago. Today's new park and recreation professionals have been told they can do anything, and they want to make an immediate impact.*

—Douglas Viara
Author
Parks & Recreation Magazine "

15

Forces Shaping the Future

James Murphy
San Francisco State University

Daniel Dustin
University of Utah

Focus Questions

Q: How does the **Flat World Paradigm**[1] relate to recreation, parks, sport management, hospitality, and tourism?

A: We live in a global environment created by the convergence of technological and political forces with a Web-enabled playing field that allows for multiple forms of collaboration without regard to geography, distance, or even language. As the global playing field flattens, this new landscape will require all service sectors to respond quickly to change. Leaders will need to become more technologically savvy and conscious of ever-changing preferences fueled by multiple constituent groups that will continually evolve with the ability to influence the direction of change.

Q: In light of the rapidity of high-speed change and the impact of technology on all aspects of our lives, what is the implication of virtual technology for the delivery of recreation, parks, sport management, hospitality, and tourism services?

A: We live in a world of **real** and **virtual leisure**. Fewer mass trends will encompass all of society because everyone has (or will have) at their disposal, literally in the palm of their hands, a portable, compact portal to the world. This empowers each of us to experience real life and virtual events and to become connected with people next door, down the street, across the nation, and globally, almost instantaneously. Virtual leisure experiences may improve our quality of life or they may detract from it. Technology is neither good nor bad; however, the quality of our leisure experiences may depend on how we use technology.

Q: How does the increasing emergence of diversity in North America complicate and/or extend leisure expression?

A: We live in an increasingly multicultural society. The challenge for leisure services professionals is to embrace subcultural, racial, ethnic, and lifestyle differences that continue to represent a greater proportion of the population mix rendering Anglo-Saxon, heterosexual, Judeo-Christian majority perspectives less of an overriding influence in setting community norms, mores, and institutional structures.

Q: How does the concept of sustainability influence recreation, parks, sport management, hospitality, and tourism?

A: Leisure services professionals will be called on to lead the charge by serving as role models and stewards of the planet's biodiversity through sustainable practices.

Q: How will a future filled with ambiguity and uncertainty influence a career in leisure services?

A: It will be incumbent on future recreation, parks, sport management, hospitality, and tourism professionals to be flexible, adaptable, inquisitive, at times "in the moment," and open to change. They should provide leisure-related guidance to their constituents while also managing their own work–life balance. Leisure services professionals should serve as role models by demonstrating how active, leisure-centered lifestyles improve quality of life.

Key Terms

Flat World Paradigm	Digital Age
Virtual leisure	Social media
Real leisure	For-benefit
Sustainability	Microtargeting
Macro trends	Transformational leisure
Micro trends	Collaborative, boundary-free
Pluralistic	Servant leaders
Green	Environmental and social justice
Carbon footprint	Advocacy
Augmented Reality Technology (ART)	Deep recreation

Forces Shaping the Future

Recreation, parks, sport management, hospitality, and tourism professionals have never been in a better position to make a positive difference in the world locally, regionally, nationally, and globally. Revenues generated from leisure services continue to increase across the planet, and in the United States, there is increasing pressure to set aside and protect more natural areas for recreation-related purposes. Local governments and nonprofit agencies are fast becoming the focal point for enhancing quality of life for communities and for promoting the sustainable use of resources. The second and third decades of the 21st century promise to be exciting and profitable for the continued growth of careers in recreation, parks, sport management, hospitality, and tourism.

Any attempt to map the future will inevitably fall short of what will occur. The world is changing at such a rapid pace that we barely have time to embrace advancing technology, new societal structures, and emerging values or to adapt and adjust our personal and professional lives. However, we know change is inevitable, and the pace of change is occuring at a faster clip.

In this chapter, we will first discuss five **macro trends** that will likely shape institutions and everyday life in the context of leisure:

- increasing diversity,
- concern for sustainability,
- promoting health and wellness,
- accelerated pace of change and new technologies, and
- the emergence of a fourth leisure services delivery sector.

We will then discuss five **micro trends** that may be even more influential than the macro trends:

- increase in individual and nature-based sports,
- smartphones,
- homeschooling,
- slowing down, and
- linguistically isolated households.

Micro trends are caused by increasing freedom, the prevalence of individual choice, and connectivity, all of which serve to buoy many kindred small, intense subgroups who aspire for more personally relevant forms of leisure expression. Toward the end of the chapter, we will discuss the significant implications these macro and micro trends have for the delivery of leisure services. Finally, we will conclude with you, the future recreation, parks, sport management, hospitality, and tourism professional, and the values you bring to the profession.

Macro Trends

Increasing Diversity

Increasingly, recreation, parks, sport management, hospitality, and tourism professionals must work within a **pluralistic** leisure services delivery framework that recognizes and accepts differences as well as embraces and honors racial, ethnic, and gendered lifestyles within overarching community and national perspectives.

Community life in North America will continue to be transformed in the years ahead by an influx of immigrants. Leisure services professionals will play a critical role in creating a welcoming environment for community members, particularly immigrant groups. This is not a new mandate. At the beginning of the 21st century, "more than 60% of the net increase in minority population growth was due to immigration, with over 75% of the U.S. immigration originating from Asia and Latin America."[2] What is changing is how important it is for leisure professionals to know more about how leisure contributes to a sense of place and community. Equally important is the understanding of how leisure has positive and negative impacts where communities are forming and restructuring due to immigration. In this regard, recreation, parks, sport management, hospitality, and tourism professionals have a part to play in easing global tensions. "Ethnic tensions and conflict occurring in the U.S., Europe, and other parts of the world show there are opportunities for race and ethnicity research to explore how leisure contributes to social conflict and community cohesion."[3] Leisure services have the potential to divide or unite us. In their ideal state, they serve as the glue that holds diverse communities together.

The leisure services profession has been "sensitive to diversity and committed to inclusion for decades."[4] According to Balmer, "demand complexity will continue to expand and become a game changer in the way we think about and deliver facilities, parks, programs, community building and other services."[5] Understanding this trend is crucial for our profession because throughout North America ethnic and culturally diverse communities have been growing rapidly. The 2010 U.S. census revealed startling trends that demonstrate how diverse our society has become:

- By 2019, no single racial or ethnic group will be a majority.
- The United States will become a plurality nation, and although non-Hispanic whites will remain the largest single group, no group will be in the majority.
- By 2060, the population aged 65 and over will represent 1 in 5 citizens. The "oldest old," those aged 85 and older, will triple in population from 5.9 million to 18.2 million.
- The number of Hispanic citizens will more than double. Nearly 1 in 3 Americans will be Hispanic compared to 1 in 6 today.
- The Asian population will more than double, reaching 34 million (8.2% of the population).
- Black citizens will increase from 41 million to 62 million (14.7% of the population).[6]

Future recreation, parks, sport management, hospitality, and tourism professionals will need to provide safe havens where all people in the community can recreate and to work to reduce racial and ethnic disparities in access to parks and other forms of leisure expression. As the field's professional makeup reflects more closely that of the overall population in any given community, more opportunities will be available for individuals from varied cultural, racial, and ethnic backgrounds to collaborate with community members to determine the leisure services and organizations most relevant to ensuring a high quality of life for all.

Concern for Sustainability

Leisure services have to become increasingly **green**. While sponsoring a myriad of activities and events, and while providing facilities, buildings, and natural areas that use a considerable amount of energy, we must minimize our **carbon footprint** and increase efficiency and cost savings. Dustin, Bricker, and Schwab warned that "the increasing divide between humans and nature jeopardizes our health in significant ways."[7] At the same time, they envisioned a future when "the individual, through a healthier lifestyle, reduces his or her carbon footprint on the larger world, while the larger world reciprocates with cleaner air, cleaner water, and an abundance of health-restoring properties."[8]

Balmer added optimistically that we are seeing a more permanent shift in lifestyle expressions toward

- conscious choice to move toward voluntary simplicity, downward mobility, and small indulgences;
- a shift to home-based, affordable leisure;
- consumptive forms of recreation falling into disfavor as energy becomes more costly, the desire to protect natural areas increases, discretionary income decreases, and pressure to restrict tax increases persists;
- dramatic shifts in tourism behavior related to all of the above, resulting in a further blending of the recreation and tourism/vacation marketplace; and
- rapid growth of lifestyles of health and sustainability.[9]

Partnering with other professions, the recreation, parks, sport management, hospitality, and tourism profession will be expected to conserve the biodiversity of the planet. A healthy earth is essential to many forms of leisure experience, so "threats to biodiversity and the consequences of its losses, including the obvious ecological consequences, as well as the impact on aesthetic, ethical, sociological, and economical aspects of our world, reveal the reality of our dependence on a healthy planet."[10] Leisure services professionals will need to understand that these relationships extend from the global level to the local level. The phrase "think globally, act locally" encourages everyone to consider the health and well-being of the planet as they take action in their local communities. Our profession will be at the forefront of teaching the public that leisure pursuits, as with any other human activity, may have positive or negative effects on the ecosystem as a whole. Imploring our constituents to act for the greater good requires that we become aware of how our actions are intertwined with and are interdependent on all other living systems.

Improving Health and Wellness

Concurrent with the "greening" of recreation, parks, sport management, hospitality, and tourism is the recognition that leisure expression, physical engagement, and participation in community life improve physical, mental, emotional, and spiritual health. Opportunities for all community members to experience natural settings must thus be seen as an essential right. To this end, leisure services providers should foster healthy living, particularly for urban populations who often lead sedentary lives. "Our physical, mental, and emotional well-being can be improved by walking, hiking, biking, climbing, running rivers, skiing, snowboarding, and snowshoeing,"[11] to name a handful of health-promoting leisure pastimes. Preventing health problems such as asthma and obesity is less expensive (and more fun!) than paying for costly medical treatment. Recreation, parks, sport management, hospitality, and tourism providers must advocate for recreation to be embraced as part of a comprehensive health promotion strategy. Service providers need to recognize that low-income, racial, and ethnic minority populations typically have less access than other population groups to parks and open spaces. We must work collaboratively with other community, regional, state, and federal partners to assure more equitable availability of, access to, and quality of recreation resources for everyone.[12]

Accelerated Pace of Change and New Technologies

We cannot predict the future with precision, but we know that change will continue rolling toward us at a faster and faster pace. Many social institutions (e.g., churches, schools, workplaces, families) do not provide sufficient clarification and assistance for people to decipher and decode forewarnings indicating that changes are upon us. Messages that represent change, even when conveyed via the Internet, social network sites, cell phones, or smartphones, often leave people baffled. They increasingly rely on their internal barometers to gauge the meaning of changes that appear in their daily lives. For example, **Augmented Reality Technology (ART)** is emerging as a tool for interacting with the world. It layers virtual imagery and information over a real-world environment. ART provides information on objects, locations, and people automatically as they pop up in real time. The technology is conveyed through smartphones that leverage Global Positioning Systems data, digital compasses, cameras, and wireless connections. In essence, "everything you carry will have much more awareness about where it is and what's around it, whether you are interested or not."[13]

Technology has dramatically changed the way people communicate. "Today Americans on average, spend more working time communicating and using media devices such as television, radios, MP3 devices, and Smartphones, than any other activities."[14] According to the PEW Interest and Life Project, mobility changes the way individuals interact with one another.[15] People expect to always have broadband on, or always be connected—whether riding in the subway, jogging along a city street, or hiking in a national park. As McLean and Hurd observed,[16] the smartphone is an example of how technology has affected individuals, families, work, and communities. As recently as 2002, a cell phone was primarily a phone. Today's smartphones have replaced cell phones and digital handheld devices and expanded their services. Many people continue to use a cell phone primarily as a phone, but many more use it to send and receive e-mail; or as a note taker, camera, video recorder, calendar, alarm clock, or timer; or to play music, read books, access navigation, and connect to online services such as social media sites, news, entertainment, or sports updates. With advanced on-screen technology, this is possible with the touch of a finger.

Balmer addressed the revolutionary changes that have resulted from the tools and toys of the information age.[17] He noted dramatic change in both personal leisure experiences and how recreation, parks, sport management, hospitality, and tourism will be driven in the future. **Digital Age** leisure will be shaped by a convergence of suppliers and distributors under single ownership (television, movies, music, and gaming are seamlessly combining to drive new entertainment). For example, before visiting a national park you could download your choice of apps that will act as a personal tour guide for your visit. Technological advances bring more information and services to our homes or vehicles through a single device and link us to social networking and an ever-growing array of free or low-cost resources, entertainment (music, movies, books), and interactive gaming that bring virtual reality to us wherever we are. The provision of virtual leisure services by both major (e.g., Microsoft) and niche (e.g., a New Delhi–based yoga studio) suppliers in direct competition with traditional local providers could result in abrupt shifts in leisure behavior and service expectations.

As detailed in Table 15.1, Balmer envisioned eight essential shifts in the way people will view their lives and in the way their expectations will be shaped through the influence of the Digital Age. People want a product that meets their specifications; they expect excellent, timely personal service; and they want it delivered quickly to the location of their choice. People will comment on their satisfaction and dissatisfaction, pressuring providers to keep their products and services top-notch so they will not lose their customer base to other providers. Service providers who make their core values highly visible and align their values with those of their customers will be the most successful. For example, Netflix had the major market share in online movie screening until they made a critical error—raising prices dramatically without informing their customers or giving them choices. Overnight dozens of new providers sprang up to fill the needs of customers that dropped Netflix in droves in search of better, lower cost service.

Recreation, parks, sport management, hospitality, and tourism professionals will have to be adept at dealing with instantaneous communication in a world without borders and provide insight, clarity, and even wisdom to their colleagues and constituents about how to live and thrive in the future. The 21st century leisure services professional will need to be especially focused on using technology to promote and advocate for removal of inequities in services via **social media** (Facebook, YouTube, Twitter, custom applications, Wikipedia, Blogs, etc.), which will be as important as face-to-face expertise in working with community members.

Table 15.1 *Digital Age Behaviors*	
Immediate	The online population demands current information and immediate gratification. If you take too long to provide what they want, they have already moved on (without explanation). Speed is of the essence.
Customized	We expect service providers to do their utmost to tweak their product to our needs. We cluster in the mass niches to provide economy of scale. We have access to 6 million customized music channels and await similar satisfaction in other areas. We demand the freedom to choose and expect others to support our freedom of expression.
Flexible	We have grown accustomed to last-minute planning, to facilitating immediate spontaneous gatherings online, and to seeing social movements explode in less than a week.
Free	We have shared music, video, movies, blogs, news, and so forth among ourselves at no cost. We gravitate to free services and are tolerant of inexpensive add-ons. We expect the world to become open source.

(cont.)

Table 15.1 (cont.)	
Interactive	We want to be heard and to influence. We have learned consumer advocacy.
Participatory	We want to participate in online critique of almost everything. As network members and consumers, we expect to codevelop and coinnovate. We believe in the power of collaboration; we expect distributed leadership.
Not fixed	We carry our ability to participate with us. The mind-set of anchoring tasks to address certain locations has been challenged. We can form a group to do something we care about almost anywhere.
My network	We want to do it with our friends, with groups that have formed around our own specific niche interests. Geographic communities are less interesting than our communities of interests.[18]

To respond most effectively to Balmer's predictions (see Table 15.1), leisure services professionals should consider

- providing a virtual presence for their organization;
- using technology to their advantage to promote social and environmental justice;
- customizing choices for their constituencies; and
- offering excellent, friendly service.

Digital Age customers demand excellent service and have competing companies from which to choose. For example, successful companies such as Zappos.com have responded to customer demands with fast, free, and easy shipping and returns. Customer service representatives are easy to reach by phone and are friendly. You can even press 5 on your phone to hear the joke of the day. This gives the customer a feeling of being connected to the Zappos.com team. Consumers want to feel good. They are highly motivated to shop where companies are friendly and making the world a better place to live. Social entrepreneurs such as TOMS® shoes do well by doing good. They give away a free pair of shoes to a child in a third world country for every pair purchased. Leisure services professionals who stay abreast of the latest technology and autonomy-promoting management strategies (e.g., R.O.W.E., "Results Only Work Environment," at Best Buy®) will be best positioned to provide services relevant to the 21st century consumer.

Emergence of a Fourth Sector

As mentioned in Chapter 2, the leisure service delivery system is evolving into less differentiated forms of service with more permeable boundaries, which are likely to blur over time (see Figure 2.1). In the past, separate and distinct public agencies provided local, state, and federal government programs, facilities, and natural areas for people to enjoy. Private nonprofit agencies primarily provided youth and group membership forms of service, and commercial for-profit organizations offered entertainment, festival, and theme park experiences.

Now, however, recreation, parks, sport management, hospitality, and tourism agencies are confronted by what the rest of society has experienced as an accelerated rate of change and traditional yet artificial barriers between organizations are being removed by a number of forces (e.g., economic changes and consumer choice). More important, all leisure services providers are increasingly realizing that traditional structural boundaries are no longer as relevant—thus the emergence of the fourth sector and the prediction that leisure services providers will increasingly move in this direction (see Figure 15.1).

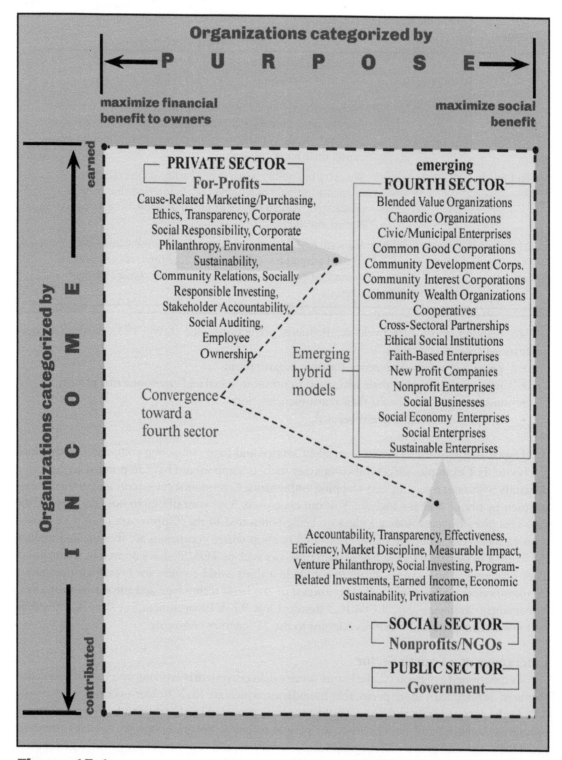

Figure 15.1. Patterns of organizational change: Emergence of a fourth sector. NGO = nongovermental organization.

What is the significance of the blurring of boundaries among commercial, for-profit, public, and nonprofit sectors? How will this melting away of strictly defined organizational missions and services impact recreation, parks, sport management, hospitality, and tourism? As discussed in Chapter 2, the mission and methods of an increasing number of organizations are becoming more similar to organizational landscapes that integrate social purposes with effective business practices (see Figures 2.1 and 2.2). The fourth sector is the result of the creation of hybrid organizations that "transcend the usual sectoral boundaries and resist easy classification within the traditional three sectors."[19]

Fourth sector organizations, or **for-benefit** organizations, may best serve the leisure needs of communities in the future because at their core they are run by socially conscious entrepreneurs who want to help society meet the requirement of sustainability—"the pursuit of lasting economic prosperity, social equity, and environmental well-being."[20] Consumers who want to better their lives, communities, and the world are drawn to these providers out of a shared purpose and meaning. Furthermore, these emerging organizations are equipped for and dedicated to being a part of the broader community and ideally affect systemic, global solutions. Thus, organizations run by conscious entrepreneurs will survive and thrive, even during economic downturns, in the 21st century.

Recreation, parks, sport management, hospitality, and tourism organizations are ideally suited for such a vision of service. Indeed, organizations that do not convert from their more rigid service structures will not be well positioned to ameliorate our social and environmental problems nor will they continue to thrive. Business-as-usual practices could even stifle or ruin various forms of leisure expression. In the face of increasing degradation of the planet from global warming, increasing ill effects of urbanization, unhealthy obese and diabetic youth, and growing out-of-control gang violence, organizations have to be more nimble to influence policies that may cut across territorial boundaries to influence the direction of public/governmental, nonprofit, and commercial, for-profit decision making.

With the emergence of fourth sector organizations, leisure services professionals will be required to have diverse educational backgrounds and work experiences that emphasize transparency, measureable impact, venture philanthropy, social investing, economic sustainability, program-related investments, and accountability. The fourth sector is designed for sustainability that benefits owners, board members, and employees of for-benefit organizations, as well as the financial supporters and constituents of public and nonprofit agencies. This type of organization will be dedicated to advancing the welfare of its stakeholders. They will be organic, strategic enterprises that lend leadership to the community to provide direct intervention and advocate for positions that solve problems. A common goal will be to improve quality of life for all, in such a way that the community at large and the environment are the ultimate beneficiaries.

Micro Trends

According to Penn, the power of individual choice has never been greater—the skill of **microtargeting**—identifying small, intense subgroups and communicating with them about their individual needs and wants—is key to working with community groups in the future.[21] The one-size-fits-all approach to the world is over. Clearly, recreation, parks, sport management, hospitality, and tourism organizations that are flexible, adaptable, and full-service in nature will be in stronger positions to identify and respond to emerging trends among subcultural groups.

An example of successful microtargeting, Penn suggested, is the model that Starbucks® followed that led to its initial success. Starbucks® structures its menu to be responsive to a multitude of coffee tastes and other specialty drink requests. The business is governed by the idea that Starbucks® customers make choices—about their coffee, milk, sweetener—and the more choices members of small, intense subgroups have about specific products or services, the greater satisfaction they feel. Starbucks® has been successful because it can be all things to all customers—it makes no bet on one set of choices over another. Rather, it focuses on the individuation and customization of experience. An important lesson to be learned from Starbucks® is that small groups, drawn together by shared needs, habits, and preferences, may create a movement that may change the direction of a product, program, or service.

North America is moving in hundreds of small directions at once. The micro trends that follow are part of the continually evolving excitement and energy within our society. Recognizing and responding to these trends is an ongoing professional challenge for all leisure services providers. Small trends show little deference to one another. For every high-profile group of young, chic up-and-comers in society, there is another group of older, old-fashioned churchgoers. For every group of gadget geeks, another group resists technology. More people are dieting than ever, but steak houses have never been so full.

Micro trends reflect the human drive toward individuality, and conventional wisdom often seeks to drive society toward conformity. The original mass-produced industrial model of the economy is being replaced by the Starbucks® economy—the multiplication of choice as the driver of personal expression and satisfaction. For every trend, there is a countertrend. For every push to modernization, there is a drive to hold on to old values. For every dash to the Internet, there are those who want to escape to the outdoors for peace and quiet. For every push to have instant information, there are people who want it long, detailed, and thoughtful. And then there are people who want a little of both, who balance their energy between embracing change and technology while enjoying trends that may seem old-fashioned.

The micro trends Penn identified include the following:

- **Increase in individual and nature-based sports**. In the period between 1999 and 2005 the number of skateboarders (+167%), kayakers and rafters (+117%), and snowboarders (+114%) far outpaced more traditional sports such as baseball, which decreased 7%, and basketball, which fell 0.7%, during the same timeframe.
- **Smartphones.** The increase in production of smartphones, iPads, or other handheld devices and subsequent decrease in cost means more people have constant and immediate access to information and may communicate with text messages, e-mails, and pictures in real time.
- **Homeschooling.** The number of families who homeschool their children has steadily increased. In the period from 1999 to 2003, the number of parents who homeschooled their children increased 30%. This figure represented 2.2% of the school-age population in the United States and 12% of finalists for the National Spelling Bee.
- **Slowing down**. Although Internet use and instant sharing of information via social networking sites has surged, some people still have long attention spans. They are represented by marathoners who take hours to finish a race, golfers who take 4.5 hours to play a round, readers who enjoy books of 400 and 500 pages, and moviegoers who enjoy sitting through films of 1.5 to 2.5 hours.
- **Linguistically isolated households.** One in 25 households (25 million people) in the United States has individuals and families where no one speaks English well or at all. Although most mainstream work settings require workers to speak English, a number of communities have lower wage earners in particular who work, play, shop, and socialize entirely in Spanish, Mandarin, or Hindi.[22]

Micro Trends and Leisure

Micro trends are accelerating the individuation of community life. We are watching groups of dedicated, intensely interested people express their individuality in new ways, putting stress on politics, religion, popular culture, family structure, and leisure services organizations. We are witnessing a disaggregation of society and the breaking down of boredom and expansion of freedom of choice that is becoming more of the cornerstone of people's overall life choices. Leisure expression has never been more central to people's way of living. The potential for personal satisfaction due to individual choice is at its highest level ever. Even with a change from more materialistic forms of leisure (represented by consumerism), people are recognizing that leisure as experience, of which they are more conscious and about which they care, has value.[23] People's growing desire for leisure experience has resulted in a desire to strengthen their bonds, despite increased social fragmentation, and pursue enjoyment with family and friends and for knowledge, self-improvement, and renewal. White Hutchinson suggested that the increasing desire for **transformational leisure** experiences (or self-actualization) is premised on the idea that people recognize that experiences contribute to making a better person beyond the purchase of things or engaging in nonenriching experiences.[24]

White Hutchinson also noted that people increasingly desire to have "high fidelity" experiences (high quality, enriching, and uplifting). A constant tension exists between fidelity and convenience (ease of getting and paying for something). Offerings that are one extreme or the other—either high in fidelity or high in convenience—tend to succeed. For example, movie theaters offer 3-D and IMAX movies or in-theater dining to compete with the convenience of in-home movies.[25] For leisure-based destinations (movie theaters, bowling alleys, national parks, etc.) to succeed, they will have to

> raise their fidelity to overcome the convenience of electronics, at-home leisure and consumers' search for value. [They] need to offer experiences that can't be found at home, and the experiences need to be high in quality and fidelity with high perceived value.[26]

The desire for transformational experiences is underscored by the higher education levels of people aged 30 to 34 compared to the generation of those aged 70 to 74. This illustrates that leisure expression is becoming more like classical leisure, as discussed in Chapter 1. At the same time, some people have argued that the rise in choice and transformational leisure threatens social cohesion. Can there be no unity, no community, no single United States or Canada? Will the expansion of choices evolve into new separate and distinct patterns rather than one unifying pattern? The number of people in contemporary society that is dividing along lines of personal choice rather than circumstance (e.g., race, gender, home ownership) is much greater than it was 50 to 60 years ago.

Increasingly, actions will be based on 51% coalitions rather than a broadly unified public because personal choices tend to pull in opposite directions and make it harder to bring people together. We may be moving away from a mass society, a faceless society, with people forced into conformity—everyone looking alike, dressing alike, and being required to think alike. Penn suggested we are now heading in the opposite direction—a future of many choices, driven by individual tastes, choices that are reinforced by the ability to connect and communicate with communities of even smaller niches with individuals looking more different by the minute.

Implications for Leisure Services

The future of recreation, parks, sport management, hospitality, and tourism has no clear direction given the magnitude of these macro and micro trends. For leisure services organizations to function effectively, they will be required to recognize that mainstream culture and national expectations of mass conformity will not resonate with the hundreds of subcultural groups where no ethnic or racial group is a majority. The profession will need to acknowledge the multiplicity of small niche interest groups within communities and adopt a **collaborative, boundary-free** leisure service delivery system approach that promotes and encourages frontline professional staff to seek out various interest groups for their input on program ideas and ways to engage them directly or remotely and to facilitate the desires people view as beneficial in their community.

Servant Leadership

Leisure services delivery must use the full range of leadership roles that embrace tolerance, outreach, developmental tasks, removal of barriers to participation, and advocacy for people's rights to enable them to engage fully in all aspects of community life. **Servant leaders** are best suited for this challenge as they have a desire to serve first (not promote organizational mechanisms), thus making the conscious choice that brings one to aspire to lead. Characteristics of servant leaders include

- commitment to the growth of people,
- building community,
- stewardship,
- empathy and healing capacity,
- awareness,
- foresight—understanding the lessons of the past,
- entrepreneurial, and
- flexibility and adaptability.[27]

The concept of servant leader suggests that the first priority of a leader should be service and putting others first.[28] The leadership emphasis for servant leaders is on empowering and helping others. Servant leaders recognize that the full continuum of leisure services delivery—direct service, information referral, enabling/facilitating, entrepreneurship, and advocacy—is necessary for any organization to be responsive to the diversity of interests, lifestyles, and subcultural values that exist in most communities. Servant leaders seek, above all, to provide services that result in public benefit. Thus, servant leaders are more likely to comprehend the complexities of a world that is increasingly evolving in ways that require flexible, visionary, compassionate, and socially conscious leaders.

Servant leaders will serve as arbiters of competing forces that both enhance and decimate recreational opportunities. Where do we, as professional recreators, go from here? According to Dustin,

> ...we human beings are biologically ill-equipped to deal effectively with the environmental problems confronting the world of today...there is a fundamental mismatch between the nature of these problems and our ability to perceive them and do something about them; and that if we are to have any hope of turning things around, we must better understand the causes of the mismatch so that we might begin to act in the light of our limitations as a species as well as our potentials.[29]

We humans, it seems, are increasingly out of step with our own nature. Our success as a species has not been in adapting to the natural world, but in transforming our world to make it more hospitable for ourselves. To date, we have been self-centered. Furthermore, politicians prove increasingly ill-suited to offer leadership to solve our growing environmental problems, which most people see as outside of themselves. In this regard, a person cannot be a leader for constructive, sustainable change unless he or she views the end result on behalf of the community, not as a way to receive a vote. Recreation, parks, sport management, hospitality, and tourism professionals of the future who embrace the fullness of the leisure service delivery system (particularly collaboration and advocacy) may emerge at the forefront as recognizable catalysts and champions for a habitable quality of life that serves the total good. Dustin recommended the following to move community members in a sustainable direction—this includes recreation, parks, sport management, hospitality, and tourism professionals:

1. **Slow down.** Live less frantic lives and become more aware of our total surroundings and the impact we have on the planet.

2. **Scale down.** Downsize our list of necessities, live more consciously below our means. "We need to measure the fullness of our lives not by the number of our possessions, but by the quality of our relationships with others and by the degree to which we continue to learn and grow intellectually, spiritually, and emotionally."[30]

3. **Step down from our anthropocentric pedestals.** We should assume a more humble position among the creations of the Earth. Dustin suggested cultivating a lifestyle characterized by reverence and restraint.[31]

Environmental and Social Justice

Recreation, parks, sport management, hospitality, and tourism professionals will be in the forefront in the future to the degree they embrace **environmental and social justice**. What this means is that our profession must work toward more sustainable practices and ensure that all people, regardless of race, ethnicity, income, national origin, or education, receive equitable treatment and opportunities for meaningful involvement in community life. Our profession will be challenged to assure the reduction of racial and ethnic disparities by promoting physical activities in public parks, playgrounds, and other recreation areas and facilities. Additionally, an ecologically sound orientation to service delivery, one that considers environmental factors as integral to recreation expression, is important for planning purposes.[32]

Taylor et al. recognized that it is critical to acknowledge that park and recreation systems are public goods and are provided as a matter of public policy:

> [First,] they are an important function of government and are found at all levels government (municipal, county, state, and federal). Eighty-percent of U.S. citizens report using public parks, and nearly one in four use them frequently. Second, park and recreation opportunities are associated with numerous benefits, including psychological (e.g., stress reduction), social (e.g., family bonding), economic (e.g., increased property values), environmental (e.g., open space), and health (e.g., benefits of exercise).[33]

Need for Advocacy

Historically, recreation, parks, sport management, hospitality, and tourism professionals have not viewed **advocacy** as their responsibility. In this context, advocacy means actively recommending and supporting change, particularly for underrepresented or underserved people or the environment. But as the impact of leisure pursuits on communities is increasingly recognized, the need for leisure services professionals to become more involved with other community services is readily apparent. The role of advocate means ensuring that all constituents are served by promoting sustainable living patterns. Becoming a core member of the community and advocating for the benefits of leisure services will be an essential role of leisure services providers in the years ahead.

The California Park and Recreation Society (CPRS) has led the way in demonstrating why parks and recreation is an essential human service. The action play that CPRS developed highlights nine missions that serve as a forward-thinking model for park and recreation programming:

- strengthen community image and sense of place
- support economic development
- strengthen safety and security
- promote health and wellness
- foster human development
- increase cultural unity
- protect environmental resources
- facilitate community problem solving
- provide recreational experiences[34]

These missions may be used to advocate convincingly for recreation, parks, sport management, hospitality, and tourism. To accomplish these missions, CPRS identified 10 core competencies that professional leaders must have: resourcefulness, knowledge of community, creativity, flexibility, and a set of skills including partnering, coalition building, mediation, facilitation, interpersonal, and the ability to multitask. Leisure services professionals must understand that they have an important responsibility to develop collaborations and partnerships with internal public service departments, public safety, and other departments to build community through volunteerism, public meetings, and focus groups and to gain legislative support by being an advocate.[35]

The Power of One

We have focused on macro and micro trends that will likely shape the future of leisure services. But in the final analysis, it is critically important for you to understand your obligation and opportunity to shape the future. With more than 300 million U.S. citizens filling the landscape, it is easy to think that one individual cannot make much of a difference. Yet as noted anthropologist Margaret Mead said, "Never doubt that a small group of thoughtful, committed citizens can change the world. Indeed, it is the only thing that ever has."[36] Your challenge is to infuse a career in recreation, parks, sport management, hospitality, or tourism with your own creativity and uniqueness to add value to the profession in support of the common good. It is up to you to create a career with meaning by putting your personal, positive stamp on things. To assist you in that quest, we leave you with six of our strongest beliefs about what our profession has to offer the larger world, as well as four general guidelines for action. We encourage you to take what we have to say and build upon it in a manner that leads you toward a fulfilling personal and professional life.

Our Professional Beliefs for Your Consideration
1. Recreation, parks, sport management, hospitality, and tourism may contribute substantially to quality of life.
2. The best way to articulate these contributions is in the context of health promotion.
3. Our society is fundamentally "out of synch" with what is really healthy for human beings and the environment. Consequently, we must reweave the American Dream in a way that is socially and environmentally conscious and sustainable for centuries to come.
4. Parks and recreation, in particular, ought to be treated as public goods, as something to which everyone in our culture should have access, as with public education.
5. When that access is compromised, the problem is ethical (i.e., it must be viewed as a matter of social and environmental justice, and it must be remedied).
6. The greatest professional challenge for recreation, parks, sport management, hospitality, and tourism professionals is to assume a proactive role in educating the citizenry about the need to develop an American way of life that ensures social and environmental justice for all.

The balance is delicate between encouraging leisure expression and ensuring access to leisure opportunities while being caretakers of the environment in a way that guarantees future generations will be able to realize their human potential and quality of life as well. Dustin et al. believe leisure services professionals are in a unique position to champion human fulfillment:

> In the name of human fulfillment, our profession can contribute to the creation of an environment that nourishes the human potential. We, as much as any farmer, physician, carpenter, or scientist, can play a vital role in orchestrating an atmosphere of hope for humankind. We can serve as principal architects of a new beginning of this planet.[37]

In closing, here are four guidelines for action to which you may refer when confronted with any challenge that requires you to balance the materialistic, tangible behaviors desired to achieve self-fulfillment, with sustainable, minimal impact expressions that benefit not only individuals but also the larger living world:

1. **Ideal of individual freedom.** We "should be committed to the ideal of individual freedom. We should act on the environment, both the internal one of the organism and the external one of society, and make it compatible with the expression of that freedom. This means society must make a concession to its members. It must give them room to grow and develop, to succeed and fail, to express their initiative, creativity, and fulfillment as individual human beings. This also means that the individual must make a concession to society. One must accept responsibility for one's behavior."[38]

2. **Commitment to expanding opportunities.** Leisure services professionals should be committed to the ideal of "expanding opportunities for choice."[39] Although some opportunities desired by the public may be in conflict with service providers' ideas/values, "the opportunities should be made available as long as they are socially acceptable."[40]

3. **Supporting the overall good of the community.** "On occasion matters of personal preference clash with matters of social principle."[41] At times, recreation, parks, sport management, hospitality, and tourism professionals will experience conflicts of individual preferences among different lifestyle and interest groups, but they should "support the social principle governing the situation."[42]

4. **Ethical principle: Reconciliation of competing individual and societal interests.** "The interplay between one's freedom to act and one's responsibility to society for one's actions is necessarily bounded by the limits of compatibility with the dynamic structure of the whole."[43] One's behavior must be in accordance not only with the welfare of humankind, but also with the welfare of the larger community of life."[44]

Recreation, parks, sport management, hospitality, and tourism professionals contribute to the quality of all life on Earth. Dustin et al. suggested that we even contribute to the very survival of humanity.[45] The stakes are high for leisure services professionals, and the world community will look to and rely upon the capable decisions being made by socially conscious servant leaders on behalf of a profession whose primary goal is to promote human dignity and fulfillment while sustaining the fragile natural world for future generations to enjoy. The recreation, parks, sport management, hospitality, and tourism profession has immense possibilities in the years ahead that may result in the emergence of the leisure services field as a fulcrum for supporting and helping to facilitate recreational experiences that foster culturally relevant, personally satisfying, and environmentally sustainable "**deep recreation.**"[46] This idea, sometimes called flow, is representative of personal desires that embrace freely chosen, intense, challenging, transformational, and intrinsically motivated experiences.

Employment opportunities in recreation, parks, sport management, hospitality, and tourism are projected to increase into the future. To the degree these professionals recognize the ways in which people desire leisure expression, ranging from momentary snippets of engagement to deeply intense, challenging, and transformational experiences, they will understand the important role they play in facilitating opportunities for choice and safeguarding the environment that supports them. Therein resides a career with meaning.

For Further Investigation

For More Research

1. Identify, research, and write a paper about macro trends affecting recreation, parks, sport management, hospitality, and tourism in your community. How does the influence of a macro trend intersect with competing or contrary micro trends in your community? Are they reconcilable?

Recommended websites:

childandnature.org/blog

www.google.com/Top/Society/Future/
   Predictions

www.markpenn.com/microtrends

www.microtrending.com

naisbitt.com

newblaze.com

slowisbeautifulcecile.blogspot.com

www.theyear2012.blogspot.com

2. Select a book or article from the recommended reading list. Read it and write a paper about what you learned and how you believe these lessons will impact recreation, parks, sport management, hospitality, and tourism.

Active Investigation

1. Choose a cause, write and send an advocacy letter supporting a position that will contribute to individual or community well-being.

2. Interview one or more professionals about the trends they see and how they believe they will affect the future of recreation, parks, sport management, hospitality, and tourism. Choose a professional who has been in the field for 10 or more years to get a long-range view. Example interview questions include the following:

   - How have you seen your job change over the years?
   - How have your constituents changed? Do you believe that your agency or business has done well keeping up with its changing needs?
   - What is the biggest challenge you see facing recreation, parks, sport management, hospitality, and tourism today? What do you think it will be 5 and 10 years from now?
   - Review the sections on macro trends and micro trends. Ask the professional how some of these are affecting his or her agency or business.

3. Go online and navigate to one of the websites listed above and join in and participate in a blog related to an issue of interest to you and see how others react to your views.

Recommended Reading

Andrews, C. (2006). *Slow is beautiful: New visions of community, leisure and joie de vivre*. Gabriola Island, Canada: New Society Publishers.

Happiness is on the decline even though we are the most affluent country in the world. No one seems to know how to exit the "fast lane." Andrews helps us understand the forces taking the joy out of our existence and provides a vision for a more fulfilling life.

Bandura, A. (2004). Health promotion by social cognitive means. *Health Education and Behavior, 31*(2), 143–164.

Bandura makes an excellent case for how recreation, among other services, contributes to health promotion.

Chivian, E., & Bernstein, A. (Eds.). (2008). *Sustaining life: How human health depends on biodiversity*. New York, NY: Oxford University Press.

This book was motivated by its UN sponsors' sense of the world's indifference to the consequences of environmental degradation. It covers a collaborative survey of biodiversity issues written and/ or reviewed for accuracy by more than 100 scientists, and the contributors illustrate how human health is inextricably tied to the health of the world's ecosystems.

Chouinard, Y. (2005). *Let my people go surfing: The education of a reluctant businessman.* New York, NY: Penguin.
As the founder of Patagonia, Chouinard provides a fascinating look inside its history. His book serves as a guide for anyone interested in creating a "new style of responsible business."

Louv, R. (2005). *Last child in the woods: Saving our children from nature-deficit disorder.* Chapel Hill, NC: Algonquin Books.
This must-read illustrates the dangers inherent in a society increasingly losing touch with nature and calls for reconnecting people, especially children, with their fundamental ground of being.

Poscente, V. (2008). *The age of speed.* Austin, TX: Bard Press.
Poscente explains that work is no longer a place but rather a state of mind. He explains how speed is both the cause of the problem and the solution to the ambiguity we face when trying to resolve the competing demands of career and personal life.

Roberts, N., Chavez, D., Lara, B., & Sheffield, E. (2009). *Serving culturally diverse visitors to forests in California: A resource guide* (General Tech. Rep. PSW-GTR-222). Albany, CA: U.S. Department of Agriculture, Forest Service, Pacific Southwest Research.
Changing demographics make it essential for recreation managers to understand how to both attract and serve ethnically diverse visitors to our forest resources. The guide provides numerous materials, best practices, and practical application tips.

Robert Wood Johnson Foundation. (2000). *Healthy places, healthy people: Promoting public health and physical activity through community design.* Princeton, NJ: Author.
This report is a white paper from a meeting that summarizes the best thinking about how the problem of physical inactivity can be addressed. Successful interventions must target both the individual and the environments in which people work and live.

Schwab, K., & Dustin, D. (Eds.). (2013.) *Just leisure: Things that we believe in.* Urbana, IL: Sagamore.
This book is a compilation of essays written by park, recreation, and tourism professionals dedicated to the proposition that a concern for social and environmental justice should underpin the delivery of leisure services. The book challenges your world view and prompts you to reassess your fundamental assumptions.

Schwartz, B. (2004). *The paradox of choice: Why less is more.* New York, NY: HarperCollins.
This psychology professor provides convincing evidence that we face too many choices on a daily basis. The bewildering array of choices is stressful because it exhausts our brains and erodes our sense of well-being. The author offers practical suggestions for reducing stress during decision making.

Wellman, D., Dustin, D., Henderson, K., & Moore, R. (2008). *Service living: Building community through public parks and recreation.* State College, PA: Venture.
This book discusses the lives of four distinguished Americans who lived a life of service: Frederick Law Olmsted, Jane Addams, Benton McKaye, and Marjorie Stoneman Douglas. The authors draw lessons from their lives that can benefit any of us who aspire to service living.

References

[1]Friedman, T. (2005). *The world is flat: A brief history of the twenty-first century.* New York, NY: Farrar, Strauss, and Giroux.

[2]Floyd, M., Bocarro, J., & Thompson, T. (2008). Research on race and ethnicity in leisure studies: A review of five major journals. *Journal of Leisure Research, 40,* 1–22.

[3]Ibid, p. 14.

[4]Balmer, K. (2011, October). *Rethinking leisure services.* Paper prepared for the 2011 National Recreation Summit, Lake Louise, AB, Canada, p. 8.

[5]Ibid.

[6]El Nasser, H., & Overberg, P. (2012, December 12). Census: Economy slows U.S. population growth. *USA Today.* Retrieved from http://www.usatoday.com/story/news/nation/2012/12/12/census-whites-us-2043/1763429/

[7]Dustin, D., Bricker, K., & Schwab, K. (2010). People and nature: Toward an ecological model of health promotion. *Journal of Leisure Sciences, 32*(1), p. 4.

[8]Dustin et al., 2010, p. 7.

[9]Balmer, 2011, p. 9.

[10]Dustin et al., 2010, p. 9.

[11]Ibid.

[12]Taylor, W., Floyd, M., Whitt-Glover, M., & Brooks, J. (2007). Environmental justice: A framework for collaboration between the public health and parks and recreation fields to study disparity in physical activity. *Journal of Physical Activity and Health, 4,* S50–S63.

[13]Kim, R. (2009, October 26). Augmenting how we see the world. *San Francisco Chronicle,* p. 8.

[14]McLean, D., & Hurd, A. (2013). *Kraus' recreation and leisure in modern society.* Burlington, MA: Jones and Bartlett Learning, p. 413.

[15]Ibid.

[16]Loc cit., p. 414.

[17]Balmer, 2011, pp. 9-10.

[18]Loc cit., p. 10.

[19]Sabeti, H. (2009). *The emerging fourth sector.* Washington, DC: The Aspen Institute, p. 2.

[20]Loc cit., p. 4.

[21]Penn, M. (2007). *Microtrends: The small forces behind tomorrow's big changes.* New York, NY: Hachette Books.

[22]Ibid.

[23]White Hutchinson Leisure and Learning Group. (2009) *The future of leisure time: A new value equation.* Retrieved September 10, 2009, from http://www.whitehutchinson.com/news/knews/2009_august/article103.shtml

[24]Loc cit., p. 7.

[25]Ibid.

[26]Loc cit., p. 9.

[27]Peete, D. (2005, June 30). Needed: Servant-leaders. *Long-Term Living,* pp. 8–9. Retrieved from http://www.ltlmagazine.com/article/needed-servant-leaders

[28]Greenleaf, R. (1991). *The servant as leader.* Indianapolis, IN: Robert K. Greenleaf Center.

[29]Dustin, D. (2012). *The wilderness within: Reflections on leisure and life.* Urbana, IL: Sagamore.

[30]Loc cit., p. 230.

[31]Ibid.

[32]Taylor et al., 2007.

[33]Taylor et al., 2007, p. S53.

[34]California Parks and Recreation Society. (1999). *Creating community in the 21st century: An action plan for parks and recreation.* Sacramento, CA: Author.

[35]Clark, J. (2006). *Human resources: Servant leadership and the parks and recreation professional.* Unpublished manuscript.

[36]Sommers, F., & Dineen, T. (1984). *Saying attributed to Margaret Mead in curing nuclear madness.* London, England: Methuen, p. 158.

[37]Dustin, D., McAvoy, L., Schultz, J., Bricker, K., Rose, J., & Schwab, K. (2011). *Stewards of access/custodians of choice: A philosophical foundation for parks, recreation, and tourism.* Urbana, IL: Sagamore, p. 112.

[38]Loc cit., p. 113.

[39]Ibid.

[40]Ibid.

[41]Loc cit., p. 114.

[42]Ibid.

[43]Laszlo, E. (1972). *The systems view of the world.* New York, NY: George Braziller, p. 75.

[44]Dustin et al, 2011, p. 114.

[45]Ibid.

[46]Murphy, J. (2007). *Whither organized parks and recreation?* Redwood City, CA: Bay Area Institute, District IV, California Parks and Recreation Society.

Index

4-H clubs, 86–87
21st Century Community Learning Centers (CCLCs), 60
501(c) 3 organizations, 79

A

A Matter of Time: Risk and Opportunity in the Non-School Hours (Carnegie Council on Adolescent Development), 58
Accepted Practices Exchange, 237
Action Without Borders, 94
Addams, Jane, 14, 30
adventure tourism, 279
advertising firms, 232
advocacy, need for, 353–354
advocates, 81–82
affinity for nature, 17, 19
after-school centers, 65–66
after-school programs, 91
agencies, mission focused, 75–76
ag-natural, 274
agritourism, 274
Air Force Combat Support and Community Service-Outdoor Recreation, 111–112
Aldrich, Dr. Tina M., xi
Alfriend, Ginny, 19, 140
Allen, Lawrence R., x
America Outdoors, 142
American Camp Association, 93
American Therapeutic Recreation Association (ATRA), 154
Americans With Disabilities Act (ADA), 159, 160, 229
amusement parks, 278–279
Anaheim, City of, 33
aquatics careers, 180–181, 184–185
Aquatics certifications, 95, 332
architectural tourism, 281
Argentina's Mendoza Valley, 281
armed forces recreation, 101–116
    See also Morale, Welfare, and Recreation (MWR)
    for further investigation, 115–116
    internships, 114–115
    overview, 101–102, 104–106
    profiles, 102–104
    resources, 113–114
Armed Forces Resort Center (AFRC), 109–110
Army MWR's Nonappropriated Fund (NAF) Management Training Program, 108

Art in the Public Interest (API), 94
Association of National Park Rangers, 142
Association for Experiential Education (AEE), 94
athlete/player development, 200
Augmented Reality Technology (ART), 345

B

backcountry settings, 89
backpacking guides, 309
Barcelona, Dr. Robert J., xi, 193
Bare, Stacy, 112
Barnthouse, Token D., xi, 101
Bay Area Ridge Trail Council, San Francisco, 141
benefits-based sports management (BBSM), 201
Better Opportunities for Single Soldiers (BOSS), 110
bicycles, 309
Big Brothers Big Sisters, 87
bluefishjobs.com, 174
boating, 307
Boston Common, 124
Bowe, Jeremy, 281
Boy Scouting, 89–90
Boys & Girls Clubs of America, 77, 79, 86
Build-a-Bear Workshop, 309, 310
Burns, Ken, 125

C

Calatrava, Santiago, 281
California Parks Company, The, 122
California Recreation and Park Society (CPRS), 35, 353–354
Camp Fire USA, 87
Camp Ton-A-Wandah, 297, 299
campgrounds, camps, 304–305
camping organizations, 88–89
campus career services, 326
campus recreation
    careers in, 174–182
    described, 167–168, 171–174
    first-year orientation programs and outdoor recreation, 182–185
    for further investigation, 189–190
    future opportunities, issues, challenges, 185–187
    graduate assistantships, 176
    profiles, 168–171
    recently completed facilities (table), 173
    resources, 187–189

role of, over student's time at college
      (table), 173
summary of career possibilities
      (table), 184–185
typical career progression (fig.), 177
Cannon, Edward, 104, 107
canoe liveries, guided trips, 307–308
carbon footprint, 344
career exploration, 323
career planning, 323
careers
      in aquatics, 180–181
      in armed forces recreation, 101–102
      in campus recreation, 167, 174–182
      in community recreation, 300–312
      in community recreation and leisure
            services, 61–68
      in event management, 229–237
      in facility management, 182–183
      in fitness, 180
      for further investigation, 44–46
      future opportunities, issues,
            challenges, 69–70
      in hospitality industry, 251–262
      how to use this book, 42–43
      leisure service delivery system, 29–37
      making right recreation-related career
            connection, 37–39
      in marketing, 208–209
      in Morale, Welfare, and Recreation
            (MWR), 106–109
      in nonprofit recreation and leisure
            services, 82–92
      in outdoor recreation, 130–139, 181–182
      preparation, technology and, 327
      in recreation, parks, sport management,
            hospitality, and tourism, 27–29
      in recreation, preparing for, 321–338
      in recreational sports, 177–179
      in sport management, 201–211
      in student activities, 179–180
      in therapeutic recreation and recreational
            therapy, 156–161
      in travel and tourism, 275–286
Carr, Tom, 18
Carter, President Jimmy, 126
casino/gaming industry, 260–262
Central Park, New York City, 16, 30, 124
certifications
      commercial recreation, 314
      and community recreation, leisure services
            careers, 62–63
      described, 331–332
      Morale, Welfare, and Recreation (MWR), 114

nonprofit agencies, 95
      in recreational therapy, 162
      resources, 70
      sport management, 213
      wine education, 290
      for working in outdoor recreation, 142
Certified Meeting Professional (CMP), 237
Certified Nonprofit Professional Alliance, 95
Certified Park and Recreation Professional
      (CPRP), 62–63, 332
Certified Playground Safety Inspector (CPSI), 332
Certified Therapeutic Recreation Specialist
      (CTRS), 83, 154, 332
Challenger League Baseball, 159
Charity Channel, The, 94
Chouinard, Yvon, 126
Christian Camping International (CCI), 94
church recreation, 88
Clark, Maxine, 310
Clinton, President Bill, 126
collaborative, boundary-free leisure, 351–352
Collette, 26
Colorado Dude Ranchers Association, 309
commercial for-profit recreation providers, 31–32
commercial sector, 199
community recreation
      benefits of, 55–59
      careers in, 61–68, 300–312
      for further investigation, 72–73, 316–317
      future opportunities, issues, challenges, 312
      and leisure services, 49–70
      overview, 295–296, 299–300
      profiles, 296–299
      resources, 70–71, 313–316
Community Youth Services (CYS),
      Olympia, WA, 86
Complete Wine Course (Zraly), 282
concessionaires
      with NGOs, 138
      sales and usage fees, 33
      concierges, 255
Confucius, 320
Conservation International (CI), 141
continuum approach, 42–43
Convention Industry Council (CIC), 230, 237
coolworks.com, 143
Costa Condordia accident, 259
cover letters, 334
Crabtree, Polly, xi, 221
cruise industry, 258–259
Cryer, Shelly, 74
culinary preparation, 253
Cultural Heritage Toolkit, 285

cultural tourism, 274, 279–280
Cummings, Kevin, 192, 194–195

D

Da Vinci Code (film), 275
Dakota Events LLC, 224
Darton College, Georgia, 179
Dedina, Serge, 271
deep recreation, 355
Department of Agriculture, 127
Department of Defense (DoD), 102
destination management companies (DMCs), 232
destination management organizations, 277–278
Dhuyvetter, Sandy, 18, 268
Digital Age, 345–346
digital age behaviors (table), 346–347
direct service, 18
"Discover the Benefits" campaign, 56
discretionary time, 5
dive and snorkel shops, 307
Dr. Shades, 256
drama, theater, and the arts, 91
dude ranches, 309
Duncan, Mary, 14
Dustin, Daniel, xi–xii, 341

E

ecotourism, 274, 279–280, 288
education, making the most of your, 325–326
enterprises, 299
entrepreneurism, 17, 20
environmentalism, 353
ePortfolio, 333
esprit de corps, 104
event management
    careers in, 229–237
    in corporate or organizational
        settings, 233–234
    for further investigation, 239–243
    history, growth of, 226–228
    in hospitality and venue settings, 234–235
    overview, 221–222, 225–226
    profiles, 222–225
    resources, 237–239
    trends, 228–229
event managers, 227
evidence-based practice, 161
expenses, 299
extramural sport, 177

F

facilitators, 82
facility management, 182–183

faith-based agencies, 87–88
federal parks, outdoor recreation in, 119–146
festival management firms, 232
financial sustainability, 129–130
First-Year Orientation Program (FOP), 182–183
fishing guides, 309
Fite Jr., Elton, 77–78
fitness, careers in, 184
fitness careers, 180
Flat World Paradigm, 341
for-benefit organizations, 349
Forest Reserve Act of 1891, 126
four Ps model of this book, 43
fourth sector
    emergence of, 347–349
    organizations, 35–36
Francis, Erica, 120–122
Frankl, Viktor E., 7
freedom, leisure and, 6–7
Friedman, Thomas, 34
Fu, Dr. Yao-Yi, xii, 245
future
    forces shaping the, 342–343
    macro trends, 343–349
    micro trends, 349–351
    what individuals can do, 354–355

G

Gamache, Mike, 17, 202
gaming/casino industry, 260–262
Gap Adventures, 33
Geddie, Dr. Morgan W., xii, 245
Gehry, Frank, 281
general recreation programming, 64–65
generalists, 39
Girl Scouting, 89–90
Girls Inc., 86
globalization and leisure service delivery
    system, 34–35
Goldbecker, Chris, 48
Golden Gate National Parks Conservancy, 222, 223
Golf 20/20, 32
Google Inc., 12
graduate assistantships in campus recreation, 176
Graham, Garrett, 297–299
gratuities, 252, 257
Gray, David E., xviii
green leisure services, 344
green spaces, 22
Green Thumb Program, New York City's, 69
green travel and tourism, 286
Greiner, Jim, xii, 295

H

Hadid, Zaha, 281
hands-on job experience, 329–330
Hargrove, Ellen, 309
Harrell, Willie, 169–171
Heads in Beds: A Reckless Memoir....
(Tomsky), 255
, health
    from green spaces, 22
    improving, 345
    recreation promoting, 13
health protection/health promotion model, 155
hedonistic behavior, 21–22
Hendricks, Dr. William, xiii, 119
Heritage tourism, 284–286
Hilton, Conrad H., 244, 255
homeschooling, 350
Hope-Johnstone, John, 20, 275, 286
horseback riding, 309
hospitality
    See also recreation, parks, sport management,
        hospitality, and tourism
    described, 10
hospitality industry
    careers in, 251–262
    described, 249–250
    for further investigation, 265–267
    future opportunities, issues,
        challenges, 262–263
    history, and today, 250–251
    overview, 245–246, 249–251
    profiles, 246–249
    resources, 263–265
hospitals, recreational therapy in, 158–159
Hot, Flat, and Crowded (Friedman), 34
hotels, affordable housing in, 262
Hull House, 14, 30
humanism, 3, 12–13
hunting guides, 309
hybrid organizational models, 36

I

Idealist, 94
incentive travel firms, 232
inclusive recreation
    described, 58
    specialists, 66–68
inclusive services, 18
income, 299
independent event firms (independents), 232
informational interviews, conducting, 45, 326
inspirational experiences in leisure, 4–5
interests, 323

International Association of Conference Center
    Administrators (IACCA), 94
International Classification of Functioning,
    Disability, and Health (ICF), 154, 156
International Ranger Federation, 142
Internet resources, 324–325
internships, 114–115, 214, 330–331
interpretation, 129
interscholastic, intercollegiate athletics,
    careers in, 205–206
interval ownership, 251
interviews
    conducting informational, 45
    informational, 326
    taking job, 334–335
intramural sports
    careers in, 184–185, 210
    described, 177
iSeek Skills Assessment, 44
*It's Not About Time: Rediscovering Leisure in a
    Changing World* (Pavelka), 7

J

Jewish Community Centers (JCC), 88
job interview, 334–335
job search, 332
job shadowing, 329
jobs. *See* careers
Johnson, Keith, 247–249

K

kayak liveries, guided trips, 307–308
kayaking, 308–309
Kay-Arora, Margaret, 76, 83
Kaye, Al, 151–153
Keirsey Temperament Sorter II, 44
Kennedy, Dr. Doug, xiii
Kitty Hawk Kites, 308
Klondike Gold Rush National Historical Park,
    Alaska, 121
Kreider, Tim, 8
Kuhlenschmidt, Megan, 50–52

L

landscape architecture, 125
Lane, Andy, 166
Law, Pamela, 103–104
leadership
    evolving roles in leisure service delivery
        system, 34
    servant leaders, 352–353
Leave No Trace/Leave No Trace Training, 95
Lee, Dr. Chang, xiii, 245

Lee, Joseph, 14
leisure
    agencies' purpose, 80
    benefits attributed to (table), 15–16
    businesses described, 300–301
    businesses overview, 295–296
    campus, 167–168
    collaborative, boundary-free, 351–352
    described, 5, 23–24
    and freedom, 6–7
    inspirational experiences, 4–5
    motivation for participation, 20–22
    multiple dimensions of (fig.), 9
    and play, 11–12
    and recreation in North American life, 3–23
    as recreational activity, 8–9
    as state of mind, 8
    transformational, 351
    virtual, 35, 185, 341
leisure ability model, 155
leisure entrepreneur, 299
leisure service delivery system
    emerging, 32–34
    evolving structure of (fig.), 31
leisure services
    careers in, 61–68
    community recreation and, 49–73
Lenz, John, 102–103
licenses
    described, 331–332
    nonprofit agencies, 95
lifestyle, 324
LifeWorkTransitions.com, 44
Lilyestrom, Amber, 195–196
LinkedIn, 327
livable communities, 56
local attractions, 278–279
local parks, outdoor recreation in, 119–146
lodging industry, 254
Long, Sheila, 52–54

M

Mackenzie, Susan Houge, 139
MacNeil, Karen, 282
management skills, 199
Man's Search for Meaning (Frankl), 7
Marbury, Kevin, 168–169
Marine Corps Community Service-Single Marine
    Program (SMP), 110
Maritz Travel, 232
marketing careers, 208–209
Marriott, William, 255
Mason, David, 82

Massachusetts Amateur Sports Foundation
    (MASF), 194, 195
Mather, Stephen T., 127
Melton, Nicholas, 252
Mesa Arizona's Parks, Recreation, and Commercial
    Facilities, 33
Michener, James, 148
microtargeting, 349
Miller, Wiley, 11
mission focused agencies, 75
Modlin, Chelsea, 122–123
Morale, Welfare, and Recreation (MWR)
    See also armed forces recreation
    careers in, 106–109, 113
    described, 104–106
    example program service areas, 108
    resources, 113–114
Morfin, Sintia, 222–223
motivation
    darker side of, 21–22
    to enter recreation-related professions, 3–4
    of recreation, parks, sport management,
        hospitality, and tourism professionals, 17–20
motorcycles, 309
Muir, John, 123, 126, 127
multidisciplinary perspective, 60–61
Multiple Use-Sustained Yield Act (MUSY), 127
multitasking, 221, 229
Murphy, James F., ix–x, 341

N

Nanus & Dobbs, 85
National AfterSchool Association (NAA), 94
National Association for Interpretation, 142
National Association of Professional Baseball, 205
National Council of Nonprofit Associations
    (NCNA), 94
national governing bodies (NGBs), 207
National Institute on Out-of-School Time
    (NIOST), 94
National Outdoor Leadership School (NOLS), 137
National Park Foundation (NPF), 136
National Park Service (NPS), 123, 222
National Parks and Conservation Association, 141
National Parks, The (documentary by Burns), 125
National Recreation and Park Association (NRPA),
    9, 14, 55, 113, 142
National Resources Defense Council (NRDC), 141
National Senior Olympic Games, 57
National Therapeutic Recreation Society
    (NTRS), 154
Nature Conservancy, The, 136
Navy MWR - Fleet Recreation, 111
needs-driven organizations, 31

networking, 328

New Hampshire Hospital, 150–151

New York City's Parks and Recreation Green Thumb Program, 69

Nintendo Wii, 162

NIRSA: Leaders in Collegiate Recreation, 171, 187

nongovernmental organizations (NGOs)
careers, 134–137

nonprofit agencies
future opportunities, issues, challenges, 92–93
resources, 93–95
roles in communities, 81–82
what you should know about, 79–80
where located, 81
who they serve, 80–81
youth-serving, 85

nonprofit community-based organizations, 30

Nonprofit Leadership Alliance, 94

nonprofit leisure organizations, 75, 78, 79–80

nonprofit organizations, 127
careers in, 82–92
characteristics of, who they serve, 79–80
for further investigation, 96–98
future opportunities, issues, challenges, 92–93
history of nonprofit leisure, leisure services, 79
location of, roles within communities, 81–82
overview, 75–76
profiles, 76–78
recreation in, 75–93
resources, 93–95

nonprofit recreation and leisure services
careers in, 82–92
in North America, 79

nonprofit sector, 199

Northern Virginia Senior Olympics, 57

nursing facilities, recreational therapy in, 159–160

O

Obama, Michelle, 127

Obama, President Barack, 126

obesity and campus recreation, 186

Octagon, 209

Oleck & Stewart, 82

Olmsted, Frederick Law, 124, 125

Olympic Games, 197

open space and recreation in North America, 124–125

outdoor organizations, 88–89

outdoor recreation
careers in, 130–139, 181–182
in federal, state, and local parks, 110–146
for further investigation, 144–146

future opportunities, issues, challenges, 140–141
overview, 119–120, 123–130, 143–144
profiles, 120–123
resources, 141–143
today, 127–128

outdoorindustryjobs.com, 143

out-of-school programs, 91

Outward Bound, 95

Outward Bound International, 90

Oyster River Youth Association (ORYA), 17, 202

P

parks
See also recreation, parks, sport management, hospitality, and tourism
outdoor recreation in federal, state, and local, 110–146
public, 9–10
working with visitors, 128–129

participation, motivation for recreation and leisure, 20–22

partnerships, 129–130

Parton, Dolly, 302

part-time work, 330

passions of recreation professionals (table), 40–42

Patricia Neal Rehabilitation Center (PNRC), 151–153

personality, 324

Peterson, Karen, 284

Pinchot, Gifford, 126

planning
career, 323
outdoor recreation, 129–130

play
leisure and, 11–12
love of, 19–20

Play and Education (Lee), 14

pluralistic leisure services, 343

Polstein, Matt, 19, 294

Porterfield, Matthew, 153

portfolio, 332–333

positive youth development (PYD), 59

Poslusny, Duane, 129

private enterprise, 31

professional organizations, 328

professional sports, careers in, 208

profit, 299

programming
general recreation, 64
site-based, 59–61
sport, 200

public good, 30

public parks described, 9–10

public recreation, 9
public relations firms, 232
public sector, 199
purple recreation, 21

Q

quality of life, 17, 18–19

R

Rec Link, 82
recreation
    See also recreation, parks, sport management,
      hospitality, and tourism
    armed forces, 101–116
    campus. *See* campus recreation
    church, 88
    community, and leisure services, 49–73
    deep, 355
    described, 9
    inclusive, 58
    and leisure in North American life, 3–23
    motivation for participation, 20–22
    in nonprofit organizations, 75–98
    open space in urban areas for, 124–125
    outdoor. *See* outdoor recreation
    preparing for career in, 321–338
    purple, 21
    -related professions, 17
    researching careers in, 324–326
    therapeutic, 149–164
    unstructured, structured, 84
recreation, parks, sport management, hospitality,
    and tourism
    careers in, 27–43
    history of, 14–17
recreation professionals
    general qualities of (table), 39–40
    passions of (table), 40–42
recreation service model, 156
recreational sports careers, 177–179, 184
recreational therapy, 149–164
    careers in, 156–161
    described, 153
    for further investigation, 163–164
    future opportunities, issues,
      challenges, 161–162
    history as profession, 154
    models of practice, 154–156
    overview, 149–150
    profiles, 150–153
    resources, 162–163
    vs. therapeutic recreation, 155
Red Cross, 95

researching careers in recreation, 324–326
resilience, 59
resources
    campus recreation, 187–189
    community recreation, 313–316
    event management, 237–239
    Internet, 324–325
    managing outdoor, 128
    Morale, Welfare, and Recreation
      (MWR), 113–114
    nonprofit organizations, 93–95
    outdoor recreation, 141–142
    outdoor recreation in parks, 141–143
    recreation and leisure services in North
      America, 23–24
    recreational therapy, therapeutic
      recreation, 162–163
    sport management, 212–214
    travel and tourism, 287–291
restaurant industry, 255, 256–257
résumé, 333
risk behaviors, 58
risk management, 186
Robinson, Debbie, 150–151
ROI (return on investment), 228
Roosevelt, Theodore, 55, 126
Ross, Dr. Craig M., xiii, 321
Roving Leader program, 59

S

Sabbach, Jamie S., 63
Salvation Army, 88
Sasidharan, Dr. Vinod, xiv, 269
Schaefer, Marcia, 246–247
Schinke & Hanrahan, 202
Schwab, Keri A., vi, ix, 3, 27
Scouting, 89–90
seasonal jobs, 82
Secretary of the Interior, 126
Senior Games, 57–58
seniors
    careers working with, 68
    programs, 70
servant leaders, 352–353
service providers, 81
Seward, Jason, 169–171
Shaw, Dr. Greg, xiv, 269
Sheffield, Emilyn A., x, 221
Shores, Dr. Kindal, xiv, 49
Sierra Club, 127, 137
Single Marine Program (SMP), 110
Sisto, Tony, xiv, 119
site-based programming, 59–61
Skalko, Thomas K., xiv–xv, 149

skills, 323
smartphones, 350
Smith, Kerrie, 100
Smith, Megan, 272
snow skiing, 309
snowmobiling, 309
social justice, 80, 353
social media
    importance in future, 346–347
    tips, 327
social services, 30
"so-importants," 18
special event and meeting planning and
    management firms, 231–232
special events, 227
Special Olympics, 159
specialized recreation and leisure services, 31
sport business, 200
sport management
    See also recreation, parks, sport management,
        hospitality, and tourism
    careers in, 201–211
    competencies, 204
    described, 10, 197
    focus for students, 204
    four major job emphases, 200–201
    for further investigation, 215–218
    future opportunities, issues,
        challenges, 214–215
    opportunities by management sector
        (table), 200
    overview, history, 196–198
    philosophies, sectors, 198–200
    professional organizations, websites, 212
    profiles, 194–196
    resources, 212–214
    and sport teams, 193–194
    websites, 212, 216
sport organizations, 91, 206–207
sport participation, 198
sport performance, 199
sport programming, 200
sports
    and campus recreation, 167
    intramural. *See* intramural sports
    popularity of, 196–197
    winter, 309
standards of practice, 161
Starbucks, 263, 349–350
state of mind, 8
state parks, outdoor recreation in, 119–146
Stegner, William, 6, 118
Step Up to Health initiative, 56
Stevens, Cheryl L., vi, ix, 3, 27, 119

Stone, Edie, 69
stress, 221
student activities, careers in, 179–180, 184
Student Conservation Association (SCA),
    122, 136, 143
"student learning imperative," 170
student organizations, 328
summer job, 330
Suren, Dr. Asuncion T., xv, 101
sustainability, concern for, 344
sustainable tourism, 279
swimming, 180–181

T

tai chi, 153
Tanning Butlers, 256
tasting rooms, 283
Taylor, Joyce, 85
technology
    and campus recreation, 168
    and career preparation, 327
teen center careers, 65–66
theme parks, 278–279
therapeutic recreation, 149–164
    careers in, 156–161
    vs. recreational therapy, 155
    resources, 162–163
third parties, 161
Tighe, Margo, 247–249
Time Bind, The (Hochschild), 7
tips, 252, 257
Tocqueville, Alexis de, 80
Tomsky, Jacob, 255
tourism
    See also recreation, parks, sport management,
        hospitality, and tourism
    described, 10–11
    how it became a profession, 273–274
    travel. *See* travel and tourism
tourism industry sectors, 274
tourism organizations, 273
traditional ownership-based model, 29
transformational leisure, 351
travel and tourism
    careers in, 275–286
    for further investigation, 291–292
    future opportunities, issues,
        challenges, 286–287
    overview, 269–270, 273–274
    professionals, 291
    profiles, 270–272
    resources, 287–291
triple bottom line (TBL), 273
Trust for Public Land, The (TPL), 136

U

University of New Hampshire (UNH), 195
Urban Revitalization and Livable Communities
    (URLC) Act, 56
U.S. Coast Guard, 105
U.S. Forest Service (USFS), 123
USAJobs, 143
Utah Office of Tourism (UOT), 270

V

values, 323
vendors, 231
venue management, 210
venues, 231
Vermont Arts Council, 285
Vermont Department of Tourism and
    Marketing, 272
Vicini, Dan, 224–225
village greens, 124
Viren, Dr. Paige P., xv, 295
virtual leisure, 35, 185, 341
vision statements, 80
volunteering, 330
volunteers, 80, 93, 96
vulnerable populations, 85

W

Washington Outfitters and Guides Association, 142
water-related businesses, 305–308
Watts, Clifton, 49
website for this book, 34
websites
        campus recreation resources, 187–189
        Morale, Welfare, and Recreation (MWR), 115
        nonprofit employment, 96–97
        sport management, 212, 216

wellness, improving, 345
What's the Economy for, Anyway? (De Graaf), 13
white-water rafting, 308–309
WiLDCOAST, 271
Wilderness Education Association (WEA), 95
Wilderness First Responder and Wilderness First
    Aid, 95
Wildwater Rafting, 296, 302
Williams, Dave, 270–271
Williams, Dr. Richard, xv, 149
Wine Bible, The (MacNeil), 282
wine tourism, 280–284
winter sports, 309
Wise, Jack, 19, 296–297
World Health Organization (WHO), 13, 154
World Is Flat, The (Friedman), 34
World Organization of Scouting, 90
World Tourism Organization (UNWTO), 10
Wounded Warrior Project (WWP), 106

Y

Yellowstone National Park, 16, 125–126, 132
YMCA (Young Men's Christian Association),
    76–77, 79, 85–86
yoga, 153
youth
        -serving nonprofit agencies, 85
        sports, 209–210
        supporting positive development, 58
YWCA (Young Women's Christian Association), 79

Z

Zappos.com, 347
Zimmermann, Dr. Jo An M., xv–xvi, 75
Zraly, Kevin, 282

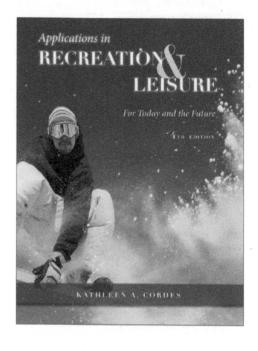
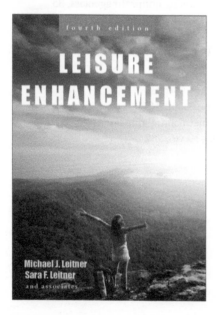